The Coming of
the Cosmic Christ

The Coming of the Cosmic Christ

The Healing of Mother Earth and the Birth of a Global Renaissance

Matthew Fox

HarperOne
An Imprint of HarperCollinsPublishers

HarperOne

Grateful acknowledgement is made for permission to reprint excerpts from the following works: *Breakthrough*, by Matthew Fox. Copyright © 1980 by Matthew Fox. Reprinted by permission of Doubleday, a division of Bantam, Doubleday, Dell Publishing Group, Inc. *Meditations with Julian of Norwich*, by Brendan Doyle, copyright © 1983 by Bear & Company; *Meditations with Meister Eckhart*, by Matthew Fox, copyright © 1983 by Bear & Company; *Meditations with Hildegard of Bingen*, by Gabriele Uhlein, copyright © 1983 by Bear & Company; *Meditations with Mechtild of Magdeburg*, by Sue Woodruff, copyright © 1982 by Bear & Company; *Meditations with Nicholas of Cusa*, by James Francis Yockey, copyright © 1987 by James Francis Yockey; all used with permission of Bear & Company, P.O. Drawer 2860, Santa Fe, NM 87504. *Psychological Reflections*, by Carl G. Jung; Jacobi and Hull, editors, vol. series 31. Copyright © 1953 by Princeton University Press. Reprinted by permission of Princeton University Press. *The Selected Poetry of Rainer Maria Rilke*, edited and translated by Stephen Mitchell. Copyright © 1982 by Stephen Mitchell. Reprinted by permission of Random House, Inc. *The Sonnets to Orpheus*, by Rainer Maria Rilke. Copyright 1985 by Stephen Mitchell. Reprinted by permission of Simon and Schuster, Inc. *Phallos: Sacred Image of the Masculine*, by Eugene Monick. Copyright © 1987 by Eugene Monick. Reprinted by permission of Intercity Books. *Archetypes: A Natural History of the Self*, by Anthony Stevens. Copyright © 1982 by Anthony Stevens. Reprinted by permission of William Morrow and Company, Inc.

Excerpts taken from *The Jerusalem Bible*. Copyright © 1966, 1967, and 1968 by Darton, Longman & Todd Ltd., and Doubleday, a division of Bantam, Doubleday, Dell Publishing Group, Inc., and used by permission of the publishers.

HarperCollins books may be purchased for educational, business, or sales promotional use. For information, please e-mail the Special Markets Department at SPsales@harpercollins.com.

HarperCollins Web site: http://www.harpercollins.com

HarperCollins®, ◼®, and HarperOne™ are trademarks of HarperCollins Publishers.

Library of Congress Cataloging-in-Publication Data

Fox, Matthew, 1940–
    The coming of the cosmic Christ.
    Bibliography: p.
    Includes index.
    1. Redemption. 2. Maysticism. 3. Cosmology. 4. Human ecology—Religious aspects—Christianity. I. Title. II. Title: Cosmic Christ.
BT775.F68   1988   230   88-45136
ISBN: 978-0-06-062915-1

HB 02.06.2023

This book is dedicated to the young, and to the youth in all of us. May we grant one another the opportunity to live out our dreams, to care for the wounded child in one another, and to pass on to others still unborn an earth as alive and diverse and wondrous as the one we have inherited.

And to my father, George T. Fox (1914–1987), who honored the young with a healthy senex.

Though we are God's sons and daughters,
we do not realize it yet.
                              Meister Eckhart

Contents

Acknowledgments

I wish to acknowledge the many persons who have challenged and encouraged me in the research and writing of this book. Of course many of these are given credit in the endnotes. Others include faculty and students at the Institute in Culture and Creation Spirituality with special thanks to Brian Swimme, Jim Conlon, Marlene Denardo, and Buck and Donna Ghosthorse. I also thank M. C. Richards, whose series of sculptures of the Johannine "I am" sayings reawakened my interest in the Cosmic Christ. My appreciation goes to David Granville, Victor Lewis, and Catherine LaFever for scintillating conversations, and to David Gentry-Akin, without whose research skills, critical editorial work, and personal support I could not have completed this project. I wish to thank Pat Feldsien for her editing skills and preparation of the index, Sue Espinosa and Jo Ann McAllister for their work with Friends of Creation Spirituality, and Clayton Carlson and Thomas Grady, publisher and editor, respectively, at Harper & Row. A special thanks to Jean Lanier and Laurence Rockefeller for a grant that allowed me to complete the research and writing of this book in swifter fashion. A word of appreciation also goes to the dancers of the Sundance at Rosebud Reservation in August, 1987, whose ordeals make this planet a more sacred place for us all.

List of Abbreviations

Frequently cited sources are identified in the text by the following abbreviations:

BDW   *Hildegard of Bingen's Book of Divine Works, with Letters and Songs*, Matthew Fox, ed. (Santa Fe, NM: Bear & Co., 1987).

BR   *Breakthrough: Meister Eckhart's Creation Spirituality in New Translation*, Matthew Fox (Garden City, NY: Doubleday & Co., 1980).

DA   *Meditations with Dante Alighieri*, James Collins (Sante Fe, NM: Bear & Co., 1984).

HB   *Meditations with Hildegard of Bingen*, Gabriel Uhlein (Santa Fe, NM: Bear & Co., 1982).

IHB   *Illuminations of Hildegard of Bingen*, Matthew Fox (Santa Fe, NM: Bear & Co., 1985).

JN   *Meditations with Julian of Norwich*, Brendan Doyle (Santa Fe, NM: Bear & Co., 1983).

ME   *Meditations with Meister Eckhart*, Matthew Fox (Santa Fe, NM: Bear & Co., 1982).

MM   *Meditations with Mechtild of Magdeburg*, Sue Woodruff (Santa Fe, NM: Bear & Co., 1982).

NC   *Meditations with Nicholas of Cusa*, James Francis Yockey (Santa Fe, NM: Bear & Co., 1987).

All biblical quotations are from the *Jerusalem Bible*, edited to reflect gender-inclusive language.

The Coming of
the Cosmic Christ

Prologue: A Dream and a Vision

Albert Einstein was once asked, "What is the most important question you can ask in life?" He answered, "Is the universe a friendly place or not?" In the first century of this era, when Jesus lived in Palestine and during the time when the Gospel stories about him were being written, the most important question in the Mediterranean civilization was, "Are the angels friend or foe?" Since angels were understood to be the driving force behind the elements of the universe, it is clear that, like Einstein, the people of that era wanted to know if the universe was a friendly place or not.

To that same question the early Christians had a definite response: Jesus represented the smiling face of God, the benignity of the universe and all its powers including the invisible angels. All the early hymns to the Cosmic Christ composed by first-century Christians celebrate the power of Jesus Christ over thrones, dominations, and angels. In other words, the early Christians had an answer to Einstein's pressing question. In the modern era, however, the Enlightenment's encroachment on religion has resulted in Christians throwing out all cosmology, all angels (which represent cosmology in the Gospels), all mention of the Cosmic Christ. I believe it is time to reclaim the Cosmic Christ.

The etymological meaning of *religion* is "to bind us back" to our sources. Religious believers and all citizens of our planet need to hear the vast and awesome mystery of the scientific story of our origins. The archetype of the Cosmic Christ encourages us to reverence our origins in a way that the anthropocentric religious paradigm of the Enlightenment era could not. It also encourages us to reverence our divinity and our responsibility as co-creators in a way that the Enlightenment paradigm did not. As Meister Eckhart put it, "though we are God's sons and daughters, we do not realize it yet."[1]

THE DREAM

This book began with a dream and ends with a vision. The dream came to me on March 15, 1986. It was a dream about the devastation our planet is currently undergoing because we lack a living cosmology.* I

---

*By the term "cosmology" I mean three things: a scientific story about the origins of our universe; mysticism that is a psychic response to our being in a universe; and art, which translates science and mysticism into images that awaken body, soul, and society. A cosmology needs all three elements to come alive: it is our joyful response (mysticism) to the awesome fact of our being in the universe (science) and our expression of that response by the art of our lives and citizenship (art).

call this devastation "matricide," or the killing of the mother, for this is how the dream spoke to me. This dream and my exegesis of it constitute part I of this book. Part II represents the bridge between dream and vision—the antidote, the cure, the resurrection. It is about the awakening to mysticism that alone, I believe, offers us hope for true healing and a deep spiritual conversion. The vision constitutes parts III–V where I present a paradigm shift for Western religion and for Christianity in particular, a shift from the "quest for the historical Jesus" to the "quest for the Cosmic Christ." In part III, I explore the sources for the Cosmic Christ in Scripture and among Christian mystics of the East and West. In part IV, I spell out some understandings of the Cosmic Christ. And in part V, I present a vision of a global renaissance of the human spirit: what a "second coming," an awakened human spirit, might effect for the survival of Mother Earth and her children.

The peril of Mother Earth and our children will not be alleviated without enlisting our spiritual heritage in the struggle. "Fight the worst with the best," advises farmer/poet/prophet Wendell Berry.[2] At a National Academy of Sciences conference in 1986 exploring the mass extinction of plants and animals on our planet, Paul R. Ehrlich of Stanford University declared, "Scientific analysis points, curiously, toward the need for a quasi-religious transformation of contemporary cultures."[3] In this book I attempt to show what this transformation would look like and how religion itself—to be true to its task—must undergo its own transformation. Not only religion but all levels of culture need to join in the struggle, as writer Harold Gilliam points out in his "State of the World" address. This

> will not be done without a quantum leap in public education and public
> pressure on leaders for action to preserve the global habitat. This is not
> the kind of understanding that comes out of a computer. It can only be
> generated by the conventional media—including press, pulpit, radio and
> TV and by the schools, which with few exceptions are doing a lamentable
> job of giving our young people insight into the ongoing degradation of the
> only planet we have.[4]

When a civilization is without a cosmology it is not only cosmically violent, but cosmically lonely and depressed. Is it possible that the real *cause* of the drug, alcohol, and entertainment addictions haunting our society is not so much the "drug lords" of other societies but the cosmic loneliness haunting our own? Perhaps alcohol is a liquid cosmology and drugs are a fast-fix cosmology for people lacking a true one. An astute observer of human nature in our time, psychiatrist Alice Miller, understands the opposite of depression not to be gaiety but *vitality*.[5] How full of vitality are we these days? And how full of vitality are our institutions of worship, education, politics, economics? Is it possible that our entire civilization is depressed because we lack the Cosmic Christ perspective?

A NEW PASCHAL MYSTERY

A second way to envision this book is to describe it as a paschal mystery story for the third millennium of Christianity and for a new era of religious belief. Using traditional theological categories, this book might be envisioned as follows:

Part I: The Crucifixion of Mother Earth (which is also the crucifixion of Jesus Christ—see Part IV) and the Mother Principle

Part II: The Resurrection of the Human Psyche by Way of an Awakened Mysticism

Parts III–V: The Coming of the Cosmic Christ Ushering in a Global Renaissance That Can Heal Mother Earth and Save Her by Changing Human Hearts and Ways

This book names the paschal mystery for the third millennium of Christianity: matricide, mysticism, and the Cosmic Christ reveal anew the paschal story we have understood as the death, resurrection, and second coming of Jesus the Christ. The death of Mother Earth (matricide) and the resurrection of the human psyche (mysticism) and the coming of the Cosmic Christ (a living cosmology) name the mystery of the divine cycle of death and rebirth and sending of the Spirit in our time. Were the human race to believe anew in this mystery a renaissance would surely occur.

THE PROPHECY OF JOEL

A third way to approach this book is to understand it as a parallel to the book of the prophet Joel. The Cosmic Christ, as I point out frequently in this book, is by no means a Christian invention or a Christian possession. The prophets as well as the wisdom writers of ancient Israel, along with the prophets of other religions including those of Native Americans, are not oblivious to a Cosmic Christ (or Cosmic Wisdom) among us. The book of Joel, written in the fifth century B.C., follows an order similar to that of this book.

Part I: Lamentation Over the Ruin of the Country (Joel 1:1–12).

Stand dismayed, you farmers, wail, you vinedressers, for the wheat, for the barley; the harvest of the field has been ruined. The vine has withered, the fig tree wilts away; pomegranate, and palm, and apple, every tree in the field is drooping. Yes, gladness has faded among the sons and daughters of the human race.

(1:11–12)

This corresponds to part I of this book, a lamentation over the pain of Mother Earth and the mother principle.

Part II: A Call to Repentance and Prayer (Joel 1:13–2:17).

How shall the devastation of the land come to an end? By a metanoia, a change of heart. Fasting, mourning, repentance are in order. Cosmic suffering needs to be acknowledged for there is "mourning among the beasts and the herds of cattle wander bewildered. . . . The earth quakes, the skies tremble, the sun and moon grow dark, the stars lose their brilliance" (1:18; 2:10). Breakthrough will come: the Day of Yahweh will awaken the people whose hearts will finally be opened up by the tragedy around and within them.

> But now, now—it is Yahweh who speaks—
> come back to me with all your heart,
> fasting, weeping, mourning.
> Let your hearts be broken, not your garments torn,
> turn to Yahweh your God again,
> for Yahweh is all tenderness and compassion.
>
> (2:12–13)

This part corresponds to that awakening of heart knowledge and of entering the darkness that is called mysticism, which is considered in part II of this book. With this breakthrough the day of Yahweh—a day of compassion and justice, of healing and celebration—can truly happen.

Parts III–V: The Prayer Is Answered, the Creator God Sends the Divine Spirit to Heal.

One scholar has written that Joel's "contribution is to prophesy the outpouring of the Spirit on all God's people in the messianic age."[6] This Joel does indeed promise. Yahweh speaks, "Now I send you corn and wine and oil, until you have enough" (Joel 2:19). Good things begin to happen, "the pastures on the heath are green again, the trees bear fruit, vine and fig tree yield abundantly. . . . The threshing-floors will be full of grain, the vats overflow with wine and oil" (2:22, 24). All this is a sign that the Divine One is in our midst.

> You will eat to your heart's content, will eat your fill,
> and praise the name of Yahweh your God
> who has treated you so wonderfully.
> . . . .
> And you will know that I am in the midst of Israel, that I am Yahweh your God.
>
> (2:26–27a)

A promise of a messianic age follows—one that blesses all people and all nations with the gift of the Divine Spirit. Peter, the friend and disciple of

Jesus, cited the following passage on the first Christian Pentecost day, understood as the Day of Yahweh (see Acts 2:16–21).

> "After this
> I will pour out my spirit on all humankind.
> Your sons and daughters shall prophesy,
> your old folks shall dream dreams,
> and your young ones see visions.
> Even on the slaves, men and women,
> will I pour out my spirit in those days.
> I will display portents in heaven and on earth,
> blood and fire and columns of smoke."
> The sun will be turned into darkness,
> and the moon into blood,
> before the day of Yahweh dawns,
> that great and terrible day.

(Joel 3:1–5)

There is deep, cosmic imagery in the announcement of this Day of Yahweh, this day of healing of the cosmic pain. The mystical awakening that foreshadows a global healing is presented as a cosmic awakening, an awakening to a living cosmology, to a Cosmic Christ alive and vital in all creatures and in all humans—young and old, slave and free, male and female. The messianic spirit is presented as nonelitist—it will be poured forth on all kinds of persons. This section of Joel corresponds to parts III–V of this book, where I present the sources and meanings of the Cosmic Christ and describe how the Coming of the Cosmic Christ might affect our understanding of sexuality; of the relations between young (puer) and old (senex); of creativity regarding lifestyles, work, and education; of folk art; of worship; and of deep ecumenism. I foresee a renaissance, "a rebirth based on a spiritual initiative," to use historian M. D. Chenu's definition, as the result of the outpouring of the Spirit. This new birth will cut through all cultures and all religions and indeed will draw forth the wisdom common to all vital mystical traditions in a global religious awakening I call "deep ecumenism." Joel too ends his prophecy with a vision of hope:

> When that day comes,
> the mountains will run with new wine
> and the hills flow with milk,
> and all the river beds of Judah
> will run with water.

(4:18)

PENANCE AND THE PARADIGM SHIFT

Joel is called both "the prophet of Pentecost" and "the prophet of penance."[7] In this book I call for a new Pentecost, a coming of the messianic spirit to the entire human race and all its religions and cultures. But I also call for penance, a deep and radical self-criticism and letting go especially among my own people, that is, among European or ex-European Christians. We need to let go of the Enlightenment and its worldview that denies mysticism and lacks a cosmology. We need to let go of a religious worldview that bores the young, trivializes Jesus Christ, and renders our spiritual heritage almost impotent. Scientist and mystic Gregory Bateson has commented that "we have lost the core of Christianity."[8] I agree, for the core must be a vital and living cosmology, a cosmological mysticism, a Cosmic Christ. No book I have ever written has shocked me more than this one, for what I have learned in the process of writing is how cheated and deprived we Westerners have been during a religious era that lacked a cosmology and lost all contact with the Cosmic Christ. As I demonstrate in part III, one cannot read the Gospels correctly without a living cosmology, yet this is what our theologians and spiritual leaders have been doing for centuries. To do penance for this sin of omission on religion's part means we must let the old paradigm go and commit ourselves with vigor to this newer, yet far more ancient, paradigm. This means the theology of the Cosmic Christ—ignored for centuries—must be reconsidered seriously today.

The penance I call for is not merely an individual *metanoia* or "change of heart." The Spirit is the One who "makes all things new" and the newness I yearn to see is a newness in the churches themselves. For this to happen the churches must confess their sins, beg forgiveness, be emptied, let go, and begin anew with the new but very ancient paradigm of the Cosmic Christ.

The churches need to beg the forgiveness of native peoples whose sense of the Cosmic Christ was never lost; forgiveness of lovers who have not been instructed in the ways of sexual mysticism that the Song of Songs celebrates; forgiveness of youth who continue to be victims of adultism at the hands of so many Western institutions including religious ones; forgiveness of artists and the creative play-er in every adult; forgiveness of women and others cheated of their spiritual heritage in an antimystical, anticosmic religious era. Once the churches have knelt and begged forgiveness, they must rise rapidly and begin contributing to the renaissance that the planet so desperately needs. They must lead with revitalized worship and with a revitalized commitment to a *deep ecumenism* flowing from a morality of reverence for all creation that in turn is born of a mystical awakening about the awe, wonder, and "radical amazement" (Rabbi Abraham Heschel's phrase) that our existence is all about.

Wendell Berry wisely declares, "Perhaps the great disaster of human history is one that happened to or within religion: that is, the conceptual division between the holy and the world, the excerpting of the Creator from the creation."[9] Mysticism is the cure to this religious dualism, yet mysticism has been ignored in most Protestant, Roman Catholic, and Jewish theological training and leadership. This book attempts to offer a way of healing the dualism between science and religion, soul and cosmos, psyche and spirit, justice making and celebrating, theology and mysticism, God and us.

If my thesis is correct that it is time to move from the quest for the historical Jesus to the quest for the Cosmic Christ, this would help to diffuse the distorted religion and pseudo-mystical movement of our time popularly known as fundamentalism and sometimes called Christofascism.[10] Enlightenment theologians—also called "liberals"—are incapable of dealing with a cosmology because they owe more to Newton, Kant, and Descartes than to the first century writers of the Gospels who believed in a living cosmology and a Cosmic Christ. One result has been that the most eschatological book of the Bible—The Book of Revelation—has been left to the fundamentalists on the right and the secular Marxists on the left. The confusion Enlightenment theologians have regarding the issue of resurrection and the empty tomb also is due to a lack of cosmology. In this book I am calling for the dismantling of liberal religion and the regrounding of faith in a mystical, prophetic, cosmological worldview—a transformation and renewal, not merely a reformation or reshuffling of a tired agenda. A radical religious awakening worthy of being called a spiritual renaissance is one that critiques both psyche (mysticism) and society (justice and prophecy). And it practices what it preaches.

The coming together of the historical Jesus and the Cosmic Christ will make Christianity whole at last. Christianity has been out of touch with its "core," its center, its sense of mystical practice and cosmic awareness. It has succumbed to a patriarchal mindset that has eroded its worship, message, and identity rendering them flat and lifeless. It is almost as weary and depressed as our civilization is. It needs the kind of dreams and visions that the prophet Joel promised would be available in abundance in the messianic age. It needs the kind of *renewal* that John XXIII dreamed of when he launched his revolution in the Vatican in the 1960s. Perhaps a new "ecumenical council" will be forthcoming in our lifetime. This one would be *deeply ecumenical* and would call forth the wisdom of *all* the world's religions. Part of its work might be to declare an ancient but forgotten doctrine: the Cosmic Christ, the "pattern that connects" all the atoms and galaxies of the universe, a pattern of divine love and justice that all creatures and all humans bear within them. Ecumenical councils of the fourth and fifth centuries declared that Jesus Christ was both God and human; what is needed if there is to be a twenty-first century for Mother Earth and her children is a spiritual vision that prays, celebrates, and lives out the reality of the Cosmic Christ who lives and breathes in Jesus and in *all* God's children, in all the prophets of religions everywhere, in all creatures of the universe.

This Cosmic Christ will make things happen, will effect a change of heart, a change of culture, a change of ways. This Cosmic Christ will lead the way to a deep sexuality; deep communication between young and old; deep creativity in lifestyles, work, and education; deep worship; deep ecumenism and interaction among all religions of the planet. John of the Cross advised his listeners to "launch out into the deep." It is time the human race did that. And if our spiritual traditions lack the vitality and vision to lead us, who will dare to do so?

A Cosmic Christ who does not accomplish the renaissance I speak of is not the true Christ but a false prophet ushering in a pseudo-mysticism. "By their fruits will you know them," Jesus advised. A true awakening to the Cosmic Christ will effect genuine results. The most basic of these will be an awakening to the sacred.

This book is about the sacred and our response to it: reverence. The sacred what? The sacred everything. The sacred creation: stars, galaxies, whales, soil, water, trees, humans, thoughts, bodies, images. The holy omnipresence of the Divine One in all things. The Western term for this image of God present in all things is "the Cosmic Christ." Poet Gerard Manley Hopkins put it this way:

In a flash, at a trumpet crash
I am all at once what Christ is, since he was what I am, and
This Jack, joke, poor potsherd, patch, matchwood, immortal
diamond,
Is immortal diamond.[11]

What creature dare deny that it is an immortal diamond? An original blessing? An image of the Divine One? It is my experience that only the human species dares to deny its divinity, dares to deny the Cosmic Christ. It is time, as Meister Eckhart put it, to "deny the denial." (ME, 40). If religion itself cannot lead the way in this denial of the denial of the Cosmic Christ, in this resurrection, ascension, and sending of the Spirit to Mother Earth by way of a resurrected humanity, then we are in deep trouble indeed. In this sense I frankly submit this book to religious thinkers and leaders as a judgment not of orthodoxy but of orthopraxis. To what work and what actions does a belief in the Cosmic Christ lead?

I believe that this book provides—not by any intention of my own—a judgment on religion itself. Can the churches themselves believe enough in the resurrection and in Pentecost to be resurrected and to become awakeners of the Spirit? Time is rapidly running out for Mother Earth and mother church. Gregory Bateson poses this sobering question to church and synagogue alike: "Is the human race rotting its mind from a slowly deteriorating religion?"[12] I believe that a slowly deteriorating religion is one that ignores or forgets its own main sources; that underestimates the human capacity for evil—in our day, the human capacity for destroying Mother Earth and her children; that fails to heal dualisms but in fact encourages them; that bores the young; that fans fires of scape-goating and encourages the sin of projection; that cannot admit its own failures and mistakes; that stands impotent vis-à-vis the powers and prin-cipalities of society; that cannot celebrate and teach people to celebrate; that substitutes moralizing for mysticism; that has no cosmology and no interest in cosmology; that denigrates science's efforts to learn about creation; that ignores the artist; that commits adultism, sexism, or an-thropocentrism; that condemns its own prophets; that alienates the *anawim* be they women, homosexuals, the poor, or the illiterate; that re-duces worship to words; that offers no vision to a tired civilization; that has forgotten its dreams; that engages in death wishes; that fails to excite the child in adults and in youth; that fails to challenge the comfortable. If Jung is correct when he says that "only the mystics bring creativity into religion,"[13] then the only way for religion to resist going rotten is to open up its heart and its theological mindset to the mystical once again.

May the Cosmic Christ redeem us from a mindless and mystic-less reli-gion. May the Cosmic Christ lead us to a saner—and less rational—cen-tury. May the Cosmic Christ bless us all so that we might be blessers instead of crucifiers of Mother Earth and the generations to come.

Part I

A Dream
"Your Mother Is Dying"
—A Crucifixion Story for Our Times

We belong to the ground
It is our power
And we must stay close to it
or maybe we will get lost.
        (Narritjin Maymuru Yirrkala, an Australian Aborigine)

The earth is at the same time mother. She is mother of all that
is natural, mother of all that is human. She is the mother of all,
for contained in her are the seeds of all.   (Hildegard of Bingen)

True religion is the original umbilical cord that binds our individual selves back to our larger, universal source. That source,
in women's religion, is the Great Mother, who is the great cosmic weaver, the divine potter, the carrier of the heavenly water jar; we participate in her substance, her nature, her
processes, her play, and her work.
        (Monica Sjöö and Barbara Mor)

Wisdom is seen as the all-encompassing divine ground of being
out of which the Trinity emerges. It creates the world, guides
it to perfection, and unites the creation with its Creator. . . .
Wisdom is the ground of being of the three persons of God.
        (Rosemary Ruether)

Before creation a presence existed
Self-contained, complete, formless, voiceless, mateless

Changeless
Which yet pervaded itself
With unending motherhood.

(Lao-Tzu)

The mother's battle for her child—with sickness, with poverty, with war, with all the forces of exploitation and callousness
that cheapen human life— needs to become a common human
battle, waged in love and in the passion for survival.

(Adrienne Rich)

A maternal theology will affirm those qualities symbolized by
the Great Mother—an assertive, whole motherhood—in all
human beings. And it will affirm the "maternal" reality—the
material reality—as continuous with the spiritual reality, and
vice versa.

(Glenys Livingstone)

Sometimes, looking at it out of the space station I imagine I'm
in, I get the definite but indescribable feeling that this my maternal planet is somehow actually breathing—faintly sighing
in her sleep—ever so slowly winking and wimpling in the be-
nign light of the sun, while her musclelike clouds writhe in
their own meteoric tempo as veritable tissues of a thing alive.

I was not brought up to think of the earth as a being. Such an
impression has come to me only in this new outer perspective
of space, which so provokes the thought that I cannot but wonder upon it. Could it? Just could the earth be alive?

(Guy Murchie)

The Earth, its life am I,
The Earth, its feet are my feet,
The Earth, its legs are my legs,
The Earth, its body is my body,
The Earth, its thoughts are my thoughts,
The Earth, its speech is my speech.

(Navajo Chant)

We enter into this life with the total knowledge we have
learned to help the Mother Earth. Our purpose is to protect

the Earth. This is why our children must be born to this world
in warmth and love, and raised with such. They must be allowed to keep their Spirit memories and use them to aid the
Mother.

(Buck Ghosthorse)

Over a year ago, while on a lecture tour, I had a dream that I realized was
an important one. Native Americans refer to such a dream as a "big
dream"—one meant not just for the individual but for the whole community. It was a Saturday night, and I was leading a retreat at Kirkridge Retreat Center in Bangor, Pennsylvania. I was exhausted and my defenses
were down. The climax of the dream contained this refrain: "Your mother is dying." Is my mother dying? Is your mother dying? Is our mother
dying? What follows is an exegesis of some possible meanings to the
dream, some possible answers to these questions.

1. Mother Earth Is Dying

The first meaning of the warning, "Your mother is dying," can be tak-
en in reference to Mother Earth. That the earth is our mother is a deeply held truth among native peoples of the Americas, Africa, Asia, and
Europe. Among Europeans, the teachings of the great Benedictine ab-
bess of the twelfth century, Hildegard of Bingen, stand out: "The earth
is at the same time mother, she is mother of all that is natural, mother of
all that is human. She is the mother of all, for contained in her are the
seeds of all" (HB, 58). Native Americans speak an ancient truth when
they say that "native languages talk of the Creation in family terms such
as 'Mother Earth,' 'Grandmother Moon,' 'The Grandfather Winds.' "[1]
Is our Mother Earth dying? Consider Bhopal; Chernobyl; Love Canal;
Times Beach, Missouri; and now—even as I write this—the Rhine River, where one thousand tons of chemicals, including eight tons of pure
mercury, were spilled—the river where Hildegard of Bingen and Meister Eckhart, the two greatest creation mystics of Western Europe, lived
and preached their message of compassion and interconnectivity with
creation. A Swiss government official reports that "the Rhine is now
dead. The whole ecosystem is destroyed due to this accident."[2] Today,
one out of two fish eaten in cities around the Mediterranean sea are im-
ported because that sea is poisoned. It seems that every month a new
ecological disaster is produced by the two-legged ones. Mother Earth is
the victim. If this continues, eventually we and our children will pay the
price. If we persist in poisoning the "mother of all," then we will ultimately poison ourselves.

Consider these facts. Agricultural practices in North America today destroy topsoil at the rate of six billion tons per year. Topsoil is the matrix of all of our lives—the lives of the plants, the animals who live on the land and eat the plants, and the humans who eat both the animals and the plants. It takes God and nature ten thousand years to produce one inch of topsoil, and the typical agricultural region contains only six inches of this precious gift. It has been estimated that the state of Iowa, as rich a state in healthy topsoil as any in the United States, will be a desert by the year 2020 if the current rate of soil depletion continues. If we continue this abuse of the land, in fifteen years the planet's fertile land will be reduced by one-third. This means that, even as the human population expands, the demands for more living space and more food will increase, yet the amount of fertile land will shrink 33 percent. Once fertile, life-giving land will be replaced by deserts of increasing size.[3]

The world's forests are disappearing at an alarming rate—one-third of the planet's total will be destroyed in the next fifteen years. Each year forest land half the size of California vanishes. Most of this destruction is occurring in Third World countries. First World corporations and governments exploit these lands in order to satiate First World appetites for beef (used in fast-food chains) and other luxury items such as sugar, coffee, tea, and cocoa.[4] In these forests dwell the world's most diverse species of plants, birds, and animals. When the forests go, many of these species will also disappear. Chinese herbal doctors, practitioners of a five-thousand-year-old medical tradition, tell me that herbs necessary for their practice are disappearing even from Chinese forests. There is no doubt that many of the world's forests contain undiscovered plants that could assist humans in controlling disease in natural ways. Yet they are disappearing with the elimination of our forests. Forests also recycle air for all of us and as they are cut down the health of the air we breathe will be seriously affected.

We now know that a species is a once-in-a-universe event, never to be repeated. Along with the forests, birds are disappearing. I mentioned this in a workshop in Montana last year and a woman told me this story. "My husband and I moved to Montana twenty years ago and have lived in the countryside all this time. When we arrived birds were so abundant that when we drove down our dirt road we had to drive very slowly as waves of birds parted as we went by. Today, when we wake up in the morning, we do not hear one bird singing." This woman was speaking of her experience in the countryside of Montana, not of New York City or Washington, D.C. Will we be the last generation to know what it means to hear a bird sing?

There are approximately ten million species of living things with whom we share this planet. These creatures range from fishes and porpoises to ash trees and rose bushes to coyotes and lions, to dogs, cats, and humans. The human is only one of these species and, indeed, among the most recent. Species as a whole have a life cycle—they are born and they eventually die. In the ordinary course of events one species disappears about every two thousand years. Currently, however, species are disappearing at the rate of one every twenty-five minutes. At this rate humankind will eliminate ten percent of the remaining species (one million of the remaining earth creatures) in the next ten years. If current rates of destruction continue, within the next one hundred years there will be no living species left on this planet—including humankind, since we are totally interdependent with all these other creatures. As Hildegard said eight centuries ago, "in the midst of all other creatures humanity is the most significant and yet the most dependent upon the others" (HB, 87).

It has been suggested that we call a United Species Conference—a conference far more representative than the United Nations is—and put this one question to the ten million representatives (one for each species): "Should the human species be allowed to continue on this planet?" The vote would most likely be 9,999,999 to 1 that we humans, with our dualistic hatred of earth, of one another, and of our own existence, be banished to some distant place in the galaxy so that Mother Earth could resume her birthing of beauty, amazement, colors, and health. Consider how the species we call whales have dwelled on this planet fifty-six million years longer than we have and yet they never found it necessary to invent Trident submarines and other fanciful ways of destroying life. We are the only species on this planet in its 4.5 billion years of existence to channel such a massive degree ($1.8 million per minute) of our human and natural resources into the design and production of weapons aimed at the destruction of ourselves and the planet. In its nuclear testing of bombs since 1945 in the Nevada desert the United States alone has already ruptured Mother Earth's womb 845 times. Mother Earth is in great pain—a pain inflicted by her own children as they commit matricide.

Consider the 1986 conference called by the National Academy of Sciences at the Smithsonian Institute in Washington, D.C.

> Speaker after speaker reported that human activity, particularly the rapid destruction of tropical forests, was dangerously reducing the earth's biological diversity. . . . They also said thousands of species were disappearing each year without humans' ever discovering them or their potential for helping humanity. . . . Norman Myers, a consultant on environment and development, said an impending "extinction spasm" was likely to produce "the greatest single setback to life's abundance and diversity since the first flickerings of life almost four billion years ago."

> Other speakers said the current rate of species extinction caused by human activity was paralleled only in major geological and climatic upheavals that changed the earth in the distant past.[5]

This report, curiously, did not make any major news program and it was reported only on page 28 of the *New York Times*. The only hope for Mother Earth is a spiritual awakening.

And how about water? Holy, holy water. If you want to know how sacred water is, then do as Native American Bill Wahpapah advised—go without it for four days. One's gratitude for the gift of water returns with that first sip! In all our probings of the frontiers of the universe, humans have yet to discover water on any other planet than our own. To the best of our knowledge, water is a unique creation of our planet. How are we treating this holy and essential gift—this original blessing without which there is no life? In the United States alone we dump eighty billion pounds of toxic waste into mother earth's lifeblood—her water—annually. In the United States one-half of our water comes from underground aquifers or cavernlike reservoirs of fresh water. A study in Massachusetts recently found that one-third of its aquifers have been poisoned. Twenty-five percent of the aquifers in California have been poisoned. In Long Island, one hundred percent have been poisoned. The human race knows no way to clean up an aquifer once it is poisoned, and a poisoned aquifer will remain contaminated for at least 100,000 years! The Environmental Protection Agency estimates that there are 50,000 toxic dump sites in our country currently leaking poisons into Mother Earth. Only twenty-two have been cleaned up as of today while $1.7 trillion have been spent on military research and equipment in the past seven years. One wonders if a sane and healthy "defense department" ought not defend the soil, the waters, the forests, the air.

Already the human race has begun to feel the effects of the wounds that we have inflicted on Mother Earth. We have begun to put our hands in her lanced side and in her crucified hands and feet. At Love Canal, for example, where poisonous chemicals were dumped in the soil, there were eighteen pregnancies. Of these, only two resulted in normal children. Three resulted in stillborn fetuses, four were spontaneous abortions, nine had birth defects including incomplete skull closures, multiple rows of teeth, cleft palate, congenital heart defects, and genetic damage. All men living at Love Canal had the DNA in their sperm cells poisoned and the human race knows no way of cleaning this up. Thus, all their offspring are likely to enter the world with poisoned genes.

In the last twenty-five years serious birth defects have doubled world over. Current statistics may not yet reflect the magnitude of the problem, yet we continue dumping dangerous chemicals into Mother Earth. Again, Hildegard warned of human folly vis-à-vis Mother Earth when she declared: "The earth should not be injured! The earth must not be destroyed! As often as the elements of the world are violated by ill-treatment, so God will cleanse them. God will cleanse them through the sufferings and hardships of humankind. All of creation God gives to humankind to use. But if this privilege is misused, then God's justice permits creation to punish humanity" (HB, 78–80).

When I speak of "original blessing" I am speaking of those blessings of healthy soil, living forests, singing birds, clean waters, and healthy DNA in our reproductive systems. These blessings form the basis of a true living economy—they constitute our essential wealth. Wealth means health. Health is blessing. And, unfortunately, we cannot take this blessing for granted any longer. Mother Earth is dying. Are we—as a student of mine recently asked—our mother's keeper? Is Mother Earth herself not the ultimate *anawim*, the most neglected of the suffering, voiceless ones today? And along with her, the soil, forests, species, birds, and waters are not being heard where legislators gather, where judges preside, and where believers gather to worship. Is the human race involved in a matricide that is also ecocide, geocide, suicide, and even deicide? Are we being kept in the dark about it by our media, government officials, and educational and religious institutions?

Consider the everyday crises that the failed nuclear reactor in Chernobyl created. Following is a report by a journalist who was in Poland at the time of Chernobyl.

> For those living within range of the fallout . . . the worst thing was the uncertainty. Should one drink the milk? Eat lettuce? Take off shoes before entering the house? Wash a cat or dog that might have tracked in the invisible poison? Keep the children out of sandboxes and off soccer fields? Shower more frequently? Turn off air conditioners and open windows? Sunbathe on the grass? Both Communist and anti-Communist governments tried to reassure their edgy populations that the levels of radiation posed no immediate danger.[6]

The issues of drinking milk, eating lettuce, sunbathing on the grass, washing off pets, letting children play outdoors takes us beyond the anthropocentric ideological battles between communist and noncommunist governments. Indeed, all the billions spent on weapons could not move this modern "cloud of unknowing" one inch from anyone's borders. Mother Earth and her pain is so much greater than patriarchy's limited agenda. Patriarchy cannot measure up to Mother Earth's immense blessings which we so easily take for granted—until tragedy strikes. As the poet Rainer Maria Rilke put it:

> In spite of all the farmer's work and worry,
> he can't reach down to where the seed is slowly
> transmuted into summer. The earth *bestows*.[7]

Yes, Mother Earth does bestow. Good health, good soil, good forests, good bodies, good minds, good souls. But are humans responding to this immense act of blessing, of bestowal?

2. The Mystical Brain Is Dying

Where does our matricidal consciousness come from? Laurens van der Post, a Belgian ecologist who was raised in Africa among a pygmy tribe, theorizes that

> the reason we exploit, damage and savage the Earth is because we are out of balance. We have lost our sense of proportion. And we cannot be proportionate unless we honour the wilderness and the natural person within ourselves. That is where the balance comes from. Our greed and aggression and corruption by power comes from cheating that first person within ourselves out of his natural inheritance.[1]

I agree that the human race as it is principally constituted today is indeed "out of balance." And from this lack of balance within we savage the world outside, with Mother Earth becoming our primary victim.

A crucial dimension of this imbalance in the West is the stunted growth of our mystical awareness and the underdevelopment of our mystical brain. Our brains are amazingly complex creations of time, nature, and divinity. Part of what we know about the brain is that the right and left hemispheres perform different tasks. The left lobe accomplishes analytic and verbal processes for us, and the right lobe accomplishes the synthetic, sensual, and mystical tasks. Western civilization, which dominates the globe today, has invested almost exclusively in left-lobe processes in education, politics, economics, and religion. Once during an evening seminar, I explained the concept of the left and right brain to a group of students. The next day I asked if anyone had had a dream they wanted to share. A woman told us of dreaming that her left brain was as big as a weather balloon that goes up to 65,000 feet and that her right brain was a dried-up prune! There lies the epitaph of Western civilization. Our right brains, our mystical brains, our maternal brains that embrace the whole and resist compartmentalization, have become dried-up prunes.

In spite of religion's reluctance to pursue its own mystical tradition and education's fear of the right brain, I continually find right brains awakening in our time: engineers and physicists, policemen and women, artists and musicians, social activists and teachers, therapists and doctors, lawyers and politicians, homemakers and students, young and old, the religious and the no-longer-religious, and even some ministers and priests! This is no small revolution. Within it lies the last great hope for Mother Earth. I believe this awakening comes from Mother Earth herself, who is not inert and passive, but very aware and sensitive that her days are numbered. With every MX missile placed on her bosom, three thousand creation mystics are coming out of the closet. Of that I am sure.

Much is happening today to awaken the mystic and maternal force in us. Of primary importance is the rejection of Newton's piecemeal consciousness, i.e., knowing the part will instruct us in the whole. The whole is greater than its parts, and the quest for the whole, for unity is a mystical quest par excellence. It is the quest of Einstein's science, sometimes referred to as the "holographic universe," meaning a living microcosm/macrocosm model. Brain researcher and neurosurgeon Karl Pribram in his book *Languages of the Brain*, and English physicist David Bohm both celebrate unity-in-diversity and diversity-in-unity as in a hologram, with "each part being in the whole and the whole being in each part."[2] Both scientists conclude that "the quintessential religious experience, the experience of mystical oneness and 'supreme identity,' might very well be a *genuine* and *legitimate* experience of this implicate and universal ground."[3] As physicist Fritjof Capra puts it, "the universe is seen as a dynamic web of interrelated events."[4] Interestingly, Hildegard of Bingen wrote of the "web of the universe" in the twelfth century.

Ours is a time of emerging awareness of the interconnectivity of all things. Mysticism is all about interconnectivity. Thus ours is a mystical time. Consider, for example from our own Western tradition, the following statements from two of our greatest mystics, Hildegard of Bingen and Meister Eckhart:

> Everything that is in the heavens, on the earth, and under the earth, is penetrated with connectedness, penetrated with relatedness.
>
> (Hildegard: HB, 41)

> All creatures are interdependent.
>
> (Eckhart: BR, 196)

> Relation is the essence of everything that is.
>
> (Eckhart: BR, 198)

> God has arranged everything in the universe in consideration of everything else.
>
> (Hildegard: HB, 65)

Clearly there was a time in Western consciousness when the right lobe was not a dried-up prune. Mother was not dying.

3. Creativity Is Dying

Another level to understanding that "our mother is dying" is the issue of human imagination and creativity. Carl Jung said that creativity emerges "from the realms of the Mothers."[1] The maternal is the place of new birth, of new wombs, of new stories, of new beginnings, of new possibilities. But how fruitful is it of late? How many abortions of imagination and imaginative individuals are performed daily and weekly in our educational, familial, and religious institutions?

A teacher of third graders for twenty-one years told me she was convinced that by the third grade 95 percent of the children in our country have lost their creativity. What efforts do our churches, synagogues, and schools make to tap the creativity of the young? What prominence does art as meditation, for example, have in education and in religion? "Imagination denied, war ruled the nations," William Blake observed nearly two centuries ago. Yet, it was not until the twentieth century that we learned how thoroughly war can rule nations, how nations like our own can spend trillions of dollars on weaponry and war preparations while its young fall into despair spawned by unnourished imaginations: apathy, dropping out, drugs, alcohol dependency, punk behavior, suicide. When war rules nations long enough it also begins to rule the nation's young. War turns inwards and against the self.

If the divine power of imagination within us all is not tapped for its beauty and surprise, ecstasy and possibilities, it will degenerate into self-loathing, self-contempt, and violence—that is, war—toward self or others. Psychoanalyst Rollo May comments on what happens when imagination is cut off:

> Imagination is the outreaching of the mind. . . . The psychotic patient could not tolerate the possibility of becoming lost in the open spaces. His capacities for abstract thought, for transcending the immediate facts in terms of the possible—what I call, in this context, imagination—were severely curtailed. He felt powerless to change the environment to make it adequate to his needs. . . . Such behavior is indicative of what life is when imaginative powers are cut off.[2]

This feeling of powerlessness is overtaking our times. From it, as Buddhist scholar Joanna Macy points out, comes despair, and despair conceals apathy. Apathy, Macy teaches, is not a lack of interest or caring, but the cover-up we create when powerlessness overwhelms us.[3] When mother imagination is dying, powerlessness takes her place.

Notice the connections, indeed the interconnectivity, between the matricide of the right or mystical brain and the matricide of the imagination. May tells us:

> In our day of dedication to facts and hard-headed objectivity, we have disparaged imagination: it gets us away from "reality"; it taints our work with "subjectivity"; and worst of all, it is often taken as the "frosting" to life rather than as the solid food. . . . Throughout Western history our dilemma has been whether imagination shall turn out to be artifice or the source of being.

> What if imagination and art are not frosting at all, but the fountainhead of human experience?[4]

If we are committing matricide of our imaginations and creativity, then in May's words, we are killing the very "source and fountainhead of our being." We are killing the soul. And, we are seriously distorting and limiting what our left brain or reason might otherwise accomplish. May believes that imagination deserves to be understood as "a principle in human life underlying even reason, for the rational functions, according to our definitions, can lead to understanding—can participate in the constituting of reality—only as they are creative."[5] The left brain cannot go it alone! No father without mother. How shall we revive our power of imagination and creativity?

4. Wisdom Is Dying

Wisdom appears universally in cultures and religions as a feminine, maternal figure. And wisdom is dying. Consider how our civilization has, under the driving influence of the patriarchal Enlightenment, produced so much knowledge and information that we have found it necessary to invent a multibillion dollar industry to store it all and retrieve it on command. Computers are the libraries of such a civilization. But what would it take to store all the wisdom we have accumulated these past three centuries? Where is the wisdom? Why has mother wisdom been treated so coarsely?

Wisdom personifies all the mothers in peril I have been naming. Wisdom is of Mother Earth, for nature contains the oldest wisdom in the universe. Wisdom requires the right brain as well as the left, for it is birthed by both analysis and synthesis. Wisdom requires imagination and nurtures it. Wisdom often comes via the creative spokespersons of a culture, in the handing on of stories, sagas, myths, images from the past and from the future. There is no mother wisdom without mother creativity. "Wisdom is found in all creative works," observed Hildegard of Bingen (IHB, 49).

Wisdom demands a cosmology, a relating to the whole, a healing of the whole when it is broken, a passion for the whole. In his study of *The Decline of Wisdom*, French philosopher Gabriel Marcel found that in all religions, East and West, wisdom was linked with our learning of and relating to the ways of the cosmos. Wisdom is never anthropocentric. Wisdom is the *magna mater*, "the great mother," who emerges from the sea, from the waters of birth and replenishment. Wisdom is playful and erotic. Wisdom seeks her beloved at any cost and does foolish things to find the beloved. "Eros is the lover of wisdom," May points out, "and the force in us that brings to birth both wisdom and beauty."[1]

Several years ago, I gave a series of lectures at the University of British Columbia in Vancouver. I was told that I could pick my own topics except the first, which was to be "Wisdom and the University." I wrestled with this topic more than I have ever wrestled with a lecturing assignment before or since. I knew that I had to speak honestly. Two hundred faculty, administrators, and students gathered for my first talk, which I began: "To speak of wisdom in a university today is a bit like talking of chastity in a brothel. No one goes to the university today for wisdom and if they do they either flunk out the first term or change their ideals rapidly." Instead of talking about wisdom and the university—which would have been a very brief lecture—I talked about why wisdom was no longer a category in education and university. "University" originally meant a place where one went to experience his or her place *in the universe*— thus, to find wisdom. Today, as a result of the Newtonian paradigm, our educational structures are built on a parts-mentality. Each area of learning—sociology, psychology, science, art, math, history, religion—is seen simply as a part. No attempt at integration, or the understanding of the whole that is wisdom, is made. The goal of education is not wisdom but getting a job.

Where eros and play are dying, cosmos and earth are also dying. And so too is mother wisdom. Matricide encompasses wisdom in its sheath of destruction.

5. The Youth Are Dying

"Mother" is a word that defines a relationship. A mother does not stand alone. She is by definition in relationship with a child. Therefore, to say "your mother is dying" is also to say that youth is dying. We see increasing evidence of this as we learn more about the numbers of suicidal youth, drugged and alcoholic youth, depressed and apathetic youth, unemployed and apparently unemployable youth, and youth who have been victims of physical, sexual, educational, and religious abuse. It is becoming more evident that the gifts youth have to offer the greater community are not being called forth. The gifts of the young are being aborted. Alice Miller speaks of children who ought to be understood "not as creatures to manipulate or to change, but as messengers from a world we once deeply knew, but we have long since forgotten."[1]

There is wisdom in the youth. The wisdom literature of Israel tells us that "by the mouths of children, babes in arms" (Ps. 8:2) is the divine majesty praised. Jesus affirmed this when he said, "unless you change and become like little children you will never enter the kingdom/queendom of heaven." (Matt. 18:3). Are these sayings merely sentimental pieties, or is there in them such earth and nature wisdom as we see in other species whose adults will sacrifice themselves so that their children might live? Are we capable any longer of sacrificing for our children? I do not mean for a new car or the perfect college education or for "all the things I never had while growing up." I mean sacrificing the worldview of matricidal patriarchy.

Native peoples teach that the ultimate norm for morality is the impact our choices have on persons living seven generations from now: If the results appear good for them, then our choices are moral ones; if not, they are immoral. What would have to change in our civilization today if we agreed on that criterion? Would we not find something else to do with the 1.8 million dollars per minute that we currently spend on weapons, for example? Might we put our imagination and creativity to work to create jobs, to preserve Mother Earth and her lushness, to limit human population, to heal and celebrate and play and challenge in holy ritual making?

Alice Miller, who has worked for over twenty years as a psychiatrist with severely depressed youth, drug addicts, and young criminals, states that she never worked with a person who abused others who was not himself or herself abused as a child. This corresponds to recent findings in America: ninety-five percent of rapists have been victims of rape. Miller points out that we have a commandment to "honor thy father and thy mother," but none to "honor thy children." She suggests Jesus became a great person because his father, Joseph, treated him as if he were a child of God. With good reason Miller asks: what would happen if all parents and all of society treated our children as if they were children of God?[2]

Our society is sick with adultism. Adults set the economic, moral, educational, worship, and work agendas. To the extent that adults are out of touch with the child in them this agenda creates a false self and an unbalanced society. The wounded child in the adult screams out for attention, compassion, and healing. Yet adults too often deny that wound and instead play out their wounded child on others. Miller demonstrates this with Adolf Hitler who was beaten daily by his father. She suggests that had Hitler had a way to express his outrage as a child, six million Jews might be alive today. The killing of the child within contributes to the killing of our communal future, our hopes and dreams. In such a society, the reigning philosophy of life becomes "everyone for oneself."

Further evidence of adultism is found in our images of God. Is God ever imaged as a child except sentimentally at Christmas? I propose that a careful analysis of God images in a matricidal society will reveal a disproportionate percentage of adult God images and few images of a youthful God. When Meister Eckhart said that "God is *novissimus*," "the newest thing there is" (BR, 112), he was celebrating an ancient tradition of the childlikeness of divinity. Divinity is not old and tired, controlling and judgmental, but spontaneous, playful, erotic, full of surprises (see Proverbs 8). A tired, pessimistic, patriarchal, adultist culture has projected its own weariness and exhaustion onto divinity—and then we wonder why the youth are dying.

Philosopher Alfred North Whitehead declared that "the death of religion comes with the repression of the high hope of adventure."[3] Adventure is our capacity to go beyond the given. A living cosmology offers adventure because it challenges us to reset all our relationships and all our images of self, work, existence, and citizenship into the vast mystery of the universe and its history. Youth desire and deserve to know that their lives are not trivial and not lacking in adventure. Otherwise youthfulness dies along with living religious passion. Meister Eckhart promises that this sense of zest and adventure is at the fingertips of all who regain their true selves—which includes their adventurous and youthful selves. "People who dwell in God," Meister Eckhart promises, "dwell in the eternal now. There, people can never grow old. There, everything is present and everything is new" (BR, 113). Eckhart teaches that the first gift of the spirit is newness, for "every action of God is new and God makes all things new" (Wis., 7:27; BR, 112). Creation stories and re-creation stories invariably begin as Genesis and the Gospel of John do, with the phrase "in the beginning." As Eckhart says, "God is the beginning and if we are united to God we become new again" (BR, 111).

6. Native Peoples, Their Religions, and Cultures Are Dying

The oldest religions on our planet are not the "great world religions" of Hinduism, Buddhism, Judaism, Islam, and Christianity, but the religions of the native peoples of the Americas, Africa, ancient Europe, Australia, Polynesia, and Asia. In these religions one finds deep memories of what essayist Frederick Turner calls "aboriginal mother love."[1] These religions arose in cultural periods that were matrifocal. They reverenced Mother Earth and her fruitfulness: they were nondualistic in their celebration of the "sacred hoop" that binds all creatures and gifts of the earth together—the rock people, the cloud people, the tree people, the finned ones, the winged ones, and the two-legged ones. By following the cycles of seasons and harmonizing with the wisdom of Mother Earth they shared in the family of creation.

Joseph Campbell observes:

> There can be no doubt that in the very earliest ages of human history the magical force and wonder of the female was no less a marvel than the universe itself; and this gave to woman a prodigious power. . . . It is, in fact, most remarkable how many primitive hunting races have the legend of a still more primitive age than their own, in which the women were the sole possessors of the magical art.[2]

Campbell believes that this wonder of the female and the mystery of maternity and its relation to the universe "has been one of the chief concerns of the masculine part of population to break, control and employ to its own ends."[3]

Consider what happened when white European Christians came to America's shores in 1492. At that time there were approximately eighty million inhabitants of the Americas. By 1550 only ten million remained. In Mexico the population on the eve of the European conquest was about twenty-five million. By 1600 only one million remained. In the West Indies there was practically a total extermination of the aboriginal peoples. In 1492 there were 1,100,000 inhabitants in Santo Domingo. By 1530 there were only 10,000 left. In 1492 there were 600,000 inhabitants of Cuba; by 1570 only 270 households remained.[4]

These facts reveal a holocaust of ineffable proportions. Bartolomé de las Casas, who observed these events firsthand, wrote that "so great is the Indians' despair that many take their own lives and they will not rear children." Las Casas took the side of the Indians in pleading their cause with the king of Spain and the pope. He said that the colonists "exterminated the Indians by their greed."[5] He believed that the Indians represented an advanced civilization in comparison with that of European Christianity. He said, "The Indians were better equipped to supervize the Spaniards and give them a way to life superior to what the Spaniards had in Castille."[6] As for the argument that Indians too had wars and an occasional ritual of human sacrifice, Las Casas commented: "The avarice of the Spaniards did more to destroy and depopulate this land than all the sacrifices and wars that took place in pagan times."[7] The Europeans accused the natives of "innate indolence" because they only grew food for their own subsistence and left themselves time and occasions for celebrations and revelries. The native peoples had room in their souls for the *via positiva*, for enjoying the fruits of Mother Earth. The European compulsion to conquer and satisfy what Turner called their "ravenous pursuit" of a "hunger beyond consumption" condemned pleasure as sinful. One is reminded of W. H. Auden's comment, "As a rule it was the pleasure-haters who became unjust."[8]

Between 1503 and 1660, 185,000 kilograms of gold and 16 million kilograms of silver arrived at one Spanish port from the Americas. Silver shipped from the New World to Spain in these 150 years was triple the total European silver reserves. The blood of the Indian peoples was the price of this greed. What happened at Auschwitz was heralded, and indeed surpassed, on American soil four centuries earlier. Las Casas believed that if ever there were cause for a "just war" that the native peoples of the Americas held such a right and that "this right will be theirs until the day of judgment."[9]

Frequently in this book I praise the wisdom of native peoples for always living out of a cosmology. But the dark side of this story—the immense suffering of native peoples that exists to this day—must also be acknowledged. This suffering is due primarily to the fact that they have been robbed of their cosmology by a white society and a religion that felt it had outgrown cosmology. I have come to think of alcohol as "liquid cosmology" because I find that cultures that were once thriving and in tune with the cosmos, when conquered by an acosmic culture, succumb readily to alcohol. One thinks of the native peoples of America as well as those of Ireland as examples of this suffering.

Our failure to live a *via positiva*, to celebrate the pleasures of the Divine Presence where we are on Mother Earth, creates a compulsion to conquer and achieve pleasure elsewhere. A story is told of European Christian missionaries who first arrived in East Africa.

In the year 1846 two German missionaries, Krapf and Rebmann, opened their first church about twenty kilometers from Mombasa among the Warabai people. They had learned the local language and offered the first Christian liturgy (they were Lutherans). The people were not impressed and said they would not return next Sunday. There ought to have been rice and plenty to eat and drink. There should have been drumming, dancing, and singing. Krapf and Rebmann told the people that they were speaking like that because they were sinners. The people asked what it meant to be a sinner. When Krapf explained the notion, the Warabai asked him who had been slandering them. When Rebmann explained that God had sent his only Son to show them his love, they said that they did not need that Son to know that God loved them. They knew that love because God had given them their lives; God gave them their children, the sun and the moon, the rain and the harvest, their children and their beer.[10]

Notice that the native peoples knew the first article of faith—that of a Creator God. They possessed a *via positiva:* they knew God loved them because of the blessings they experienced in life, which they attributed to God.

Hildegard teaches that Adam's sin was a failure in eros—he did not enjoy deeply enough the delights of earth. Her exegesis of the fall in the Garden of Eden is related to the fact that in both Hebrew (*hokmah*) and Latin (*sapere, sapientia*) the word for wisdom means "to taste." "Taste and see the Lord is good," says the Psalmist (34:8). Humans need to drink in and taste the pleasures of existence lest they be driven to limitless greed and insatiable consumption.

Laurens van der Post tells of the wisdom he learned from the bush people of Africa. They do not feel the cosmic loneliness, the "staggering loss of identity and meaning that we in the modern world experience. The one outstanding characteristic of these people as I knew them, and which distinguished them from us, was that wherever they went, they felt they were known."[11] Why is this? Because they saw their world as a family, including the cosmos and all creation. As Frederick Turner observes, from the Native American perspective myth and cosmos go together. Cosmos is a "thou." "Celebration of life" is the purpose of myths of native peoples. Myth allows no dualism.

Aboriginal mother love was imperiled by Europeans schooled in hatred of creation and sacralization of dualism. The Great Mother archetypes of native peoples everywhere have been practically exterminated by patriarchal holocausts and colonialism. There is Spider Woman and White Buffalo Woman in the Americas; there is Gaia and Athena in Europe; there is Oshun and Yemaya (among others) in Africa; there is Sophia in Greece and Shekinah in Israel. Aboriginal mother love is in us all. As one Hopi scholar and practitioner says, "every Hopi issues from the mother principle."[12] Without Spider Woman no creation would ever take place. The goddess in everyone has been dying, along with creation, Mother Earth, and wisdom. So said my dream.

7. Mother Church Is Dying

Mother church is deeply entangled in the lethal embraces of matricidal patriarchy. Fundamentalism is a planetary phenomenon in religions today: Islam, Judaism, and Protestant biblical literalists all have their kind; Roman Catholics whose hearts and souls wait for papal order demonstrate their kind. This fundamentalism is the result of a deep-seated fear triggered by the breakup of cultural patterns. The move from one era of civilization to another causes anxiety, especially among those whose egos are weak and whose sense of mother love, earth love, wisdom, and love as children has been truncated or aborted.

Religious fundamentalism exemplifies identification with the oppressor—the very hatred of mother that caused it is embraced and intensified by fundamentalism. Fundamentalism is patriarchy gone berserk. It is banishment of the mother in us all and in our traditions. It results from mysticism repressed and denied, and it always leads to scapegoating—the projected hatred of others. It occurs when the mother principle is rendered a shadow, that is, a repressed part of the personal or collective psyche.

Four images of Church come to me in these last days of the twentieth century. The first comes from a woman who had worked for many years with prostitutes on the streets of Chicago. She was asked if she had any support from the churches in caring for these women. "No," she replied, "none whatsoever." "What do you think of the Church?" she was asked. Her reply: "I see the Church as a very, very old grandmother who does not see well anymore, does not hear well anymore, and does not get out much anymore. She is clinging too tightly to life. Though we love her dearly, we should let her die."

Another image is a giant, patriarchal dinosaur that is dying. Unfortunately, it is dying a graceless death with its giant tail whipping about, killing anything within range. The biggest problem is that it is dying on top of its own treasure of mystics and prophets, of good news and wisdom stories, of cosmic sacramental powers. We must stand clear of the lethal tail, keep our distance by knowledge of history and good sense of humor, and retain our conscience. At the same time we must convince the dinosaur to roll over, so that we can rescue its treasure for the next millennium of spiritual practice.

This image is close to another—a burning building. Time is short, and we must rescue what is valuable from that burning edifice we are familiar with as Church.

The final image is "mother church" succumbing to being an almost exclusively father church. Any organization that is run exclusively by fathers, from the fathers' point of view and for the fathers' benefit will succumb to competition and jealousy and will remain out of touch with the deeper pain of our times—that of Mother Earth, mother wisdom, and mother peoples. My dream included a vivid altar scene where priests had grouped around the celebrant of the Mass. There was an air of deep suspicion. Finally, the male priests ripped a mask off the celebrant, revealing that she was female. "Caw-Caw-Caw" shouted all the male priests in unison. "Cawing" is the sound of death and death wishes. There was a reptilian kind of energy and hatred in that dream that parallels some of the reptilian language toward the *anawim* in our society and toward those who work with them that is emerging today from fundamentalist forms of Christianity.

An almost fashionable fascism arises wherever religion or society repress the mother principle in the name of patriarchy. Power struggles, not mutual love, support, and solidarity, characterize such systems. This same kind of competition can be observed in fundamentalist church structures. The authoritarian character who thrives in such a system "is essentially sado-masochistic," according to psychiatrist Anthony Stevens,[1] and is compelled to categorize others as either strong or weak. He worships the former and has contempt for the latter. "The very sight of a powerless person makes him want to attack, dominate and humiliate him," writes psychiatrist Erich Fromm. Every sadist has a masochistic side: the bullying adult is trying to free himself from having been bullied as a child. Such a person deeply enjoys submission to a leader, God, or fate. "As a monk he will be dictatorial with lay brethren but totally submissive to the Abbot and the Rule of the Order. . . . 'The Führer is always right,' cried Goebbels."[2] Or, in religious parlance: "The pope is always right," or "The Bible—as our leader interprets it—is always right."

A mother-hating psychology and a mother-hating worldview come together in the following manner, as Stevens describes it: "The authoritarian character is thus the individual basis of a collective fascism, where the social and political structure is dominated by an order imposed by a single masculine authority. Fascism is the ultimate expression of father-dominance. . . . it is perhaps not without significance that Nazism took root in the German 'Fatherland.' "[3]

In a fascist society or religion two areas of the self are aborted or forbidden to develop naturally: sexuality and aggression. Persons are not educated to be true selves but to wear false personas modeled, as Stevens writes, "on the demands of the parents and not on the needs of the Self."[4] The child thus instructed often channels these powers of sexuality and aggression into self-loathing and self-contempt. I call this the original sin mentality—the notion that I came into the world despised, unwanted, ugly, and powerless. It may be displaced onto a scapegoat, for example, racial minorities, women, or homosexuals. It can be transformed into worship of the oppressor who is "always right." Finally, it can be eroticized in sado-masochistic fantasies and practices. This kind of energy pervades patriarchal institutions including the church. According to Stevens,

> eroticized aggression directed against weaker individuals is the essence of *sadism*, while that directed against the Self in deference to the worshipped tyrant is the essence of masochism. The sadist is one who has incorporated the coercive parent; the masochist one whom the parent has devoured. Sadism seeks unrestricted power through Self-identification with authority; masochism seeks to be absorbed by authority so as passively to participate in its power and its glory and atone for sin.[5]

When mother church is dying, perverse energies are unleashed. Sado-masochism substitutes for morality; control for prayer; moralizing and condemnation for play and celebration; and a self-centeredness and preoccupation with human-made games and rules substitute for cosmic adventure, interest, wonder, and living ritual.

The profound power of the maternal energy or the Great Mother archetype can be used negatively or positively. Maternal creativity and loving can be misused and become destructive and hateful. Some psychologists call this the Terrible Mother archetype. The rule of the Good Mother results in peace and contentment, that of the Terrible Mother activates inconsolable grief and pain in the child and fury in the mother. Mothers can become battering mothers and devouring parents whose "resentment and hostility deny the child satisfaction of his legitimate needs."[6]

The primal relationship between a good mother and her children is characterized by "basic trust," as psychologist Erik Erikson teaches. Indeed, this basic trust is of creation itself, of "the world" since the young child does not distinguish between mother and world. Eros is the lesson learned in such a relationship. "The most wonderful feature of the primal relationship . . . is that it is ruled by Eros: it is perfused with love. The moment the mother-child dyad is formed, Eros is constellated." Mother deprivation accomplishes the opposite resulting in a kind of abortion of eros, a stifling of trust and love of life. When maternal care is lacking, children develop "rickets of the soul." According to Stevens, this fact is true not only for human children but also other mammals such as rhesus monkeys, which, if deprived of mother love, enter adult life with "their social and sexual capacities permanently damaged: both males and females are sexually incompetent and make hopeless parents, treating their young with the same concern as inanimate objects."[7] The quest for adventure, the increase of courage—from the French word for "big heart"—the enlargement of heart knowledge and heart power are all thwarted and even aborted when love of mother, love of world, and with it, love of self are lost. One ironic result is that the child never leaves the mother and tends to internalize the self-hatred that he or she has picked up by innuendo from the parent. The second birth myths speak of and that Jesus shared with Nicodemus is frustrated. There is, as Stevens says, a "failure to get free of the mother: the hero languishes in her belly forever, ingested, engulfed, 'absorbed.' " The Terrible Mother thus "enhances the male's primordial fear of woman, and she can so sap his masculine confidence as to make it impossible for him even to attempt the dragon-fight," the great adventure. One is reminded of Alfred North Whitehead's warning that the death of religion comes with the repression of the high hope of adventure. Stevens maintains that the child devoured by the mother "may adopt a posture of meek submissiveness to veil his smouldering resentment, his beleaguered sexuality achieving some relief in a masochistic and onanistic glorification of his servitude, as the phallic attributes of the Terrible Mother become eroticized."[8]

Members of a religion whose motherliness is dying might expect to experience much that is analogous to spiritual masochism. Stevens is pointing out how phallic a Terrible Mother becomes. An alliance forms between devouring father and devouring mother in which the child becomes the food for furious and avenging parents.

Lest some think my dream is too hard on churches and churchpeople, a study of history reveals how often prophetic warnings have come from within the Church. The reality of Church can be expressed in many forms. Many ways of understanding the Church throughout history have eventually yielded to new ways. Some of our present forms need to die so that newer, more creative, and more life-giving forms can be birthed. It is idolatrous to overidentify the Spirit of the Divine One with any one form or expression of forms. Fascism is a patriarchal heresy. St. Hildegard of Bingen, referred to as a "great saint" by John Paul II, once declared to Pope Anastasius IV:

> "O man, you who sit on the papal throne, you despise God when you don't hurl from yourself the evil but, even worse, embrace it and kiss it by silently tolerating corrupt men. . . . And you, O Rome, are like one in the throes of death. . . . For you don't love the King's daughter, justice."
>
> (BDW, 275)

Hildegard writes abbots and priors about the "crimes" that monks and clergy commit "against justice" (BDW, 299) and she preaches against the laziness of clergy and their refusal to study and to preach and to change their hearts. The Church as we have known it is dying.

8. Mother Love (Compassion) Is Dying

The Hebrew word for compassion is derived from the word for womb. Womb love, mother love, creative love are all part of the power we know as compassion. It is here that Jesus' teaching to be "compassionate as your Creator in heaven is compassionate" (Luke, 6:36) is explicitly a maternal revelation of divinity. Jesus seized elements in his Jewish tradition that were most maternal—the wisdom sayings and the call to compassion. This invitation to divine motherhood seriously challenged the religious system of his day. The crucifixion of Jesus was the logical result of his frontal assault on patriarchy. Perhaps this helps underscore the deep meaning of the Last Supper where his promise of Eucharist was essentially this: Eat me—the Divine Son—and drink me—the Divine Blood—instead of allowing yourselves to be eaten and devoured by avenging parents. The eucharistic meal becomes an invitation to all God's children to stop being food for devouring parents and to start being food for a divinely blessed universe and its joyful Maker and Sustainer. There is a promise of maternal eros in all this—the eros of food and drink, of common banqueting, and of returning to a lost mother love—that of divinity itself.

Religion and culture that represses and distorts the maternal will also repress the ancient tradition of God as Mother and of the goddess in every person. Jesus came to restore that truth to the patriarchal and militaristic culture of his day. He also came to awaken the creativity in every person, i.e., every mother, male as well as female. The story of his resurrection accomplished this creative awakening at the psychic level. Psychologist Otto Rank, who was not a Christian, insists that this story as developed by Jesus and Paul constitutes the "greatest revolution in human history"[1] because it invites all humans to let go of their fear of death. When we can do that, Rank feels, we can get on with our divine destiny, which is to create.

The mother church of Western Christianity inherited the Roman Empire with the Edict of Milan in 312. In that century the patriarchal and dualistic theologian Augustine of Hippo put forward a theology that legitimized the lack of mother love, i.e., conscription of Christians into the military, "just wars" in the name of Christ, coercion of minority groups such as Donatists, and rendering women into shadows and scapegoats ("Man but not woman is made in the image and likeness of God," he wrote).[2] We accurately refer to that era as the "patristic age" or the age of the fathers. Only today are we beginning to free ourselves from this abortion of the maternal in the womb of the church begun sixteen centuries ago.

It is time for a second birth from mother church. Just as Jesus told Nicodemus that one must be born again, so too those who are engulfed in mother church's womb need to be born again in the womb of mother cosmos. This second birth is crucial for the redemption of the Church, which is always in need of reformation (*semper reformanda*) and desperately in need of renewal today.

True redemption is always about compassion—an awakening of passion with God and all God's creation and children, especially the suffering ones. Compassion is not about pity or feeling sorry for others. It is born of shared interdependence, an intuition of and sense of awe for the wondrous fact that we all live and swim in one primordial divine womb, we live in fetal waters of cosmic grace! Not only must we celebrate this, but we must struggle for those who are drowning in our midst because they are so deeply wounded by poverty of soul, body, or both.

The mark of the true Church, the believing Church, will always be as Jesus said it ought to be: wherever compassion is found. In the future it will be compassion making—celebrating, healing, justice making—the living out of shared interdependence that will define the Church and its leadership. For it is there that royal personhood is celebrated and the kingdom/queendom of God that Jesus promised was already among us.

I believe that in the future fascist religious sects will bind together and that those committed to compassion as the norm of the Gospels and of other religions will bind together. The latter will be doing something about the mother who is dying, mother love, God as Mother, the mother in each of us and the divine image or goddess in each of us. This is the message of my dream.

During the Apollo mission in 1969, astronaut Rusty Schweikert was let out of the capsule on an umbilical cord. Usually NASA keeps one compulsively busy up there—lest a mystical experience might perhaps break through— but a peculiar and indeed synchronistic thing happened to Schweikert. Just as he emerged from the capsule, something went wrong within the capsule; both Mission Control in Houston and the remaining astronauts had to concentrate on the problem. This left Rusty all alone floating around Mother Earth in complete cosmic silence. During this time, Rusty had two profound conversion experiences, both of which I believe were awakenings to compassion. He looked back on Mother Earth, "a shining gem against a totally black backdrop," and realized everything he cherished was on that gem—his family and land, music and human history with its folly and its grandeur; he was so overcome that he wanted to "hug and kiss that gem like a mother does her firstborn child." Mother love, compassion flowed through his psyche perhaps for the very first time. Trained as a jet fighter pilot, he was a typical "macho man," but a breakthrough of his own powers of maternity came washing over him at that moment in space. All the pent-up power of compassionate maternal energy overcame him. Imagine what might happen if these vast reservoirs of incredible power were unleashed in all men, nations, and institutions of the West and East! Schweikert's second awakening in space was a political one. He was a red, white, and blue American who believed what he had always been taught—that the world is divided between the "communist world and the free world."[3] Yet, while floating around Mother Earth he saw that rivers flowed indiscriminately between Russia and Europe; that ocean currents served communist, socialist, and capitalist nations alike; that clouds did not stop at borders to test for political ideology; and that *there are no nations*. Nations exist in the mind of the human race alone. It is nations that spend a million dollars a minute on weapons and they have no existence except what the human mind gives them. Interdependence is what really exists.

On returning to NASA, Schweikert was not debriefed by any spiritual director about his mystical experiences. He confesses to having wandered about in a state of stupor for six months, bumping into walls while asking himself repeatedly this one question: "Why did God do this to me?" Finally, he concluded that God did this *through him* so that others might hear the message. What message? Compassion, I suggest. Interdependence. Eros. Shared beauty on this shining, glistening planet.

It cost about forty million dollars for Rusty Schweikert to have his sexual and political awakening to compassion. That figure reveals how close to death mother is in our culture. One hopes the rest of us can awaken to compassion less expensively. My dream tells me it is possible.

9. Our Mother Is Dying, but Not Dead

I have described and exegeted above what was for me a very revelatory dream about the death of the mother in Western culture. Matricide—the killing of the mother principle—is being committed against Mother Earth, mother brain and mother creativity; against mother religions and mother wisdom; against youth, against mother church, mother compassion and fatherhood as well. A student of mine recently posed the question: Am I my mother's keeper? This is the moral and spiritual question of our time. Evidence is slim that Westerners have taken that responsibility at all seriously—or even playfully—the past four hundred years. Patriarchal agendas and cultural presuppositions, patriarchal educational and religious institutions have left us all with maternal blood on our hands: The blood of Mother Earth crucified, of mother brain atrophied, of mother wisdom dried-up, and of mother church turned devouring parent.

The Vatican is rendering itself impotent by eating its most creative sons and daughters—those who are striving to reintroduce gospel Good News into a civilization gone mad with militarism and dualism. In addition to married couples and religious sisters receiving the Vatican's wrath, there is an ever enlarging list of creative theologians and churchmen and churchwomen. And, like patriarchal institutions everywhere, the Vatican continues to spend more money than it takes in, the 1984 debt of $36 million grew to $61.8 million in 1987.

What is it about patriarchy that renders it so arrogant and yet so stupid in our time? Is it those people and institutions that lack the maternal principle or are busy fighting, repressing, or trying to forget it who are intrinsically power hungry, greedy, and unbalanced? Isn't it interesting that the late Pope John Paul I, who only lived thirty days as pope, but who was determined to clean up financial and other scandals in the Vatican, made the following pronouncement shortly before his sudden death: "God is both mother and father, but God is more mother than father."[1]

The dream I have described and exegeted is, I believe, a dream about the reigning dis-ease of our time. Its symptom is matricide, the killing of the maternal in and all around us. But the dis-ease itself is patriarchy, the period of Western civilization from about 4500 B.C. to today when matricidal characteristics we have been discussing came to dominate the human psyche, institutions, and decision making. Significantly, my dream did not say "your mother is dead," but "your mother is dying." There is still hope, there is still something we can do to turn things around (metanoia), to convert and change our ways. What does it take to bring the healthy mother back to balance with the healthy father in us all? I believe the answer lies in a deep mystical awakening the likes of which the planet has never witnessed before—a mystical awakening that is truly planetary, that draws out the wisdom and the mystic, the player and the justice maker from the wisdom traditions of all religions and cultures. Such a mystical awakening would surely birth that "peace on earth" for which creation longs—the promise given two thousand years ago in Bethlehem. Peace on earth cannot happen without peace with the earth and peace among all earth creatures. For humans to be part of the peace process, to cease being warriors against Mother Earth, a great awakening must take place. That awakening, I am convinced, will be an awakening in our mystical consciousness. It is already well underway.

Part II

Mysticism
A Resurrection Story for Our Times

Work of the eyes is done, now
go and do heart-work

(Rainer Maria Rilke)

If you wish your heart to be bright, you must do a little work.
. . . .
If metal can be polished
to a mirror-like finish—
what polishing does the mirror
of the heart require?

(Rumi)

Normal consciousness is a state of stupor, in which sensibility
to the wholly real and responsiveness to the stimuli of the spirit
are reduced. The mystics, knowing that man is involved in a
hidden history of the cosmos, endeavor to awake from the
drowsiness and apathy and to regain the state of wakefulness
for their enchanted souls.

(Abraham Heschel)

Although no more than seven dwelling places were discussed,
in each of these there are many others below and above and to
the sides, with lovely gardens and fountains and labyrinths,
such delightful things that you would want to be dissolved in
praises of the great God who created the soul in His own image
and likeness.

(Teresa of Avila)

Future and past cannot live off the present forms of religious experience for these are too shallow; the future can live only from the most primordial communion with the sacred.

(Thomas Berry)

God cannot catch us
Unless we stay in the unconscious room
Of our hearts.

(Patrick Kavanagh)

Mere purposive rationality unaided by such phenomena as art, religion, dreams, and the like, is necessarily pathologic and destructive of life.

(Gregory Bateson)

The brain's importance to the body is suggested by the fact that, while it has only 2 percent of the body's weight, its operation uses 20 percent of the body's oxygen and blood. . . . . The complexity of a single human brain is comparable to all the telephone switchboards, exchanges and wiring patterns of computers, radio, TV and other electric equipment on Earth.

(Guy Murchie)

The epitome of irrationality is the marvel of creation itself.

(Otto Rank)

Everything is full and pure at its source and precisely there, not outside.

(Meister Eckhart)

The concepts of science show strong similarities to the concepts of the mystics. . . . The philosophy of mystical traditions, the perennial philosophy, is the most consistent philosophical background to modern science.

(Fritjof Capra)

In orthodox Christianity there is a dangerous inclination to abandon the ecstatic dimension of our relatedness to God. . . .

By contrast, the great saints kept the fire of ecstasy alive and understood our capacity to praise God in creation as a form of participation in life's ecstasy.

(Dorothee Soelle)

One who knows distances
out to the outermost star
is astonished when he discovers
the magnificent space in your hearts.

(Rainer Maria Rilke)

How wonderful is the wisdom in the Godhead's heart.
It is the heart that sees the primordial eternity of every creature.

(Hildegard of Bingen)

O seekers, remember, all distances are traversed by those who yearn to be near the source of their being.

(Kabir)

There in the lucky dark,
none to observe me, darkness far and wide;
no sign for me to mark,
no other light, no guide
except for my heart—the fire, the fire inside!

(John of the Cross)

It is easier to sail many thousands of miles through cold and storm and cannibals, in a government ship, with five hundred men and boys to assist one, than it is to explore the private sea, the Atlantic and Pacific Ocean of one's being alone.

(Henry David Thoreau)

There must be new contact between men and the earth; the earth must be newly seen and heard and felt and smelled and tasted; there must be a renewal of the wisdom that comes with knowing clearly the pain and the pleasure and the risk and the responsibility of being alive in this world.

(Wendell Berry)

If it is true that Mother Earth and the mother principle are being crucified in our time as we considered in part I, then it is also true that those
committing this matricide, namely the human race, can cease the killing.
But how will this be done? How will we move from crucifixion or matricide to healthy living? The link, I believe, lies in the human psyche's capacity for resurrection: for aliveness, wakefulness, awareness, and
rebirth—in short, mysticism. Yet the West is ignorant of mysticism and
of its own mystics for reasons we will explore. If we can awaken to an
authentic mysticism, then a resurrection of Mother Earth is possible.

10. The Etymology of Mysticism

What is meant by mysticism? Let us begin our exploration with the
etymological meanings of the word.

The word *mysticism* comes from the Greek *mystikos,* which seems to
have two basic meanings: to "shut one's senses" and to "enter the mysteries." These two meanings are related because one is more fully open
to the mysteries to the extent that one, paradoxically, has learned to shut
one's senses (i.e., has ceased projecting and is open-minded). The two
spiritual traditions of the West, that of fall-redemption or ascetic spirituality, and that of creation-centered or original blessing spirituality, will
interpret the word *mystikos* differently. The former will interpret the
phrase "shut one's senses" in the sense of *mortification* (from the Latin
"to put to death") of senses. Thus we find in fall-redemption spiritual
writers a great deal of writing on "mortification of the senses." When a
mortification-of-the-senses ideology links up with a distrust of body and
nature, then we equate mysticism with an asceticism understood as control over passion, senses, and self. Such denigration of the blessing that
passions are, serves well a basic patriarchal ideology of "power-over"
others: persons, creatures, Mother Earth, creation itself. "You cannot
undervalue the body and elevate the soul," Wendell Berry warns.

The ascetic (fall-redemption) tradition in Christian spirituality strongly advocates a mortification of the senses. A book published early in this
century, *Directorium Asceticum: Guide to the Spiritual Life,* which included a
preface and an imprimatur by a cardinal and was translated into several
languages, informs us of a nun so holy that "she never allowed herself to
look at or touch any part of her person, even such as decency does not
require us to veil." When she was sick in bed she asked her spiritual director's permission to wear stockings "since she considered it unbecom-
ing to touch one naked foot with another." In the same volume we learn
that Bishop St. Hugh, "though compelled by his pastoral charge to deal
with women, . . . had never for forty years looked one in the face." And
St. Aloysius, we are informed, "never fixed his eyes on the countenance

of any woman, not even of his own mother." Not only are women excluded from the male mystic's experience in this ascetic tradition, but so is the rest of creation. We are told that St. Laurence Justinian "even when he might blamelessly have used his eyes, abstained from contemplating the beauty of the country, and the foliage of the trees which grew in his private garden." A holy nun called Sara lived in a monastery of Scythia near a fountain for forty years and "never cast one single look at it."[1] This perverse understanding of mysticism as mortification of the senses renders the term "mysticism" pejorative in the West.

The creation-centered tradition does not traffic in "mortification of the senses" because it recognizes passion, body, senses, and sensuality as part of that divine gift, that original blessing, that touches the depths of awe and gratitude in our lives. There is no regret for being body in the creation tradition and no need to punish the body or to seek mastery over it or over others. Compassion is the basic energy force and indeed moral norm of this tradition and, as Meister Eckhart put it, "compassion begins at home with my body and soul" (BR, 423). How can we be compassionate toward others if we are not compassionate toward that basic gift we have all received, namely our bodies? The creation tradition understands the discipline of "shutting one's senses" as developing our capacity for letting go of sensory input at times, that we might sink into silence and nothingness, experience solitude and celebrate it and learn from it. One might say that the "shutting of senses" means to pull the plug regularly on the television set or to go out occasionally to the desert, into the woods, or to the sea to *just be*. There is no moral imperative for shutting down the senses because they are evil or "out of control." Rather, we let go of sensory input because the input itself may be poisonous or polluted, or simply overwhelming to soul and body. Thus one does "shut off one's senses" as a kind of purification—*not* because the senses are evil but because they are such blessings that they deserve a housecleaning in order to be renewed and restored. The purification is not so much of the senses as of the sensory input to which they have been subjected. Psychologist Arthur Deikmann calls this process "deautomatization." The senses can be so bombarded by the onslaught of day-to-day input that true beauty is lost or forgotten. I have referred to these awakening and cleansing exercises as "tactical ecstacies" in *Whee! We, wee All the Way Home: A Guide to Sensual, Prophetic Spirituality.*[2] They are means and not ends. The end is to *awaken* rather than *deaden* the senses.

The second meaning of *mystikos*, "to enter the mysteries," also has very different meanings in fall-redemption and creation-centered ideologies. In the fall-redemption tradition, "enter the mysteries" has come to mean the mysteries of cult, of sacraments defined usually as ecclesiastical liturgical rites. The creation-centered tradition backs up, so to speak, to the primal sacrament, the primal mystery that is the universe itself. It calls for a spiritual awakening to the mystery of the universe and our existence in it. Reentering that mystery is a fundamentally holy act, a sacred discipline. We must call upon the spiritual athlete within ourselves to enter that mystery fully. (Here is where the creation tradition "redeems" the word "ascetic," which originally meant to be an athlete—not an athlete at mortifying one's senses but an athlete at engaging the mystery of one's existence in the context of the mystery of the universe.) The universe is, after all, the proper setting for and the source of all energy for rendering ritual, cults, and sacraments effective. Thus, by returning to the mystery of the universe as a starting point for the mystical journey, the creation tradition deanthropocentrizes liturgy and gives it life again. In this fuller context of a mysticism grounded in the ultimate mystery of the universe itself, liturgy receives its primary power, its primary source for its symbols and its work of healing and empowerment. Cosmologist Brian Swimme, in *The Universe Is a Green Dragon*, provides the basis for a renewed mysticism of the sacraments beginning with the primal sacraments of the sea, land, life, fire, wind. He writes:

> We sometimes fall into the delusion that power is elsewhere, that we are unable to find access to it. Nothing could be further from the truth. The universe oozes with power, waiting for anyone who wishes to embrace it. But because the powers of cosmic dynamics are invisible, we need to remind ourselves of their universal presence. Who reminds us? The rivers, plains, galaxies, hurricanes, lightning branches, and all our living companions.[3]

Not only is the universe a great mystery and therefore a source of mysticism, but our bodies are too. One person's brain is more complex than all the electronic circuitry in existence. The human heart daily accomplishes work equivalent to lifting a ton from the ground to the top of a five-story building. According to scientist Guy Murchie the body can be understood as a corporation with one hundred organs, two hundred bones, six hundred muscles, trillions of cells and octillions of atoms, all working together to make a whole person. "No one could critically examine it without a respect amounting to awe."[4] The body, like the universe, is a source of awe and therefore a source of mysticism.

The creation tradition understands mysticism primarily as our entering the fullness of the mystery of our existence, the gift and blessing of creation itself. The mysterious universe we enter includes the universe of our minds and imaginations, memories and bodies as well as the mysteries of the cosmos itself. But given the wounds of the human condition, to enter these mysteries as fully as possible some letting go is needed, some returning to a space of emptiness and openness and primal ability to wonder. To enter the mystery and be unable to wonder is to miss the power and splendor of the journey—and to miss the power and splendor of the Giver of the Journey, the Giver of Creation, the Giver of the Gift.

11. The Denial of the Mystic

About twenty years ago during the so-called "sexual revolution," Western society dealt with the issue of the denial of our sexuality. This awakening to our sexuality was a long process evolving over a period of at least a century. It was set in motion by modern psychology, beginning with Sigmund Freud. About ten years ago, with the pioneer work of physician Elisabeth Kübler-Ross and of Pulitzer-prize-winning author Ernest Becker, we began to deal in earnest with the denial of death. It is time now to address the pressing issue of Western society's dangerous and dismal denial of the mystic.

Our denial of the mystic is evident in the way we treat Mother Earth as object and, indeed, in the way we generally treat the maternal principle as negative force in our lives. The mystic may well be understood as the shadow side of the Western personality. Why should we explore this unknown and often repressed element of our psyches and personalities? Hildegard of Bingen says that the worst thing the devil can say to the human race is: "O, human, you do not even know who you are" (IHB, 104). If we are mystics but do not know we are mystics, then we are indeed in the clutches of the demonic, for we do not even know who we are.

Alice Miller tells us that depression is the result of being "separated from one's true self."[1] The mystical dimension of our psyches is part of our true self but our culture teaches us to deny it and thus educates us for depression which eventually leads to despair. Miller evaluates our culture as one enmeshed in depression and believes that our century is unique for its commitment to depression. This depressive culture is the end result of a civilization that, for the past three hundred years, has denigrated the mystic. Miller also defines the opposite of depression, not as gaiety or absence of pain, but as "vitality."

While doing a workshop on the mystical journey according to Meister Eckhart's four paths, a woman told me this story: "I told my psychiatrist this week that I thought I might be a mystic. Her response was: 'You probably have epilepsy. Take these chemical tests over the weekend, and we will discuss it next week.'" The woman went on: "You know, after hearing Meister Eckhart and you expound on mysticism, I think I might quit my psychiatrist next week. I'm not at all sure I have any need for her any longer. Your workshop has pretty much convinced me that I am a mystic after all." Two months later I met this woman again. She had terminated psychiatric treatment, was saving money, and enjoying life more as a mystic.

Is this story an isolated instance? Certainly not. In my numerous travels throughout North America, Europe, and Australia, to do workshops/ playshops in creation mysticism over the past fifteen years, I have encountered the same reality: all kinds of persons are waking up to the mystic within them today. Yet how seldom this awakening, this resurrection that presages the awakening and resurrection of Mother Earth herself is welcomed or nourished in our society. Gregory Bateson calls the repression of the mystical "pathological" and cultural historian Jose Arguelles declares that a "dictatorship of reason" in the modern era of Western culture has "banished mysticism as a branch of the insane."[2]

Historian of religions Huston Smith comments on what he calls "Christianity's ambivalence toward its mystics."[3] The Christian West has indeed been ambivalent toward its mystics. Few of us know the greatest of the mystics of our own Western heritage—Meister Eckhart, for example, who was condemned by his own church six centuries ago and still awaits a liberation from that stigma. Yet Eastern wise persons, such as D. T. Suzuki, know that Eckhart was the greatest Zen thinker of the West. Few Westerners know Hildegard of Bingen, an extraordinary woman gifted in science, poetry, music, drama, mysticism; she was also a social reformer. How many theology students have studied the works of Julian of Norwich or Eckhart from the perspective of their contribution to theology? How many Protestants know that one of Martin Luther's most important influences—by his own admission—was the *Theologia Germanica*, a mystical work of the fourteenth century from the Eckhartian school of spirituality? Or that John Tauler, a student of Eckhart, deeply influenced Luther? The liberal Protestant theologian of our century, Reinhold Niebuhr, called mysticism a "heresy,"[4] and Anders Nygren, bishop of Lund, called it "the acme of egocentric piety."[5] Students in Protestant, Roman Catholic, and rabbinic seminaries do not generally receive solid courses on the mystical tradition of Judaism and Christianity. I once lectured at a prominent Protestant seminary located at a famous Ivy League school and was told by a student (who said she and others had "begged for courses on the mystics") that the dean of the theology school and other professors felt that "mysticism is a fad." Recently I received a letter from a person who, like so many others, had found it necessary to leave his Western faith roots in order to "get serious" about meditation and mystical practices. He wrote: "It is ironic, as you certainly know, that we have to leave the seminary, and even get outside the Church, as I have done in order to discover the wealth of our Christian heritage of mysticism and especially the great mystics of the Dominican Order which were rarely spoken about in my seminary background. But here [where he has started a center dedicated to spiritual practice] we are deeply immersed in the mystical experience."[6]

We deny the mystic also when we publish amateurish extrapolations about mysticism. One book I read recently laboriously argued that mystical experiences were only possible as a result of elaborate ascetic practices. The author went into great detail about the many rules that had to be observed precisely in order to attain mystical experiences. Finally he reached his crescendo: if the reader fulfills all these rules correctly, you might, by the time you are fifty-two years old, have your first mystical experience! Anti-intellectualism remains a sad inheritance of the sentimental era of pseudo-mysticism that prevailed when religion cut itself off from cosmology in the West. This kind of bad theology contributes to a pejorative understanding of mysticism. Over the years, at least thirty Protestant ministers, from many denominations, have told me that the only teaching they received on mysticism in the seminary was that it "begins with *mist* and ends in *schism*." The basic mystical literature of Israel is, of course, the wonderful wisdom literature of the Hebrew Bible. The Psalms, the Song of Songs, the books of Proverbs, Sirach, Ecclesiastes, and Job are the literature that Jesus Christ, himself a Jew, knew so intimately. Yet, Christian ministers rarely receive much instruction in the mystical literature of Israel.

Because the wisdom literature of Israel is universalist, because like all mysticism it is deeply feminist, cosmic, creation-centered, and filled with mystery that moves the heart; because it is erotic, playful, and full of creativity and invitation to the same—it does not "fit" the agenda either of patriarchal education or of patriarchal religion which has defined itself biblically as *Heilsgeschichte* or "salvation history" for the past few centuries. Much of the wisdom literature of Israel came from Egypt where a mother goddess was worshipped. Isis was from Ethiopia—thus we are speaking of a black mother goddess as being behind much of this biblical literature.[7] Another reason mysticism doesn't fit well with patriarchal education and religion is mysticism cannot fit into the wineskin of exclusively left-brain religion or education. Thus, we have so little of it even among our trained religious leaders.

The denial of mysticism by churches and synagogues is a deep and enduring scandal that is no longer tolerable. The reason human civilization is tired, depressed, unimaginative in dealing with unemployment, pollution, youth despair, injustice, and inequality is that we "do not even know who we are," as Hildegard put it. We are out of touch with our "true selves," as Alice Miller puts it. A civilization that denies the mystic is no civilization at all. It offers no hope and no adventure, no challenge worthy of sacrifice and joy to its youth or its artists. It offers no festivity, no sabbath, no living ritual to its people. And no deep healing. Such a culture actually promotes negative addictions: drugs, crime, alcohol, consumerism, militarism. It encourages us to seek outside stimulants to provide meaning for life and defense from enemies because it is so woefully out of touch with the *power inside*. It relegates the poor to still greater poverty and the comfortable to an infinite deluge of luxury items, and those in the middle to resentment toward both poor and rich. For such a culture knows nothing and teaches nothing about authentic empowerment. Such a culture will trivialize the deepest riches of the human spirit and will fail to employ persons in the good work that art and creativity are all about.

12. The Rise of Pseudo-Mysticism

The mystic lies deep in every person. To deny it is to invite the emergence of pseudo-mysticisms and ersatz mysticisms that catch our personal and collective imaginations. Jesus warned his followers about "false prophets" who would come as wolves in sheep's clothing. So too it is necessary today to be mindful of false mystics and false movements that come disguised in mystical trappings. The test for authentic mysticism is justice making and compassion, as Jesus taught. I believe that contemporary civilization, in addition to denying the mystic, is also swamped in pseudo-mysticisms. Among these are the following:

Nationalism. Nationalism has become a kind of mystical fever for many citizens of our planet. There is some truth to celebrating the community that one hopes a people are, but excessive commitment and zeal on the nation's behalf arises psychologically from a dissatisfaction with the "inner person" who is so ignored that the "outer person" takes over, having been excited by calls to nationalistic mysticism. In the name of the idol called National Security, the modern nation-state seems willing to spend any amount of money—to the tune of $1.8 million per minute around the globe today. Nation-state security is a pseudo-mysticism which deprives the poor and unemployed of the basic necessities of life and thus denies their right to a decent life.

Militarism. The ideology of the nation state raised to a level of mystical commitment paves the way for the pseudo-mysticism of war. The thrill of holding an automatic weapon in one's hands or of new, faster, and more destructive weaponry and technological gadgets are all indicative of this pseudo-mysticism. Rambo might well be canonized as the patron saint of militarism. Notice, of course, how pseudo-mysticisms link up together—that of nationalism marries very conveniently that of militarism.

Fascism. Fascist mysticism is always mysticism without justice. Justice is the test of authentic mysticism. Without justice mysticism can very easily become a negative power, a release of the demonic instead of the divine. The Nazis would torture people in the afternoon and then return to their homes at night and cry as they listened to Wagner or Beethoven. Sentimentalism—feelings for family, state, or one's beloved cut off from justice—is part of a pathological mysticism. The Nazis succeeded partly by manipulating mystical techniques such as chanting, processing, and lighting candles in the darkness to achieve a sense of "entering the mysteries." One wonders if the German people would have been so gullible to these misuses of mysticism if healthy mysticism had been taught them by their religious traditions.

Technology. Inventions fascinate—as well they should, for human imagination and ingenuity are among the most awe-inspiring inventions of the universe. But the implicit promise of our civilization is that salvation will come from technology. "Buick saves" was the basis of a well-financed ad campaign a few years ago. The mythology that a new invention will prevent war—the press has called it Star Wars—is a good example of the mystical yearning we have for peace which can be projected onto ersatz objects of mysticism. Peace has more to do with what goes on inside the human person than with what we invent outside ourselves. To ignore and deny the mystic inside encourages the idolatry of technology.

Consumerism. Consumerism promotes the idea that things we buy will give us the satisfaction, excitement, and meaning in life that we so desperately seek. Yet consumer goods are themselves their own evidence against the false mysticism they offer. Constantly invented and infinitely advertised, they cannot ultimately satisfy and therefore offer no authentic mysticism. The human race cannot in fact buy its way or eat its way out of the boredom that results when true mysticism is lacking.

Fundamentalism. Fundamentalism is another pseudo-mysticism in our time, whether it come from the Protestant literalism of the Bible and the television evangelist's "word of God" message; from the literalism of Roman Catholics looking for salvation by way of papal pronouncements or Muslims hanging on the word of the Ayatollah Khomeini. Because these fundamentalism movements always lack the integrality of justice, deep violence lurks just beneath their sentimentalisms. Sadly, they have the power to seduce into their narrowly sectarian ways the young who are searching for true community and vision. Christofascism has no sense of the past. It is invariably antihistorical and anti-intellectual. Spawned by an ignorance of tradition, its "loss of roots and lack of tradition neuroticize the masses and prepare them for collective hysteria," Carl Jung observed.[1] What logically follows, according to Jung, is a "collective therapy, which consists in abolition of liberty and terrorization."[2] The rise of cults is a response to the lack of healthy mysticism in today's religious institutions.

New Ageism. Certain New Age practices are also pseudo-mysticisms. Interpreting so-called "past life experiences" in an excessively literal way without considering the possible metaphorical meanings is an example.

Invariably, I have found that persons dealing with "past lives" are working out—often in a very commendable and creative way—the deep suffering and pain from their present life. This connection is lost when the preoccupation with past lives loses its metaphorical base. The result is a severe underestimation of one's present responsibilities and opportunities. Excessive preoccupation with states of consciousness that elicit levitation, for example, is also a pseudo-mysticism. Again, the power of the mystic to relate to healing society is a key ingredient to testing the spirits. "By their fruits you will know them," advised Jesus.

Asceticism. The effort to define mysticism as asceticism has paralleled the era of Newton. There is something mechanistic and machinelike about defining mysticism as ascetic practices, that somehow to inflict bodily pain on oneself will result in a communion with the Divine. This is not true mysticism, as Meister Eckhart says: "Asceticism is of no great importance for it reveals a greater ego rather than a lesser one; more self-consciousness instead of less" (ME, 58).

Mystiques. The mystique of heroes, performers, popes, ball players, nations, presidents, rock singers is pseudo-mysticism born of projection. A true mystic no longer projects but faces "isness" itself as the divine revelation. Sadly, our media feed us with entertainment that encourages us to displace our own greatness onto others.

Psychologism. Psychologism, the reduction of spirituality to psychological categories, is prominent today. In seminary training where more attention is given to CPE (Clinical Pastoral Education) than to mystical development, an entire generation of would-be spiritual leaders is often forfeited to the god of counseling. As psychologist James Hillman puts it, psychology has the power to kill the spirit. "Psychological counseling then literalizes problems and, by killing the possibility of seeing through to their madness, kills the spirit."[3] Otto Rank had similar concerns when he wrote of moving "beyond psychology" to mysticism and creativity. While psychology is often a useful and necessary tool, the Spirit is too vast to be restricted to psychology alone.

Never devoid of mystical energy and yearnings, a society that denies the mystic and lacks a prophetic religion to insist on the primary role of the mystic within every psyche and every community, will fall into various forms of pathological pseudo-mysticisms. Mysticism is identified exclusively with the pseudo-mystical phenomenon we have described here and those who equate it with egotism, heresy, pathological religion, or kookiness become justified in doing so. This equation of mysticism with sickness—which Freud among others fell victim to—perpetuates the denial of the mystic in the individual and in society. Pessimism increases. And depression. And despair. And disempowerment. And then apathy.

Mysticism may be denied, but mysticism is not dead. Though Newtonian attitudes have dominated science, education, and religion for three hundred years, mysticism still lives. In fact, its resurrection occurs more among scientists than among theologians or church leaders. "I want to know the mind of God. The rest is all details." Who made this observation? Was it Teresa of Avila? John of the Cross? Meister Eckhart? It was Albert Einstein. He also said, "The most beautiful experience we can have is the mysterious. It is the fundamental emotion which stands at the cradle of true art and true science. Whoever does not know it and can no longer wonder, no longer marvel, is as good as dead."[4]

Other scientists, standing on Einstein's shoulders, are also exploring mysticism. Nobel laureate Roger Sperry has written that "current concepts of the mind-brain relation involve a direct break with the long-established materialist and behaviorist doctrine that has dominated neuroscience for many decades. Instead of renouncing or ignoring consciousness, the new interpretation gives full recognition to the primacy of inner conscious awareness as a causal reality."[5] Physicists Fritjof Capra and Brian Swimme, by their work on cosmology and mysticism, have opened the door for a more mystical view of the world. Capra maintains that

> the concepts of science show strong similarities to the concepts of the mystics. I feel on much firmer ground with this assertion than I did ten years ago. It's not just physics that has parallels to mysticism, it's also biology, psychology and various other sciences. . . . The philosophy of mystical traditions, the perennial philosophy, is the most consistent philosophical background to modern science at all these levels.[6]

Just as modern science effectively denied mysticism to our culture for three hundred years, so too the post-Einstinian scientific era is launching an era of mystical awareness. It is more important than ever, therefore, to examine mysticism in a critical fashion.

13. Twenty-one Running, Working, Experiential Definitions of Mysticism

What *is* authentic mysticism? Etymological definitions aside, efforts to define mysticism invariably end in frustration and despair because definitions are the quest of the left brain which seeks to analyze and to separate. But mysticism is a right-brain experience. That there *are realities* such as mysticism that resist definitions is good news! Mysticism is beyond the control of anyone—even the mystic! It is impossible to develop a single definition that fully does justice to the experience called mysticism, but that does not condemn us to vague, essentially noncommunicable meanings. It simply means that mysticism demands our respect and resists control at all times—even at the level of language itself. In this section I will present twenty-one "running definitions," working definitions of mysticism. My approach is nonlinear and best understood as a circle, with each of the definitions feeding into it. By exposure to each of these "definitions" the reader will begin to feel and make connections with his or her own mysticism, for the purpose of *defining* mysticism here is to *elicit* the mystic within each person. Hopefully in this process, we will demystify mysticism and reveal its generic meanings, and thereby encourage common practice and understanding of its great power. A basic teaching of all in the creation mystical tradition is this: *everyone* is a mystic.

1. EXPERIENCE. The first meaning of mysticism is experience itself. As Kabir, the great creation mystic of India, put it in the fifteenth century, "I say only what I have seen with my own eyes—and you keep quoting the Scriptures!" He goes on, "Experience, O seeker, is the essence of all things."[1] The mystic is keen on the *experience* of the Divine and will not settle for theory alone or knowing *about* the Divine. "Taste and see the Lord is good," says the Psalmist in the wisdom tradition of Israel. There is no such thing as vicarious mysticism—no one can experience life and divinity on our behalf.

Poet Rainer Maria Rilke celebrated the richness of experience in this passage of his novel, *The Notebooks of Malte Laurids Brigge:*

> Verses are not, as people imagine, simply feelings (those one has early enough),—they are experiences. For the sake of a single verse, one must see many cities, men and things, one must know the animals, one must feel how the birds fly and know the gesture with which the little flowers open in the morning. One must be able to think back to roads in unknown regions, to unexpected meetings and to partings one had long seen coming; to days of childhood that are still unexplained, to parents whom one had to hurt when they brought one some joy and one did not grasp it (it was a joy for someone else); to childhood illnesses that so strangely begin with such a number of profound and grave transformations, to days in rooms withdrawn and quiet and to mornings by the sea, to the sea itself, to seas, to nights of travel that rushed along on high and flew with all the stars—and many nights of love, none of which was like the others, of the screams of women in labor, and of light, white, sleeping women in childbed, closing again. But one must also have been beside the dying, must have sat beside the dead in the room with the open window and the fitful noises. And still it is not yet enough to have memories. One must be able to forget them when they are many and one must have the great patience to wait until they come again. For it is not yet the memories themselves. Not till they have turned to blood within us, to glance and gesture, nameless and no longer to be distinguished from ourselves— not till then can it happen that in a most rare hour the first word of a verse arises in their midst and goes forth from them.[2]

Though Rilke is describing the source of poetic inspiration, he is also describing where mysticism takes place. The mystic is one whose "blood within" has been turned by his or her deep, unforgettable, and therefore truthful experiences. Where would the history of the Spirit be if Paul had not yielded to his experience of falling from a horse? If Hildegard had not grounded her adult life on the experiences of mandalas that both healed and instructed her? If Francis of Assisi had not responded to the call to "repair my church?" If Julian had not recorded her "visions" from her meditations on the feast day of the Holy Cross? If Luther had not responded to his experience of liberation on reading Romans? If Martin Luther King, Jr., had not trusted his experience of prayer?

King was about two weeks into the bus boycott that he had organized in Montgomery, Alabama. He was receiving phone calls threatening him and his family daily. Finally he received a call at midnight that said, "If you aren't out of town in three days, we're going to blow your brains out, and blow up your house." King comments:

> I sat there and thought about a beautiful little daughter who had just been born. . . . I started thinking about a dedicated, devoted and loyal wife, who was over there asleep. . . . And I discovered that religion had to become real to me, and I had to know God for myself. And I bowed down over that cup of coffee. I never will forget it. . . . I prayed a prayer, and I prayed out loud that night. . . . "I'm faltering. I'm losing my courage. And I can't let the people see me like this because if they see me weak and losing my courage, they will begin to get weak." . . . And it seemed at that moment that I could hear an inner voice saying to me, "Martin Luther, stand up for righteousness. Stand up for justice. Stand up for truth. And lo I will be with you, even until the end of the world." He promised never to leave me, never to leave me alone. No never alone.[3]

There is a *trust* implicit in the mystic's reliance on experience—a trust of the universe, a trust of what is and what occurs to us, yes, a trust of oneself. As Meister Eckhart says, "Why is it that some people do not bear fruit? . . . Because they have no trust either in God or in themselves. Love cannot distrust" (ME, 82). Carl Jung complains that modern people get their experiences from words and dictionaries to such an extent that we are surprised when we meet up with a real live cow and we actually experience its smell. The dictionary said nothing about the smell so, given our word-orientation bias, we were unprepared for the full reality of "cow."[4] To know a cow is to *experience* a cow—not read about one.

2. NONDUALISM. Another dimension to mysticism is nondualism. Our mystical experiences are *unitive* experiences. They may occur on a dark night with the sparkling stars in the sky; at the ocean; in the mountains or fields; with friends or family; with ideas; in lovemaking; in play; with music and dance and art of all kinds; in work; in suffering and in letting go. What all mystical experiences share in common is this experience of

nonseparation, of nondualism. "Separate yourself from all twoness," Meister Eckhart advises. "Be one in one, one with one, one from one" (ME, 128). Or as the great English-speaking mystic, Julian of Norwich, put it, "Between God and the soul there is no between" (JN, 77). Here Julian is celebrating the end of the primary dualism—that between humans and divinity. The mystics promise that within each of us there is a capacity—the experience of the "no between"—to be united and not separate. Mysticism announces the end of alienation and the beginning of communion, the end of either/or relationships (which form the essence of dualism) and the beginning of unity. Yet the unity that the mystics celebrate is not a loss of self or a dissolution of differences, but a unity of creativity, a coming together of different existences. Eckhart says that "the soul becomes God but God does not become the soul" (ME, 69). There is a unity in diversity, a diversity in the union of love.

3. COMPASSION. Compassion is another word for the unitive experience and therefore another name for mysticism. Compassion is the "keen awareness of the interdependence of all living things which are all part of one another and involved in one another," as Thomas Merton observed two hours before his untimely death. A dualistic culture is uneasy with the deep, true meaning of compassion and sentimentalizes or relegates it to a lifestyle for "bleeding hearts." In truth, compassion is the very origin and goal—as well as the process—of creation mysticism. "The first outburst of everything God does," Meister Eckhart says, "is compassion" (BR, 44). This means that all creatures as children of God hold compassion in common. Compassion is our universal heritage, our God-origin and our God-destiny. Compassion unites us, it forms the common "field" that all creatures share. The mystic intuits this, feels it, experiences it, tries to live it out in some fashion. Kabir celebrates this when he declares, "I am like a pitcher of clay floating in the water, water inside, water outside. Now suddenly with a touch of the guru the pitcher is broken. Inside, outside, o friends, all one." The dualism of inside and outside is broken through in this image. The separation between the human and the divine is broken through for Kabir as he says, "O friend, Kabir has looked for him everywhere, but to no avail. For Kabir and he are one, not two. When a drop is merged into the ocean how is it to be seen as distinct? When the ocean is submerged in the drop, who can say what is what?"[5] Divinity is not outside us. We are in God and God is in us. That is the unitive experience of the mystics East or West. Its technical name is *panentheism*, which means that "God is in all things and all things are in God."[6]

4. CONNECTION MAKING. Not only is mysticism about experiencing unity and nondualism, it is also about making unity and making connections where connections have been lost, forgotten, or covered up. As part of this process, we must get out of the way so that the connections and interdependencies that already exist might emerge. We connect our ex-

periences with those of others. We connect—by symbols, stories, and myths, music and colors, form and ritual—with one another's deep and often unspoken experiences of life's mysteries.[7] The artist is, by definition, a maker of connections and therefore a mystic. In the process of creating connections are made between clay and the person, for example, and between the stars that made the clay and the clay that is the person. Connections of time and space, of human and nonhuman, of past and future, all coming to be in the present moment—all these connection-making events are mystical events as well.

5. RADICAL AMAZEMENT. Abraham Heschel defines mysticism as "radical amazement." The mystic in us is the one moved to radical amazement by the *awe* of things. "Awe is the beginning of wisdom," Heschel declares, "awe precedes faith." And praise too "precedes faith."[8] Heschel is being true to the great mystical literature of Israel, the wisdom literature of the Bible, when he makes these observations. Einstein is also working from this tradition when he defines mysticism as being able to wonder, marvel, and be rapt in awe.[9] Humans exist for awe's sake—to be radically amazed and to draw radical amazement from one another. That is our task. It is a mystical task, a task that demands we overcome the temptation to take our existence for granted. Awe is the opposite of "taking for granted." If awe precedes faith, then there can be no living faith without it. Translators with no appreciation for the mystical have mistakenly rendered the Hebrew word for "awe" as "fear." Heschel knows better. Awe is the beginning of wisdom; awe contains an element of terror—the universe that birthed us is terror-filled. The fear experienced in the face of terror is not the fear of guilt but a fear of WOW!—a reverential fear based on a realization of the greatness of our existence, of our being included in the amazing twenty-billion-year drama that is the universe. Awe is our passion involved in yielding to the radical amazement that surrounds our lives. If the beginning of wisdom is awe, then awe must be the starting point of creation mysticism. Awe is a three-letter word for the *via positiva*, the first of the four paths of creation spirituality.[10]

6. AFFIRMATION OF THE WORLD AS A WHOLE. Philosopher Josef Peiper defines mysticism as "an affirmation of the world as a whole."[11] "To become divine," Gandhi notes, "is to become attuned to the whole of creation."[12] The mystic is neither neutral nor bitter or cynical toward the world. The mystic has taken in enough of the blessing of the world to be radically amazed by it and, therefore, to *affirm* it. To embrace the "world as a whole" is to embrace a cosmology. What the mystic affirms is not the world laid waste by human neglect, sin, and greed, but the world *as a whole*. This affirmation enables us to receive sustenance, challenge, and power from the whole.

Andrew Weil, M.D., in his book on drugs and mysticism, says that the paranoid and the mystic share much in common: paranoid persons believe there is a conspiracy in the universe against them, mystics believe there is a conspiracy in the universe on their behalf.[13] The mystic has a sense of the whole, an apprehension of it, a yearning for it. It is a benevolent yearning, a yearning for what King referred to as the ultimate "beloved community." The mystic tastes, on occasion, the sense of a beloved community in its universal or cosmic dimension. King points out that in the Gospel of John we are told, "God loved the *world* so much that God gave the divine Child" (John 3:16). If God's love is for the whole world, ours must be also.

7. RIGHT-BRAIN. As we discussed earlier, our brains are divided into right and left hemispheres. The left brain operates the motor functions of the right side of our body, while the right brain operates motor functions of the left side. It is generally recognized that the left lobe operates functions of analysis and verbalization, while the right lobe is primarily responsible for synthesis, for connection making, for experiences of the whole. Mystical ability is physiologically located in the right lobe of the brain as we saw in part I above.

Psychiatrist Anthony Stevens speaks of the "imperialism" of the left brain in our culture and its social institutions. He writes:

> Ever since the Renaissance, stress has increasingly been laid on the need to develop left hemispheric functions at the expense of the right. Encouragement of the left hemisphere begins early in life with the emphasis placed in all Western primary schools on the need for proficiency in the three Rs (writing, reading and arithmetic). Although right hemispheric activities such as art, drama, dancing and music are given a place in curriculum, fewer resources and fewer hours are allocated to them than to left-sided disciplines such as mathematics, languages, physics and chemistry; and at times of economic retrenchment it is invariably the right-sided activities which are pruned or curtailed.[14]

The curtailing of right brain activities in Western education that Stevens laments also applies to the training of religious leaders of Protestant, Roman Catholic, and Jewish traditions. (See chapter 11 on "The Denial of the Mystic.") *Heilsgeschichte*—"salvation history"—has prevailed as the dominant agenda of patriarchal theological education during the Newtonian era. The more mystical literature, for example wisdom literature in the Hebrew Bible, has seldom been taught. Yet I remember as a teenager growing up in the Roman Catholic tradition I was allured more to Mass on Saturdays than on Sundays. It was some years before I understood why. Saturday Mass at that time was almost always celebrated in honor of Mary the mother of Jesus. The biblical readings were drawn from the wisdom literature of Israel and were pregnant with mystical and cosmological images and references. I was utterly fascinated by their mystery: they spoke to my heart. They nurtured my own right brain that was starving under the constraints of the macho-oriented culture of the 1950s. In a typical passage, Wisdom speaks:

> From everlasting I was firmly set,
>   from the beginning, before earth came into being.
> The deep was not, when I was born,
>   there were no springs to gush with water.
> Before the mountains were settled,
>   before the hills, I came to birth.

(Prov. 8:23–25; see vss. 26–36)

8. SELF-CRITICAL. Mysticism is always self-critical. Mystics learn to let go of projection onto others and are able to see the dualism in themselves as well as in others. Self-knowledge is often heralded by mystics like Teresa of Avila and Catherine of Siena as the "foundation," "basement," or "cell" of the spiritual journey. The mystic is willing to undertake a critical examination of the self and to refrain from projecting the dark, unexamined shadows lurking in the self onto others.

The mystic not only avoids projection but also avoids the internalization of self-hatred. Many people go through life deeply wounded by internalized oppression—deeply believing false images of themselves or their origins that others have projected onto them. Being self-critical entails a willingness to own that which is blessing in oneself. One must let go of internalized oppression and dare to see oneself again as an image of God, as an original blessing, as a co-creator with divinity. Self-love is a rare and radical kind of love because it requires a trust of our right to be here and of the universe's love of us.

Part of the radical self-criticism to which the mystic must be open is the willingness to criticize religion. Often religion goes uncriticized in a secularized culture because deep down it regards religion as powerless. *It remains for those who have been touched by the power of religious faith to love religion enough to criticize it.* This is why the authentic mystic is frequently such a threat to organized religion. Jesus' crucifixion is an archetypal example of this often repeated phenomenon. Carl Jung maintains that "only the mystic brings what is creative to religion itself. . . . The creative mystic was ever a cross for the Church, but it is to him that we owe what is best in humanity."[15]

9. HEART KNOWLEDGE. The mystic trusts the experience of the heart. As the Irish poet Patrick Kavanagh puts it:

> God cannot catch us
> Unless we stay in the unconscious room
> Of our hearts.[16]

The mystic gradually learns ways of awakening the heart, strengthening it, expanding it, watering it, and enabling it to reach its full, cosmic, potential for joy. When he was imprisoned and tortured for his efforts to revitalize his Carmelite religious community, John of the Cross gradually realized he was dying. He faced a dilemma: if he was caught escaping he would be tortured to death; if he remained in his cell he would probably die also. He chose the greater risk; he would die escaping, if he had to die. Surprisingly, he succeeded in escaping and wrote the following poem to name that strength in him which inspired his daring decision:

> There in the lucky dark,
> none to observe me, darkness far and wide;
> no sign for me to mark,
> no other light, no guide
> except for my heart—the fire, the fire inside![17]

The "fire inside" was the flame of his heart that urged on John of the Cross to his own survival. Heart knowledge urges the mystic on. In the Hebrew Bible, the new covenant between Yahweh and humanity promised by the prophet Jeremiah is a covenant *of the heart*.

> Deep within them I will plant my Law, writing it on their hearts. Then I will be their God and they shall be my people. There will be no further need for neighbor to try to teach neighbor, or brother to say to brother, "Learn to know Yahweh!" No, they will all know me, the least no less than the greatest!—it is Yahweh who speaks.
>
> (Jer. 31: 33–34)

Part of awakening the heart is awakening the body. The heart, after all, is found in the body, not in the head. Body prayer, bodily art as meditation practices, and breathing meditations all assist in opening up the heart.

One indicator of pseudo-mysticism is antagonism between faith and science or between heart and head. A creation mystic never enters into heart knowledge at the expense of head knowledge. The two aspects (right and left brain) should never be at odds. The genius and heroic courage of the thirteenth-century philosopher, Thomas Aquinas lies largely in his resistance to the dualism between heart and head, faith and science promoted by the sentimental and anti-intellectual theological tradition of his day. He insisted that the divinity one finds by reason does not differ from the divinity one finds by faith. This is why he appealed to Aristotle—a "pagan" scientist whose work was regarded as the most important and controversial of Aquinas's day—to develop his own cosmology.

In the past few hundred years, during the demise of cosmology and mysticism, much of faith has succumbed to the rational tendencies of secular culture. Heart knowledge has been greatly undervalued in the liberal agenda. Instead, a great deal of intellectual conflict has characterized the debate between science and religion. Sentimentalists or anti-intellectuals known as fundamentalists cling only to their feelings about a personal savior and tolerate no interference from head knowledge, theological, psychological, or scientific. These persons want to replay Scopes's trials in America or reinstitute inquisitions at the Vatican. Otto Rank, a prophetic psychiatrist, comments on the head/heart dialectic in modern culture. Using the terms, "rational/irrational," he observes that although humans think, talk, and even act rationally, we all "live irrationally":

> Our age was up to recently so highly rationalized that the irrational had only the neurotic form of expression. But to attempt to cure this result of rationalism by more rationality is just as contradictory as a war to end wars, or an effort to strengthen a weakening democracy by more democracy.[18]

Rank is telling us why the so-called mysticism of the modern era, such as the emphasis on mortification of senses cited earlier, has been so deeply neurotic. How can we avoid this dilemma of *either* neurotic irrationality *or* excessive rationality? Rank offers a solution: "The only remedy is an acceptance of the fundamental irrationality of the human being and life in general . . . a real allowance for its dynamic functioning in human behavior, which would not be lifelike without it." Rank is saying that the human race must realize that *all of life is mystical*, i.e., irrational. Rank believes that the awe we feel toward creation is the greatest of our "irrational" experiences when he says, "The epitome of irrationality is the marvel of creation itself."[19] Rank goes on:

> When such a constructive and dynamic expression of the irrational together with the rational life is not permitted it breaks through in violent distortions which manifest themselves individually as neurosis and culturally as various forms of revolutionary movements which succeed *because* they are irrational and not in spite of it.[20]

When the irrational and mystical is repressed, Rank warns us, it will emerge in perverted forms, i.e., as personal neurosis or as cultural violence. Rank believes that to recover the irrational or mystical, not at the expense of the rational but in tandem with it, would lead to an authentic awakening of the richest possibilities of humanity. He maintains: "Granted an acceptance of the fundamental irrationality of the human being and life in general with allowance for its dynamic functioning in human behavior, we have the basis for the emergence of everything of which mankind is capable in personal and social capacity for betterment."[21] Irish poet Patrick Kavanagh makes the same point this way:

> I have a feeling
> That through the hole in reason's ceiling
> We can fly to knowledge
> Without ever going to college.[22]

10. A RETURN TO THE SOURCE. Mysticism demands a return to our origins. Meister Eckhart says, "Everything is full and pure in its source and

precisely there, not outside" (BR, 427). Kabir says, "O seekers, remember, all distances are traversed by those who yearn to be near the source of their being."[25] If you have ever yearned to be "near the source of your being," you have had mystical yearnings! Meister Eckhart is constantly talking about this return to the source, "When I dwelt in the ground, in the bottom, in the stream and in the source of the Godhead, no one asked me where I was going or what I was doing." He invites us to "return to God and the core, the soil, the ground, the stream and the source of the Godhead" (BR, 77). When we do that, we derive a living energy for our work and recover our work as an expression of our truest self, our deepest being. "When word and work are returned to their source and origin," Eckhart promises, "then all work is accomplished divinely in God. And there too the soul loses itself in a wonderful enchantment" (ME, 116). This hints that we get lost in the source, lost in enchantment and grace, even in the midst of our toughest work.

John of the Cross also celebrates mysticism as a return to our source and its mystery. He writes of a "spring that brims and flows":

Its source I do not know because it has none.
And yet from this, I know, all sources come,
 Although by night.

I know that no created thing could be so fair
And that both earth and heaven drink from there,
 Although by night.

Its radiance is never clouded and in this
I know that all light has its genesis,
 Although by night.
. . . .
The current welling from this fountain's source
I know to be as mighty as its force,
 Although by night.[24]

In understanding mysticism as a "return to our source," we recover the etymological meaning of the word religion itself. As we discussed earlier, "religion" is derived from the Latin word *religare,* meaning "to bind again or to bind back." Mysticism is a binding back or a rebonding with our very source.

11. FEMINIST. Mary Giles, in *The Feminist Mystic,* says simply, "the mystic is feminist."[25] Just as patriarchal consciousness is characterized by its dualism and its denigration of mysticism, so a way of seeing the world that is more feminist will include the mystical. People who see the world in this way will practice values of interdependence and communion rather than dualism; of celebration and delight rather than competition; of compassion rather than legalism; of nurturance rather than judgment. The mystics' ability to let go and undergo the apophatic divinity, the

hidden God who is "without a name" as Eckhart puts it (ME, 42), is of particular interest to women and others who have not had their own voices celebrated through history. Theologian Dorothee Soelle tells how a "hidden feminist" inside her resisted the "so-called scientific language devoid of a sense of emotional awareness" that she found in male-dominated theology. "I was helped," she declares, "by the language of the mystics."[26] When Meister Eckhart says, "I pray God to rid me of God" (ME, 50) he is encouraging the kind of letting go of language that Soelle and many other feminists find necessary if divinity is to emerge in greater fullness.

The image of "returning to our Source" is a deeply maternal one, whether it conjures up memories of our mother's womb or of the ocean or of the Divine One in whom we all live, move, and have our being. This is feminist imagery and it is telling that Eckhart's favored term for the source is not God but "the Godhead." The Godhead is that side of divinity that is not active in creation and history but is silent and does not act. Like a big, cosmic mother, the Godhead just is. "Isness" needs no justification.

12. PANENTHEISTIC. Healthy mysticism is panentheistic. This means that it is not theistic, which envisions divinity "out there" or even "in here" in a dualistic manner that separates creation from divinity. Panentheism means "all things in God and God in all things." This is the way mystics envision the relationship of world, self, and God. Mechtild of Magdeburg, for example, says, "The day of my spiritual awakening was the day I saw and knew I saw all things in God and God in all things" (MM, 42). Panentheism melts the dualism of inside and outside—like fish in water and the water in the fish, creation is in God and God is in creation. Meister Eckhart says that "ignorant people falsely imagine that God created all things" in such a way that they are outside divinity (BR, 73). For "God is in all things. The more divinity is in things, the more divinity is outside of things" (BR, 73). (See 1 John 4:16.)

Over the years I have met many serious spiritual seekers who called themselves atheist. Yet I have come to realize that most atheism is a rejection of theism and most atheists are persons who have never had panentheism or mysticism named for them in a culture where theistic relations to divinity are celebrated at the expense of mystical or panentheistic ones. I do believe that if the only option I was given by which to envision creation's relationship to divinity was theism that I would be an atheist too.

13. BIRTHING IMAGES. Every mystic is a birther of images. Part of the "radical" or critical consciousness of the mystic is a deep intuition that inherited language is not adequate for the task of naming the deep experiences of life. The mystic's trust of experience produces a consequent distrust of the namers of experience for us. When an American presi-

dent refers to the MX missile as a "Peacemaker," mystics sense that the inherited language is inadequate to the task at hand. Language can be redeemed only in a return to experience, which is language's source. It is out of deep experience that language is reborn. This rebirth occurs through the generation of new images, for images are closer to our experience than words. Images are the midwives between experience and language. A mystical awakening will entail an awakening of the power of images to heal, to name, to excite, to teach. Poet Rainer Maria Rilke used to say that words are the last resort for expressing what happens deep within ourselves.

The greatest mystics of the Middle Ages were among the birthers of our contemporary Western languages. Each was at the heart of the battle for a new language in order to name a new experience. Each was engaged in what we might call the search for "new wineskins." Francis of Assisi and Dante were launchers of the Italian language. Francis's *Canticle to the Sun* has long been considered among the finest poems in the Italian language. Meister Eckhart was at the forefront of launching the German language, which contributed to his condemnation, for at his trial he was accused of "confusing the peasants"[27] by preaching to them in their own language. He did not preach in Latin because he was willing to risk his theological reputation by communicating with people in language they understood. His preaching in these peasant dialects contributed to birthing a powerful new force, the German language, for naming people's experience. Julian of Norwich has been called "the first English woman of letters"[28] because she helped to launch the English language along with that mystic contemporary of Meister Eckhart, Geoffrey Chaucer. John of the Cross wrote the finest poetry that has ever been written in the Spanish language. Though educated in Latin, he knew the power of communicating his deepest experiences in a fresher wineskin and chose Spanish for that purpose.

Is every artist not a birther of images? Thus, every mystic is an artist and every true artist is a mystic. This should come as no surprise if one has grasped the meaning and interconnection of the preceding "running definitions" of mysticism I have proposed. Does the artist not image? Does the artist not return to origins? Does the artist not toy with the "irrational" and entertain the right brain as well as the left? Are not the great mystic-prophets those who lived out their images and created spaces where others could live out theirs? Is it not the artist, whom writer James Joyce calls the "priest of the imagination," who articulates the journeys of depth for the people? Who therefore names the mystical journey?

In the creation tradition, all people are mystics. Mysticism is not elitist; it touches the true self in each one of us. All people are artists as well. All persons are both artist and mystic because all are called to be in touch with the true self, the deep experience that is theirs, and to utter images from that silent space. The artist in us utters the images, shares the experience. Art cut off from its mystical roots becomes sterile and egotistic, an instrument of elitism or consumptionism. It is aligned with competition rather than compassion, which is the basis of community. The gift of the true artist is always a gift to the community, even if it involves criticizing the community. It comes from the depths and is gifted to the depths of another. Every person has a gift to give the community and is therefore an artist. Our primary effort in education and child rearing ought to center around the eliciting, the leading out (from the Latin *educere* from which we derive our word "education") of the gift that is the mystic within. This is why art as meditation is a sine qua non for educating the mystic in one another. Native peoples know the truth of these things—all in the community are artists with gifts to express and images to share. The native traditions have not lost this truth because they have not lost faith in the mystic lying within each individual, whose gifts are *for the people*, for the entire community.

The gifts of all the great artists of our race were due in part to the fact that they were mystics. Does the music of Mozart, the challenge of Mahler, the painting of da Vinci, the burning vision of poet Adrienne Rich not do precisely this: awaken the mystic in each of us who encounters such expressions of grace and beauty? Is not art like existence itself, a source of awe and wonder and therefore still one more source for our mysticism? Great artists have invariably been great mystics and great mystics have been great artists—poets of the soul. We will never understand the true gift of the artist until we understand that the source of their gifts is in fact the mystical agenda. I believe this helps to explain why both artist and mystic have been reduced to a peripheral role during the modern, Newtonian era.

14. SILENCE. Mysticism is dialectical. The mystic approaches reality from a "both/and" rather than an "either/or" perspective. While the mystic is passionate about imaging and sensitive to language, its death and its possibilities for rebirth, the mystic is also a befriender of silence. Returning to the source of one's being is rarely an experience that can be expressed in words. Kabir says, "Anyone who has had a taste of this love is so enchanted that he is stricken with silence."[29] Have you ever been "stricken with silence"? If so, you have tasted the ineffable; you have had a mystical experience. Silence is too often defined as "the absence of something" when it is much more than that. Silence is also a search for something, a search for the depths, for the source. Many of the mystical awakenings experienced by astronauts and *cosmo*nauts in space have been triggered by the cosmic silence they have encountered there. Similar things happen to persons swimming in the depths of the sea or spelunking in the caves of Mother Earth. Silence moves people. That is why

it is so essential to meditation practices, including the art of listening to
our images. Being, one might say, is silent. We must embrace silence in
order to experience being. Then—and only then—does it speak deep
truths to us. As Rilke says: "Being-silent. Who keeps innerly silent/
touches the roots of speech."[30]

Meister Eckhart, like Kabir and other mystics, celebrates silence.
"Wherever this word is to be heard, it must occur in stillness and in silence," Eckhart declares (BR, 260). Nicholas of Cusa writes that "in the
end, the mystical study of the Divine leads to freedom and silence where
the vision of the invisible God/dess is conceded to us" (NC, 76). Silence
is about being-with instead of proselytizing or selling the ego. Kabir says,
"O dear friend, when you have a gem in your hand you don't go out in
the street announcing it."[31] In other words, befriend the gem in silence
for a while. Silence is another instance of the refusal to project that is so
basic to the mystical consciousness. There is a time for silence as there is
a time for images, a time for speech, and a time for work. The mystic in
us yearns for silent time and for our letting go of images. "Quit flapping
your gums about God," Meister Eckhart advises, for "the most beautiful
thing which a person can say about God would be for that person to remain silent from the wisdom of an inner wealth" (ME, 182). The silence
of which the mystics speak is that suspended moment at the well, at the
source of being, of images, of creativity—that power from which the
words come and from which they derive their power. Poet and potter
M. C. Richards reflects, "Where do my words come from? . . . from the
silence behind the words"—from the silence of the preexistent word
that is "in the beginning."[32]

That power from which the dance or the painting or the music or the
struggle or the love or the lovemaking comes is silence. A left-brain culture will be ill at ease with silence. It will be excessively wordy. Words can
obscure the presence and power of the Divine as they so often do in worship services that have lost touch with their mystical roots and have succumbed to secularization. The fear of silence runs deep in a culture void
of mysticism. Gregory Bateson celebrates the need and power of silence
when he says:

> Noncommunication of certain sorts is needed if we are to maintain the "sa-
> cred." . . . There are many matters and many circumstances in which con-
> sciousness is undesirable and silence is golden, so that secrecy can be used as
> a marker to tell us that we are approaching holy ground. Then if we had
> enough instances of the unuttered, we could begin to reach for a definition
> of the "sacred."[33]

15. NOTHINGNESS AND DARKNESS. The mystic has plunged into the
darkness and has tasted nothingness itself. Mysticism not only takes one
into the awe of what we see in the light of day but also into the depths of
what we see—or fail to see—in the dark. Nicholas of Cusa writes about

the darkness that left-brained experts or scholars cannot penetrate when he says that "the scholars are deficient in that they are afraid to enter the darkness. Reason shuns it and is afraid to steal in. But in avoiding the darkness reason does not arrive at a vision of the invisible" (NC, 64).

Mysticism takes us into the darkness of what Jung calls the "lavishing mother"[34]—the darkness of pain and doubt—and allows us to be there. What the mystics call the "dark night of the soul" is not an elitist experience reserved for professional pray-ers. Such "nights" are realities for every person and every culture. The difference lies in how one responds to the experience: some allow the darkness to penetrate them and others resist and deny it. Joanna Macy teaches us that apathy is born from the denial of pain.[35] The presence of apathy is an indication that we are not being mystical. Apathy results when we flee from the mystical invitation to be with the darkness.

The mystics dare to talk about nothingness, about our experiences of no-thing-ness. The mystics do not shelter us from the truth that emptiness is as real as fullness, that subtraction and letting go are as authentic and necessary a means to truth as are addition and adding to. "The soul grows by subtraction rather than by addition," Meister Eckhart teaches (BR, 183). Our nothingness experiences are lessons in wisdom, preludes to compassion. They put us in touch with the depths of others who also undergo the truth of the nothingness of being. King, on emerging from one of his early prison experiences, commented, "I think I received a new understanding of the meaning of suffering. I came away more convinced than ever before that unearned suffering is redemptive."[36] The mystics dare the dark and the suffering that accompanies true vulnerability. Suffering can make our souls grow larger.

16. CHILDLIKE PLAYFULNESS. A mystic is a child at play—the mystic within us is the child within us. Meister Eckhart frequently defines mysticism as "unselfconsciousness." He urges people to develop their unselfconsciousness. Is this not what children have in abundance? To the extent that adults allow children to be children and do not project adultism onto them, all children are active mystics. Jesus celebrated the child on many occasions, as when he admonished adults that "until you change and become as little children you will never enter the kingdom-/queendom of God" (Matt. 18:3). Play and fantasy are about letting our unselfconsciousness have the stage for a while. So much of adult living, work, preparation for work is about self-consciousness. The mystic in each of us is eager to play. On the indispensable connection between play and creativity, Carl Jung remarks poignantly, "From the standpoint of the intellect everything else is nothing but fantasy. But what great thing ever came into existence that was not first fantasy?"[37] The "great things" that mystics bring into existence—Eckhart talks of how we birth God—all depend on fantasy. Jung continues, "All the works of human-

ity have their origin in creative imagination. What right, then, have we to disparage fantasy? . . . Fantasy is not a sickness but a natural and vital activity which helps the seeds of psychic development to grow."[38] While Freud disparaged mysticism for its experience of returning to the womb and to one's origins as "infantile regression," Jung sees in this return a healthy revivifying of the creative powers.

> Every good idea and all creative work are the offspring of the imagination, and have their source in what one is pleased to call infantile fantasy. Not the artist alone but every creative individual owes all that is greatest in his or her life to fantasy. . . . Without this playing with fantasy no creative work has ever yet come to birth.[39]

Whether it is God playing with wisdom before the creation of the world (see Proverbs 7), or the artist playing with forms and shapes, or the musician playing with sounds and chords, or the teacher playing with ideas, or lovers playing with one another's bodies, or the contemplative playing with God, there can be no living mysticism, no creativity, without play. The divinity that the mystic encounters is invariably a youthful, childlike divinity—the child within is the divine child.

17. PSYCHIC JUSTICE. Mysticism can also be understood as psychic justice. All people have a left and a right lobe in their brains. We live in a culture that essentially develops and rewards only the left lobe, and thus we are out of balance, out of harmony. Injustice means being out of balance. We are psychically unjust, psychically unbalanced to the extent that we operate from the left lobes of our brains exclusively.

Mysticism brings justice—harmony and balance—back to our brains, bodies, and psyches. Mysticism is personalized justice. The proper translation and real meaning of the biblical term "righteousness" ought to be "mysticism" or internalized justice. Mysticism brings back the balance of right and left lobe, of light and dark, of passion and silence, of being and doing, of play and seriousness, of love and of letting go of love, of work and art, which are so often lacking when peace and justice movements lack a mystical grounding. When the personalized justice that mysticism brings is lacking in the psyche, psychic injustice is projected onto society and its institutions. In this way social injustice is rooted in personal injustice or vice versa. Thus, to educate the mystic is to educate for peace instead of for war. The mystic wrestles with the wars we carry on inside of ourselves—the "psychic battleground." This provides a training ground for the social battles that need to be fought in the name of justice. The battles the mystic undergoes teach a sense of personal understanding and compassion toward the "enemy" that sometimes is missing when one hasn't confronted one's own psychic battles. In other words, by confronting one's projections and by healing psychic injustice, the mystic clears the way for a more effective struggle for social justice. The scientific word for justice today is *homeostasis,* which is the quest for balance and equilibrium that is found in all organisms and even in the universe itself. Mysticism is about returning homeostasis to the human mind.

18. PROPHETIC. A prophet is a mystic in action.[40] The prophet, as Heschel teaches, is one who interferes with injustice. Thus, the mystic is invariably dangerous and always in trouble; the mystic is prophetic. Hildegard of Bingen at the age of 81 was excommunicated along with her entire convent of nuns for burying a young revolutionary on their property; Francis of Assisi had his order snatched from him while he was still alive—a fact that resulted in his stigmata or physical identification with the wounds of the crucified Jesus Christ. Thomas Aquinas's death was precipitated by his constant battles with secularists on the one hand and anthropocentric religious spiritualists on the other. The last year of his life he had a nervous breakdown and was unable to write or speak. He was condemned, not once or twice, but three times before his eventual canonization. Mechtild of Magdeburg was literally driven from town to town because she was a Beguine (a member of the women's movement of the thirteenth century) and dared to criticize those in power for their greed and indifference to the plight of the poor, the young, and the sick. Meister Eckhart was condemned a week after he died and though in reality he is the greatest Christian mystic of the West, he remains on the condemned list to this day. Like Hildegard, he remains practically unknown in mainline Christianity. Julian of Norwich was ignored for two centuries after her death, her great mystical work, *Revelations of Divine Love*, being published for the first time in the seventeenth century.

The mystic must be a prophet because a certain psychic balance is required of the mystic—an investment of one's energies into the social arena, which is often so essential after so much inner and personal experience. Mystics need to risk danger and prophecy. They are unable to contain all they have experienced. People today sometimes fall into a kind of blissfulness that ignores the sufferings of others and fails to develop one's powers for compassion. This is pseudo-mysticism. It is precisely the dialectic or tension between mysticism and prophecy that keeps people and the communities they create sane. A balance within (achieved through mysticism) becomes projected healthily beyond us as a balance of justice and harmony through the very struggle for justice. Injustice outside us challenges complacent ego protectiveness within us. Mysticism is not about security. As theologian Dietrich Bonhoeffer put it, "peace is the opposite of security."[41]

19. BEING-WITH-BEING. One of the gifts mysticism brings to the prophetic struggle is a rooting of the struggle not at the superficial levels of righteousness or guilt or compulsion or winning but at the level of being. Mysticism is about *being-with-being*: being-with-being in silence, in experience, in awe, in connection making, in nondualism, but also about being with suffering beings, with the victims of self-hate and oppression. In

different ways every creature on our planet is such a suffering individual. Mysticism moves the struggle for justice beyond blame and anger to new possibilities. That is the spiritual genius of Gandhi, King and others who embrace nonviolence as a means of absorbing the hatred and pain of others into new arenas of energy making and creativity. Meister Eckhart speaks to the relation of justice making and being when he writes, "For the just person, to act justly is to live; justice is her life; her being alive, her being to the very extent that she is just. . . . in God, action and being are one" (ME, 96). Eckhart concludes that "people ought to think less about what they should do and more about what they are. . . . Because if you are just, then your works are also just" (ME, 97). Eckhart promises that as our work for justice becomes more and more grounded in our mystical roots of being-with-being, then true and profound creativity can happen. We become co-creators and birthers of new creation:

> All virtue of the just and every work of the just is nothing other than the Son—who is the New Creation—being born from the Father. In the depths of our being, where justice and work are done, we work one work and a New Creation with God (ME, 94).

20. TRUE SELF. The mystic in us, by ever exploring depths of one's experiences—whether of light or of darkness, of joy or of suffering—is unleashing and creating what Paul calls the "inner person," the true self. Co-creation happens here, for the birth of the mystic is a birth *with God* of what is divine and truly oneself. It is the outward birth of the image of God from within. Each self is a unique mirror of divinity and therefore each person births a unique creation when he or she lets the true self be born. The creativity required in this birthing is one of authentic empowerment. It comes from where the divine dwells within the community—that is from the bowels of its "amongness," as Jesus speaks of when he says, "The kingdom/queendom of God is *among* you"—and it comes from within the individual. The Divine One is the "One who is with us," *Emmanuel,* "God with us." God is with us especially at the level of the true self, at the level of being unique images of God. Indeed, one can talk of God depending on us to mirror divinity, to recall the image of divinity that each of us is to divinity itself. Looking in a mirror is an intimate thing—it cannot be done at a distance. The true self that is the image of God is also a connecting link with the being it images. The work of co-creating with God is an intimate work of being-with God.

Meister Eckhart, in his treatise on how every one is an aristocrat or royal person, makes the distinction between the "external person" and the "inner person," a distinction that strikingly parallels Alice Miller's "false self" or "as-if self" that a wounded child creates in order to be loved and the "true self" who is the part of ourselves which accepts unconditional love.[42] Eckhart says that the inner person "is hidden within us. . . . Scripture calls this person a new person, a heavenly person, a young person, a friend, and a royal person" (BR, 510). He also teaches that the inner person is "the soil in which God has sown his likeness and image and in which he sows the good seed, the roots of all wisdom, all skills, all virtues, all goodness—the seed of the divine nature (2 Pet. 1:4). The seed of the divine nature is God's Son, the Word of God (Luke 8:11)" (BR, 511). Thus, for Eckhart, the true self or inner person is nothing less than the Cosmic Christ inside each of us. The inner person is "the good tree of which our Lord says that it always bears good fruit and never evil fruit" (BR, 511). Alice Miller writes that "soul murder" occurs when an individual is denied access to his or her true self. In a culture that denies the mystic, i.e., the development of the true self, soul murder is a regular event.

21. GLOBALLY ECUMENICAL. Without mysticism there will be no "deep ecumenism," no unleashing of the power of wisdom from *all* the world's religious traditions. Without this I am convinced there will never be global peace or justice since the human race needs spiritual depths and disciplines, celebrations and rituals, to awaken its better selves. The promise of ecumenism, the coming together of religions, has been thwarted because world religions have not been relating at the level of mysticism. The Western tradition appears to have nothing to offer on a mystical level because its religious institutions are unaware of their mystical heritage. With the awakening of a living cosmology, a living mysticism, new possibilities for relating and interacting among all the spiritualities of humankind will begin to emerge. Not only the so-called "major world religions" but also the more ancient and more earth-centered traditions of the native peoples of the Americas, Africa, Europe, Australia, and Asia need to be tapped for their wisdom. If ecumenism were to shift from position papers to prayer, from the classrooms of academia to the sweat lodges and the sun dances and the solstice rituals of native peoples' religions, a new era would finally begin for planet earth and her peoples. The creation mystical traditions are universalist traditions since all peoples share creation and the maker of creation in common. As Kabir said, "Now beyond caste or creed am I!"[43] Kabir, of fifteenth-century India, was considered both Hindu and Moslem. He bridged within himself the two spiritual traditions. The earth yearns for an era of unsurpassed religious creativity that can be experienced if we dare to awaken the mystic within ourselves and our traditions.

The Second Vatican Council paved the way for this kind of global ecumenism when, in what may well prove to be its most prophetic document, *On Non-Christian Religions (Nostra Aetate)*, it declared, "From ancient times down to the present there has existed among diverse peoples a certain perception of that hidden power which hovers over the course of things and over the events of human life. . . . *The Catholic Church rejects nothing which is true and holy in these religions.*"[44] The document wisely calls on Christians to "make common cause of safeguarding and fostering social justice, moral values, peace and freedom" among all religions and to pay special attention to the rituals, the "ways and sacred ceremonies" that "answer the restless searchings of the human heart" among all religions. Not so wisely, however, does the document instruct Christians to "forget the past." Justice requires an acknowledgment of the pain and suffering of native peoples caused by Christian avengers who completely lacked a mystical consciousness.[45] The history of Christians' behavior toward native religions is not an enviable one. We must ask forgiveness through dialogue and prayer before true "forgetting" can take place. A mystical consciousness gives us the freedom to let go and to ask for forgiveness. Churches need to pray for such gifts of the Spirit as the capacity to ask forgiveness. Only in this way can honest ecumenism happen at a deep and effective level.

I believe that these twenty-one definitions of mysticism give us certain tests that we can put to mystical claims to discern whether they are authentic or bogus. The first of these tests that I have alluded to already is that of *justice*. Is mystical energy being awakened to make more justice, that is more healing and *oneing* (Julian of Norwich's word) in the world? A second test is that of an *intellectual life*. True mysticism never exists at the expense of the left hemisphere of the brain; it is never anti-intellectual. "All science comes from God," declares Hildegard of Bingen (IHB, 14). A third test is *paradox and humor*. The mystics, so respectful of the diversity of things and of the omnipresence of divinity, realize that the universe does not subsist on linear logic alone. If it did, divinity could not be at home here. Another test is *fertility*. "By their fruits you will know them," advised Jesus. What fruits result from our mysticism or claims to it? Another test is what Eckhart calls *unselfconsciousness*. Childlike awe and wonder and spontaneity ought to return to adults becoming true to the mystic inside them. Still another test is *dialectical consciousness*—an ability to embrace the both/and instead of settling for dualistic either/or's. Finally, a growing facility to *experience the Cosmic Christ in all things*. Or, as Meister Eckhart puts it, "to such a person God shines in all things" (BR, 223) and in the mystic who is you "all things become for you nothing but God" (BR, 249).

By examining the etymological meanings and then elaborating on these twenty-one running, working, definitions of mysticism we hopefully have opened the door for the psychic resurrection that healthy mysticism can make happen. A student of mine wrote recently that "from my childhood I have had mystical experiences but I did not know what they were." The ability to name our experiences is a necessary part of empowerment. It is also a necessary ingredient to community building, for the isolation of the mystic in us and in our society is a tragedy. A common language, such as that offered in this chapter, can foster possible common action in the name of mysticism. Mystics must come out of the closets, must gather to share their stories that we might set fire again to our tired and cold civilization. These stories can inspire us to acts of prophecy which can awaken our hearts, renew our cultures, and hasten the resurrection of Mother Earth.

14. The Historical Jesus as Mystic and Teacher of Mysticism

Christians must reclaim the historical Jesus as a mystic and a teacher of mysticism. The working, running characteristics of mysticism are basic to the person of Jesus and his preaching based on the surest versions of the gospels. Theologian Edward Schillebeeckx tells us that Jesus' "Abba *experience*" (his mystical experience with God the Creator or Father/ Mother) was basic to his entire life and preaching:

> What Jesus had to say about God as man's salvation springs directly from his personal experience of God, of the reality which in his own, for the time extraordinary, way he referred to as *Abba*, a concept borrowed from the Jewish family life of the period. . . . [This experience] could be the source of his assured proclamation of God's coming rule and at the same time the 'power- house' of a way of living and course of conduct anticipating the praxis of the kingdom of God.[1]

It is clear from this discussion that Jesus had undergone deeply the first two notes of mysticism—*experience (trust)* and *nondualism.* The relation between Father and child in the term *Abba* or "papa" is a deeply intimate, i.e., nondualistic one. In turn Jesus teaches his disciples to be intimate with the Father, to pray "our Father," and to experience nondualism. In this context Paul teaches followers of Jesus to "cry out 'Abba, Father!' " (Rom. 8:15). Paul also takes to heart the teaching of Jesus about the non-dualism between humans and divinity when he writes in the same passage, "everyone moved by the Spirit is a son or daughter of God. . . . heirs of God and coheirs with Christ" (8:14, 17) for "the Spirit of God has made its home in you" (8:9). A development of the mysticism of Jesus is achieved in John's Gospel when Jesus says, "The Father and I are one" (John 10:30). The very heart of Jesus' preaching—that of the nearness of the kingdom of God—is a promise of the "nearness" (i.e., the nondualism) of God's reign and presence among people. The nearness promised by Jesus is both a nearness of space—*among* or *within* you—and of time— *is* among you. There is also a nearness of time intended in the eschatological dimensions to Jesus' preaching the kingdom; there is an urgency about the "not yet" dimension to the kingdom and that is why "judgment" is at hand. The kingdom of God will erupt any minute and with it a new opportunity for persons to make breakthrough decisions.

Compassion is the thrust of Jesus' message about the kingdom and about our role in it. The summary to his Sermon on the Mount as presented in Luke's Gospel is, "Be you compassionate as your Creator in heaven is compassionate" (Luke 6:36). Notice how this challenge is a nondualistic one: for the Jew only God is "the compassionate One" but Jesus invites his followers to embrace their divinity by calling them to exercise the divine power called compassion. *Connection making* is integral to Jesus' deliberately chosen method of teaching through parables. Before he could create these stories of connections between leaven and the kingdom, between brides and bridegrooms and the kingdom, between fishing and the kingdom, between sowing and the kingdom, between harvesting and the kingdom, between lost coins and sought-after pearls and the kingdom—he had to experience, as every artist does, the *process* of connection making. His parables are fresh, unique stories born out of that mystical experience. The parables demand that his hearers also engage in connection making. His stories are not moral lessons or elaborate allegories but require the listener's participation just as a *koan* between a Buddhist guru and a disciple does.

Radical amazement and *awe* also play a powerful role in Jesus' personal experience and teaching. He demands conversion, a change of heart (*metanoia*), on the part of his followers in order that they might fully grasp the radical nature of his vision. Jesus was so committed to his vision of God's reign that he was willing to risk everything, including death, rather than abandon that vision. The kingdom/queendom of God is no small thing, though it comes from "the little ones." We fail to realize how it is that the people who hear and trust him "drop their fishing nets and follow." We know what an important part *affirmation of the world as a whole* played in Jesus' preaching because this is precisely what distinguished his eschatology from that of the dire, pessimistic apocalyptism that was current in his day (some of which can be found in John the Baptist's preaching). His news was Good News and Glad Tidings about blessing and responsibility for the world. It was never a denunciation of individuals or of creation. Yet, he did denounce the attitudes and actions of persons and groups who interfered with the affirmation of others, especially the poor and "little ones": "They tie up heavy burdens and lay them on other's shoulders, but will they lift a finger to move them? Not they! . . . [You] have neglected the weightier matters of the Law—justice, mercy, good faith!" (Matt. 23:4–23). The world as a whole is affirmed as the dwelling place of God's creatures. Among the creatures Jesus celebrates are the human outcasts—lepers, sinners, tax collectors, fishers, widows, and orphans. He affirms them as part of the sacredness of "the world as a whole." He requires that his followers do likewise: "As often as you do this to the least of these you do it to me" (Matt. 25:40). The kingdom of God is creation itself.

Jesus employed his *right brain*. He attended the synagogue and chanted in praise of God. His was an essentially nonlinear culture that was governed by oral rather than written tradition. He was attuned to nature and valued solitude, especially at the critical decision-making times of his life. He was not a lawyer or a theologian but a storyteller who announced the Good News. Storytellers work out of the right brain and speak to the right brain of others with messages of intellectual depth that strongly challenge left brains.

There is no question that Jesus was a *self-critical* person whose message of criticism evoked a response in his listeners. He dared displace Moses' authority with his own ("You have heard it said in the Law, but I say to you"); he overturned the selling tables in the Temple; he forgave sins; he challenged religious authority and taboos, including his justice towards women, foreigners (the Samaritan and the woman at the well), and children. All of this critical consciousness comes from his mysticism and leads to his death. Jesus would not have been crucified had his message and person not been radical and critical. His was also a mysticism of *heart knowledge* for Jesus speaks from the heart and to the heart. He insists that pollutions do not come from outside the mind or heart in the matter of obeying external laws but from within. Adultery is committed "in the heart" and persons are to pray and fast not "so people can see them" but "in that secret place, and your Creator who sees all that is done in secret" will respond (Matt. 5:28; 6:6, 18).

Jesus is often *returning to the source* of his being. His *Abba* prayer is an example of that. So too is his use of the term "Father" in his teaching about prayer and living. Heart knowledge leads one back to the source, to the One who blesses, to the One who is with us, to the Creator. That Jesus was a *feminist* is evident as he presents an almost unique view of women for a man of his time, culture, and religion. Chauvinistic language, imagery, and concerns are absent from his teachings. He was at home with women and with men; he had both male and female relationships and followers. His call to compassion is a call to a more maternal, compassionate way of life. Women were the first to believe in his resurrection and to pass on the good news.

Jesus as presented in the synoptic Gospels is *panentheistic.* The emphasis in Matthew's Gospel on Jesus as *Emmanuel,* God-with-us (Matt. 1:22), is an emphasis on the immanent presence of divinity in Jesus and in the world by way of Jesus' presence. In his preaching on the "amongness" of the kingdom/queendom of God, Jesus preaches a truly panentheistic mysticism. "The kingdom/queendom of God is not coming with signs to be observed; nor will they say, 'Lo, here it is!' or 'There!' for behold, the kingdom of God is in the midst of you" (Luke 17:20–21). *Already* the kingdom/queendom of God is among you, just as panentheism teaches. We are in the kingdom and the kingdom is in us. The past is here and the present is here and even the future is here, for "the future battle is already taking place, now, in the present," as exegete Norman Perrin puts it in his comments on this passage.[2] Perhaps the most important word in this celebrated pericope of Jesus' pronouncement on the immanence of God's realm is the word *behold*, since Jesus' often shocking parables have as their primary purpose to *get people to behold*, to get people to wake up and see, to behold what is already in their midst. (See Matt. 13:13–17.) He startles his Jewish listeners, for example, by getting them to *behold* the divine compassion in a "good Samaritan" (Luke 10:30–36). At the time of Jesus most Jews could never see the divine presence in Samaritans who were sworn enemies.

What is it we are always being told to behold in Jesus' parables? The divine presence everywhere. For this "beholding" to take place, a breakthrough has to happen in our consciousness. As John Dominic Crossan puts it, an "inbreaking of the kingdom" happens to the person hearing Jesus' parables about the kingdom. Thus "does the kingdom of God break abruptly into a person's consciousness and demand the overturn of prior values, closed options, set judgments, and established conclusions."[3] In my categories, part of the inbreaking of the kingdom is the movement from theism to panentheism itself. C. H. Dodd calls the promise that the "kingdom of God is among you" evidence of the "instantaneousness and ubiquitous" nature of the kingdom of God, which "is not localized in space (or time)." It is already "within your hands, within your power."[4] The kingdom of God spoken of as a Seed Growing Secretly in Mark 4:26–29 is depicted as "a present fact" and a "present crisis." For "something has now happened which never happened before."[5] Jesus has seen something that so many others have missed: that all is in God and God is in all. Or, that all is in the kingdom/queendom of God and the kingdom/queendom of God is in all. For Jesus the kingdom/queendom of God is *a panentheistic realm.* Because there are sinners in the kingdom or weeds among the farmers' crop does not denigrate from the fact of panentheism (Matt. 13:24–30).[6] The Dragnet that the kingdom is (Matt. 13:47–48) "involves an undiscriminating appeal to men of every class and type," says Dodd.[7] It would be difficult to imagine a more panentheistic image than that of the dragnet that Jesus invents in that story. Leaven in bread is another deeply panentheistic image that Jesus (in Matt. 13:33; Luke 13:20–21) applies to the kingdom/queendom of God. Like Jesus' ministry leaven had in it "no element of coercion, but in it the power of God's kingdom worked from within, mightily permeating the dead lump of religious Judaism in His time."[8] How rich the theme of panentheism is in Jesus' parables and preaching about the kingdom/queendom of God! Even small experiences of creation, such as mustard seeds, contain the divine. Exegete Pheme Perkins writes, "Jesus' nature parables are not romantic poetry. They hope to awaken us to a vision of the presence of God that is dependable even in situations that might appear to be full of loss. . . . The common world is pictured as a place of God's transforming presence." Is this not another way of saying "all is in God and God is in all?" Is this awakening to panentheism not at the heart of Jesus' awakening all to the kingdom/queendom of God?

Jesus' ministry was one of *birthing images*—his parables indicate a fertile imagination wrestling with efforts at new images for the kingdom of God and for the role of humans in bringing it about. He also elicited immense image birthing from others—the Gospels and the Epistles of the New Testament testify to his power to elicit images from others. Jesus was an artist in his parables and his storytelling, in his preaching of the kingdom/queendom of God and in his healing of the sick, in relating to the dispossessed and the outcast. On numerous occasions Jesus took symbolic actions related to his religious traditions that reveal his deep intuition such as his decision to go to Jerusalem during Passover when the sacrifice of the lamb was being celebrated. His Last Supper indicates his awareness that he was to be the lamb sacrificed.

Silence was evident in Jesus' way. He talks of not praying "long prayers like the pagans" but brief prayers that are to the point (Matt. 6:7). He speaks about the "secrets of the heart" (Matt. 5:28). While the stories and sayings he relates in the Gospels are very rich, they really are not numerous. His message is more one of action than of speech. Thus his actions of healing are often done in silence and flow from a deep sense of silence. At his trial and torture, he apparently had little to say to his tormentors. The admonition to pray "behind closed doors" (Matt. 6:6) suggests a kind of silence, as does his going alone into the desert to pray. We are told that his mother on several occasions "pondered events in her heart" (Luke 2:19), a prayer of silence.

Jesus' decision to enter Jerusalem during Passover, when sentiment against him was strong, led to an experience of *nothingness and darkness* that is archetypal in human history—his cruel and premature death by crucifixion. He chose to align himself with those in society for whom darkness and death were an ever-present reality even before he confronted his own intense darkness and death on the cross. He wrestled with spirits of psychic darkness in temptations to temporal kingship or success as well as with the death of friends and betrayal by them. He associated with those who lived "in darkness"—the social outcasts. His acts of healing presume an empathetic understanding of the darkness and suffering of others.

Jesus was also a *child at play*. Perhaps this is what allowed him to break laws and taboos so easily—"the Sabbath is for people, not people for the Sabbath" (Mark 2:27)—and to give birth to new images. His respect for children is explicit, not sentimental or patronizing. Children are teachers of adults—"unless you adults change and become like children you will never enter the kingdom/queendom of God" (Matt. 18:3). The evangelists, writing during the persecution of Jesus' followers, are more concerned with the events of Jesus' death than with his sense of humor and play. Yet, play and childlikeness were a part of the disciple's experience of Jesus. Jesus was involved in *psychic justice*—what being "pure of heart" (Matt. 5:8) is all about. He sought inner justice as well as outer justice. "Blessed are those who suffer persecution for justice' sake, for theirs is the kingdom/queendom of heaven" (Matt. 5:10). He desired a cleansing of the heart as well as the Temple, for God dwells in both. One of the oldest terms used in reference to Jesus was that of *prophet,* and he did not discourage that title. The first time he speaks in the Gospel of Luke he refers to himself as a prophet (Luke 4:24). He did what prophets do—announce the Glad Tidings—and he suffered what prophets suffer, as he said.

The ancient tradition of Judaism that God is the One-who-is-with-us (Emmanuel) can be traced back to the oldest Biblical writer, the Yahwist author of Genesis. The theme of being-with God was surely Jesus' raw experience in his *Abba* prayer. The theme of being-with-being helps to explain his preaching about the kingdom/queendom. Being with the Maker of all being is certainly *being-with-being.* The God Jesus worshipped as a Jew was the one who called himself "I am" or "I will be" (Exod. 3:14). Jesus' being-with-being was developed in his intense relationships with persons and with processes of nature, which he employed in his parables. No falling sparrows or fish or weeds or rocks escape his observations, his being-with.

Jesus, like all of us, wrestled with his *true self:* his destiny, his task, his decision making. He wrestled alone in prayer and together with those who were closest to him. He called others to become more truly themselves, to be true to their hearts and true to the perspective of the kingdom/queendom of God in their midst. He called for *metanoia* (conversion) and he got a response. He called persons to let go of fear and lack of trust, in order that the kingdom/queendom might take root in them. "Set your hearts on the divine realm first, and on divine righteousness, and all those other things will be given you as well" (Matt. 6:33). With the true self God is well pleased. Jesus is *globally ecumenical* in the sense that his teaching is universal—he breaks taboos and proclaims salvation to both Jews and non-Jews, to sinners and the saved. Foreigners, such as Samaritans, are heroes in his parables.

That Jesus was a mystic, both in his person and his proclamation, has been sorely neglected by Christian theology. The reader is invited to pursue this methodology more deeply by reflecting on the person, teachings, and example of Jesus through the prism of the mystical characteristics offered here. Albert Schweitzer was one of the few Christians of this century who had the courage to call Jesus a mystic, but he insisted that Jesus was a mystic and teacher of mysticism only in an eschatological sense, that is in terms of the Coming of the Son of Man in the future.[10] I believe that Jesus was a mystic in the fullest sense of the term because he lived the mystery of his relationship with the Creator and taught others to do the same. He truly "entered the mysteries" and invited others to follow him. He extended this invitation within the context of his preaching of a kingdom/queendom that was both present and yet to come, both eschatological and already among us. Indeed, his teaching was eschatological in that it was meant to trigger the mysticism of his hearers and thus bring about the future reign of God. His parables were designed to do this both in content and in form. The purpose of his parables was breakthrough and *metanoia:* seeing the world in a new way, a Good News way. This is not so much eschatology as a future event as it is the future come home, the future starting here and now. "Thy kingdom/queendom come on earth as it is in heaven" (Matt. 6:10). Jesus' mysticism was both eschatological *and* prophetic. His followers must also embrace a mysticism with these dimensions. The letters of Paul and the Gospels fall into this category of eschatological but prophetic mysticism. So too does the history of Christian mysticism *when it is healthy.* When it falls into disease, it loses the prophetic dimension.

The earliest sources we have of Jesus' life and teachings reveal this mystical dimension. In the theology of Paul we encounter a highly developed mysticism "in Christ," and in the "death and resurrection of Christ" (see Paul's epistles, especially Romans and 1 Corinthians). This mysticism does not deny the pain of the world, yet it images all suffering in the context of the resurrection. We shall explore this theme more fully in the next section of this book. In doing so we begin to open the door to the healing of Mother Earth's pain, the dream with which we began this book and the issue that binds all persons on this planet together in the task of a prophetic and eschatological mysticism.

Part III

From the Quest for the Historical Jesus to the Quest for the Cosmic Christ
A Paradigm Shift for Western Religion

In him were created all things in heaven and on earth: everything visible and everything invisible.

(Colossians 1:16)

Christ exists in all things that are.

(Gregory of Nazianzus)

The Logos of God has become human so that you might learn from a human being how a human being may become divine.

(Clement of Alexandria)

It is God whom human beings know in every creature.

(Hildegard of Bingen)

Each creature is a witness to God's power and omnipotence; and its beauty is a witness to the divine wisdom. . . . Every creature participates in some way in the likeness of the Divine Essence.

(Thomas Aquinas)

The Incarnation accomplished the following: That God became human and that humans became God and sharers in the divine nature.

(Thomas Aquinas)

Each of us is a mirror of eternal contemplation, with a reflection that must surely be that of the living Son of God with all his works.

(Mechtild of Magdeburg)

God is constantly speaking only one thing. God's speaking is one thing. In this one utterance God speaks the Son and at the same time the Holy Spirit and all creatures.

(Meister Eckhart)

See! I am God. See! I am in everything. See! I never lift my hands off my works, nor will I ever. See! I lead everything toward the purpose for which I ordained it, without beginning, by the same Power, Wisdom and Love by which I created it. How could anything be amiss?

(Julian of Norwich)

Divinity is the enfolding and unfolding of everything that is. Divinity is in all things in such a way that all things are in divinity.

(Nicholas of Cusa)

The Enlightenment's quest of the historical Jesus was made possible, and made necessary, when Enlightenment philosophy deposed the Cosmic Christ.

(Jaroslav Pelikan)

Our age and that age of the first century have more in common than we think. . . . Both times can be characterized as cosmically scared, frightened ages, caught under principalities and powers where tiny little human beings just know that they cannot do much, that they are not in control, that they are just caught.

(Krister Stendahl)

The reception of a new paradigm often necessitates a redefinition of the corresponding science. Some old problems may be

relegated to another science or declared entirely "unscientif-
ic." Others that were previously non-existent or trivial may,
with a new paradigm, become the very archetypes of significant scientific achievement.

(Thomas Kuhn)

People do not put new wine into old wineskins; if they do, the
skins burst, the wine runs out, and the skins are lost. No. They
put new wine into fresh skins and both are preserved.

(Jesus)

This third nature of Christ (neither human nor divine, but cosmic)—has not noticeably attracted the explicit attention of the
faithful or of theologians.

(Teilhard de Chardin)

A few years ago I referred to the term "the Cosmic Christ" in a television show being taped under the direction of a Methodist minister. She
asked, "What is 'the Cosmic Christ?' I've never heard the phrase before." This woman was a well-read and recently educated minister, having been ordained about five years. I have since learned that very few
graduates of Christian seminaries—Protestant or Catholic—have been
exposed to the theology of the Cosmic Christ. Theologian and scientist
Teilhard de Chardin complained that he could not find either theologians or lay people interested in the Cosmic Christ. Why is this concept
so foreign to Christianity today?

Lutheran scholar of church history, Jaroslav Pelikan, believes it is the
result of the Enlightenment. "Enlightenment philosophy deposed the
cosmic Christ," he writes.[1] One might expect that, when rationalism and
patriarchal mindsets drive out mysticism, intuition, imagination, and
above all cosmology, the Cosmic Christ would be banished as well. If humanity can survive without a cosmology, why would it need a Cosmic
Christ? If the human mind has "outgrown" mysticism, why would it
need a Cosmic Christ? In an anthropocentric era of culture, education,
and religion, there is no need of a Cosmic Christ. Such a concept is an
embarrassment. If Newton is correct and our universe it essentially a
machine, who needs a Cosmic Christ? There is no mystery in a machine-
universe. The concept of "mystery" itself is reduced to the level of an
"unsolved problem." Mystery as the dark silence behind all being and
the deep, unfathomable presence that grounds all being is banished.
The Enlightenment banished mystery and mysticism, relegating the latter to extraordinary states of consciousness on the periphery of things,
and consequently, it banished the Cosmic Christ. As Lutheran scholar

Joseph Sittler observed, the rationalism and pietism that infiltrated Christianity from the seventeenth century to the present also "turned down the blaze of the . . . vision [of the Cosmic Christ] so radically that it . . . was effective only as a moral or mystical incandescence."[2]

We see in this brief account of the loss of a Cosmic Christ theology the power of culture—in this case the Enlightenment movement—to influence spirituality. The Christian West was too alienated from its own creation mystical tradition to resist this secular effort to eliminate a living cosmology symbolized religiously by the "Cosmic Christ." Augustine's theology, which heavily influenced the philosophy of Descartes, has no cosmic Christ.[3] Augustine's preoccupation with human guilt and salvation and his promotion of an introspective conscience,[4] offered no resistance to a cultural movement that sought to eliminate the cosmos, the maternal principle in the psyche, and with it the Cosmic Christ. In effect, theologians responded to the Enlightenment by putting aside the concept of Cosmic Christ, and with it most other attempts to see the world and faith in nonanthropocentric ways. As white, Western culture decimated native populations by acts of colonialism—populations that worshipped a Cosmic Christ because they worshipped in a living cosmology—the Western church lost its Cosmic Christ. Theologian Krister Stendahl wisely criticizes Rudolf Bultmann for his anthropocentrism and indeed the entire theological enterprise of our time:

> We [Christians] happen to be more interested in ourselves than in God or in the fate of his creation. . . . Rudolf Bultmann's whole theological enterprise has *one* great mistake from which all others emanate: he takes for granted that basically the center of gravity—the center from which all interpretation springs—is anthropology, the doctrine of man.[5]

Instead of the Cosmic Christ, the Enlightenment challenged Christian theology to go in search of the "historical Jesus." The quest for the historical Jesus has dominated christological studies for two centuries. Pelikan, commenting on how this quest has been undertaken *at the expense of the Cosmic Christ,* says, "The Enlightenment's quest of the Historical Jesus was made possible and made necessary when Enlightenment philosophy deposed the Cosmic Christ."[6]

I believe the issue today for the third millennium of Christianity—if the earth is to survive into the next century—is the *quest for the Cosmic Christ.* The movement from the Enlightenment's quest for the historical Jesus to today's quest for the Cosmic Christ names the paradigm shift that religion and theology presently need to undergo. One cannot explore the meaning and power of the Cosmic Christ without a living cosmology, a living mysticism, and the spiritual discipline of art as meditation. *The holy trinity of science (knowledge of creation), mysticism (experiential union with creation and its unnameable mysteries), and art (expression of our awe at creation) is what constitute a living cosmology.* Every theologian must embark on these pathways and awaken them within if the theological enterprise is to accomplish its task in our time. This will require a deep letting go of the old paradigms of education and theology. The old wineskins of an anthropocentric, rationalistic, antimystical, antimaternal worldview cannot contain the new wine of creativity that is exploding wherever minds, and hearts and bodies are being baptized into a living cosmology, into the living Cosmic Christ. Perhaps it is time to back huge moving vans up to our seminaries, load up the immense theological paraphernalia that has accumulated around the theme of the historical Jesus, and channel religion's resources in another direction— the quest for the Cosmic Christ.

What has been accomplished in the period of the quest for the historical Jesus is by no means lost in our pursuit of the Cosmic Christ. It may be that we could not understand the dynamic character of the Cosmic Christ without access to twentieth-century scientific revelations of the radically dynamic and creative nature of our universe from the very first millisecond of its existence. A theology of the Cosmic Christ must be grounded in the historical Jesus, in his words, in his liberating deeds (cf. liberation theology), in his life and orthopraxis. The Cosmic Christ is not a doctrine that is believed in and lived out *at the expense of the historical Jesus.* Rather, a dialectic is in order, a dance between time (Jesus) and space (Christ); between the personal and the cosmic; between the prophetic and the mystical. The dance is a dance away from anthropocentrism.

Nevertheless, in calling for a paradigm shift in theology and religion itself we are not talking about an easy change of consciousness or a simplistic change of agenda. To move from a "personal Savior" Christianity—which is what an anthropocentric and antimystical Christianity gives us—to a "Cosmic Christ" Christianity calls for *metanoia*, a change of perspective by all those who do theology and by those schools which claim to teach theology. It will no longer be possible to teach theology without art as meditation, without spiritual disciplines that are grounded in the body and that arouse the imagination, as an integral part of the curriculum. Just as science has its laboratory hours for teaching the methods of scientific inquiry, so too theology requires laboratories in painting, clay, ritual, massage, and music to teach the art of mystical development. Churches and synagogues require laboratories of prayer where the "prune brain" that the right lobe has become can be watered, nourished, and developed. The Cosmic Christ cannot find a home in a left-brained setting alone. No exclusively left-brained individual or institution, whether of education or of worship, can welcome the Cosmic Christ.

15. The Quest for the Cosmic Christ— A Paradigm Shift

To understand fully the implications in shifting from the quest for the historical Jesus to the quest for the Cosmic Christ, it may prove valuable to look at the classic work by Thomas Kuhn on paradigm shifts in science, *The Structure of Scientific Revolutions.* Among the various descriptions of a new paradigm, Kuhn offers the following:

- see nature in a new way
- a shift of vision
- a transformation of vision
- a conversion
- a map or a director for making a map
- a switch in visual gestalt[1]

A paradigm or worldview or vision, Kuhn believes, is a *community* issue, not a private one. Reeducation is greatly needed during the era of a paradigm shift. It will require different roles of different persons—indeed it may require an entirely different kind of person. Otto Rank refers to this when he says, "New personality types are created during social and spiritual crises of religious, political or economic origin."[2]

Kuhn explains the origins of paradigm shifts in the following manner. First, an anomaly awakens us to new questions. An anomaly is "a phenomenon for which one's paradigm had not readied the investigator." Mother Earth's survival and the murder of the mother principle in general constitutes such an anomaly. The war on nature and on Mother Earth that proceeds unabatedly and without interference by organized religion provides a startling anomaly indeed. Often, Kuhn believes, there is a growing awareness that "something is amiss" in one's worldview. This awareness produces breakthrough. What he calls "paradigm-induced anticipations"[3] are violated.

The second step in a paradigm shift is a crisis or breakdown. What prophets call a "tearing up and knocking down" is necessary. Kuhn calls it a kind of "paradigm destruction so a new paradigm can emerge. . . . Einstein's theory can be accepted only with the recognition that Newton's was wrong." An example of such an upheaval may be a deep insecurity in one's profession that precedes new paradigm shift. Such an insecurity can be observed among clergy and hierarchy in Western churches today. In the sixteenth century, Ptolemaic astronomy failed to solve the scientific problems being addressed and thus it was time, "to give a competitor a chance," comments Kuhn. I would suggest a religious parallel: Augustine has failed to solve the problems of religion for the West, and thus, it is time to give a less sexist, less dualistic, less anthropocentric religious paradigm its chance. This paradigm can be found in a creation-centered mysticism, one that leads to a cosmology in action. There is a "failure to fit" in the old paradigm, Kuhn reports. I suggest that religion's "failure to fit" is evident in the fact that fewer than ten percent of European Catholics, for example, attend worship on a regular basis. Everywhere the youth are voting against the current religious paradigm with their feet—they are walking out of the church.

The worship being offered is taking place in the context of a failed paradigm. So too are definitions of religious life and spiritual leadership. Often the new paradigm comes in the middle of the night to the young, Kuhn observes.⁴

According to Kuhn, there is a transition period between paradigms in which one can expect "a large but never complete overlap between the problems that can be solved by the old and by the new paradigm. But there will also be a decisive difference in the modes of solution." Different rules with a different universe of discourse will characterize the familiar and the old paradigm. What characterizes the new paradigm? It is more aesthetic; neater; simpler than the old. What was once considered "trivial" in the previous paradigm— and here I include Mother Earth, wisdom literature of the Bible, science, art, mysticism and the Cosmic Christ—"may, with a new paradigm, become the very archetypes of significant scientific achievement." One result of such a paradigm shift may be a "redefinition of the corresponding science." I believe that an awakening to the mystical requires such a redefinition in Western theology and church practice—one, for example, that quests after the Cosmic Christ with the same vigor employed in the search for the historical Jesus since the Enlightenment. Another result may well be a "revolution in world view."⁵

Kuhn warns that resistance will often accompany a paradigm shift. I would add that denial does also—the denial that everything is not right in Christianity, or in Western education, or in our very definitions of what constitute theological education and ministerial training, or in the prevailing worldview of patriarchal religion in general. I detect a kind of "denial of death" when religious believers are first exposed to creation theology because persons resist hearing that Augustine on whom we have depended for so long, might have misled us on many basic issues. Resistance is a sign that something deep is being challenged, and a paradigm shift is a deep movement indeed. "The decision to reject one paradigm is always simultaneously the decision to accept another, and the judgment leading to that decision involves the comparison of both paradigms with nature and with each other."⁶ In other words, a paradigm shift requires generosity, courage, and sacrifice. Otto Rank put it this way:

> We are at one of those crises in human history in which once again we must sacrifice one thing if we want the full enjoyment of another. . . . There seems to be a spiritual law whereby nothing can be wholly won or enjoyed without something being given up or sacrificed for it.⁷

Surrender, Rank insists, is always a "freely chosen decision."⁸ The surrender of an overly anthropocentric Jesus and an overly anthropocentric and antimystical religious vision is part of the process of letting go— one might say, part of the way of the cross in our day—that is required if a new and living paradigm such as the Cosmic Christ is to replace both the quest for the personal savior of fundamentalism and the quest for "salvation by footnotes" to which a rationalistic theology succumbs.

In my earlier book, *Original Blessing*, I named the religious paradigm shift of our time as one from original sin to original blessing. In terms of the history of spirituality, this paradigm shift is from the three stages of purification, illumination, and union that mysticism inherited from Proclus and Plotinus (*not* from Jesus or the Hebrew Bible since neither of these thinkers was either Jewish or Christian) to the four paths of delight (*via positiva*), letting go (*via negativa*), creativity (*via creativa*), compassion, i.e., celebration and justicemaking (*via transformativa*). Today "to enter the mysteries" means to enter the mysteries of the four paths of creation spirituality—mysteries of delight, darkness, birthing, compassion. In this section we will explore more fully how the paradigm shift can also be named as moving from the quest for the historical Jesus to the quest for the Cosmic Christ.

Though I am approaching this paradigm shift from a theological perspective, it should be emphasized that this shift will affect every aspect of our culture. Kuhn's study, which outlined the dynamics of a paradigm shift, is a study of such a shift in science. A scientific paradigm is the most basic of all paradigms in a culture, and it is changing radically in our time. But the religious paradigm is, from the point of view of culture itself, of immense importance, as sociologist Robert Bellah points out. "No one has changed a great nation," he writes, "without appealing to its soul. . . . Culture is the key to revolution; religion is the key to culture."[9] The "Jesus" dimension to religion paralleled the individualism of the Enlightenment and industrial age. A "cosmic" dimension to the Jesus story parallels an emerging age in which Mother Earth yearns to see from the human race a living cosmology, an awakened creativity and a deeper commitment to compassion. When scientific and religious shifts occur together a new civilization, a "new soul,"[10] is born. A living cosmology is, by definition, science, mysticism, and art creating together a vision for existence.

Jesus Christ himself spoke of a paradigm shift when he presented the image of the old and new wineskins. A wineskin in Jesus' culture was the container on which one's life depended for surviving the long, hot journey through the desert. If the wineskin sprung a leak, it was a life and death matter. The wineskin was portable and supple. A fermenting process went on inside subjecting it to considerable stress. A dried-up wineskin was a dangerous companion for the journey.

In keeping with this image I am proposing that our current religious wineskin, which lacks the Cosmic Christ, is not only dangerously dried-up but also leaking badly. The wine, the energy and power of the Good News, cannot be contained, much less allowed to develop and ferment, in these old wineskins. Without a living cosmology our tradition cannot sustain us for the adventurous journey to which so many feel themselves called. Jesus put it quite directly: "People do not put new wine into old wineskins; if they do, the skins burst; the wine same as before runs out, and the skins are lost. No. They put new wine into fresh skins and both are preserved" (Matt. 9:17). A paradigm shift is clearly both a spiritual and a cultural event of great significance.

We shall now consider the Cosmic Christ from the viewpoint of its sources in Scripture, in the history of Christian mysticism (especially that of the creation mystics of the Middle Ages), and in its meaning for today: Does a new theology of the Cosmic Christ offer the hope of a *revitalized* Paschal mystery for the third millennium of Christianity? Does the Cosmic Christ represent a true second coming, an ushering in of a spiritual and cultural renaissance that can heal the most poignant and urgent pain of our time—the crucifixion of Mother Earth?

16. Biblical Sources for Belief in the Cosmic Christ

By returning to our sources, we gain an impetus for and an understanding about the rich doctrine of the Cosmic Christ that Christianity largely has hidden within its bosom for centuries. As Joseph Sittler put it, "the theological magnificence of Cosmic Christology lies for the most part, still tightly folded in the Church's innermost heart and memory."[1] Teilhard de Chardin calls the Cosmic Christ the "third nature" of Christ, meaning that it takes us beyond the fourth-century conciliar definitions of Christ's human and divine natures into a third realm, "neither human nor divine, but cosmic." He comments that this has "not noticeably attracted the explicit attention of the faithful or of theologians." Clearly Chardin saw the paradigm shift that was implicit in powerful celebration of the Cosmic Christ.

In this section I will present a basic recovery of the Cosmic Christ from biblical sources, beginning with the tradition in Israel and concluding with the hymns to the Cosmic Christ and the Gospel stories from the New Testament.

THE COSMIC CHRIST IN ISRAEL

PREEXISTENT WISDOM. The Cosmic Christ was present in Israel and in the Hebrew Bible principally as cosmic wisdom. Preexistent wisdom is celebrated in Israel on numerous occasions. In the book of Job the penetrating question is asked, "Where does wisdom come from?" (Job 28:12, 20) and in Baruch wisdom is celebrated as the divine attribute by which God governs the world (Bar. 3:9–4:4). Wisdom is personified in Proverbs (1:20–33; 8:1–36; 9:1–6) in passages such as the following:

> Wisdom calls aloud in the streets,
> she raises her voice in the public squares;
> she calls out at the street corners,
> she delivers her message at the city gates.
>
> (Prov. 1:20–21)

> Yahweh created me when his purpose first unfolded,
> before the oldest of his works.
> From everlasting I was firmly set,
> from the beginning, before earth came into being.
> The deep was not, when I was born,
> there were no springs to gush with water.
> Before the mountains were settled,
> before the hills, I came to birth;
> before he made the earth, the countryside,
> or the first grains of the world's dust.
> When he fixed the heavens firm, I was there
>
> (Prov. 8:22–26)

> Come and eat my bread,
> drink the wine I have prepared!
>
> (Prov. 9:5)

Sirach 24 also celebrates this preexistent wisdom:

> Alone I encircled the vault of the sky,
> and I walked on the bottom of the deeps.
> Over the waves of the sea and over the whole earth,
> and over every people and nation I have held sway. . . .
> From eternity, in the beginning, he created me,
> and for eternity I shall remain.
> . . . .
> Approach me, you who desire me,
> and take your fill of my fruits.
>
> (Sir. 24:5–6, 9, 26)

The book of Wisdom instructs us that Wisdom "pervades and permeates all things" (8:24). She is "a breath of the power of God" and "a reflection of the eternal light, untarnished mirror of God's active power, image of his goodness" (7:25, 26). The power of Wisdom is great:

> Although alone, she can do all;
> herself unchanging, she makes all things new.
> In each generation she passes into holy souls,
> she makes them friends of God and prophets.
> . . . .
> She deploys her strength from one end of the earth to the
> other,
> ordering all things for good.
>
> (Wis. 7:27; 8:1)

It is Wisdom who "knows God's works and was present when God made the world" (9:9), and it is Wisdom who is worthy to govern with justice and sit on the Father's throne (9:13).

The wisdom texts of Israel play prominently in the Cosmic Christ texts of the Christian Scriptures. Christ is the source of true wisdom that comes from God (1 Cor. 1:30). John 1 and John 5 grow out of the Cosmic Christ texts of Sirach 24. The experience of the Cosmic Christ was expressed in the earliest Christian writings that eventually became the New Testament. Very often these passages are hymns that were sung at liturgical gatherings—hymns to the Cosmic Christ. We need to emphasize how basic this doctrine was to the earliest believers in Jesus who were instructed by the disciples themselves. These believers lived in a world that "had great interest in the cosmos," as Schillebeeckx comments.[3] The mystery religions and goddess religions of the period were not as anthropocentric and rationalistic as our recent Western culture has become. It is in this context that the celebration of the Cosmic Christ answered a yearning in the human heart on the one hand and distinguished the new believers in Jesus from their counterparts on the other. There were significant contrasts between those who believed in Jesus as the Cosmic Christ and those who were initiated into other forms of cosmic spirituality. Later we will do an exegesis of some of the Christian Scriptures that are central to a Cosmic Christ theology and mysticism.

THE PROPHETS. The Cosmic Christ is present in the prophets and in certain messianic expectations. As Abraham Heschel puts it, "what concerns the prophet is the human event as a divine experience. History to us is the record of human experience; to the prophet it is a record of God's experience."[4] The experience of God as integral to human history is the experience of the suffering, the pathos, the anguish, and the anger of God who suffers when innocent victims suffer from injustice. This is surely an instance of the Comic Christ as the universal suffering one. The God of the prophets is everywhere. " 'Am I a God close at hand, and not a God far off?' says the Lord. 'Can anyone hide oneself in secret places where I shall not see them? Do I not fill heaven and earth?' says the Lord" (Jer. 23:23–24). A universal awakening is promised wherein "all nations shall flow to the mountain of the house of the Lord" (Isa. 2:2–3) and war among nations will cease. "For the earth shall be full of the knowledge of the Lord as the waters cover the sea" (Isa. 11:9). Because justice is the primary preoccupation of the prophet whose task is to penetrate human history with the divine desire, and because justice for Israel is a cosmological issue—the universe itself is understood to stand on pillars of righteousness and justice—it follow that the prophets cannot operate without a living cosmology, without a sense of the Cosmic Christ. Human injustice makes Mother Earth suffer.

> The earth shall disclose the blood shed upon her,
> And shall no longer cover up her slain.
>
> (Isa. 26:21)

> The world languishes and withers,
> The heavens languish together with the earth.
> The earth lies polluted under its inhabitants,
> For they have transgressed the laws,
> Violated the statutes, broken the everlasting covenant.
>
> (Isa. 24:4–5)

The messianic vision of the prophets offers redemption from the sinful and anthropocentric ways of humanity. The redemption promised is a universal one. "The God of Israel is also the God of her enemies. . . . They will live together when they worship together," comments Heschel.[5] We see this also in Zechariah, "Many nations shall join themselves to the Lord in that day, and shall be My people" (2:15) and in Isaiah, "My house shall be called a house of prayer for all people" (56:7).

There is only one history. "Have we not all one Creator? Has not one God created us? Why then are we faithless to one another, profaning the covenant of our ancestors?" asks the prophet Malachi (2:10). "The prophet," says Heschel, "may be regarded as the first universal man in history" because he addresses his message to all peoples.[6] Isaiah spoke to God's plan "concerning the whole earth" (14:26) and spoke to "all you inhabitants of the world, you who dwell on the earth" (18:3). Jeremiah was appointed "a prophet to the nations" (1:5) and Amos spoke in the name of the God who wields the destiny of all nations (9:7). Justice is a universal issue common to all expressions of the Cosmic Christ through the word of God or the gift of creation. In addition, the prophet is pictured as a kind of preexistent figure, not unlike the preexistence of cosmic wisdom itself. Consider, for example, Jeremiah's calling as prophet:

> The word of Yahweh was addressed to me, saying,
> "Before I formed you in the womb I knew you,
> before you came to birth I consecrated you;
> I have appointed you as prophet to the nations."
>
> (Jer. 1:4–5)

The fact that Jesus saw himself in the prophetic tradition made it quite natural for his followers to understand him as the Cosmic Christ, the one "anointed . . . to bring the good news to the poor, to proclaim liberty to captives and to the blind new sight, to set the downtrodden free, to proclaim the Lord's year of favor" (Luke 4:18–19).

APOCALYPTIC LITERATURE. The Cosmic Christ is present in Israel's tradition of apocalyptic literature. Apocalyptic literature is steeped in angelology and in visions of cosmic happenings. Angels always denote a cosmology because, as theologian Rob van der Hart puts it, "Angels were put in charge of the cosmic order." The reason angels abound in apocalyptic literature is that crisis times produce angels, according to van der Hart.[7] In the book of Daniel the expression "the son of man coming on the clouds of heaven" (7:13–14) who receives "dominion, glory and kingship" is said to stand for Israel herself, the Chosen People seen as a cosmic body. This phrase, "son of man," became Jesus' favorite expression to refer to himself in the Gospels. It is connected to notions of the weakness of the human person and to the suffering servant of Isaiah. "The Son of Man has not come to be served but to serve" (Mark 10:45). At the same time, however, this title also identifies "a figure of cosmic power." As one scholar puts it:

> While suffering is central to the concept of Son of Man, power and glory are too. In fact, the titles Son of Man and Son of God are functionally very similar. The Son of Man forgives sins, has authority over the Sabbath, rises from the dead, and comes in the glory of the Father accompanied by the holy angels, with great power and glory. He assembles his chosen ones from all over the earth, initiates the last drama of world history, vindicates his ministry, and presides as eschatological judge.[8]

In other words, the Son of Man category is deeply cosmological in both the Hebrew Bible and the Christian Scriptures. C. H. Dodd believes that the "Son of Man" as applied to Jesus in John's Gospel may connect to Hellenistic traditions about a heavenly person who is the prototype of humankind and is the true human who dwells in all good humans.[9] Written during times of persecution, the book of Daniel—as so much of apocalyptic literature—was a source of exhortation and encouragement that the Jews not abandon their faith. Apocalyptic literature emphasizes the end-times and the nearness of the Day of Judgment for the persecuting powers that be. While apocalyptic literature found its way into the Gospels, the fullest expression of this literary genre in Christianity found in the book of Revelation. In that book we find the rich imagery of the Cosmic Christ displayed in an apocalyptic vein, or what biblical scholar Elisabeth Schüssler Fiorenza calls the "science fiction" genre of the Bible.

NEW TESTAMENT HYMNS IN CELEBRATION OF THE COSMIC CHRIST

PHILIPPIANS 2:1–24. Paul ushers in this cosmic hymn with a call to compassionate behavior for those who "participate in the Spirit": "Complete my joy by being of the same mind, having the same love, being in full accord and of one mind. Do nothing from selfishness or conceit. . . . Let each of you look to the interests of others. Have this mind among yourselves, which you have in Christ Jesus" (2:2–5). Then he launches into the hymn:

Who, though he was in the form of God,
did not count equality with God
a thing to be grasped,
but emptied himself,
taking the form of a servant
being born in the likeness of humanity.
And being found in human form
he humbled himself and became obedient unto death
even death on a cross.
Therefore God has highly exalted him
and bestowed on him the name
which is above every name,
that at the name of Jesus
every knee should bow
in heaven and earth and under the earth,
and every tongue confess that Jesus Christ is Lord,
to the glory of God the Creator.

(2:6–11)

Paul, who definitely wrote this letter—probably about A.D. 56–57—is celebrating Jesus as exalted by God to be a new cosmic ruler. The early Christians who sang this hymn are employing the cosmology of the Hellenistic world of their time, the threefold division of the universe into heaven, earth, and the under-the-earth realm. Jesus rules all. Jewish theology is also employed here. Jesus being in "the form of God" alludes to the "image and likeness of God" motif accorded the original Adam in Gen. 1:26–27. But Jesus was emptied and treated as a "servant" or "slave." Here we could have an allusion to the suffering servant theme of Isaiah—and here too we have one of the shocking differences between Cosmic Christ mysticism and other cosmic mysticisms: the historical cross is central to grounding the Christ. The Cosmic Christ is a wounded person, one who died on a cross (scholars believe that Paul added the phrase "even death on a cross" to the original hymn). It is necessary to understand Cosmic Christ mysticism in the historical context of the cross, but this raises a question: Without a Cosmic Christ mysticism does the understanding of the cross become distorted, overly personalized, anthropocentralized, and indeed trivialized? Does a true—that is, a cosmological mysticism of the cross—get reduced to a *mystique* of the cross?[10]

Schillebeeckx, commenting on this passage, says "the striking thing is that this lordship of Christ is not related to the community or the church of God, as is *almost* exclusively the case in Paul, but to the *universe*." There is an ascension or exaltation motif in this hymn but no mention of resurrection as such. Yet Christ for Paul is "the one who has risen from the dead and is alive." The universe plays a bigger role in this passage than does the church. "Paul is no stranger to the idea that Christ is not just Lord of the church, but Lord of the universe."[11] Paul writes in a more eschatological context of the Cosmic Christ in 1 Corinthians: "When everything is subjected to him, then the Son himself will be subject in his turn to the One who subjected all things to him, so that God may be all in all" (15:28).

The hymn in Philippians also relates to Isa. 45:22–25 where all the nations are invited by Yahweh to give a "bowing of the knee and swearing of the tongue" in homage. An enthronement motif is celebrated here, that of Jesus Christ as royal person of all creation, though himself humble, human, and a victim of oppression. Jesus is *not* an angel but a man who has suffered—this was probably shocking to the cosmologists of the Middle East of that time. The motif is one of incarnation and exaltation. Paul follows up on the hymn as he began—with a call to compassionate behavior: "Do all things without grumbling" and "be glad and rejoice with me" (vss. 15, 18).

ROMANS 8:14–39. In this passage, Paul is celebrating a Cosmic Christ. "The whole creation is eagerly waiting for God to reveal the divine sons and daughters. . . . From the beginning till now the entire creation, as we know, has been groaning in one great act of giving birth; and not only creation, but all of us who possess the firstfruits of the Spirit" (8:19, 22–23). He celebrates here the *Abba* prayer that Jesus prayed and that we are called to pray, for "everyone moved by the Spirit is a son or daughter of God . . . and child of God . . . and coheirs with Christ" (vss. 14, 17). Once again Paul's sense of our experience with the Cosmic Christ is not a vague "feeling good," but a grounding in the suffering that accompanies prophetic misunderstanding and persecution. "Nothing therefore can come between us and the love of Christ, even if we are . . . being persecuted." We triumph through such trials (vss. 35–37). Paul ends this rich celebration of our union with the Cosmic Christ with a hymn to the four corners of the universe: "For I am certain of this: neither death nor life, no angel, no prince, nothing that exists, nothing still to come, not any power or height or depth, nor any created thing, can ever come between us and the love of God made visible in Christ Jesus our Lord" (vss. 38, 39). Here again Paul displaces the supposed rulers of the cosmos with Christ. In Paul's time most of these cosmic forces would have been considered hostile to humanity. This is another instance of the Glad Tidings of Jesus, tidings that touch the entire universe, not just human affairs.

Once again the biblical theme of our being "images of God" is raised in this passage of the Cosmic Christ. "God co-operates with all those who love God. . . . they are the ones God chose specially long ago and intended to become true images of the divine Son so that this Son might be the eldest of many sisters and brothers" (Rom. 8:28–29). Christ is celebrated as the perfect image of God, the second and "better" Adam and yet as a sibling to all other humans who are also images of God. This passage is placed within the fuller context of Paul's letter that depicts our lives as a struggle. Paul resists temptations to presume that Christ mysticism takes us out of the world or out of the daily struggle. The "not-yet" dimension to his mysticism is evident: "we are not saved yet—it is something we must wait for with patience" (vs. 25). Paul grounds his christological mysticism in the Jewish history of Jesus in the passage that immediately follows when he says that his "brothers of Israel" are "descended from the patriarchs and from their flesh and blood came Christ who is above all, God for ever blessed!" (9:4–5). The Cosmic Christ is fully grounded in a history, in a people, in flesh and blood. The Incarnate Christ is seen in a dialectical relationship to the Christ of cosmology.

COLOSSIANS 1:15–20. In this letter, written about A.D. 61–63 and certainly of the Pauline school if not of Paul directly, we find another ancient hymn to the Cosmic Christ. The author places it in the context of compassionate living: "lead a life worthy of the Lord, fully pleasing to that one, bearing fruit in every good work and increasing in the knowledge of God" (1:10). The cosmic hymn follows:

> He is the image of the invisible God, the first-born of all creation; for in him all things were created, in heaven and on earth, visible and invisible, whether thrones or dominions or principalities or authorities—all things were created through him and for him. He is before all things, and in him all things hold together. He is the first-born from the dead, that in everything he might be preeminent. For in him all the fullness of God was pleased to dwell, and through him to reconcile to himself all things, whether on earth or in heaven, making peace by his death on the cross.
>
> (1:15–20)

The phrase "all things" is repeated six times in this brief passage and we are told that "all things hold together" in Christ. Peace among all things happens through him. This is cosmic redemption indeed. Joseph Sittler calls this passage a "vast Christic vision"[12] that Christians have turned down and effectively ignored for centuries. Christ's preexistence as the "first-born of all creation" is like that of Wisdom who accompanied God in creation (Prov. 8:22; Sir. 1:4, 24:9; Wis. 9:9). Thus Jesus is seen as human and time-bound as well as preexisting and transcending. All the creatures of heaven and earth are "in Christ." Due to this theology of the Cosmic Christ "there is no longer any reason for cosmic anxiety, the great problem of life in those days," says Schillebeeckx. Christ is also the "first-born of the dead" in whom the fullness of God dwells. The hymn, which borrows so much from other religions, is deeply ecumenical. For this reason Schillebeeckx maintains that "the hymn is not afraid of what might be called 'modernism,' in comparison with traditional faith. . . . Here is a universal concept from the syncretism of late antiquity."[13]

While this deeply cosmic and mystical hymn celebrates the "fullness" of Christ throughout creation, the overall thrust of Colossians is not so much space as time. The author emphasizes the church as the body of Christ at a practical and behavioral level. Prior to their experience of the Christ, the hearers of this letter are seen as "enemies in the way that you used to think and the evil things that you did" (1:21). Now they are "holy, pure and blameless—as long as you persevere and stand firm on the solid base of the faith" (1:21, 23). The letter warns against false ascetic practices (2:16–23) and urges the hearers to recognize in Christ "the one who is the head of every Sovereignty and Power" (2:9).

EPHESIANS 1:3–14. The Letter to the Ephesians was written about the same period as that to the Colossians. The author of Ephesians was familiar with the Colossians text whereas the reverse is not true. The author is at least close to Paul and of the Pauline school; some scholars believe that it might have been Paul. Beginning with a cosmic hymn to Christ, this epistle, like Colossians, culminates in a call to compassionate living, in this case to a reconciliation of Jew and pagan. The hymn reads in part:

> Blessed be the God and Creator of our Lord Jesus Christ, who has blessed us in Christ with every spiritual blessing in the heavenly places, even as God chose us in Christ before the foundation of the world. . . . For God has made known to us in all wisdom and insight the mystery of the divine will, according to the divine purpose which God set forth in Christ as a plan for the fullness of time, to unite all things in Christ, things in heaven and things on earth.
>
> (1:3–4; 9–10)

The author pictures Christ as a cosmic ruler. "God has put all things under Christ's feet and has made Christ the head over all things for the church, which is his body, the fullness of the one who fills all in all" (1:22–23). Christ is both head of the universe and head of the church, who "fills all in all." As in Stoic teaching, the author pictures the universe as a living human; but unlike Stoic teaching, the universe depicted is not static but dynamic—there is much more to come. Here we have one more instance of an eschatological dimension to Christ mysticism that distinguishes it from other mysticisms of the time. Christ has been "raised from the dead" and sits "in heavenly places far above all rule and authority and power and dominion, and above every name that is named, not only in this age but also in that which is to come" (1:20–21). The church is meant to signify the historical presence of this cosmic and reconciling Christ, to be a microcosm of the macrocosmic order that Christ brings to the universe. The author demands compassionate behavior. Christ Jesus created "one single New Human in himself out of the two people [of Jew and non-Jew] . . . in his own person he killed the hostility" (2:15–16). Christians are urged to be "one house" and "one body" built on the cornerstone of Christ and the peace he brings. Schillebeeckx comments that the author is sympathetic to the "universal cosmic awareness" of his culture but that he emphasizes how the "historical responsibility of the church is to be taken seriously. . . . If any book lays the foundations for a political theology in the New Testament, it is Ephesians."[14] Once again, the cosmic and the historical come together in Christ mysticism. The letter is Good News to its readers because it assures them not to be afraid of the cosmos and its rulers, including fate and destiny. Christ frees one from such anxieties. Notice that the message is *not* that the Christian believer is to withdraw from a cosmology and live out a psychologized and introverted existence—but to relate anew to all the universe with hope and "power." God is celebrated in a deeply mystical way as being "Parent of all, over all, through all and within all" (4:6). Christ brings humans to a realization of this as the "founder of universal peace."[15] Ephesians emphasizes the historical and prophetic dimension of the Cosmic Christ and calls the Church to fulfill its task of being a place for peace and reconciliation.

In this letter, the creative dimension of a living cosmology is emphasized by the author. We are told that "we are God's work of art, created in Christ Jesus to live the good life as from the beginning God had meant us to live it" (2:10). Truly art, mysticism, and scientific worldview come together in this letter as they do whenever a cosmology is viable and vibrant.

The call for the "new person" is a call for a person remade in the cosmic peace and reconciliation that Christ brings. Ephesians also calls for deep ecumenism: the reconciliation of Jew and pagan is a practical result of the cosmic reconciliation that the Cosmic Christ brings. Schillebeeckx argues that the author of Ephesians thinks "in historical and ecclesiastical rather than in cosmic terms."[16] This interjects a dualism between cosmos and history and between cosmos and Church. I propose instead that in Ephesians both church and history are seen in the context of the cosmos.

When we incorporate a Cosmic Christ into our theology an interesting question arises for ecclesiology: Is the definition of Church as "people of God" too anthropocentric? The authors we have been reading—and the hymns sung by the earliest Christian believers—celebrate Christ within the cosmos, and persons "in Christ" and the Church as a microcosm of Christ within the cosmos. To omit this trivializes our concept of Church and invites institutional sins and divisions that have haunted the Church for centuries. Arrogance abounds when the cosmos is left out or appropriated unconsciously to oneself or one's institutions. Humans, as individuals and as communities, are more likely to celebrate diversity and to be creative if they live within a cosmos rather than limited human assemblies upon which they strive to invoke the grace of God.

HEBREWS 1:1–4. This letter, whose author is unknown to us, was written about A.D. 67 to an exclusively Jewish Christian audience, perhaps even

Jewish priests. The letter begins with a typical Cosmic Christ motif—a combination of sacred space (cosmos) *and* sacred time (prophet):

> At various times in the past and in various different ways, God spoke to our ancestors through the prophets; but in our own time, the last days, God has spoken to us through the child, the child that God appointed to inherit everything and through whom was made everything that is. Christ is the radiant light of God's glory and the perfect copy of God's nature, sustaining the universe by his powerful command; and now that Christ has destroyed the defilement of sin, he has gone to take his place in heaven at the right hand of divine Majesty. So Christ is now as far above the angels as the title which he has inherited is higher than their own name. God has never said to any angel: "You are my Child, today I have become your Parent"; or: "I will be a Parent to you and you will be my child."
>
> (Heb. 1:1-5)

The author of this letter rejects the idea of angels ruling the universe in favor of the Cosmic Christ (another name for this Christ is high priest), who is fully human and has suffered as all humans do. We see the themes of eschatological exaltation of the Cosmic Christ on the one hand—how else will cosmic powers be tamed and therefore humans be "free"—and the human, suffering prophet and servant on the other. After discussing Jesus' death, the author says that "it was essential that he should in this way become completely like his sisters and brothers so that he could be a compassionate and trustworthy high priest of God's religion" (2:17). On the one hand Christ is exalted, on the other he is a brother who has learned compassion in the way we all learn it—through suffering.

Christ is a "priest" in the Letter to the Hebrews. The term "Christ" means "the anointed one" and, in the context of the author of Hebrews, versed as he is in the Jewish priesthood, "Christ" and "priest" are practically synonymous. This in itself is a statement on the Cosmic Christ, because the priest is a cosmic mediator in this respect, not a preserver of cult as such but a bearer of the prophetic gift of divine compassion that permeates the universe. Schillebeeckx believes that this letter actually "demythologizes the Jewish image of priesthood. For the author, the love of the human Jesus who suffers for others in faithfulness to God and in solidarity with the history of human suffering, is priesthood in the true sense of the word: bringing men to God."[17] I believe the message is even less anthropocentric—and less sexist—than that: Jesus as priest is the Cosmic Christ who reconciles all creation in God by healing the human consciousness that has been at war with creation. Jesus' death is a sin offering that wiped out all sin and thereby initiated a new covenant.

JOHN 1:1–18. John's Gospel, composed about A.D. 90, develops the themes of the Cosmic Christ considered earlier. The author has been exposed to these themes in Christian worship and in Paul's letters. The

Prologue to John situates all of Jesus' life and ministry in a cosmological context. It celebrates Christ as the *Logos* or "Word" of God as well as the wisdom of God present with God at the creation of the world. Yet, as in other texts, Jesus is also seen in a grounded, earthy, and historical context. He "pitched his tent among us" and "was in the world"; witnesses including John the Baptist and the Johannine authors saw him and lived with him (1:14–15). This text, like so many of the others we have considered, was "probably an early Christian hymn that the evangelist has annotated and incorporated into his Gospel."[18] The hymn begins:

> In the beginning was the Word:
> the Word was with God
> and the Word was God.
> This Word was with God in the beginning.
> Through it all things came to be,
> not one thing had its being but through it.
> All that came to be had life in it
> and that life was the light of people,
> a light that shines in the dark
> a light that darkness could not overpower.
> . . . .
> But to all who did accept this Word
> it gave power to become children of God,
> to all who believe in the name of the one
> who was born not out of human stock
> or urge of the flesh
> or human will
> but of God's self.
> The Word was made flesh;
> it pitched its tent among us,
> and we saw its glory,
> the glory that is the one's as the one Child of God
> full of grace and truth.
> . . . .
> Indeed, from this one's fullness we have all of us received.
>   (John 1:1–5; 12–14; 16)

Here Jesus Christ (that name is not used until v. 17) is celebrated in a cosmological context. As we discussed earlier, the Stoic use of *Logos* denotes a static world principle; the use of Christ as *Logos* is dynamic—all things come into being through him, all have life and power to overcome darkness because of him. This Word itself is light entering the world and empowering people to become children of God. It bespeaks glory or *doxa* and resides "nearest (God's) heart" (v. 18) even though it makes its tent among humans. John is clearly describing a new creation story, one which echoes the creation story of Genesis in its opening words, "In the beginning." The Word is with God " in the beginning" just as wisdom is. The Word, therefore, is not only word but also wisdom. Cosmological Wisdom texts are alluded to throughout this passage as, for example, in the tent-pitching image. The book of Sirach also celebrates such primordial wisdom:

> I came forth from the mouth of the Most High
> and I covered the earth like mist.
> I had my tent in the heights,
> and my throne in a pillar of cloud.
> . . . .
> Over the waves of the sea and over the whole earth
> and over every people and nation I have held sway.
> Among all these I searched for rest,
> and I looked to see in whose territory I might pitch camp.
> Then the Creator of all things instructed me,
> and . . . fixed a place for my tent.
> God said, "Pitch your tent in Jacob,
> make Israel your inheritance."
> From eternity, in the beginning, God created me,
> and for eternity I shall remain.
>
> (Sir. 24:3–14)

This rich cosmological poetry is incorporated by the author of John's Gospel into the imagery for Jesus Christ, who was "with God in the beginning" but is also "Word made flesh."

The term "glory" or *doxa* is prominent in this hymn and in the other texts that celebrate the Cosmic Christ. Glory and its synonym "beauty" are cosmological categories. In the Scriptures, their use indicates a cosmological awareness on the part of the author. Glory in the Hebrew Bible signifies divine power and holiness, often manifested as light—light is the first element created in the Genesis story. Yahweh is the "king of glory" and Yahweh's glory "fills the earth" (Ps. 24:8; Isa. 6:3). Creation announces divine glory, for "the heavens declare the glory of God and the firmament proclaims God's handiwork" (Ps. 19:2). Divine glory is also revealed in God's care for people. In the New Testament glory is described as "power, splendor, light." God's glory is manifested in holiness and power. Glory is understood eschatologically— Christ will come in the glory of the Creator (Mark 8:38). Those who follow Christ will share in his suffering and his glory. The Spirit will give glory to the preachers of God's hidden wisdom. This glory surpasses that which Moses experienced on Mount Sinai. "We all, with faces unveiled, reflecting as in a mirror the glory of the Lord, are being transformed into this one's very image from glory to glory, as through the Spirit of the Lord" (2 Cor. 3:18). Christ's glory is thus shared with those who follow him. It is not only shared, but it also grows and develops, revealing the dynamic nature of the Cosmic Christ's relationship to his disciples. The growth in glory is a growth in becoming the image of God, which Christ has already achieved in its fullest dimensions. We are told that the Cosmic

Christ in us is a relative thing, a divine presence that can increase and develop. For Christ's glory is that of the "only child of the Creator"— yet we have all received from that one's "fullness" (John 1:14, 16). The Cosmic Christ bears divine glory and elicits it from others.

John's Gospel lacks a transfiguration experience, which is a Cosmic Christ *glory* manifestation for the synoptic Gospels as we will see below. However, John stresses the divine *doxa* ("glory") through Jesus' miraculous signs (cf. 2:11), through the "glory" of the cross, and through Jesus' passing on of glory to his disciples (17:22). Nature (for example, thunderstorms) and history (for example, the manna in the desert) both manifest divine glory in the Hebrew Bible. Wisdom is a pure effusion of God's glory (Wis. 7:25). The preexistence of wisdom (which we saw above is the Cosmic Christ) is named in John 17:5 as "the glory that Jesus had with the Creator before the world existed" and stems "from the love that the Creator had for Jesus before the creation of the world" (17:24; 1:1).[19] Thus, the Cosmic Christ is named whenever the category of "glory" is employed in the Scriptures.

THE REVELATION TO JOHN. Apocalyptic literature is deeply cosmological. Elisabeth Schüssler Fiorenza compares it to science fiction, and Krister Stendahl compares it to a horror movie. The book of Revelation presents abundant imagery that develops a cosmological Christology. As Schüssler Fiorenza notes, the key question in the book of Revelation is a deeply political one: "Who is the true Lord of this world?"[20] Is it the emperors of Rome as the Roman Empire would want its citizens to believe? Is the emperor of Rome to be worshipped, as was his desire in promoting an imperial cult? Is the true Lord to be found in powers and institutions including the merchants and shipbuilders of the empire? The entire book is an argument that Jesus Christ is "Lord and God and King of the world,"[21] not human emperors or empire-builders. The word "Lord," when used in an anthropocentric context as it often is today, connotes lord/serf relationships of the feudal era. In English, the term "Lord" carries aristocratic connotations as in the title, "Lord Dorly." For these reasons it is often shunned as a title for Jesus by many feminists and others. Yet it had no anthropocentric meaning for the early Christian writers. The word "Lord" meant ruler of the universe, governor of the universe. It was a thoroughly *cosmic* title. In the Hebrew Bible, Yahweh is called "the Lord" of the whole earth whose glory fills the earth because Yahweh created the heavens and the earth. In the New Testament "the term, 'the Lord,' as applied to Christ, takes on a special theological significance. . . . [It expresses] most emphatically the divine 'Lordship' of Christ."[22] The term "Lord," then, is a term for the Cosmic Christ in the early church, and it is often richly employed in that context.

There are numerous allusions to the Cosmic Christ in the Revelation to John:

Jesus Christ [is] the faithful witness, the First-born from the dead, the Ruler of the kings of the earth. He loves us and has washed away our sins with his blood, and made us a line of kings and queens, priests to serve his God and Creator; to him, then, be glory and power for ever and ever. Amen. It is he who is coming on the clouds; everyone will see him, even those who pierced him, and all the races of the earth will mourn over him (1:5-7).

In this passage we see many of the themes associated with the Cosmic Christ in other biblical texts: Ruler of the earth; the crucifixion; the cloud as a symbol of theophany; "glory"; and the universalism wherein all nations will know him. Christ is pictured as eschatological judge of the nations who holds stars and angels in his hands (1:10-20).

Revelation 4 and 5 address the central question of the book: who is ruler of this world? The answer given is clear: it is God the Creator who sits on the divine throne (a "central image repeated again and again like a keynote throughout the whole book" as Schüssler Fiorenza says) together with Christ who "exercised true lordship over the world." Animals "glorify and honor and give thanks to the One sitting on the throne" (4:9) and elders praise him, "You made all the universe and it was only by your will that everything was made and exists" (4:11). Christ is imaged as the Lamb slain for the entire human race; to him this song of praise is sung:

> Because you were sacrificed, and with your blood
> you bought people for God
> of every race, language, people and nation
> and made them a line of royal people and priests,
> to serve our God and to rule the world.
>
> (5:9-10)

The Cosmic Christ has rendered all a holy nation, a royal people. All creation joins in this hymn to the Cosmic Christ:

> Then I heard all the living things in creation—everything that lives in the air, and on the ground, and under the ground, and in the sea, crying, "To the One who is sitting on the throne and to the Lamb, be all praise, honor, glory and power, for ever and ever." And the four animals said, "Amen" (5:13-14).

According to Schüssler Fiorenza, Christ is pictured as Lamb twenty-eight times in this book and this "always signifies the resurrected Christ." The Cosmic Lamb who was innocent and sacrificed symbolizes "Jesus Christ as ruler of the world and its destiny."[24] This is a deeply political position to take for it sets the Cosmic Christ, whom believers regarded as the *true* ruler of the earth, against the emperors who claimed that right for themselves. This is no abstract thesis on the part of the author of Revelation. At the time it was written, persecution of Christians for refusing to honor the emperor in cultic worship was demoralizing and splitting the churches. True well-being or salvation is from the Cosmic Christ and *not* from the empire and its rulers. This Cosmic Lamb "will lead them to springs of living water; and God will wipe away all tears from their eyes" (7:17). The Lamb is the Cosmic Christ for "the Lamb is the Lord of lords and the King of kings" (17:14). Comments Schüssler Fiorenza:

> According to Revelation, final salvation does not just pertain to the soul and spiritual realities. It is the abolishment of all dehumanization and suffering and at the same time the fullness of human well-being . . . a rectification of the great tribulation with its sufferings of war, peacelessness, hunger, and inflation, pestilence, persecution, and death.[25]

The principle theme of the preaching of Jesus in the Gospels is the nearness of the kingdom/queendom of God. There is no doubt that the author of Revelation has this theme in mind when speaking of the antiempire attitudes of believers in the Lamb. "The kingdom of the world has become the kingdom of our Lord and of the Christ, and God will reign for ever and ever" (11:15). Included in this waking up to the kingdom/queendom will be a struggle against those who damage creation, for we are told that "the time has come to destroy those who are destroying the earth" (11:18).

A goddess figure appears who is Queen of Heaven and she births a child who is a messianic king and the Cosmic Christ (12:1–17). "The 'birth of the Messiah' is here therefore not the historical birth of Jesus but his exaltation and enthronement as the 'firstborn of the dead' and the beginning of the new creation." One reason for the quantity of cosmic imagery in Revelation is that the struggle against the empire is clearly seen as a struggle against cosmic powers and principalities of evil. "The whole world had marveled and followed the beast," we are told, and the beast "mouthed its blasphemies against God, against God's name, God's heavenly Tent and all those who are sheltered there. It was allowed to make war against the saints and conquer them, and given power over every race, people, language and nation" (13:3, 6–7). Satan is the origin of the power of the beast. Again, the author is speaking very specifically about the demonic oppression that Christians and others suffered under the "Roman usurpation of God's power." According to Schüssler Fiorenza, to call the Cosmic Christ "Lord" is to oppose the empire's teaching that Augustus is "Lord and Savior."[26]

Those who choose to worship the Creator God, "maker of heaven and earth and sea and every water-spring" (14:7), will be liberated just as the Israelites were led through the Red Sea out of Egypt. An immense universalism characterizes the author's hymn to the Cosmic Christ—the Lamb, who like Moses, leads the way to salvation. "All the pagans will come and adore you for the many acts of justice you have shown" (15:4). All the nations will celebrate the wedding feast of the Lamb. Schüssler Fiorenza says:

The universal cosmic salvation by far exceeds that prefigured in the Church. The cosmic universal dimensions of the new city of God are intermingled with paradisaical features of the new creation. Not only the faithful Christians but all those whose names were registered in the book of life at the final judgment, according to their works, will share in its glory, splendor, and eternal life.[27]

The Cosmic Christ is called "the Word of God" who is "a warrior for justice" (19:13, 11). He is "the King of kings and Lord of lords" (19:16). He is the "Alpha and Omega," and he promises a new, more just world—one lighted by the glory of the Cosmic Lamb (21:23). God is a God-with-us who together with the Lamb constitutes the Temple itself.

> Then I saw a new heaven and a new earth; the first heaven and the first earth had disappeared now. . . . Here God lives among people. God will be at home among them; they shall be God's people, and God will be their God whose name is God-with-them. God will wipe away all tears from their eyes; there will be no more death, and no more mourning or sadness. The world of the past has gone. Then the One sitting on the throne spoke: "Now I am making the whole of creation new. . . . I will give water from the well of life free to anybody who is thirsty" (21:1, 3–6).

The author of Revelation found in the rich imagery of the Cosmic Christ, Lord of earth, Cosmic Lamb, a source of empowerment to all Christian and non-Christian alike, suffering under the Roman Empire. The wounded Cosmic Christ ushers in visions and possibilities of relieving the injustices that create so many wounded ones on earth.

COSMIC CHRIST THEMES IN THE GOSPELS AND ACTS

While many Christians are familiar with Cosmic Christ hymns we have been considering, most of which are found in the Epistles, very little attention has been given to the Cosmic Christology in the Gospels themselves. I propose that each of the major events of Jesus' life is presented in the Gospels within a viable cosmology. The Cosmic Christ lies at the heart of the stories surrounding the historical Jesus.[28] Furthermore, as we shall see, each of the synoptic Gospels has, like John's Gospel, a Prologue to the Cosmic Christ.

INFANCY NARRATIVES. The infancy narratives represent, as biblical scholar Raymond Brown indicates, a gradually developing Christology on the part of the writers of the Gospels of Matthew and Luke. Thus, there is no infancy story in the earlier Gospel of Mark. In this respect these stories are analogous to the Prologue of John's Gospel: what he describes as the preexistence of the Word, Matthew and Luke celebrate as a unique conception—a conception by the Holy Spirit, the same Spirit that hovered over the waters in Genesis. What immediately precedes the annunciation and infancy story in the prologue of Matthew's Gospel is the genealogy of Jesus (Matt. 1:1–17). As Schillebeeckx points out, this genealogy or "book of coming to be—corresponds with the tōl 'dōt [i.e., the birth] of the world in Genesis."[29] Matthew's genealogy is a cosmic Christ statement putting Jesus' birth in the context of the history of the universe. "The infancy stories," Brown comments, "have become truly an infancy gospel."[30] The infancy stories are the gospel in miniature, a kind of microcosmic gospel that briefly parallels the macrocosmic story of the Gospel. Here we learn of the Messiah who is worshipped by some—the magi and the shepherds—and hated by others— Herod (in Matthew) and those who contradict the sign (in Luke 2:34). The same mixed response to the mature Jesus and his message is described in the fuller Gospel story.

But in the Matthean infancy narrative, those who do the worshipping are in each instance placed in a cosmological setting. The magi, who travel from afar, follow a star proclaiming the birth of the Messiah. They are scientists or astrologers, presented as very respectable persons. "There is not the slightest hint of conversion or of false practice in Matthew's description of the magi; they are wholly admirable. They represent the best of pagan lore and religious perceptivity which has come to seek Jesus through revelation in nature."[31] The infancy story is a "gospel in miniature" with "a passion and rejection, as well as success."[32] The magi worship by the star and by the Scriptures; but Herod, who rejects Jesus, represents the chief priests and scribes who will later crucify him. There is a universalism to the story—not only because nature plays so prominent a part in revelation, but also because the magi are gentiles or pagans, and the slaughtering of the innocents is not restricted to any one household. This slaughter of the innocents represents a crucifixion event, for Jesus too was an innocent one.

In the Lucan story of the annunciation the angel tells Mary that "The Holy Spirit will overshadow you" (1:35). Recall that an angel denoted cosmology in the first century. The word for "overshadow" is used in the Hebrew Bible to describe God's presence in the sanctuary, and in the Gospels it is used for the transfiguration story "where a cloud of glory overshadows." Clouds denote cosmology and theophany in ancient Israel not only for obvious physical reasons—because a cloud brings shade and needed rain to a desert people—but also because the cloud accompanies the mountain theophany of Moses and the glory of God settles there. When the tabernacle was built a cloud covered it and the glory of God filled it. Glory, cloud, and tabernacle or in later Judaism, Shekinah, all denote the divine presence, i.e., the presence of the Cosmic Christ (see John 1:14). Thus we have in Luke's infancy account, in addition to a new creation story, a new transfiguration story (see Luke 9:34). A cloud signaling the divine presence "overshadowed" those gathered and from it came the voice saying, "This is my beloved son." Similarly, in Luke's annunciation story, Jesus is named the "Son of God." Jesus is also a "new creation"; he is "totally God's work" because Mary is a virgin in Luke's account and because he is begotten by the same Spirit that begot creation in Genesis 1.[33]

When, in Luke's Gospel, the birth occurs, a cosmic symphony ensues. "And suddenly with the angel there was a great throng of the heavenly host, praising God and singing: 'Glory to God in the highest heavens, and peace to persons who enjoy God's favor' " (Luke 2:13–14). The angels announce the birth to the shepherds, and because of the angels "the glory of the Lord shone around them" (2:9). This is another theophany, a heavenly canticle sung about the *glory* of divinity, i.e., the Cosmic Christ being born in the child Jesus. The canticle echoes Isaiah: "Holy, holy, holy is the Lord of Hosts; the whole earth is full of God's glory," the seraphim sing in Isaiah.[34] Peace on earth is promised with the birth of this Cosmic Child. Truly this is "good news of great joy which will be for the whole people" (Luke 2:10). Indeed, this *is* a summary of the Good News of the entire Gospel story and the Paschal mystery of Jesus.

How will the shepherds know who the Messiah is? By visiting a manger. The manger too has cosmic connotations. These people were shepherds who lived outdoors and tended sheep. They were close to the non-two-legged ones. Isaiah said, "The ox knows its owner and the donkey knows the manger of its Lord, but Israel has not known me" (Isa. 1:3). The prophet Isaiah knew that animals can be closer to the source of wisdom than the two-legged ones. As Thomas Merton used to comment, "Never forget that every non-two-legged creature is a saint."[35]

JESUS' BAPTISM AND TEMPTATION IN THE DESERT. Just as John (the latest Gospel), Luke, and Matthew begin with the Cosmic Christ, so does Mark (the earliest Gospel). Marcan scholar D. E. Nineham calls the baptism and temptation of Jesus in the desert (Mark 1:1–13) the "curtain-raiser" and "prologue" to the Gospel. "St. Mark is doing in his prologue something very similar to what St. Matthew and St. Luke were doing in their stories of supernatural birth and infancy, and what St. John was doing in his preliminary teaching (John 1:1–18)."[36] What is the heart of this "curtain-raiser" story of Jesus' baptism? The baptism is presented as a cosmic event. "The heavens were torn apart" and "the Spirit, like a dove, descended on him. And a voice came from heaven, 'You are my Son, the Beloved; my favor rests on you!' " (Mark 1:9–11). The image of the sky opening up is from the prophet Isaiah, "O, that you would tear the heavens open and come down" (Isa. 64:1). People in Jesus' time expected the Messiah to come in such a context. According to the *Testament of 12 Patriarchs* composed about 109 B.C., "The heavens shall be opened and from the temple of glory shall come upon him sanctification with the Father's voice as from Abraham to Isaac."[37] Mark pictures Jesus anointed as the Messiah at his baptism much as the book of Acts reports when it says "God anointed him with the Holy Spirit and with power" at his baptism (Acts 10:38).

Jesus' temptation in the desert is also set in a definite cosmological context. "The Spirit," we are told, "drove him into the wilderness" where he was "tempted by Satan. He was with the wild beasts and the angels looked after him" (Mark 1:12–13). Nineham comments that "the wilderness was traditionally the haunt of evil spirits" and in this passage in Mark "the great eschatological battle is joined."[38] To encounter Satan in the desert is to wrestle with the cosmic forces of evil, with the powers and principalities. "For it is not against human enemies that we have to struggle, but against Sovereignties and the Powers who originate the darkness in this world, the spiritual army of evil in the heavens," warns the author of Ephesians (6:12). The angels were thought to govern the four elements of creation and the various domains of the universe including stars, plants, animals, and meteors.[39] The wild beasts remind one of the tame beasts at the manger in Luke's prologue. It was believed by the Jewish people that "when messiah comes, all animals will once again be tame and live in harmony."[40]

The sky opening up, the wilderness, the desert, the wild beasts, Satan, the angels—all fill out a cosmological picture of Jesus' first activities in Mark's Gospel. They set a cosmological tone for the rest of the Gospel. The Gospels of Matthew and Luke flesh out the details of this cosmic struggle involving Jesus: a struggle over the nature of his relationship to God, his calling as a son of Israel, and indeed of Israel's calling as well.

THE TRANSFIGURATION (MATT. 17:1–8; MARK 9:2–9; LUKE 9:28–36; 2 PET. 1:16–18). The transfiguration has been called "the true centerpoint of Mark's gospel, the revelation of Jesus' glorious and transcendent Sonship."[41] It contains motifs from Jesus' baptism, resurrection, crucifixion, and ascension. Eastern Orthodox Christianity—which has never forsaken the Cosmic Christ as has the West—considers the Feast of the Transfiguration to be the pivotal point of the liturgical year. It is pivotal, I suggest, because it celebrates the historical Jesus who is finally recognized by his disciples through the transfiguration event as the Cosmic Christ. Each of the four accounts of the event are explicit about this, and Peter's letter especially emphasizes the point of the theophanic experience they shared. Notice the use of the cosmological term "glory" and how God is called "Sublime Glory" in this text:

> It was not any cleverly invented myths that we were repeating when we brought you the knowledge of the power and the coming of our Lord Jesus Christ; we had seen his majesty for ourselves. He was honored and glorified by God and the Creator, when the Sublime Glory itself spoke to him and said, "This is my Son, the Beloved; he enjoys my favor." We heard this ourselves, spoken from heaven, when we were with him on the holy mountain (2 Pet. 1:16– 18).

The witnesses of the transfiguration include the earthly companions of the historical Jesus: Peter, John, and James. The other witnesses reported were Moses, who had his own mountaintop experiences of divinity in the bestowing of the covenant (Exod. 19:3–25), and Elijah, a prophet popular among the Jewish people at the time the Gospels were written and often viewed as the precursor of the Messiah. Only Moses and Elijah, among the great figures of the Hebrew Bible, were allowed to gaze upon the divine presence and survive. Only they could endure the awe of divinity[42] (see Exod. 33:18–21).

Clearly the theophany in the transfiguration event parallels others from the Hebrew Bible wherein divinity is revealed at the mountaintop or wrapped in a cloud. Peter's references to building a tent also remind one of the "tent of meeting" that Moses pitched for the gathering of the people and in which "Yahweh would speak with Moses face to face, as one speaks with a friend" (Exod. 33:11). A pillar of cloud was stationed at the tent's entrance (Exod. 33:10). The words spoken of Jesus on the mountaintop—"This is my Son, the Beloved; he enjoys my favor. Listen to him"—parallel those spoken at his baptism (Matt. 3:17). These in turn recall the servant tradition of Isaiah 42:1 and 49:3. Another cosmological reference to Christ is presented as the spirit that descends over Jesus and anoints him for his messianic mission, the same Spirit who hovered over the waters at creation (Gen. 1:2). Thus, a new creation story, a Cosmic Christ event, is alluded to in the baptism of Jesus when it was revealed to Jesus that he was a Cosmic Christ just as the transfiguration event is a revelation to others of Jesus' being a Cosmic Christ.

Schillebeeckx points out that the reason John's Gospel lacks a transfiguration scene is because the entire life of Jesus as presented in that Gospel is "an event of glorification," as for example the Cana event and the raising of Lazarus from the dead.[44] The Cosmic Christ theology therefore permeates the Gospel in its entirety.

The Eastern Orthodox tradition, as represented by theologian Nicolas Berdyaev, celebrates some of the implications of a Cosmic Christ theology of the transfiguration. Berdyaev writes:

> The central idea of the Eastern Fathers was that of *theosis*, the divinization of all creatures, the transfiguration of the world, the idea of the cosmos and not the idea of personal salvation. . . . Only later Christian consciousness began to value the idea of hell more than the idea of the transfiguration and divinization of the world. . . . The kingdom of God is the transfiguration of the world, universal resurrection, a new heaven and a new earth."[43]

THE CRUCIFIXION AND RESURRECTION. As we have seen, the image of Christ conquering death is frequently brought up in the context of the Cosmic Christ. The resurrection stories must also be seen in the context of a Cosmic Christ. The resurrection stories must also be seen in the context of a Cosmic Christ resurrected who has power even and *especially* over the cosmic forces of death. The cosmic fear and despair that permeates cultures and individuals are powerless if Christ, who brings life, reigns instead. The crucifixion is presented as a cosmic event: "darkness was over the whole land" (Mark 15:33); the sun was eclipsed" (Luke 23:44); "the earth quaked; the rocks were split; the tombs opened and the bodies of many holy men rose from the dead" (Matt. 27:52–53). In Mark's gospel we read that "the veil of the Temple was torn in two from top to bottom" (15:39) at the death of Jesus. This is an image of the cosmos torn in two since "the Temple reproduced in 'shadow' form the structure of the universe."[45]

The crucifixion is an intimate part of the transfiguration story in which, in the midst of the theophany of Jesus at the mountaintop, allusions are also made to his death. (Mark's Gospel is especially developed in this regard.) This dialectic of exaltation and crucifixion, which John would develop still more deeply in his Gospel, is one more instance of Jesus' followers insisting that the Cosmic Christ and the suffering, prophetic Jesus must be seen as coming together in the same person. The Cosmic Christ is always presented with wounds. The wounds are those of the historical Jesus, the suffering servant or the prophet who is persecuted and crucified for announcing Good News.

According to Raymond Brown, an integral part of the mystery of the resurrection is that all the Gospel stories about it take place in cosmology different from that in which we live our everyday lives. The "risen Jesus" is "exempt from usual laws of space," Brown says. "Our language of space-time experience breaks down when it is used to describe the eschatological."[46] Time and space are freely dealt with in the resurrection narratives. Luke, for example, includes the ascension and the giving of the Spirit as part of the resurrection event. He also "employs categories of space" that are always cosmological categories in the Scriptures: Jesus is lifted up on a cloud and a mighty gust of "spirit-wind" sweeps down from heaven.[47] Angels, always signals of a cosmology to first-century thinkers, are integral to the resurrection story (cf. Mark 16:7; Matt. 28:7; John 20:11–13). Brown points out that their presence at the resurrection was emphasized even in the pre-Marcan period of the early church.[48] The earliest attempt to describe the resurrection is found in the noncanonical *Gospel of Peter* written in the second century A.D. We see here how cosmological that story is; the resurrected Jesus is a universal person, a Cosmic Christ: "They saw again three men come out of the sepulcher, two of them sustaining the other, and a cross following them. The heads of the two reached to heaven, but the head of him whom they led by the hand outreached the heavens."[49]

In Matthew the resurrection is accompanied by an apocalyptic cosmic event, an earthquake accompanied by "an angel of the Lord" who descends from heaven and rolls back the stone.

An important dimension of the resurrection story are the appearances of the risen Jesus. The disciples did not say, they saw the historical Jesus after Easter, but the "risen Lord." Jesus is no longer simply Jesus, but "Lord," a cosmic identification. Brown comments:

> The post-resurrectional confession is not simply "We have seen Jesus" but "We have seen *the Lord*" (John 20:18, 25; 21:7; Luke 24:34). Since "Lord" is a christological evaluation of Jesus, the evangelists are telling us that the witnesses . . . saw that Jesus had been transferred into the realm of Lordship which is the realm of God.[50]

Indeed, the risen Lord *is* the Cosmic Christ. The book of Acts implies that it was through the resurrection that Jesus was made Lord (Acts 2:32, 36). As Brown says, "the whole New Testament agrees that the resurrected Jesus was the vehicle of *doxa* because the resurrection was the mighty act of God par excellence."[51] The resurrection is a major "glory" (*doxa*) event, a manifestation of the Cosmic Christ. Schillebeeckx concurs with this conclusion: "In antiquity, anthropology and ethics are seen against a cosmic background, i.e., one determined by heavenly spirits. Therefore Jesus' resurrection is *ipso facto* an enthronement of the Lord Jesus over all angelic powers." For the same reason and because "to sin is to subject oneself to heavenly powers [Eph. 2:1-3; see 2 Cor. 4:4]," the crucifixion of Jesus on the cross results in a cosmological triumph over sin.[52]

THE ASCENSION. The exaltation of Jesus as the Cosmic Christ is part of that dimension of the resurrection story that we call Christ's ascension (Acts 1:2-14). While only Luke in Acts (1:3, 12) and in his Gospel (24:50) treats the event as historical, many other scripture texts treat it as primal in the early church's grasp of the Christ event. We are told that Christ, following on his resurrection, took his place in heaven at the right hand of God. (We have seen allusions to this in the texts from Romans, Ephesians, and Hebrews considered earlier. Cf. Col. 3:1-3.) Christ is enthroned upon the clouds in complete glory and reigns above all heavenly powers. From there, he will come in the parousia (the end of time).

Ephesians celebrates the ascension event (see 4:3-16) as an occasion for the sending of the spirit that will make persons "grow in all ways into Christ, who is the head" (4:15) for he has risen "higher than all the heavens to fill all things" (4:10). Just as Jesus has joined the Creator God who is "Parent of all, over all, through all and within all" (4:6), so too do we receive the power to "make a unity in the work of service, building up the body of Christ" (4:12).

Notice in this brief sentence from Mark the number of cosmological terms that are present: "Then they will see the Son of Man coming in clouds with great power and glory" (13:26). The sending of the Spirit follows this elevation and glorification of the Cosmic Christ. Church tradition has honored this by either combining Easter and Ascension in one feast, as it did in the early church, or in celebrating Pentecost shortly after Ascension as is its current liturgical practice. As we shall see in our section on worship, the biblical readings currently assigned to Ascension Thursday are among the most cosmological texts of the Bible.

PENTECOST. The sending of the Spirit is a cosmic event (Acts 2:1–4). The breathing forth of the Spirit from Jesus is key to both the resurrection and ascension stories, as Raymond Brown indicates. A new creation is implicit in the sending of the Spirit, the One Spirit who hovered over the waters at the first creation. God is the One who "breathed into the human's nostrils the breath of life" (Gen. 2:7), who "fashioned us and . . . breathed into us a living spirit" (Wis. 15:11). On Pentecost the gift of the Spirit is bestowed on individuals that they might embrace their prophetic task. The Tower of Babel story depicts the cosmic chaos that ensues when humans project their order on the universe instead of yielding to divine order.[54] Thus the healing of the divisions of Babel at the first Pentecost is a deeply cosmic event; it represents the triumph of creation over chaos, of the divine plan over anthropocentric agendas. It marks the end of babbling and the beginning of communication.

The story of Pentecost could hardly be couched in more cosmic imagery than it is. All four elements play a role—wind (air), fire (of tongues), earth (all the nations thereof), and water (baptism). The physics of the first century is explicitly invoked.

> Suddenly they heard what sounded like a powerful wind from heaven, the noise of which filled the entire house in which they were sitting; and something appeared to them that seemed like tongues of fire; these separated and came to rest on the head of each of them. They were all filled with the Holy Spirit and began to speak foreign languages as the Spirit gave them the gift of speech. Now there were devout people living in Jerusalem from every nation under heaven, and at this sound they all assembled, everyone bewildered to hear these people speaking their own language.
>
> (Acts 2:2–6)

Peter's address is taken from the prophet Joel and is richly cosmic and universal in its imagery:

> In the days to come—it is the Lord who speaks—
> I will pour out my spirit on all humankind
> Their sons and daughters shall prophesy,
> your young people shall see visions,
> your old people shall dream dreams.
> . . . .
> I will display portents in heaven above
> and signs on earth below.
> The sun will be turned into darkness
> and the moon into blood
> before the great Day of the Lord dawns.
> All who call on the name of the Lord will be saved.
>
> (Acts 2:17–21)

The confession of faith with which Peter ends his address is a confession in Jesus as Cosmic Christ. "For this reason the whole House of Israel can be certain that God has made this Jesus whom you crucified both Lord and Christ" (Acts 2:36).

In this section on the quest for the Cosmic Christ in the Scriptures we have learned of the Cosmic Christ tradition in the Hebrew Bible and the all-pervading role that the Cosmic Christ perspective plays not only in the cosmic hymns of the epistles and Revelation but also in the Gospels themselves. To pursue this quest further I offer a simple way to reread the Bible in search of the Cosmic Christ. Each time you see the following terms in the Scriptures, be thinking "Einstein," "cosmology," "Cosmic Christ":

1. *Angels.* As we have seen, angels represent the number one cosmological question in the Mediterranean area in the first century A.D. "Are they friends or foes?" The same question Einstein asked about our universe, "Is it friendly or not?"

2. *Lord.* The word *kyrios* or "Lord" means the Ruler of the universe—one who makes the universe go around. A cosmological title.

3. *Cloud.* In apocalyptic literature divinity often rides the clouds, which are also frequent settings for theophanies. To a desert people like the Israelites, clouds bring the miracle of shade and on occasion the miracle of rain! Biblical scholar D. E. Nineham identifies the voice coming out of the "cloud" in the transfiguration scene with "the voice of God himself; for, in the later Jewish writings, the cloud was *par excellence* the vehicle of God's *Shekinah* [i.e., the dwelling presence of God] and the medium in and through which he manifested himself"[55] (see Cf. Exod. 16:10; 19:9; 19:16; 25:15; Num. 14:10; Ezek. 1:4–28).

4. *Glory.* The word "glory" (*doxa*) connotes the divine radiance and beauty that fills the universe. It is a cosmological term.

5. *Wilderness and mountains.* Divine theophanies take place at those cosmological places of power and energy denoted by mountains and by the wilderness where the human encounters the terror and beauty of the divine and of powerful creatures other than the human through whom the divine is also manifested.

6. *Evil.* The struggle with evil is a wrestling with cosmological forces, "powers and principalities," bigger than humans alone.

I believe that rereading our Scriptures mindful of these six categories will aid us in realizing the immensely rich theology of the Cosmic Christ in our biblical heritage. As we do this we may find ourselves responded to like the disciples at the first Pentecost about whom it was said, "these people are full of new wine" (Acts 2:13).

17. The Cosmic Christ and Creation Mystics— Greek Fathers

Philosopher Henri-Louis Bergson said in a lecture that "the extent of our future is very much dependent on how far back we go into the past."

If we are to recover the powerful tradition of the Cosmic Christ we need to look at those periods in our history when this tradition was alive and healthy. As we have seen, Scripture is far richer in a Cosmic Christ theology than we have been taught. One wonders if the Greek Fathers were aware of this theology.

In a recent study entitled *Jesus Through the Centuries: His Place in the History of Culture*, Jaroslav Pelikan (whose mother, not incidentally, was Eastern Orthodox), devotes a chapter to "the Cosmic Christ." He focuses on the Christian philosophers of the fourth and fifth centuries and presents their definition of the Cosmic Christ in the following fashion: Christ is "the divine clue to the structure of reality (metaphysics) and, within metaphysics, to the riddle of being (ontology)." Christ is the one who has "sovereignty over the universe" and he is the "first born from the dead." The Cosmic Christ gives meaning to the cosmos. He is divine wisdom as opposed to worldly wisdom and, as Basil of Caesarea puts it, "the Word of God [who] pervades the creation" from the beginning to the present day; Christ is "God's Co-operator." Christ also represents the "reason" and "mind" of the cosmos, for to be without *Logos (alogos)* is to be insane. Concerning the Cosmic Christ Gregory of Nazianzus says, "This name [Logos] was given to him because he exists in all things that are." Jesus Christ is the "second person" of the Trinity and also the Cosmic Christ. Humanity participates in this presence of the Cosmic Christ by "mirroring forth the presence of the creating Logos" (Gregory of Nyssa). Divine reason finds a home in human reason and thus order and harmony are brought to human affairs and to the universe itself. "All things are held together" by the Cosmic Christ, according to Basil, and thus the universe is not absurd but permeated with "the Logos of God who is over all and who governs all" (Athanasius).[1]

One can see in the patristic tradition of the Cosmic Christ a natural connection to the scriptural testimonies presented earlier. One is struck by how fully immersed so many thinkers of the patristic period were in a cosmology and therefore in a Cosmic Christ. As Pelikan observes, "It was characteristic of the Greek Christian philosophers of the fourth and fifth centuries that by contrast with the later Christian individualism manifest especially in Western thought, they always viewed humanity and the cosmos in close proximity."[2] He fails to note the reason for this lack of cosmic thought in Western religion: contemporaneous with this interest in the Cosmic Christ in Eastern Christianity lived Augustine of Hippo (354–430), whose interest was not in the cosmos but in psychological introspection and the question of personal guilt and salvation. He, more than any other Western figure, influenced the Christian West to be individualistic. The individualism of Descartes, who in the seventeenth century would declare "I think, therefore I am," is immediately traceable to Augustine.

Along with a lively interest in the cosmos, the Greek Fathers also celebrated the divinity of humankind associated with the coming of the Cosmic Christ. We are "partakers in the divine nature," wrote Peter (2 Pet. 1:4). Clement of Alexandria elaborates on Peter's idea: "The Logos of God has become human so that you might learn from a human being how a human being may become divine."[3] This idea echoes that of Iranaeus, an Easterner who came West in the second century: "God became a human being in order that human beings might become God," he wrote.[4] A theology of the Cosmic Christ is not embarrassed by the deification of humans. Precisely because this deification is seen in a *cosmic* and gratuitous context, there is nothing to fear—rather, a joyful response is called for. With deification comes responsibility—responsibility for creation itself. Jesus as the Cosmic Christ was understood by the Fathers as the goal of the cosmos as well as the beginning, the Omega as well as the Alpha. Through him would come, as Gregory of Nyssa put it, "the restitution of all things, and with the re-formation of the world humanity also shall be changed from the transient and the earthly to the incorruptible and the eternal."[5] While the Fathers attempted to ground this theology of *Logos* and Cosmic Christ in the incarnation and earthly Jesus, they were not noticeably successful in doing so, for their platonic dualisms often failed to equip them with a love of earth and earthiness upon which a theology of the Cosmic Christ must be grounded.[6]

Nevertheless, we do have in the fourth century a cosmological theology, and therefore a Cosmic Christ. At that time cosmology was important. The same was true, as we will see, for the creation mystics in the Middle Ages. The same has *not* been true, however, of the theology of the last three centuries in the West. But, with Einstein's fascination with the mystery of the universe banishing Newton's and Descartes' nonmystical or mechanistic cosmology, a new era of the Cosmic Christ is emerging. And with it, perhaps, a new way and a new power by which to love Mother Earth and her children, ourselves included.

18. The Cosmic Christ and Creation Mystics— The Medieval West

The creation-centered mystics of the Middle Ages in the West celebrated the Cosmic Christ with vigor. From Hildegard of Bingen (twelfth century) to Francis of Assisi, Thomas Aquinas, Mechtild of Magdeburg, Dante, and Meister Eckhart (thirteenth and fourteenth centuries), to Julian of Norwich (fourteenth and fifteenth centuries) and Nicolas of Cusa (fifteenth century), a cosmology and a Cosmic Christology was celebrated. We shall take a brief look at each of these mystics for their naming of the Cosmic Christ experience.

HILDEGARD OF BINGEN. Hildegard of Bingen (1098–1179) placed her entire theology in a cosmological setting. Her *ideas* about the universe as well as her *method* of thinking and sharing these ideas are cosmologically oriented. Hildegard composed a series of songs, "The Symphony of the Harmony of Heavenly Revelations," in which she expressed musically and poetically her deep mystical experiences of the Cosmic Christ. She believed that singing of words reveals their true meaning directly to the soul through bodily vibrations. Even today these songs evoke mystical experiences in those who sing them. Her music is cosmic; it demands an almost cosmic amount of breath to sing, as students in our Institute who have been singing if for years are aware. It jumps from mode to mode—much as the universe does in its activity.

She painted mandalas, or psychocosmograms, to elicit an experience of the Christ. In one of her paintings, "The Man in Sapphire Blue," she depicts what she calls the "golden and fiery ropes of the Universe" that hold "all things together" (IHB, 23). She emphasized that "the Man in Sapphire Blue" dwells in every person as a power of divine compassion to heal. Another painting depicts the universe as residing within the belly of divinity, who is called a "Lady Named Love" (IHB, 39). It is an amazing picture of panentheism—all creatures in God and God in all creatures. The feet of the figure represent the two thrones of justice and righteousness (i.e., mysticism) that support the universe.[1]

"It is God whom human beings know in every creature," Hildegard wrote (IHB, 40). Notice how nonanthropocentric the Cosmic Christ is: it is the divine image or "mirror" that "glistens and glitters" in every creature (IHB, 68). Sounding much like the wisdom passages of the Hebrew Bible that we considered earlier and that the writers of the New Testament drew deeply from, Hildegard writes:

> I, the fiery life of divine wisdom,
> I ignite the beauty of the plains,
> I sparkle the waters,
> I burn in the sun, and the moon, and the stars.
> With wisdom I order all rightly.
> . . . .
> I adorn all the earth.
> I am the breeze that nurtures all things green.
> . . . .
> I am the rain coming from the dew
> that causes the grasses to laugh with the joy of life.
> I call forth tears, the aroma of holy work.
> I am the yearning for good.

(HB, 30–31)

Hildegard offers her own theology of the *Logos*, or "Word" of God, when she says that Christ is the Word because "by the sound of his voice the entire creation was awakened and called to itself" (IHB, 28). Christ is the "Son of justice" who enlightens every creature. "Every creature becomes illuminated by the brightness of his light" (IHB, 37). Here she elaborates on a "Word of God" theology:

> Without the Word of God no creature has meaning.
> God's Word is in all creation, visible and invisible.
> The Word is living, being, spirit, all verdant greening,
>   all creativity.
> This Word manifests in every creature.
> Now this is how the spirit is in the flesh—the Word is
>   indivisible from God.
>
> (HB, 49)

Hildegard is not haunted by anthropocentrism; she interprets the "Word made flesh" language of John's Gospel as immediately speaking about the divine presence in nature itself. In another passage she writes that "there is no creature that does not have a radiance. Be it greenness or seed, blossom or beauty, it could not be creation without it" (HB, 24). For Hildegard the term "radiance" is a technical term denoting the light and illumination that God is. Just as every ray of the sun is the sun, so every ray of God is God (though not all of God). Thus, every creature is a ray of God, a radiance of God, a divine expression of God. Hildegard has God the Creator speak:

> I who am the Ancient of Days, do declare that I am the day by myself alone. I am the day that does not shine by the sun; rather by me the sun is ignited. . . . I have created mirrors in which I consider all the wonders of my originality which will never cease. I have prepared for myself these mirror forms so that they may resonate in a song of praise. For I have a voice like the thunderbolt by which I keep in motion the entire universe in the living sounds of all creation. This I have done, I who am the Ancient of Days.
>
> (BDW, 128)

One *feels* with the right brain as well as learns with the left brain about a living cosmological mysticism when reading Hildegard of Bingen. Like the Eastern Fathers of the fourth century, Hildegard is not afraid of the theme of divinization or deification. "Divinity is aimed at humanity," she states (HB, 89), and it is especially in our creativity that the divine shines forth. "Humanity alone is called to assist God. Humankind is called to co-create" (HB, 106). Hildegard is less anthropocentric than the fourth-century Greek Fathers in applying the "good news" of our divinization. For example, she teaches that humans "have a natural longing for other creatures and we feel a glow of love for them. We often seek out nature in a spirit of delight" (BDW, 129). The "nameless" God of Creation is worshipped "by all creatures," she teaches (BDW, 142) because every creature has a "spiritual life" (IHB, 53). The earth is holy and must "not be injured, must not be destroyed" (HB, 78). Much more on Hildegard's understanding of the Cosmic Christ can be gleaned from her writings, paintings and music, which are becoming increasingly available in English.[2]

FRANCIS OF ASSISI. Francis (1181–1226) follows the cosmic or creation-centered tradition of Hildegard and of the Celtic tradition that flourished not only in Rhineland where Hildegard lived, was trained, and did her work but also in northern Italy where Francis lived.[3] Francis, like Hildegard, grounded his sense of the Cosmic Christ in a struggle for church reform and renewal. Hildegard fought in her letters and her sermons for church renewal while Francis sought to create a lifestyle that would displace avarice and the systems of both lingering feudalism and emerging capitalism. His greatest written work—the "Canticle of Brother Sun"—should be considered through the prism of the Cosmic Christ that we are elaborating.[4] Remember that with Francis, as with Hildegard, we are talking about a mystic—someone who has internalized the experience of a living cosmology—not someone who is just writing *about* the Christ. Francis composed this great poem toward the end of his life; it echoes many of the richest themes of the Cosmic Christ.

Francis begins his poem with words we have often seen in conjunction with the Cosmic Christ theophanies of the Scriptures: "Lord" and "Glory." He understands that glory comes from the divine source of all things.

> Most high, all-powerful, all good Lord!
> All praise is yours, all glory, all honor
> and all blessing.

Like the canticles of Luke's Gospel and the Hebrew Bible, he sings praise and blessing back to their source.

> To you alone, Most High, do they belong.
> No mortal lips are worthy
> To pronounce your name.

Here Francis names the emptying and letting go processes that are sung about in Philippians 2. For true praise to emerge, it must come from an empty space deep within the individual. The Divine Transcendence is not easily named, it is shrouded in deep, unutterable mystery and demands quiet reverence. Yet, Francis acknowledges and celebrates divinity in its creative and creaturely manifestations. The divine is incarnated in the flesh of nature. He continues:

> All praise be yours, my Lord, through all that you have made,
> and first my Lord Brother Sun,
> Who brings the day; and light you give to us through him.
> How beautiful he is, how radiant in all his splendour!
> Of you, Most High, he bears the likeness.

Notice how "radiance," the term that excited Hildegard, also excites Francis to praise the "likeness" of divinity in the "light" and the "day" of his "Lord Brother Sun." Francis is following the order of Genesis 1—this is *his* creation story—and of John 1 in praising first the gift of light through the sun. (He is also following the order of contemporary cosmology that understands the creation to have begun as a 700,000-year fireball.) Sun and light were indeed the origin of things. Is Francis also alluding to Jesus as the preexistent light, the "first-born" among all creatures, when he speaks of "Brother Sun" and the "light you give to us through him"? By calling the sun "Lord," Francis not only celebrates panentheism but he also rejects "lords" of the feudal era, those whom he spent his life fighting politically by his rejection of feudal privilege, and economically by his devotion to poverty.

Francis is not sexist. Here again he is like Hildegard and the sexually balanced Celtic tradition that so deeply influenced him. His poem continually balances the male and the female aspects of the universe:

All praise be yours, my Lord, through Sister Moon and Stars;
   In the heavens you have made them bright
   and precious and fair.

Again, the themes of light, splendor, and illumination are continued as Francis celebrates the "brightness" of the moon and stars. Notice how the Cosmic Christ—"the light who enlightens all who have life"—is present in all creatures, and *therefore* all creatures are brother and sister to one another. Francis takes seriously the idea of the family of all creation, the interconnectivity of all creatures. All are bound together and connected by the divine light. He continues his poem, praising "Brothers Wind and Air . . . and all the weather's moods," "Sister Water" who is "so useful, precious and pure," and "Brother Fire through whom you brighten up the night" and who is "full of power and strength." And, he praises next, our mother and sister Earth:

All praise be yours, my Lord, through Sister Earth, our mother,
   Who feeds us in her sovereignty and produces
   Various fruits and colored flowers and herbs.

For Francis, Mother Earth is a royal person. The dignity and the independence of a sovereign reside in the earth who is both mother and sister. She is praised for birthing fruits, flowers, and herbs—that is, food, beauty, and healing powers. All this is the Cosmic Christ at work in nature. Francis is hinting at the tradition of the motherhood of God and, in fact, of Jesus that was celebrated in his time.

It is clear from what we have discussed that Francis's poem is a celebration of the ancient cosmology and its physics of earth, air, fire (light), water. The poem now turns from the Cosmic Christ in nature to the Cosmic Christ in the two-legged ones. Like the teaching we have seen in the Scriptures, a prophetic dimension is at the heart of the experience of the Cosmic Christ enfleshed in humanity. Francis celebrates, therefore the power in humans to forgive, to endure suffering, to be instruments of peacemaking. Scholars tell us that at the time he composed these stanzas Francis was asked to negotiate disputes between warring factions in his hometown, so the stanzas have a ring of *praxis* and not just theory. Notice, however, with what subtlety he moves from the word "herbs," i.e., the symbol for *nature's* healing powers, to the *human's* powers of healing and "granting pardon." This, again, confirms how grounded he was in his cosmology: human wisdom derives *from* nature's wisdom and not the other way around.

> All praise be yours, my Lord, through those who grant pardon
> for love of you; through those who endure sickness
> and trial.
> Happy those who endure in peace,
> By you, Most High, they will be crowned.

There seems to be a subtle resemblance to the Beatitudes in Jesus' Sermon on the Mount in Francis's claim of happiness for those who endure in peace. "Blessed are the peacemakers," he is saying in his own way.

Francis concludes his poem with a section in praise of "Sister Death," added when he realized he was dying. He reiterates the story of the Cosmic Christ who comes to conquer the forces of death and to relieve the cosmic anxiety over death through his own death and resurrection.

> All praise be yours, my Lord, through Sister Death,
> from whose embrace no mortal can escape.
> Woe to those who die in mortal sin!
> Happy those She finds doing your will!
> The second death can do no harm to them.

Death for Francis is not to be feared but celebrated as part of the cosmic process. Many deaths, including baptism and other conversion experiences, precede our physical death. Francis experienced many of these including the moment, which he considered the greatest act of his life, when he embraced and kissed the leper. For Francis that was a conversion experience, a kind of death and rebirth. Francis tells us not to fear the "second death" or judgment day if we are "doing God's will." What is that will? It is simply this:

> Praise and bless my Lord, and give him thanks,
> and serve him with great humility.

THOMAS AQUINAS. Thomas Aquinas (1225–1274) is seldom recognized as a mystic. Rationalistic interpreters of his thought, more influenced by the Enlightenment's banishment of the Cosmic Christ than by Aquinas himself, have overidentified him with left-brain "scholasticism"; he has thus been dismissed as a serious cosmological thinker. It is curious that seven hundred years after his death the majority of his biblical commentaries, which are his least scholastic works, have yet to be translated into English.

Yet Aquinas was so serious about a living cosmology that he dared develop his theology based on the science of the "pagan" Aristotle. Aristotle's cosmology was a totally new and extremely controversial discovery for Western Christianity at the time of Aquinas. (Aristotelian philosophy arrived in the West—as did Scholasticism—not through Christianity but through Islam.) In Aristotle and in Denys the Areopagite, Aquinas found an antidote for the lack of a Cosmic Christ in Augustine and for the excessively individualistic piety, based on Augustine, that dominated the Western church. (Neoplatonism had also subtly encouraged this individualistic piety by its distrust of nature and creation.)

Aquinas paid a high price for his daring intellectual adventure of constructing a Christian cosmology on a pre-Christian scientific paradigm. He was driven to an early death by fierce opposition to his work by the Augustinian Christians on the right wing and the secularist Aristotelians, led by Siger of Bribant, on the left. Controversial even after his death, Aquinas was condemned three times, twice by the bishop of Paris and once by the bishop of Canterbury.

Following are excerpts from the rich cosmological writings of Aquinas. Would that those who have called themselves "Thomists" through the years were as committed to a Cosmic Christ as brother Thomas was.

"Creatures can be called God's words," Aquinas says, because they "manifest God's mind just like effects manifest their causes."[5] Jesus is also a creature and of him Aquinas says, "The Incarnate Word is like a word of speech. Just as sensible sounds express what we think, so too Christ's body expresses the Eternal Word."[6] The Cosmic Christ is "both expressive and creative of the universe."[7] It is this Christ who is "the primary source of newness and renovation."[8] To Aquinas the universe is an essentially friendly place. When we lack a cosmology, we incur a kind of cosmic anxiety. "A person may imagine that he is subject to certain forces when in point of fact he is above them, all because he is ignorant of nature and of his place in the cosmos. We are warned by Jeremiah: 'Be not afraid of the signs of heaven which the heathen fear' (Jer. 10:2)."[9] God, Aquinas teaches, is the "spring and source of all goodness" and flows over into all creatures—God is the main river and creatures are the tributaries of goodness.[10] This explains how it happens that "the mind is kindled into loving divine goodness by dwelling on creatures."[11] Aquinas calls every creature a "witness to God insofar as each creature is a witness to God's power and omnipotence; and its beauty is a witness to the divine wisdom."[12] Indeed, "the whole world" is God's work of art—"a certain representation of the divine wisdom conceived within the mind of the Father."[13] The Word, who is Christ, "encompasses all things, preserving them" and thus "nothing was made outside of the Word"; the word is "per se life, always perfect life."[14] But the Cosmic Christ is not restricted to Jesus alone for Aquinas who says, "Every creature participates in some way in the likeness of the Divine Essence."[15] The Trinity is at work—the creator with Cosmic Christ and Spirit together—in a dynamic fashion in all of creation. "An image of the Trinity pulsates in all conscious and loving creatures to the extent that they too conceive words and expand in love."[16] Thus, wherever there is creativity, the Cosmic Christ is at work. Nor are individuals alone images of God, rather "the whole cosmos is."[17] Like Hildegard and Francis before him, Aquinas images the being of things—that gift of existence that is "most like God" in them—as light. "The being of things is itself their light and the measure of the being of a thing is the measure of its light."[18]

Aquinas repeats the deification theme as the reason why Christ became human. While this theme was seldom developed in Western theology, Aquinas says:

> The Son of God became human in order that humans might become gods and become the children of God.[19]

> The Incarnation accomplished the following: That God became human and that humans became God and sharers in the divine nature[20] (Cf. 2 Pet. 1:4).

> We are meant to become more like God.[21]

> The only begotten Son of God, intending to make us *partakers of the divine nature* (2 Pet. 1:4), took our nature on himself, becoming a human so he might make humans gods.[22]

> We are called God's children by taking on the likeness of his natural and only begotten Son who is himself begotten wisdom.[23]

These brief selections and comments on Aquinas's theology make it clear that the tradition of the Cosmic Christ was alive and real in his work and in his struggle to recapture a living cosmology for the Christian West. His work in this regard was brought to fruition by three of his disciples: Mechtild, Dante, and Meister Eckhart.

MECHTILD OF MAGDEBURG. Mechtild of Magdeburg (c. 1210–c. 1280), laywoman and social activist, Beguine and critic of society and church, had Dominicans as spiritual directors. These persons grounded her in Aquinas's spirituality—even though Aquinas was deeply suspect and was condemned four years before Mechtild's death—including a deep appreciation for a living cosmology and the Cosmic Christ. Her spiritual directors encouraged her writing and saw to it that her book *The Flowing Light of the Godhead*, was translated promptly into Latin. Her written work was a spiritual journal that she kept from the time she was in her twenties to the time of her death in her early seventies. It is remarkable how this uneducated laywoman—centuries before there were religious sisters in the Roman Catholic Church—developed a spirituality of the Cosmic Christ in imaginative and practical depth. Following are some of her writings on that subject:

You ask me where God dwells: I will tell you.
There is no Lord in the whole world who lives in all [his]
dwellings at once except God alone.

(MM, 29)

Notice how she is developing here the biblical theme of the kingdom of God. Her language is suspiciously similar to the question Jesus' disciples put to him in Luke's Gospel: "Tell us when the kingdom of God was to come," they inquire, and Jesus answers: "Do not look here or there. For the kingdom/queendom of God is among you"; (Luke 17:20–21). Mechtild is interpreting the term "among" to mean that divinity is in all things. She then equates this experience of the omnipresence of divinity with Jesus when she tells this story:

> One day I saw with the eyes of my eternity
> in bliss and without effort, a stone.
> This stone was like a great mountain
> and was of assorted colors.
> It tasted sweet, like heavenly herbs.
> I asked the sweet stone: Who are you?
> It replied: "I am Jesus."

(MM, 108)

This story of a meditation experience Mechtild had "in bliss and without effort" is also a story of a personal encounter with the Cosmic Christ. Other examples of Cosmic Christ encounters abound in Mechtild's writings. In the following passage she describes how every human is a bearer of the Cosmic Christ:

> In heaven, our origin, before each soul and body
> therein gleamed the reflection of the Holy Trinity.
> . . . .
> Each of us is a mirror of eternal contemplation,
> with a reflection that must surely be that of the
> living Son of God with all his works.

(MM, 32)

Just as Jesus is an image of the Godhead, so too are we. Mechtild describes the following conversation between the soul and God.

> O soul, you are perfect—Rejoice!
> For you alone are like God.
> . . . .
> Come racing like a hunted deer.
> For you are the image of my Divine Godhead.
> You are a foundation of my Divine Being.
> This is why the pure lamb laid itself
> on its own image in the stall of your body.

(MM, 45)

Mechtild once again personalizes the biblical theme of the Cosmic Christ, being "all in all" (1 Cor. 15:28). She describes the breakthrough the soul experiences in waking up:

> Woman! Your soul has slept from childhood on.
> Now it is awakened by the light of true love.
> . . . .
> Now, she sees clearly, she recognizes for the first time
> How God is All in All.
>
> (MM, 82)

How does Mechtild wake up to see God "all in all"? By panentheism. "The day of my spiritual awakening was the day I saw and knew I saw all things in God and God in all things" (MM, 42). Part of our awakening is our awakening to our nearness to God:

> I who am Divine am truly in you.
> I can never be sundered from you:
> However far we be parted, never can we be separated.
> I am in you and you are in Me.
> We could not be any closer.
> We two are fused into one, poured into a single mould.
> Thus, unwearied, we shall remain forever.
>
> (MM, 46)

Also part of our awakening is our awakening to our divinity. "The soul is a god with God. This is why God says to the soul: 'I am the God of all gods; but you are the goddess of all creatures' " (MM, 33). And again:

> As soon as the soul begins to grow the dust of sin falls away
> and the soul becomes a god with God.
> Then, what God wills the soul wills.
> Otherwise, God and soul would not be united
> in so beautiful a union.
>
> (MM, 83)

The result of the Cosmic Christ being awakened in us is celebrated by Mechtild as our creative work of compassion.

> When are we like God? I will tell you.
> In so far as we love compassion and practice it steadfastly,
> to that extent do we resemble the heavenly Creator
> who practices these things ceaselessly in us.
>
> (MM, 119)

Thus Mechtild concludes that to experience the Cosmic Christ is to become an instrument of divine compassion. This deeply biblical teaching is identical to that of Hildegard in her mandala of "The Man in Sapphire Blue" who brings compassion and dwells in all of us (IHB, 22–25).

The Cosmic Christ is present in our suffering and darkness as well. God says to Mechtild when she undergoes suffering, "I will take this burden first and clasp it close to Myself and that way you may more easily bear it" (MM, 62). Mechtild replies, "Lord, I will tear the heart of my soul in two and you must lay therein. You must lay yourself in the wounds of my soul" (MM, 66).

The Cosmic Christ is also present in play,

> I, God, am your playmate!
> I will lead the child in you in wonderful ways
> for I have chosen you.
> Beloved child, come swiftly to Me
> for I am truly in you.
>
> (MM, 47)

DANTE ALIGHIERI. Dante Alighieri (1265–1321), like all the other creation mystics we are recalling here, lived out in practice what he believed about the Cosmic Christ. Like Hildegard, Francis, Aquinas, and Mechtild, Dante was in constant political trouble. A layman, mystic, and elected official in Florence, he was "a fearless opponent of papal military power, greed, and corruption. As a result he was condemned to permanent exile and death by burning if he ever returned to Florence."[24] He wandered around Italy for over twenty years, cut off from his homeland, and his friends and relatives. During this period he composed his great work, *The Divine Comedy.* One might call the poem an experience of the Cosmic Christ in art. In this poem Dante elaborates a cosmology and a Cosmic Christ. Dante's vision is a cosmological one. For him, the "glory of God" that "moves all things penetrates the universe" (DA, 95). For Dante, the human is made of the "eternal beauties" of the "sparks of God."

> These sparks, human souls,
> which come directly from God,
> have no end:
> they are imprinted forever
> with the stamp of God's beauty.
>
> (DA, 16)

What is the purpose of creation in Dante's view? It is to awaken the divine "I am," the Cosmic Christ, in all creatures.

> God created . . . so that God's creation, God's splendor,
> might joyfully declare as it shines back:
> I subsist, I stand under, I am!
>
> (DA, 117)

The structure of *The Divine Comedy* has been identified as Dante's own "paschal mystery" for it begins in hell on Good Friday and emerges from that pit on Easter Sunday. At the culmination of his journey depicted in the *The Divine Comedy,* upon his heavenly vision, Dante describes his soul as being in a microcosmic/macrocosmic relationship with the uni-

verse. He tells us that "my desire and my will were turning in harmony
like a wheel that is moved evenly by the Love who moves the sun and the
other stars" (DA, 130). Thus it is Love that moves the universe—a point
that Hildegard also taught. Dante describes the Son who is the Cosmic
Christ, as a "great Light," an "Eternal Light" that reflects the light
from the Creator (DA, 128). Like "rainbow to rainbow" they interact
with each other (DA, 128). The great light is also expressed in the human person:

> The circle of reflected light
> seemed depicted with our human image within itself.
> I desired to see how our image was conformed
> to the divine circle
> and has a place in it.
>
> (DA, 129)

By an act of illumination (also a Hildegard word), his mind experienced a "flash of grace" and an insight into how Love moves sun, stars
and all things of the cosmos. But the eternal light is not restricted to humans alone; it is "scattered on leaves throughout the world" (DA, 127).
God is the "dazzling light" that constitutes "the creative center of all life
and movement. In that Point every *where* and every *when* are centered"
(DA, 117). Thus, time and space come together in the eternal now of
divinity embedded in creation. Dante and companion Beatrice travel
from star to star and planet to planet—theirs is truly a cosmic journey.
Likewise, Dante understands Jesus' life and death on earth as being of
cosmic consequence:

> The Divine Person who assumed our nature
> suffered death on the cross,
> a death which shook the earth,
> opened heaven,
> and pleased God.
> From the first day of creation
> to the last night
> there has never been,
> nor will there be,
> so exalted and magnificent an act!
>
> (DA, 105)

It is evident that Dante celebrated his prophetic and mystical cosmology with a grasp of the Cosmic Christ.

MEISTER ECKHART. No Christian mystic has so richly developed the
theme of the Cosmic Christ as Meister Eckhart (1260–1327), who stands
indebted to his predecessors, Hildegard and Francis, Aquinas and Mechtild. He was Dante's contemporary. Truly a follower of the Cosmic
Christ and the prophetic Jesus, Eckhart was condemned by the church a
week following his death—a condemnation that scholars agree shows all

the earmarks of a political attack on him and the oppressed with whom he worked so closely: women who were Beguines, the peasants to whom he preached in their own dialect, and the former nobility who had lost their holdings.[25]

Eckhart celebrates the *Logos* or "word" of God as applying to each and every creature: "All creatures are words of God. My mouth expresses and reveals God but the existence of a stone does the same and people often recognize more from actions than from words" (BR, 58–59). Here Eckhart celebrates both stones *and* actions as being "words of God." He is hinting, therefore, that Christ as the word of God is found in stones and actions as well as in the words we express. He continues, "All creatures are gladly doing the best they can to express God. . . . They all cry out to come back there where they have flowed out" (BR, 59). Eckhart reveals a certain serenity and joy at the efforts by all creatures to live up to their task as "words of God" or images of the Cosmic Christ. In saying they are all "doing their best," Eckhart implies that we should criticize creatures less and sit at their feet more to learn of the image of God working in and through them. Eckhart stresses how there is only one Word of God, only one Cosmic Christ. He writes, "God is constantly speaking only one thing. God's speaking is one thing. In this one utterance God speaks the Son and at the same time the Holy Spirit and all creatures" (BR, 66). Divinity, Eckhart maintains, is omnipresent.

> People think God has only become a human being *there*—in his historical incarnation—but that is not so; for God is *here*—in this very place—just as much incarnate as in a human being long ago. And this is why God has become a human being: that God might give birth to you as the only begotten Son, and as no less.
>
> (BR, 66)

In applying the "Word of God" theology uniquely to humans, Eckhart writes, "In this Word the Creator speaks my spirit, your spirit, and the spirit of every person who resembles the Word. And in this utterance you and I are true sons and daughters of God, as the Word itself is child of the Creator" (BR, 340).

Eckhart celebrates the seed of God in every person when he says that "the seed of divine nature is the Son of God, the Word of God" (BR, 352). "The seed of God is in us. . . . Now the seed of a pear tree grows into a pear tree, a hazel seed into a hazel tree, the seed of God into God" (BR, 118). People become other Christs by the presence of this seed or Word. "Your human nature and that of the divine Word are no different. . . . In the just person there is fulfilled what the Holy Spirit and the prophets said about Christ" (BR, 104). Persons are called to be the mystic and prophet that Jesus was each in his or her own way. "It is given to every person to become the child of God, substantially indeed in Christ, but in himself or herself by adoption through grace" (BR, 347).

This means that humans "do Christ's work" and "behave exactly like Jesus" (who does the works of the Christ) (BR, 347). Complaining that many people follow Christ "like a falcon follows a woman carrying tripe or sausages," Eckhart emphasizes that to follow Christ means to "mold yourself in all your works on his pattern" (BR, 347). To follow is to work, not just to pursue as a "wolf does a carcass or a fly does a pot" that smells (BR, 347).

It is in sowing "the good seed, the root of all wisdom, all knowledge, all virtue and all goodness" that "God has sowed his image and his likeness" in all creatures (BR, 352). Because all creatures contain the Word of God and express it, there is a radical equality of being that needs to be reverenced. "God poured the divine being in equal measure to all creatures, to each as much as it can receive. This is a good lesson for us that we should love all creatures equally with everything which we have received from God" (BR, 92). Because "equality gives strength in all things," the lives of animals as well as children energize adults and drive out their fear (BR, 99). "The greatest blessing in heaven and on earth is based on equality" Eckhart says, in an observation as political as it is ecological (BR, 98). After all, if "isness is God" (BR, 89), then it is at the level of "isness" that all things first express the Cosmic Christ and at that level all things are equal.

Eckhart's stress on the Word as a seed is an implication of the creativity experienced through the Cosmic Christ. The Creator is constantly creating and the universe is constantly being created. Eckhart says, "I have often said God is creating this entire world full and entire in this present now" (BR, 65). Where in particular is this creativity taking place? In the human depth and imagination. Eckhart continues, "There where time never penetrates, where no image shines in, in the innermost and highest aspect of the soul God creates the entire cosmos" (BR, 65). Eckhart is here applying the tradition of the preexistence of Christ and Christ as co-creator to humans or, if you will, to the Cosmic Christ in humans, (see BR, 214–215). The world is created in us as it is created in Christ. Indeed, the birthing of the Cosmic Christ is the purpose of the incarnation. "God is *here*—in this very place—just as much incarnate as in a human being long ago. And this is why God has become a human being: that Divinity might give birth to you as its only begotten Son, and as no less" (BR, 66). Divinity wants to birth the Cosmic Christ in each and every individual. "The Creator gives birth to the divine child in the innermost part of the soul and gives birth to you with its only begotten Son as no less" (BR, 66). How do we know that God is birthing the Cosmic Christ in us? By our ability to find the Cosmic Christ in other creatures. Eckhart writes, "Lay hold of God in all things and this will be a sign of your birth, a sign that God has given birth in you as the only begotten Son, and nothing less" (BR, 67).

Thus it is still not enough that we experience the Cosmic Christ in self and others—we are also to birth the Cosmic Christ just as Mary birthed Jesus who was Christ. "God lies in the maternity bed, like a woman who has given birth, in every good soul which has abandoned its self-centeredness and received the indwelling of God" (BR, 93). Thus Eckhart sees the "indwelling" tradition as being radically creative. He continues, "What help is it to me that the Creator gives birth to the Son unless I too give birth to him? It is for this reason that God gives birth to the divine child in a perfect soul and lies in the maternity bed so that God can give birth to the child again in all his/her works" (BR, 93). Such a person will be like Joseph the son of Jacob of whom it was said, "I don't regard him as a human being, but as a god, for God shines from his works" (Gen. 39:23; BR, 93). The vital presence of the Cosmic Christ and the increased presence that is brought about by human creativity delights God and gives God pleasure. Eckhart maintains "God loves all creatures as God. . . . God enjoys all creatures, not as creatures, but enjoys the creatures as God. In the same enjoyment in which God enjoys the God-self, God enjoys all things" (BR, 76). Eckhart also understands the presence of the Cosmic Christ in the suffering of the world. If every creature is a word of God, then the suffering of every creature is the suffering of the word of God. And the work of compassion to heal one another's suffering is the work of relieving the suffering of the Christ. (See BR, 432; 155–159; 417–477.)

Eckhart's theology of the Cosmic Christ is so richly developed, no doubt, because his creation-centered spirituality presumes a living cosmology. His work also presumes the internalization of that cosmology in a living mysticism. Eckhart's entire work—like that of Hildegard of Bingen—can be understood as a treatise on the Cosmic Christ.

JULIAN OF NORWICH. Still another champion of the Cosmic Christ in the Middle Ages was Julian of Norwich (c. 1342–1415). Julian, who chose to live as a hermitess in the middle of the bustling city of Norwich, celebrated the "inness" of God in all creatures. She writes, "In my understanding I saw God in a point. In seeing this I saw that God is in all things. God works in creatures because God is in the mid-point of everything" (JN, 37). Julian has God speak to the same issue of the divine centering: "See! I am God. See! I am in everything. See! I lead everything toward the purpose for which I ordained it, without beginning, by the same Power, Wisdom and Love by which I created it. How could anything be amiss?" (JN, 39). Julian applies this centering presence that is so much a part of panentheism—to Christ as found in Jesus:

> Our Lord Jesus oftentimes said:
> "This I am. This I am.
> I am what you love.
> I am what you enjoy.
> I am what you serve.

> I am what you long for.
> I am what you desire.
> I am what you intend.
> I am all that is."
>
> (JN, 47)

Julian is basing her own "I am" sayings on the divine "I am" sayings of John's Gospel, which are in turn based on the great "I am" of Exodus 3:14, when Moses asked God for the divine name and God said, "Tell them I am who am [or I am who will be]." Julian also presents a *Logos* or "Word of God" theology when she has God speak again, saying, "That which is impossible for you is not impossible for me: I will preserve my word in all things and I will make all things well" (JN, 58). Here Julian emphasizes the healing power of the Cosmic Christ who, as the Word present in all things, can "make all things well." This making all things well constitutes the great work of divinity. She writes, "This is the Great Deed that Our Lord will do" (JN, 58). For Julian, all creatures are enclosed in the Christ at the same time that Christ is in all creatures—a Christological panentheism. Christ is the one "in whom we are all enclosed and he in us" (JN, 90). She rightly intuits that this relationship has something deeply *maternal* about it, just as we are also all enclosed in "the deep Wisdom of the Trinity [who] is our Mother" (JN, 90). Here she is drawing on the Godhead as Mother theme we have seen in Eckhart and other creation mystics. She develops these same images further when she writes, "Our Substance—of the same nature as Jesus'—is also enclosed in Him with the blessed soul of Christ sitting restfully in the Godhead" (JN, 97).

For Julian, as for the other creation mystics we have considered, a celebration of the Cosmic Christ includes an entering into the wounds of the crucified prophet, Jesus. Indeed, she sees the crucifixion as a cosmic event involving all of nature and all its pain and suffering:

> I saw a great oneing between Christ and us
> because when he was in pain we were in pain.
> All creatures of God's creation that can suffer pain
> suffered with him.
> The sky and the earth failed at the time of Christ's dying
> because he too was part of nature (JN, 44).

Julian draws on biblical texts treated earlier that portray the death of Jesus as a significant cosmological event. She underscores the interdependence of all creatures and of all suffering with Jesus as the Christ.

Julian refers to the theme of the preexistence of the Cosmic Christ by putting it in the context of our own preexistence. "I saw that God never *began* to love us," she declares. "We have *always* been in God's foreknowledge, known and loved from without beginning" (JN, 88). All creatures—images of the preexistent Cosmic Christ—came to be at once. Julian says, "We were all created at the same time: and in our creation we were knit and oned to God. By this we are kept as luminous and noble as when we were created" (JN, 100). This celebration of our preexistence, however, does not force Julian into neglecting the future or the realization of it. Julian maintains "the soul that realizes on earth that it is the home and kingdom of our Lord Jesus is made like him and oned to him" (JN, 115). Thus, like Eckhart, she sees our earthly task as one of preparing a home for the kingdom/queendom of God here and now. Her sense of the Cosmic Christ links up once again with the teachings of Jesus that the kingdom/queendom of God is among us now.

NICHOLAS OF CUSA. Inheritor of much of the creation-centered spirituality of his fellow Rhineland mystics Hildegard of Bingen and Meister Eckhart, Nicholas of Cusa (1400–1464) was a scientist, lawyer, critical historian, philosopher, humanist, mystic, Vatican diplomat, and cardinal in the Roman Catholic church. So deep is his grasp of a living cosmology that David Bohm, one of the most creative physicists of our time, of Birbeck College, London, cites Cusa as a precursor for his work. Cusa's rich grasp of the Cosmic Christ is very evident in his thought. Says Cusa:

> If anyone held that all things are in created wisdom, and if another person held and said that all created things are in the Logos, would they not be saying the same thing? Even though there seems to be a difference in expression, yet they express the same idea, for the Logos of creation in whom all things were created can be nothing other than divine wisdom.
>
> (NC, 112)

Cusa's is truly a wisdom-oriented spirituality. Cusa maintains that "wisdom is eternal, for it precedes every beginning and all created reality" (NC, 113). Wisdom is nonelitist, it is to be found "everywhere" (NC, 88). Wisdom is "burning in all things" and "allures us with a certain foretaste of its sweetness only to be swept toward it with a wonderful desire" (NC, 33). Wisdom is "the animating power of things" (NC, 79); it is found especially in the heart:

> Wisdom is shouting in the streets. It is simply not enough for those seeking wisdom merely to read about it. Wisdom must be discovered. And once discovered it must be learned by heart. You will not find wisdom in your books for it is not of your books, but of the books of our God/dess.
>
> (NC, 87)

Like Eckhart, Cusa celebrates how "every creature is a word of God and a book about God" (ME, 14). Indeed, Cusa sees the face of God revealed in the mirror or divine image that each creature is: "Divinity shines forth in creatures as the truth of a reflected image" (NC, 122).

> There is only one mirror without flaw: the Divine, in whom what is revealed is received as it is. For this mirror is not essentially different from

any existing thing. Rather in every existing thing it is that which is: it is the universal form of being.

(NC, 131)

When we gaze on one another we gaze on the Cosmic Christ because "in all faces is seen the Face of faces, veiled in a billion riddles—yet unveiled it is not seen, until, at last, above all faces we enter into a certain secret and mystical silence of a face" (NC, 139).

While we taste eternal wisdom "in every tastable thing" and this Cosmic Christ or cosmic Wisdom is the "delight in everything delightful," what is more amazing is that wisdom itself "tastes us. And there is nothing more delicious to comprehend" (NC, 98–99). Cusa celebrates the "power of wisdom that burns forth" in the human person—"in the parts of the body" including "the harmony and movement of the various organs" and in "the spirit of the mind which is capable of wondrous arts" (NC, 39). Cusa, like all creation mystics, is a panentheist: "The absolute, Divine Mind, is all that is in everything that is. . . . Divinity is the enfolding and unfolding of everything that is. Divinity is in all things in such a way that all things are in divinity" (NC, 28f).

And we, who are other Christs and mirrors of divinity, are also panentheistic in our capacities of love, knowledge, and creativity. Cusa writes: "The human mind is the all of its dreams. . . . Mind itself supposing itself to encompass, survey, and comprehend all things thus concludes that it is in everything and everything is in it" (NC, 28–29).

Creatures can be said to be divine, for "whatever is found in creatures is found in the Divine. This is to say it is divine" (NC, 41). Humans are divine—but not fully (NC, 41). Cusa continues: "We are, as it were, a human deity. Humans are also the universe, but not absolutely since we are human. Humanity is therefore a microcosm, or in truth, a human universe. Thus humanity itself encloses both God and the universe in its human power" (NC, 42). God gives divinity to creatures but our capacity for reception is limited. Cusa writes, "The Divine Giver does not give anything other than divinity . . . But this gift cannot be received as it is given. . . . Therefore the infinite is received finitely" (NC, 129).

Nicholas of Cusa worked with the Greek church to effect a union with Rome and wrote a book on the need for a universal religion that was a greater expression of cosmic wisdom than was any single church tradition. His was truly a universal and ecumenical vision, as demonstrated when he writes:

Humanity will find that it is not a diversity of creeds, but the very same creed which is everywhere proposed. . . . There cannot but be one wisdom. . . . Humans must therefore all agree that there is but one most simple wisdom whose power is infinite; and everyone, in explaining the intensity of this beauty, must discover that it is a supreme and terrible beauty (NC, 110–111).

Truly we have in Nicholas of Cusa another example of a champion of the Cosmic Christ who did not hesitate to draw visionary ecclesiological conclusions from his theology.[26]

19. Scripture, Tradition, and the Cosmic Christ

In this section we have examined the Cosmic Christ as celebrated in Judaism, in the hymns to the Cosmic Christ, and in the events of Jesus' life as related in the Christian Scriptures. We have also seen the theology of the Cosmic Christ richly developed in the Greek Fathers of the fourth century church and the creation-centered medieval mystics of the Western church. Each of the biblical sources we have considered grounds the Cosmic Christ in history, in place, in prophetic activity, in human suffering. Indeed that is the paschal story: divinity was enfleshed in Jesus who announced the Good News and was crucified for it. Yet death—the cosmic law that all living things dread—did not overcome him, for he was resurrected and exalted, still offering Good News to creation and its inhabitants by sending the Spirit.

In studying the Gospels we find that each begins explicitly with a cosmology. In John 1 Christ is the one "through whom all things came to be." The infancy narratives in Luke and Matthew are deeply cosmological with the angels playing a key role. Mark's Gospel, which begins with Jesus' baptism and wilderness experience (including his wrestling with the devil and being comforted by angels) also opens with a cosmology. The book of Revelation is deeply cosmological as well as deeply political, insisting as it does that Christians are to honor the *true* Lord of the universe and not self-proclaimed lords in emperor's clothing in ancient Rome. This book has been practically ignored during the Enlightenment era of theology by liberal theologians for whom a cosmology and a symbolic consciousness is acutely embarrassing. No wonder the fundamentalists claimed this book as their own, interpreting it with their peculiar literalism and buttressing American empire building with it. The eschatological vision of this book remains to be discovered by scholars willing to make the move from the quest for the historical Jesus to the quest for the Cosmic Christ.

From the Gospels we have also learned that a living cosmology and the Cosmic Christ are present in and vital to each of the major events of Jesus' life: his birth, baptism, transfiguration, preaching, crucifixion, resurrection, ascension, sending of the Spirit. All take place in an explicitly cosmological context. We find key words in the New Testament that always connote a Cosmic Christ such as angels, glory, cloud, Lord. Henceforth, in reading the Christian Scriptures, each time we see these categories employed we should think: living cosmology; Cosmic Christ; Einstein. Enlightenment theologians—stuck in their anthropocentrism—were embarrassed by biblical cosmology. We need to take pride in it and re-vision our understanding of our biblical heritage accordingly.

In studying the ancient hymns of the early church we have found that the Cosmic Christ is never presented apart from the crucifixion, apart from the wounds. The Cosmic Christ is pictured as a cosmic lamb slain for all who suffer unjustly. We also learn that the Cosmic Christ is dy-namic and not static (as was the Stoic Christ figure)—there is a sense in which the Cosmic Christ is "not-yet," i.e., needing still to be birthed and coming again in the future. A new future is offered by this coming of the dynamic Christ. We learn that the Cosmic Christ is a universal concept and an ecumenical one. All nations, peoples, and creatures are invited to experience the divine "I am" within them. The Cosmic Christ is not the sole possession of Christians. Jewish wisdom literature, the prophets, and the apocalyptic writings are steeped in a living cosmology—indeed the messianic times will be marked by cosmic awakenings. The settings of the cosmic hymns in the Christian Scriptures remind us that we are to model our behavior after the Cosmic Christ—a call to wisdom being the basis of our moralities rather than mere inherited cultural mores. Mo-rality—the choices we make regarding our behavior—is to be grounded in the Cosmic Christ. (See Col. 3:10–11.) Given the rich tradition of the Cosmic Christ found both in the ancient hymns *and* in the Gospel events of Jesus' life, one wonders how much of the Gospel has been missed dur-ing the recent era when the Cosmic Christ was, in Pelikan's words, "de-posed." In this section we have also considered how vital the theme of the Cosmic Christ was to the Greek theologians of the patristic era and how richly developed this tradition became in the West through the cre-ation mystics of the Middle Ages. Hildegard of Bingen, Francis of As-sissi, Thomas Aquinas, Mechtild of Magdeburg, Meister Eckhart, Dante, Julian of Norwich, Nicholas of Cusa—all these Western mystics display a rich theology of the Cosmic Christ. Perhaps the reason they do so is the Middle Ages represents the last time that there was a living cos-mology in the West. When a living cosmology is lost, as happened with the Enlightenment, there is no need of a Cosmic Christ. But when a liv-ing cosmology emerges again, as in our time, we depend on the wisdom of our ancestors in faith who developed an understanding and experi-ence of the Cosmic Christ at the very heart of their mysticism.

What I have offered in this section is only the beginning of an ambi-tious task that must be pursued if we are to recover the Cosmic Christ. How wonderful it would be if more biblical scholars and theologians would develop this study by carrying on a full-fledged quest for the Cos-mic Christ.

In part IV we will pursue further the various meanings of the Cosmic Christ that have emerged from our study of these biblical and historical sources.

Part IV

Who Is the Cosmic Christ?

The spirit of the Lord, indeed, fills the whole world, and that which holds all things together knows every word that is said.

(Wis. 1:7)

Moses said to God: "If they ask me what your name is, what am I to tell them?" And God said to Moses, "I Am who I Am." This, he added, "is what you must say to the children of Israel": "I AM has sent me to you."

(Exodus 3:13–14)

Before Abraham came to be, I am.

(Jesus)

And if the earthly no longer knows your name,
whisper to the silent earth: I'm flowing
To the flashing water say: I am.

(Rainer Maria Rilke)

The cosmos is fundamentally and primarily living. . . . Christ, through his Incarnation, is internal to the world, . . . rooted in the world, even in the very heart of the tiniest atom. . . . Nothing seems to me more vital, from the point of view of human energy, than the appearance and eventually, the systematic cultivation of such a "cosmic sense."

(Teilhard de Chardin)

Inspired by the idea that not only is God necessary to man, but that man is also necessary to God, that man's actions are vital to all worlds and affect the course of transcendent events, the Kabbalistic preachers and popular writers sought to imbue all people with the consciousness of the supreme importance of all actions. . . . An architect of hidden worlds, *every pious Jew is, partly, the messiah.*

(Abraham Heschel)

Divine am I inside and out, and I make holy whatever I touch or am touched from.
. . . .
Why should I wish to see God better than this day?
I see something of God each hour of the twenty-four, and each moment then,
In the faces of men and women I see God, and in my own face in the glass;
I find letters from God dropped in the street, and every one is signed by God's name.

(Walt Whitman)

What pattern connects the crab to the lobster and the orchid to the primrose and all four of them to me? And me to you?

(Gregory Bateson)

In Christ were created all things in heaven and on earth: everything visible and invisible. . . . Before anything was created, Christ existed, and Christ holds all things in unity.

(Col. 1:15–17)

And we, with our unveiled faces reflecting like mirrors the glory of the Lord, all grow brighter and brighter as we are turned into the image that we reflect.

(2 Cor. 3:18)

God has made known to us in all wisdom and insight the mystery of the divine will, according to the divine purpose which God set forth in Christ as a plan for the fullness of time, to unite all things in Christ, things in heaven and things on earth.

(Eph. 1:9–10)

Christ is the radiant light of God's glory and the perfect copy
of God's nature, sustaining the universe by God's powerful
command.

(Hebrews 1:3)

The Word was with God in the beginning. Through the Word
all things came to be, not one thing had its being but through
this Word.

(John 1:1–3)

Who is a holy person? The one who is aware of others'
suffering.

(Kabir)

The heart that breaks open can contain the whole universe.
. . . All is registered in the "boundless heart" of the bodhisattva. Through our deepest and innermost responses to our
world—to hunger and torture and the threat of annihilation—we touch that boundless heart.

(Joanna Macy)

20. Naming the Cosmic Christ

Scientist Gregory Bateson asks a disturbing and critical question of religion: "Is the human race rotting its mind with slowly deteriorating religion?"[1] Bateson both strikes at the heart of the problem and offers the
hint of a solution when he speaks of a "rotting of the mind." Without
mind and mindfulness, religion is reduced to mere acts of will. Even well-
intentioned acts of charity do not make up for the loss of mind—knowing our place in the universe. For there is no mind without cosmos. The
Cosmic Christ, therefore, brings mind back to religion. In light of the
identification between mind (or psyche) and cosmos, let us consider in
this chapter the various meanings of the term Cosmic Christ.

THE COSMIC CHRIST—CREATOR OF MINDFULNESS

Healthy religion—that grounded in deep spiritual experience and tradition, that which celebrates and educates the mystic within and among

us—does not rot the mind by creating mindlessness. A mindless religion is sentimental and anti-intellectual, and it lacks a cosmology. In such a spiritual consciousness believers wallow in their own personal feelings so deeply that they never emerge to join the struggle of compassion to relieve others' pain and to make both justice and celebration happen on a community scale. Just as Anne Douglas calls sentimentalism "rancid political consciousness," so I would call mindless religion "rancid cosmic consciousness."[2] A healthy religion does just the opposite—it creates *mindfulness*. The Cosmic Christ awakens mindfulness, which instructs persons in their need and right to experience the presence of divinity around and through them. It opens their minds and hearts to the universe, to what is and to where we are: citizens of a vast twenty-billion-year history that is still unfinished and which we are called to complete; citizens of a universe of one hundred billion galaxies, of which ours is a mysteriously small one. A mindful religion, then, awakens the mind rather than dulls it; it praises the mind rather than diminishes it; it resurrects the mind rather than rots it.

How can religion accomplish this task of mindfulness? One way is by taking in the wisdom of scientists whose task is to explore the universe and to explain to us what is. "Isness is God," Meister Eckhart wrote (BR, 89), and Hildegard declared that "all science comes from God" (IHB, 14). Thomas Aquinas sought a rapprochement between science and religion in order to create a living cosmology. He warned that "mistakes about creatures contribute to mistakes about God."[3] Our failure to develop and appreciate a living cosmology has led to a reliance on a distorted theology. When science and mysticism interpenetrate, new visions can be born. A renaissance happens not from outside in but from inside out. The soul stirs. And new images are born. And lived out. And taken to amazing heights of adventure and risk and new possibilities. The young are excited by this call to adventure. I recall giving a presentation with physicist Brian Swimme one evening at a university campus. Following our presentation, a woman approached me with tears in her eyes. "I brought my sixteen-year-old daughter with me tonight," she said. "She is very bright and dropped out of high school six months ago. None of us knew what she would be doing in the future. Halfway through your dialogue she turned to me and said, 'Mom, now I know what I want to do with the rest of my life.'" What happened to this young woman as a result of experiencing a theologian and a scientist in dialogue? She was awakened to her role in a living cosmology; she was assured that her life and her life decisions regarding education, work, and relationship *were not trivial*—that she is indeed part of a twenty-billion-year history and mystery and that she has a cosmic task to perform.

A recovery of the Cosmic Christ awakens mindfulness and allows a living cosmology to emerge. The Cosmic Christ can usher in an era of a living cosmology, for there is only one "isness" in the world. Scientist and religious believer are not in search of different worlds or other universes than what is.

THE COSMIC CHRIST—THE PATTERN THAT CONNECTS

Gregory Bateson wrestled the last ten years of his life with this most pressing question: "What is the pattern that connects?"[1] What connects the crab nebula in the sky with the genes of a crawfish on earth or the genes in our bodies? The spiritual tradition proposes that the Cosmic Christ is "the pattern that connects." The ancient hymn of the letter to the Colossians states:

> He is the image of the unseen God and the first-born of all creation, for in him were created all things in heaven and on earth: everything visible and everything invisible. . . . Before anything was created, he existed, and *he holds all things in unity* (Col. 1:15–17; emphasis mine).

Does it matter that our spiritual tradition has a name for the Cosmic Christ and a grounding in a particular historical person who incarnates that Christlikeness? How would a scientist respond to this naming of "the pattern that connects"? The Cosmic Christ, seen as "the pattern that connects," affirms the scientific quest for such a pattern. It offers hope by insisting on the interconnectivity of all things and on the power of the human mind and spirit to experience personally this common glue among things.

The Cosmic Christ *personalizes* and localizes the experience of the "pattern that connects" in a manner that is utterly nontrivial. It grounds this interconnectivity in the cosmic experience of the joy and suffering of the historical Jesus: the Colossians hymn ends with a statement about the price this human, Jesus, had to pay for incarnating the Cosmic Christ. The crucial connection is made between our moral behavior and our knowledge and love of the universe. Not even scientists are exempt from acting out the wisdom of the universe. "God wanted all maturity to be found in him and all things to be reconciled through him, and for him everything in heaven and everything on earth, when he made peace by his death on the cross" (Col. 1: 19–20). Irony and paradox are also celebrated in this passage—peace comes from violent injustice in the crucifixion of an innocent man. The cosmic pain that the cross represents is named. Our sacrifices are cosmic in size; our suffering is cosmic in scope; and the peace too is cosmic in its promise. The paradox is that this "pattern that connects" also disconnects. Continuity and discontinuity accompany one another. A violent wrenching—even on divinity's part in letting Jesus die an ignominious death—produces cosmic peace. A death—any death—is always a disconnection. Yet this particularly ignominious and cosmic death on a cross, violent in its disconnection of humanity and divinity, of justice and injustice, of light and darkness, does in the last analysis, *connect*. It connects heaven and earth, past and future, divinity and humanity, all of creation: "everything in heaven and everything on earth."

The cosmic peace coming by way of the cross instructs us in a second way of mindfulness: emptying. This *kenosis*, or "emptying," is also connected to mindfulness and to the entrance of the Cosmic Christ into our psyches. "Only those who have dared to let go can dare to re-enter" warns Meister Eckhart (ME, 67). The Cosmic Christ hymn of Philippians also celebrates this way to mindfulness. Emptying precedes filling. "His state was divine, yet he did not cling to his equality with God but emptied himself to assume the condition of a slave, and became as humans are; and being as all humans are, he was humbler yet, even to accepting death, death on a cross" (Phil. 2:6–8). Paradoxically, out of this emptying, fullness occurs. "But God raised him on high and gave him the name which is above all other names so that *all beings in the heavens, on the earth and in the underworld*, should bend the knee at the name of Jesus and that every tongue should acclaim Jesus Christ as Lord, to the glory of God the Creator" (Phil. 2:9–11). Again the pattern connects divinity and earthiness; emptiness and fullness; suffering and accomplishment. It connects all creatures in the entire universe.

To believe in this "pattern that connects" is to start connecting once again. For all belief is about practice, not just theory. Belief is not belief if it is not launched into *praxis*. The practice of making and seeking connections, and of seeking even "the pattern that connects," can now begin in earnest. This enterprise will require those "new wineskins" or "new paradigms" that a living cosmology represented by the Cosmic Christ ushers in. These wineskins will offer themselves as vessels for the Spirit rising afresh among the young in all institutions of church and society; making new connections between world religions; reconnecting our lifestyles to our capacities for creativity, imagination, play, suffering, sexuality, knowledge, and wisdom itself. Embracing the Cosmic Christ will demand a paradigm shift, and it will empower us for that shift:

A shift from

from anthropocentrism	to a living cosmology
from Newton	to Einstein
from parts-mentality	to wholeness
from rationalism	to mysticism
from obedience as a prime moral virtue	to creativity as a prime moral virtue
from personal salvation	to communal healing, i.e., compassion as salvation
from theism (God outside us)	to panentheism (God in us and us in God)

from fall-redemption religion	to creation-centered spirituality
from the ascetic	to the aesthetic.

Consider how the right-hand column that represents the new paradigm is all about "patterns that connect"—cosmology; Einstein; wholeness; mysticism; creativity; compassion; panentheism; creation-centered spirituality; beauty—each new wineskin is a connecting wineskin. Truly the Cosmic Christ ushers in an era of connection making.

The Cosmic Christ is the *divine* pattern that connects in the person of Jesus Christ (but by no means is limited to that person). The divine pattern of connectivity *was made flesh and set up its tent among us* (John 1:14). In a special way the "us" includes the dispossessed—those least connected, those least established and least part of the connections that "the establishment" has to offer. Jesus offered connections to the dispossessed in particular: to the lepers, women, slaves, sinners, and outcasts of society. He connected with them not only by conversation and scandalous associations at meals but by undergoing the death of the unconnected, the death of the dispossessed on Golgotha. The historical person of Jesus offers a "pattern that connects" substantially different from the *anima mundi* ("soul of the world") tradition of Platonism, which lacks all concern and therefore connection with the *anawim*, the little and forgotten ones, the oppressed victims of social injustice. The Cosmic Christ liberates all persons and thus, like Moses of old, leads a new exodus from the bondage and pessimistic news of a Newtonian, mechanistic universe so ripe with competition, winners and losers, dualisms, anthropocentrism, and the boredom that comes when our exciting universe is pictured as a machine bereft of mystery and mysticism. The Cosmic Christ is local and historical, indeed intimate to human history. The Cosmic Christ might be living next door or even inside one's deepest and truest self. The reign of God may well be among us after all.

THE COSMIC CHRIST—BEARER OF COHERENCE

Sociologist Robert Bellah describes how Western culture has become a "culture of separation." He cites the poet John Donne who aptly wrote of our disease: "Tis all in peeces, all cohaerence gone."[2] The Cosmic Christ ushers in an era of coherence, of ending the separations, divisions, dualisms, piecemealness that characterize a world without mysticism, a society without a living cosmology. A cosmos is always a *whole*, a unity, a state of coherence even if the coherence seemingly exists for a time only in the hearts and imaginations of the people, only in hope. The Cosmic Christ unites psyche and cosmos once again. In 1875, theologian J. B. Lightfoot wrote that Christ was the "principle of cohesion in the universe. He impresses upon creation that unity and solidarity which makes it a cosmos instead of a chaos. Thus (to take one instance) the action of gravitation, which keeps in their places things fixed and regulates the motions of things moving, is an expression of His mind."[3] The opposite of cohesion is chaos. The Cosmic Christ redeemed us from chaos. (In the bible the opposite of chaos is creation and the justice intrinsic to creation. Thus injustice is always a return to chaos.) One way the Cosmic Christ moves us from chaos to cohesion is by bringing hope—the hope that coherence is possible—back to the psyche and thus back to the human race and its institutions. Unimaginable gulfs between Northern and Southern nations, between rich and poor, between employed and unemployed, between men and women, between heterosexuals and homosexuals—these are all expressions of the fact that our civilization lacks coherence, that it is chaotic. Radical changes are required if the Cosmic Christ is to be embraced as one who ushers in an era of coherence. Instead of the differences, the coherences will be sought after. For example, what does the two-thirds of our world that is poor and exploited have to give the one-third of our world that is affluent? Surely one gift is challenging the meaninglessness in a society that lacks authentic mysticism. What do the poor, the unemployed, women, and the homosexual have to give the wealthy, the employed, the men and the heterosexual in our society?

Coherence would demand some societal answers to these questions. The Cosmic Christ as represented in Jesus connects the poverty of the materially impoverished with the poverty of the spiritually impoverished. He challenges the comfortable and the complacent, the affluent and the privileged *with their own poverty.* The rich young man in Luke's Gospel went away sad because he could not let go of his riches to experience the presence of the Divine One. Thus all suffering and all poverty is connected as is all glory and all beauty. Suffering is not piecemeal; it is not meaningless. All suffering is coherent, it coheres in the Cosmic Christ (who is crucified and wounded) and it coheres in divinity as well as in humanity. It coheres on earth as well as in heaven. The "recapitulation" theme of Ephesians means to "bring together parts which have been scattered and separated." This is the meaning of "making peace."[4]

THE COSMIC CHRIST NEEDING TO BE BORN

It is not enough to celebrate the Cosmic Christ as "the pattern that connects" and the "bearer of coherence" as expressed in Jesus. There is a real sense in which the Cosmic Christ is not born yet. Even in Jesus the Cosmic Christ has yet to come to full birth, for those who say they believe in Jesus have scarcely brought forth the Cosmic Christ at all on the mass scale that Mother Earth requires. One might speak, then, of the already born Cosmic Christ (realized eschatology) who we see only "in a mirror and darkly" (1 Cor. 13:12) and of the not-yet-born Cosmic

Christ (unrealized eschatology) who is the Christ of justice, of creativity, of compassion in self and society that yearns to be born and is eager to be born *in us.* "What good is it to me," Meister Eckhart asked, "if the son of God was born to Mary 1400 years ago but is not born in my person and in my culture and in my time?" (BR, 336). At the level of "isness" the Cosmic Christ already exists as a "glittering, glistening mirror of Divinity" (Hildegard's phrase) in every creature (IHB, 68). But in the human species, capable of consciousness as we are, this has little or no effect if we are unaware of it. "What good is it to me if I am a king and do not know I am a king?" asks Meister Eckhart (BR, 137). The name "Christ" means "the anointed one." All of us are anointed ones. We are all royal persons, creative, godly, divine, persons of beauty and of grace. We are all Cosmic Christs, "other Christs." But what good is this if we do not know it? Everyone is a sun of God as well as a son or a daughter of God, but very few believe it or know it. Those who do Meister Eckhart calls "the enlightened ones" (BR, 464).

We are all called, like the Cosmic Christ, to radiate the divine presence to/with/from one another. "And we, with our unveiled faces reflecting like mirrors the glory of the Lord, all grow brighter and brighter as we are turned into the image that we reflect" (2 Cor. 3:18). Notice how Paul is speaking of our *increasing* from glory to glory as we turn "brighter and brighter." Earlier, we saw that "glory" is a cosmological term in the Scriptures and here we learn that all the divine glory in the universe has not occurred yet. Humanity has the power and responsibility to increase the glory that is the divine presence in the cosmos. Teilhard de Chardin thought that "besides his mystical body, Christ also has a cosmic body spread throughout the universe. And just as the mystical Christ has still to attain his full growth, so too has the cosmic Christ."[5] Meister Eckhart teaches that "we are all meant to be mothers of God" (BR, 329) and thus we are all called to birth the Cosmic Christ in self and society. We are called to be bearers of this new paradigm, this living cosmology and its new wineskins; we are called to be "patterns that connect" and "bearers of coherence" to a society of separation. Evelyn Underhill also grasped this sense of the Cosmic Christ yearning to be born:

> The Incarnation, which is for popular Christianity synonymous with the historical birth and earthly life of Christ, is for the mystic not only this but also a perpetual Cosmic and personal process. It is an everlasting bringing forth, in the universe and also in the individual ascending soul, of the divine and perfect Life, the pure character of God.[6]

Underhill correctly connects our vocation to birth the Cosmic Christ with the essential mystical task. Theologian Rob van der Hart, writing from the perspective of the biblical teaching on angels—which is an element of the biblical perspective on a living cosmology—also sees the call to give birth to cosmic order or coherence:

The cosmic order, so relevant for peace on earth, does not at all appear to be something given, something which can be taken for granted. *It is something to be achieved*—achieved through a continual integration of the powerful and frightening angelic wills. "Thy will be done on earth as it is in heaven."[7]

The birthing of the Cosmic Christ is itself a cosmic act involving cosmic labor pains. It will not come cheaply. "Frightening angelic wills" will encountered. Or, as Eckhart put it, "we are heirs of the *fearful* creative power of God" (BR, 405). To truly give birth to something new is an awesome responsibility.

The Cosmic Christ educes power and responsibility from those who dare to allow the mystic to be born in and through them. Indeed, one wonders if the overwhelming silence surrounding the Cosmic Christ in Christian history might not be due to a fear to undergo the birth pangs and the responsibility to which the Cosmic Christ calls persons. Carl Jung grasped the essential challenge and adventure demanded of us by the Cosmic Christ when he said that, because of the incarnation the human is involved

> in a new responsibility. He can no longer wriggle out of it on the plea of his littleness and nothingness, for the dark God has slipped the atom bomb and chemical weapons into his hands and given him the power to empty out the apocalyptic vials of wrath on his fellow creatures. Since he has been granted an almost godlike power, he can no longer remain blind and unconscious. He must know something of God's nature and of metaphysical processes if he is to understand himself and thereby achieve gnosis of the Divine.[8]

Like Hildegard, Jung is calling us to "know who we are." We are divine and human, animal and demon. We are Cosmic Christs. Meister Eckhart says:

> There is only one birth—and this birth takes place in the being and in the ground and core of the soul. . . . Not only is the Son of the heavenly Creator born in this darkness—but you too are born there as a child of the same heavenly Creator and none other. And the Creator extends this same power to you out of the divine maternity bed located in the Godhead to eternally give birth. . . . The fruitful person gives birth out of the very same foundation from which the Creator begets the eternal Word. It is from this core that one becomes fruitfully pregnant (ME, 78–80).

Because we are Cosmic Christs and because we are called to birth the yet unborn Cosmic Christ we are, like Jesus, prophets of order (justice) over chaos (disorder and injustice). This is why Eckhart can declare that "all virtue of the just and every work of the just is nothing other than the Son—who is the New Creation—being born from the Creator. In the depths of our being, where justice and work are one, we work one work and a New Creation with God" (ME, 94). He is back to his original statement that there is only one work—the work of the Cosmic Christ who declared in the person of Jesus, "I and the Creator are one. . . . Whatever the Creator does the Son does too" (John 1:30; 5:19). This same Cosmic Christ incarnated in the person of Jesus was given "glory" by the Creator and was "loved before the foundation of the world" (17:24). He desires that those who follow in his footsteps also do the works of the Cosmic Christ. "Whoever believes in me will perform the same works as I do myself, he will perform even greater works" (14:12). This is possible because of our mystical and panentheistic relationship to the Creator. "On that day you will understand that I am in my Creator and you in me and I in you" (14:20). Jesus teaches us about the vast dream of the Cosmic Christ yearning to be born in us—a dream about glory and fruitfulness. "It is to the glory of my Creator that you should bear much fruit, and then you will be my disciples. . . . Go out and bear fruit, fruit that will last" (John 15:8, 16).

JESUS AS THE COSMIC CHRIST—ONE BIRTH, ONE DEATH, ONE WORK

Paul celebrates the theme of our being other Christs and our growing into other Christs when he says, "I live now not with my own life but with the life of Christ who lives in me" (Gal. 2:20). He sees his work as a preacher of Good News (Gal. 1:16) to be that of giving birth to the Christ. "I must go through the pain of giving birth to you all over again, until Christ is formed in you" (Gal. 4:19). Jesus Christ becomes, then, two persons for us. First, he is the crucified one who lives in all of us—"I have been crucified with Christ" and become "dead to the Law," Paul declares (Gal. 2:19). Perhaps today this "dead to the Law" motif means dead to the law of Newtonian mechanism, the dead law of a dead paradigm. Second, Jesus is the power of the mystical life resurging in all of us. Because he is the one who denies death, he is the one who calls to life and to resurrection, to mysticism and the connection to all that is. Connecting life and death is truly a "pattern that connects." Just as the King was made a royal person through anointing with oil, so Christ, "the anointed one," calls us to be like him: royal persons—persons of dignity and responsibility, of beauty and of creativity; bearers of healing and makers of justice. We are called to be other Christs ourselves.[9] Yet to hear the call to be other Christs, we must be awakened. Jesus is an awakener.

The awakening he brings is essential because so many of us are asleep and as good as dead. It is Jesus who raises from the dead, who arouses us from our slumber, who awakens and excites to new life. How can he do this so effectively? Because he is the "first-born of the dead" (Col. 1:18). He has visited Hades and the land of the living dead, the underworlds of sleepfulness and dulled minds, cold hearts and limp imaginations. He has been to "the pit" and back again. In this journey, Jesus connects life and death, heaven and hell, earth and heaven, future and past; he is the "pattern that connects."

All creatures bear the image of the Cosmic Christ though many do not know it. Humans, however, bear both the image *and* likeness of the Cosmic Christ for they are capable of the creativity that is unique to God. Our works and the fruits they bear are closer to the divine work (and therefore, necessarily, to the demonic) than those of other creatures.

THE COSMIC CHRIST—CONNECTOR OF TIME AND SPACE

The Cosmic Christ as incarnated in Jesus also connects space and time. As prophet, Jesus is a time-person, an announcer of the new times, the end times, the time of justice's arrival, the time of liberation for the captives and sight for the blind, and the time of the arrival of the kingdom/queendom of God in our midst. But Jesus, like the rest of us, lived out his time and indeed—because he was so true to his prophetic vocation—his time was cut short. Because death is always so final an event—even and especially for this Son of God—no one can ever bring back the time that Jesus lost and will never live out. His was truly an *untimely* death if ever there was one. The great contribution of the Jewish prophets to the human race is surely the sense of time as prophetic, urgent, unbound by cyclical inevitability; time is an occasion for the divine breakthrough, for the coming of new life, deeper justice, truer peace. In this regard, Jesus the prophet does not disappoint. And the Cosmic Christ, bearing the wounds of time and of death, does not repress or allow us to forget the timeliness of the crucified Christ.

The past one hundred years of science have reawakened the human race to the power and dimension of time. Surely our dawning awareness of evolution and our gradual appreciation of the vast distances of time represented by the age of the earth (four and a half billion years) and the universe (about twenty billion years) fill us with a new awe at the mystery of our origins. All things are in flux; all things evolve; all things come and go; all things are in time and birthing in their time. Time and history are integral to all mystery. This is a cosmic law.

A deep connection exists between the time consciousness of today's science and the time consciousness of Jesus Christ. One of Jesus' essential contributions, like that of the Jewish prophets before him, is the call to the human to celebrate one's time, one's lifetime, one another's lifetimes—and not to take time for granted. We are called to give birth in our times to "fruit that will last" (John 15:16) and to the Cosmic Christ who, as "the pattern that connects," connects all time.

Another contribution of this "pattern that connects" who is Jesus the Christ is the connection of time and space. The West has indeed awakened its time consciousness through the work of science this past century, but our space consciousness remains dormant. Just as I understand our time consciousness to be our prophetic soul, so I see our space consciousness as our mystical soul or psyche. And, as I suggested in part II, our civilization is not in touch with its mystical powers. The Cosmic Christ awakens us precisely to this dimension that sleeps fitfully within us. The mystical experience is invariably one of the suspension of time— "Where did the time go?" we ask after undergoing such an experience. Space takes over, spacefulness—with emphasis on the *fullness*, the *pleroma*. That space is filled by divine experience, by the eternal now, by forgetfulness of all but the glory—the beautiful presence of the divine loved one. The Cosmic Christ travels not just in time but also in space. Our space-full moments are precious and memorable—they ought to be the grounding point for all morality and decision making. Eckhart says God is *spatiosissimus*, the most spacious thing there is. Here we are all given permission—at last—to celebrate our spacefulness. Jesus dares to confuse the space known as heaven with the space known as earth—"thy will be done on earth as it is in heaven." The resurrection is nothing if not a conquest of time and place (death on Golgotha) by space—that is by an empty (space-filled) tomb where sadness and death no longer are granted place. Where grief comes to an end. Where life, new but mysterious, is resurrected against all odds and all pessimism and all cynicism and all sadness. Where a return to the land of the living (walking, talking, and eating at Emmaus) and to the origin of the cosmos (ascension) and the sending of the spirit (Pentecost) is accomplished.

Without a healthy sense of space and mysticism, time becomes idolatrous—either the idolatry of time that a culture of "progress" has been heralding for one hundred years (years that have culminated in at least as much degradation as progress), or an idolatry of guilt and apocalyptic shouting that deadens all space consciousness and therefore all powers of imagination and creativity to resurrect the human spirit and thus redeem the times. Today some scientists are sounding as pessimistic as some fundamentalist preachers. Both camps lack mysticism and a sense of the Cosmic Christ who, like every mystic, operates paradoxically and snatches hope from despair, light from darkness, life from death, and youthfulness from oldness. All who are in this Christ, Paul declares, are themselves a "New Creation" (2 Cor. 15:17).

On today's spiritual scene we see two distortions (in addition to fundamentalism which is not mature enough to be called a spirituality). One distortion occurs in certain trends in the New Age movement which are all space and no time; all consciousness and no conscience; all mysticism and no prophecy; all past life experiences, angelic encounters, untold bliss, and no critique of injustice or acknowledgment of the suffering and death that the toll of time takes. In short, no body. To these movements the Cosmic Christ says, "Enter time. Behold my wounds. Love your neighbor. Set the captives free." A second distortion occurs among good-intentioned persons working intensely and sacrificing much for peace and justice—in other words, struggling to right the times, to see the messianic times happen, to taste the promise of peace and justice flowing like waters, as the prophets promised. The danger is too much time consciousness cut off from mysticism or space consciousness embroils and attaches one to the struggle of time that leads to burn out, pessimism, lack of creativity, spirit, and imagination. To these persons the Cosmic Christ says, "Behold the universe. Behold its fulsome mysteries. Behold its glory which is that of my Creator. Behold your universe within, your ever-expanding psyche, your powers of creativity, wetness, rebirth, generativity, youthfulness. Behold your connection to all things, great and small. Beauty abounds. Partake of it. You are of it. 'Be still and know that I am God' (Ps. 46:10). And you are too."

Technology has refashioned drastically our notions of space. "Space" has now emerged as a term denoting another frontier for human exploration and conquest, as in the common phrase, "conquer space." While technology has allowed us to exult in the vast awe and wonder of our planet floating in space, to visit other stars, and to stretch our telescopes and thus ears and eyes into the very moment of the origins of time and space, it has also brought the human shadow into space. What we call Star Wars is an example of exporting our militarism into outer space. We lack the inner, psychic space of mysticism that would allow us to let go of war, dualism, and unresolved oppressions. To this distorted attitude toward space the Cosmic Christ says, "Let your compulsion to conquer go. Let your militarism go. Listen to your inner space for the divine and project *that*—its glory and beauty, its hope and justice—into other spaces. Cease making space over into your own image and start reimaging yourselves in light of space. Do unto space what you would have space do unto you. And love space as yourself."

By uniting time and space the Cosmic Christ challenges twentieth and twenty-first century citizens to get on with the deep work of the universe. Just as Einstein alerted our century to the interconnectivity of time and space, the Cosmic Christ awakens us to the lessons of interpenetration between the experiences of history and mystery, of prophecy and mysticism, of time and space. In what manner are time and space the historical revelation and display of the divine kingdom/queendom at play? Who can answer this question if not the human species? And how will it ever be addressed except in *practice* as much as in theory?

THE COSMIC CHRIST—CONNECTOR OF MICROCOSM AND MACROCOSM

Another connection that the Cosmic Christ makes is that between the tiny and the magnificent, between the microcosm and the macrocosm. The Cosmic Christ ushers in an era of a psychology—not of ego and ego maintenance, though for some that will always have a role to play—but of microcosm/macrocosm. This means we must ask how we relate to the rest of the universe?—to the tiniest neutron and proton as well as to the whirling, whistling, ranting galaxies light years in advance of our own. The Cosmic Christ is a "pattern that connects" proton and galaxy, human and neutron, human and supernovas. The Cosmic Christ assures us that *nothing is trivial* for nothing is unconnected to the whole. All is a source of awe, wonder, wisdom, and the presence of the divine. All is revelation; all is unfinished; all is "eagerly waiting for God to reveal the divine sons and daughters. . . . From the beginning until now the entire creation as we know, has been groaning in one great act of giving birth" (Rom. 8:19, 22). Carl Jung celebrates the return of a micro/macrocosmic psychology when he says that "the ancient and long obsolete idea of man as a microcosm contains a supreme psychological truth that has yet to be discovered."[10] The new cosmology is indeed rediscovering the power of this truth of micro/macrocosm. When we learn, for example, that all the elements of our bodies were birthed in a supernova explosion in space billions of years ago, that discovery awakens and excites awe at our very existence, and awe, as the Scriptures tell us, is the beginning of wisdom. And, as Heschel noted earlier, "awe precedes faith." *Without awe there simply is no faith.* With awe anything can happen. Anything can be born or reborn—even the Cosmic Christ, the "pattern that connects" all things in heaven and on earth and in between.

The early Christians were more sensitive to the space/time connection than subsequent generations have been. The idol that salvation history became in theological education since the Enlightenment is just one instance of modern Christianity's unbalanced tilt in favor of time and at the expense of space. The early church represented in Ephesians and Colossians responded to the Christ event with a space/time awareness. Good Friday is time; Easter is space. The Sabbath is space, play, and the forgetfulness of time. Jesus is time; Christ is space. Mysticism *and* prophecy both play a role and a dialectical one in that tradition. Consider, for example, this beautiful blend of both that the Letter to the Hebrews expresses. First comes the time consciousness:

> At various times in the past and in various ways God spoke to our ancestors through the prophets; but in our own time, the last days, God has spoken to us through the child (Heb. 1:1–2).

Next, the space consciousness:

> This child God has appointed to inherit everything and through whom God made everything there is. The child is the radiant light of God's glory and the perfect copy of the divine nature, sustaining the universe by his powerful command . . . who has gone to take his place in heaven at the right hand of divine Majesty. So he is now as far above the angels as the title which he has inherited is higher than their own name (Heb. 1:2–4).

Clearly the Cosmic Christ holds the power to reconnect Christians in a balanced experience of time and space, of prophecy and mysticism, of history and mystery. The incarnation story—that the Divine One, the Ancient One, the Wisdom of the Ages took form as a newborn human infant, "like us in every way save sin" (Heb. 4:15)—is a story of microcosm/macrocosm if there ever has been one. For the ultimate marriage of micro/macro is that of the human and the divine.

21. Jesus Christ as Mother Earth Crucified and Resurrected

The Maori people, the native people of New Zealand, have a saying that "the Land is a Mother who never dies." I wish this beautiful saying were as true today as it has been for the tens of thousands of years of Maori existence. However, as we saw in part I of this book, matricide is a reality. The killing of Mother Earth in our time is *the number one ethical, spiritual, and human issue of our planet.* While writing this book, I have heard daily reports about the devastation of our planet—its ozone layers, its tropical rain forests, its soil, its waters, its species of wildlife going extinct, its vegetation and plant and fish and animal life, its children. All this is beginning, at last, to awaken the human consciousness to its folly. The facts are coming out; we are being educated. As theologian/geologist Thomas Berry has put it:

> The earth will not be reduced to abject servitude. After all man's assaults the majesty of the earth stands over against him with an inscrutable countenance. There are gathering signs of a response in the form of massive retaliation. The game is a game but only if it leads to larger life. Else the game is no longer a creative experience but a struggle to the death, a struggle which man cannot win.[1]

In a similar vein Hildegard of Bingen warned us eight hundred years ago not to interfere with the "web of the universe" in our dealings with nature. She wrote:

> The earth should not be injured, the earth should not be destroyed. As often as the elements of the world are violated by ill-treatment, so God will cleanse them. God will cleanse them through the sufferings, through the hardships of humankind. All of creation God gives to humankind to use. But if this privilege is misused, God's justice permits creation to punish humanity (HB, 77–80).

Clearly, creation is responding to the injustice that humanity has inflicted on it. Does the Cosmic Christ speak to this most pressing of all human and earth needs in our time? Does the Cosmic Christ contribute to the healing of Mother Earth and the battle against matricide? Can the Cosmic Christ help to raise mother from the dead? I believe so.

WHO IS THE COSMIC CHRIST? / 145

The first generation of Christians were, like all religious people of the Mediterranean basin, deeply cosmological. They understood the Christ event, the experience of the Christ in the person of Jesus, as a deeply cosmic happening. They believed that Jesus accomplished nothing less than a cosmic healing, a cosmic redemption.

The belief in the power of Jesus Christ as Lord over the chaotic forces of creation found an expression in the phrase, "Jesus is sun of justice." This cosmological title has been employed from the first century to today. The idea of Jesus as the sun, the light of lights that banishes darkness and sadness, is behind the tradition of celebrating his birth at the dark time of the year, near the winter solstice. Christmas is proof of the cosmological consciousness of centuries of pre-Newtonian Christianity. I do not believe, however, that this symbol of Jesus as the sun is appropriate for the third millennium of Christianity. It is evident, for example, that the secularization of Christmas has practically devastated any glimmering power that was once associated with that feast. Secularization has occurred in part because the cosmological symbolism was gradually lost on the people of faith who failed to cherish a living memory of a living cosmic person.

I believe the appropriate symbol of the Cosmic Christ who became incarnate in Jesus is that of Jesus as Mother Earth crucified yet rising daily. Why do I believe this? First, because Mother Earth is being crucified in our time and is deeply wounded. Like Jesus at Golgotha, she is innocent of any crime, "like us in every way save sin" (Heb. 4:15). She has blessed us for four and one-half billion years by providing water; separating continents; establishing just the correct amounts of oxygen, hydrogen, and ozone in our atmosphere for us; birthing flowers, plants, animals, fishes, birds to delight us and bless us with their gifts and their work of making air and soil healthy and welcoming to us. In short, earth loved us—and still does—even though we crucify her daily.

Yet, like Jesus, she rises from her tomb every day. Easter is not a once-in-a-liturgical-year event for Mother Earth. Rather, wounded, yet rising, Mother Earth blesses us each day as we wake from our sleep. Like the risen Jesus she has the power to walk through closed doors, through the closed hearts of the people to wish them peace, to breathe the common breath (*ruah*) of life upon them as the source of rebirth and creativity.

Jesus can be symbolized as Mother Earth because he called himself mother when he wept over Jerusalem: "O Jerusalem, Jerusalem, killing the prophets and stoning those who are sent to you! How often would I have gathered your children together as a mother hen gathers her brood under her wings, and you would not! Behold, your house is forsaken" (Luke 13:34–35). If Jesus could be so moved by his mother love for Jerusalem, how deeply would his laments resound for Mother Earth today? He who wants to gather the children together as a hen gathers her brood under her wings is in fact the one who leads the lament for the holy city, that is, for the planet itself. The house—that is, our home that is Mother Earth—is forsaken. Humans continue killing the prophets and stoning those who are sent to awaken them to the pain of Mother Earth. In Jesus' words the "house" that is forsaken is the Temple itself. Yet Mother Earth is the temple, the sacred precinct in which holy creation dwells and praises God. Jesus' mission and message were rejected in his lifetime—that is what his crucifixion symbolizes. That air of rejection is what makes our mistreatment of Mother Earth so poignant. She has sought our good as Jesus sought the good of the people of Jerusalem, only to be rejected. Notice too that it is the children whom Jesus as Mother is weeping for. It is the children, the generations to come, who will suffer most from the devastation of the planet's beauty and fruitfulness. Is not Mother Earth like Jesus in this respect?—weeping for her children's imperiled future and yearning to take *all* the children—including the adult ones— under her wings for protection? The passage in the Gospels ends with a warning: "Yes, I promise you, you shall not see me till the time comes when you say: 'Blessings on him who comes in the name of the Lord!'" (Luke 13:35; cf. Matt. 23:37–39). (The blessing that Jesus refers to is that of Psalm 118 (vs. 26), a psalm of pilgrim and messianic celebration.) It is a return to a blessing consciousness, an awareness of the original blessing that Mother Earth is and has been to humans, that alone can reestablish the holy relationship between earth and us.

The tradition of Jesus as Mother, prevalent among creation mystics, was developed richly by Julian of Norwich. She celebrates our being enclosed in the womb of Jesus when she writes, "Jesus is our true Mother in whom we are endlessly carried and out of whom we will never come" (JN, 99). This panentheistic imagery is similar to John's Gospel when Jesus speaks of our being "in him." "Make my home in me, as I make mine in you" (John 15:4; Cf. 17:21, 23). Julian continues, "In Jesus we have the skillful and wise keeping of our Sensuality as well as our restoring and liberation; for He is our Mother, brother, and liberator" (JN, 101). Julian pictures Jesus as a mother who keeps or guards our earthiness and sensuality. She connects motherhood to the wisdom of God and defines a mother's service as that which is "nearest, readiest and surest" (JN, 104–105). Our "Mother Christ" also leads us in light through this life that passes (JN, 132). Part of Julian's development of Jesus as Mother is that she also develops in great depth the theme of God as Mother: "God is the true Father and Mother of natures" (JN, 106).

Jesus Christ also symbolizes earth because, like every human, he is made of earth and is dependent on earth for his sustenance. Hildegard of Bingen talks of how earth is doubly divinized—first because it is so holy and second because it provided the body by which the Son of God was made human flesh. Furthermore, Christ is said to be the "first-born" and the "first-fruit" (Rom. 8:28; 1 Cor. 15:20, 23). These deep earth images appropriated by Paul are part of the Jewish paschal imagery of fertility rites which celebrate Passover as "a re-enactment of the cosmogony or creation." What are the "first fruits"? These "were regarded as the most precious and vital elements of all they represented—family, flock, harvest. Their sacrifice gave hope of well-being and fertility—in a word, of life."[2] The first fruits were sacrificed for the people in a special way, as was Jesus. Jesus is the "true vine" (John 15:1). "I am the vine, you are the branches. Those who remain in me, with me in them bear fruit in plenty" (John 15:5). Like every earthling, this person who is the "perfect image of the Creator"—thus the perfect Cosmic Christ—and is both first-born and first fruit is an inheritor of twenty billion years of struggle and birthing by the universe. He is an earth-creature and more radically so than any of the rest of us because he is the most precious, vital representative of earth's amazing fertility. Earth has accomplished a uniquely divine act in birthing Jesus Christ, a birth that the Gospel stories tell us took place like the original creation itself: with the spirit of God hovering over the fetal waters of Mary's womb birthing a New Creation.

Jesus' sensitivity to the pain of the universe was unique and deep. He identified totally with the *anawim*, the suffering and oppressed ones. "Then it will be their turn to ask, 'Lord, when did we see you hungry or thirsty, a stranger or naked, sick or in prison, and did not come to your help?' Then he will answer, 'I tell you solemnly, in so far as you neglected to do this to one of the least of these, you neglected to do it to me' " (Matt. 25:44–45). Is Mother Earth today not hungry and thirsty, a stranger and naked, sick and imprisoned? Then Jesus is Mother Earth—Mother Earth as *anawim*, Mother Earth as the one without a voice, the neglected and oppressed one. In Luke's Gospel Jesus' first pronouncement is that he is a prophet like Isaiah foretold. "The spirit of the Lord has been given to me, for God has anointed me. God has sent me to bring the good news to the poor, to proclaim liberty to captives and to the blind new sight, to set the downtrodden free, to proclaim the Lord's year of favor" (Luke 4:18). Is Jesus, the Christ, not sent to bring Good News to Mother Earth who is poor, to proclaim liberty to Mother Earth who is captive to human greed and rapaciousness, to give sight to the blind two-legged ones who ignore the gifts of Mother Earth, to set free Mother Earth who is downtrodden?

Wisdom has been made flesh not only in Jesus the Christ but in *all expressions of the Cosmic Christ*. Since "every creature is a word of God" as Meister Eckhart put it, it follows that Mother Earth is a special word of God: a unique expression of divine wisdom, of divine maternity and caring, of divine creativity and fruitfulness. Consider her immense accomplishments and how many other "words of God"—every creature of this planet—depend ultimately on the survival and flourishing of Mother Earth herself. Jesus, the Son of God, was utterly dependent on Mother

Earth as all humans are—here lies the scandal of Bethlehem that preceded the scandal of the cross. Mother Earth never disappointed or failed Jesus. He did not starve nor was he spiritually deprived by his experience of creation. In fact, his parables all incorporate his rich experience of creation and its blessings. He died at the hands of men (I use the word advisedly) just as Mother Earth is dying at the hands of a patriarchal civilization gone mad with its attraction to matricide. Both Jesus and Mother Earth appear to be victims of the same pathology. Mother Earth is not failing humans; rather we are failing Mother Earth.

What is this pathology that is killing Mother Earth and therefore killing Jesus Christ all over again? Otto Rank calls it an "ideological need in man to blot out the mother-origin in order to deny his mortal nature."[3] The Cosmic Christ challenges matricide at its very core—at the level of the fear of death, the flight from our mortality that Otto Rank feels dominates the era of patriarchy. The Cosmic Christ celebrates all that is human, all that is earthly, and therefore all that is mortal. There is no need to "blot out" our origins—in fact, as we saw in part II, a "return to our origins" is one of the rich gifts granted us by a living and healthy mysticism. The Cosmic Christ allows us, invites us, indeed challenges us to overcome the destructive fear of nature that lies behind so much of the pathology and matricide of our time. Says Rank:

> That man so easily loses sight of his natural self and thus distorts reality to the point of madness is deeply rooted in his fear of natural forces threatening not only from without but even more from within, in his own nature. . . . But there is a limit to all his efforts to control as long as death awaits the presumptuous conqueror of nature.[4]

Notice how Rank identifies the matricide principle with the compulsion to control, and how once again it is our mortality that tells us of the limits of control. Thus, we need to fight our mortality if we wish to live forever in a civilization of control.

The Cosmic Christ cuts through this fear of mortality in many ways, not least of which is the resurrection which puts to rest all anxiety about death and, therefore, the excessive need to control. No wonder Rank himself, who was not a Christian but a Jew, called the resurrection story the "greatest revolutionary idea" in human history. It offers us a way out of patriarchy's matricidal tendencies, a way beyond our fear of death, a way beyond male envy of the female capacity for creativity, a way to open up creativity for all. As Eckhart put it, "we are *all* meant to be mothers of God" (ME, 74). Rank (in the passage cited above) sees the cause of matricide as our losing sight of our "natural self." The flight from nature, from our animality, from our being original blessings yet finite creatures, from creation—this Rank labels as the source of our matricidal temptations. Have the churches and synagogues done a good job in celebrating our "natural self" and teaching us to celebrate it? A creation-centered spirituality, of course, does exactly that. But a fall-redemption theology—the most influential tradition in Western religion—fails to do so. When such ideology prevails, religion itself contributes to the cause of matricide in the West.

I have been arguing that the new symbol of Jesus as Mother Earth crucified yet rising holds power to awaken humans to the survival of Mother Earth, to the elimination of matricide, and to their own best selves as mystics, prophets, and creative persons. Just as the symbol of Jesus as sun of justice was effectively operative over much of the past nineteen hundred years of Christianity, so the symbol of which I speak holds the capacity to launch a global spirituality of untold dimensions appropriate for the third millennium. In addition to awakening Christians to their oldest and deepest traditions—that of a living cosmology—it will also awaken other persons of goodwill since peace toward Mother Earth is a prelude to peace on earth. Increasingly, persons of goodwill are beginning to see this with clarity. The bottom line is not that Christianity survive into the next millennium. In fact, I propose that Christianity as we know it will *not* survive for we know it now in wineskins that are brittle, old, and leaking. Nothing will survive if Mother Earth does not survive. The issue is the survival, and indeed the thriving, of Mother Earth. Christianity can assist by, among other things, lending the rich symbolism of the Paschal mystery to the survival of Mother Earth.

22. A Paschal Mystery for the Third Millennium of Christianity

In proposing that Mother Earth can be understood as Jesus Christ crucified I am invoking the ancient Jewish and Christian tradition of the paschal mystery. I am offering a new wineskin with which to grasp and live out that paschal mystery for the third millennium. A living cosmology such as the Cosmic Christ ushers in provides a new and challenging context in which to re-vision the tradition of the paschal mystery. Let us examine briefly the heart of that tradition.

One theologian defines the paschal mystery as "the Easter mystery of the passion, resurrection and ascension of Christ, the salvation prefigured in the Old Testament, consisting of the conquest of death and the gift of life, hence the origin of the Church and of the sacraments, especially baptism and the Eucharist."[1] I am proposing that in a Cosmic Christ context the paschal mystery takes on new power, deep meaning, and moral passion when we understand it as the passion, resurrection, and ascension of Mother Earth conceived as Jesus Christ crucified, resurrected, and ascended. It is, then, the life, death, and resurrection of Mother Earth. Within this context, the rebirth of the Church and the sacraments can occur as we shall see in part V below. It is important to note that the origin of the Jewish feasts of the Passover was not in terms of salvation history but in terms of Mother Earth worship. They were celebrations of cosmological space and time:

> Both Passover and mazzot were of pre-Israelite origin. The Passover was originally a rite of nomad shepherds, performed in the night of the full moon at the spring equinox for the protecting and well-being of themselves and their flocks. . . . The mazzot belonged to the culture of a farming population, who marked the break between old and new at the beginning of the harvest by eating unleavened bread which contained no flour from the crops of the previous year. Hence Passover and mazzot were two nature-feasts which were "historicized" by the Israelites.[2]

The fertility rite tradition was not altogether lost in Israel which chose the sensual and cosmological Song of Songs text as the Passover reading in the synagogue. The paschal mystery of Jesus Christ is traditionally linked to the Passover theology of the Jewish people that centers on the three saving acts of Yahweh. First, Israel is spared death by way of the blood of the Passover lamb used as a sign to protect the people. Second, Israel is led out of bondage in Egypt. Third, Israel passes through the Red Sea, where the parting of the waters signify a passage through the birthing channel, a clear image of the new birth. Thus the Passover is an exodus as well as a transition—a "crossing over" from death to life, from slavery to freedom, from oldness to new birth into a land of promise and rest.

The liturgical or sacramental aspect of the Passover consisted essentially of a memorial celebration that would revive the liberating events. The Passover was considered the "feast of feasts" in Israel; it commemorated the very birth-day of Israel, the launching of the history that was Israel. The ritual was a symbolic reenactment of the departure and liberation. It was also a sacrificial meal; "the lamb or kid to be eaten at home was first sacrificed in the temple. . . . The Passover blood had expiatory value."[3]

In the New Testament version of the Christ event, the Jewish Passover was the "hour" toward which Jesus deliberately moved. He was killed as our "paschal lamb," our Passover (1 Cor. 5:17; John 19:34, 36). In the synoptic Gospels his farewell meal is related to the Passover meal of the Jews. The story of his sacrificial death is directly related to the expiatory value of the blood of the Passover lamb. Just as the blood of the Passover lamb had expiatory value, so too does the death of Jesus: the Church is birthed from Jesus' side at his crucifixion and a new covenant is established between Yahweh and Yahweh's people. Salvation is understood as liberation from bondage.

Each meal we eat today is like a "farewell meal" of Mother Earth since, when we eat, we always eat Mother Earth. Mother Earth, then, is a constantly sacrificed "paschal lamb" whose blood is spilled for our healing, nourishment, and salvation.

Can Mother Earth expect a salvation today comparable to the tradition of the paschal mystery? Can she expect to be spared death by way of a sacrificial offering? Is the nailing of Mother Earth to the cross not expiation enough with which to awaken the human race? And might not a new Israel, one that goes toward the ends of the earth and welcomes all God's creation, emerge from such a restored covenant? After all, the first covenant in the Scriptures is not that between God and Israel but between creation and humans—it is the rainbow (see Gen. 9:12–17). The rainbow is neither Jewish nor Christian, neither Islamic nor atheist. It belongs to all creation. It is a cosmic covenant. And it is a direct progeny of Mother Earth and her wonders of sunlight and rain, earth and sky. If the Cosmic Christ can awaken us to the power of Mother Earth to revivify ancient rituals such as Passover, how much else can be renewed by a Cosmic Christ perspective?

23. Redeeming Redemption—The Cosmic Christ as Redeemer of Cosmic Pain

The Good News we yearn to hear and that Mother Earth herself yearns to feel is that salvation is about solidarity: solidarity with God, neighbor, and all of God's creatures. The idea of a private salvation is utterly obsolete. Only a Newtonian worldview of piecemealness could have spawned the popular heresy that salvation is an individualistic or private matter. In a world of interdependence there is simply no such thing as private salvation. "All are sent or no one is sent," Meister Eckhart writes (ME, 114). Salvation is about God becoming "all in all," Paul tells us (1 Cor. 15:28). The hymns to the Cosmic Christ that we considered in part III as well as the overwhelming interest in cosmology that we found in the Gospels all attest to the cosmic sense of redemption and healing. Perhaps the power of this Good News is best summarized by Kabir, who asked, "Who is a holy person? A holy person is one who is aware of others' sufferings."[1] Notice he does *not* say a holy person is one who understands one's own suffering but the sufferings of others. Of course, to understand the suffering of others one must truly entertain the guests of pain and suffering in oneself. But to stop there—with only one's own pain—is pure sentimentalism. Sentimentalism and fundamentalism go together. Those who indulge exclusively in their personal salvation and their personal savior do so in direct contradiction to the entire teaching of the Cosmic Christ crucified for all. Salvation must be universal in the sense of comprehensive, a healing of all the cosmos' pain, or it is not salvation at all. The trivialization of religion comes precisely from the failure to appreciate cosmic suffering and therefore cosmic healing or redemption.

The Cosmic Christ will usher in an era when the whole notion of private salvation has gone the way of Newtonianism, which represents the cosmology on which the preoccupation of pietism and personal salvation has constructed itself. The Cosmic Christ leads us to explore suffering and new levels of truth and honesty instead of covering it up. For example, given humanity's destructive power represented not only in the nuclear weapons buildup but also in nuclear power plants such as Chernobyl or in chemical factories such as Bhopal in India, is it not evident that the *demonic* aspect of human power is cosmic in scope? In other words, we can no longer limit our powers of destruction to "personal" or even "interpersonal" infliction of pain. National boundaries can no longer fence out the pain humans are capable of inflicting on Mother Earth and her children. The innocent *do get hurt and will get hurt.* The Laplanders of Finland, whose entire culture and economic survival depends on the reindeer, were able to market exactly six reindeer after the Chernobyl event. Notice the interdependence here of human and four-legged one: because the innocent reindeer were unjustly poisoned by Chernobyl, the innocent Laplanders were as well.

Since the pain, suffering, and sin are cosmic—bigger than we can control and far more complex in space and time than we can imagine—the redemption must be cosmic as well. If the demonic aspect of the human psyche is capable of inflicting such cosmic pain, isn't the *divine* aspect of this same psyche also capable of effecting cosmic healing? The Cosmic Christ insists on this possibility and can show us the way! Cosmic redemption is a response to cosmic evil. To be human is to be *capax universi* as Thomas Aquinas put it—"capable of the universe." Our capacity for the universe is both divine and demonic, both positive and negative, both glory and shadow. Our struggle is against "powers and principalities," according to Paul (Eph. 6:12). In a living cosmology there is no such thing as being "merely human." The Christ or heavenly Messiah will disarm cosmic forces. Christ, we are told, "disarmed the principalities and powers and made a public example of them." In this sense, he set us free from being under the law—from being "subjected to the guardians and trustees, to the elemental spirits of the universe (Gal 4:1–3). All they can offer is a 'particular' balance of the cosmic forces, a 'Law and Order,' which puts freedom in a straightjacket."[2]

The Cosmic Christ wrestled within Jesus to establish the balance of cosmic forces and to make a cosmic warrior of him. Jesus' temptations in the desert were *cosmic* temptations, a wrestling with powers and principalities symbolized by the devil as we saw in part III. The Letter to the Hebrews develops the cosmic suffering that Jesus underwent in his wrestling with the Cosmic Christ yearning to be born fully in him. We are instructed in that letter that to be human "means to be subjected to higher heavenly powers. . . . Because he lives in a world which is subject to good and evil spirits, and show solidarity with all men, Jesus can be tempted (4:15) and suffer (2:10–14; 5:7; 2:16–18;12:2–3). Like the *kenosis* or "emptying," theme of Philippians 2, the theme of Hebrews emphasizes that Jesus is a lowly person because the human is lower than the angels and in some ways subjected to them. The angels represent the cosmic forces. Jesus shares our cosmic vulnerability as humans in a universe vaster and farther beyond our reach or ability to control than we dare imagine. Thus the struggle of Jesus as human "is set in a cosmic perspective in which the world of spirits belongs to a higher reality than the earthly world of men."[3]

The compassionate solidarity that Jesus learns comes from the cosmic suffering he undergoes. The same is true of us. We imbibe the healing power of the Cosmos Christ to the extent that we are emptied of mere personal suffering to experience all suffering as cosmic or shared suffering. Joanna Macy puts it this way: "The heart that breaks open can contain the whole universe. Your heart is that large: trust it. Keep breathing." Essentially, there is only one heart—the heart of the cosmic Christ who is also the bodhisattva, one who is fully committed to the enlightenment of every creature on earth. Macy continues, "All is registered in the 'boundless heart' of the bodhisattva. Through our deepest and innermost responses to our world—to hunger and torture and the threat of annihilation—we touch that boundless heart. It is the web we have woven as interconnected systems—or synapses in the mind of God."[4] This is why the creation mystics all invite us to explore the dark, to taste the pain, to make the deep journey into the underworld of grief, anger and pain: the Cosmic Christ is there and accompanies us on our journeys. We are in pain together. Macy advises:

> Experience the pain. Let us not fear its impact on ourselves or others. We will not shatter, for we are not objects that can break. Nor will we get stuck in this pain for it is dynamic, it flows through us. Drop our defenses, let us stay present to its flow, express it—in words, movements and sounds.[5]

The Cosmic Christ is present wherever there is pain. The Cosmic Christ unites all this pain in the one divine heart, in the one divine—but wounded—body of the Christ which is the body of the universe. The Cosmic Christ is the crucified and suffering one in every creature, just as much as the Cosmic Christ is the radiant one, the divine mirror glistening and glittering in every creature. Divinity is not spared suffering—that is the lesson of the Cosmic Christ who suffers.

Wherever injustice reigns the Cosmic Christ is crucified again. This also means that wherever justice is fought for and prevails; wherever healing takes place and is passed on; wherever compassion prevails, the Cosmic Christ is healing, redeeming, liberating on a cosmic scale. The Cosmic Christ leads the way to cosmic redemption.

24. The Cosmic Christ—Revealer of the Divine "I Am" in Every Creature

As we saw in the Greek Fathers and in the medieval mystics, one of the most common themes in Cosmic Christ theology is a celebration of how common and omnipresent divinity is. Divinity is found in all creatures. The divine name from Exodus 3:14, "I Am who I Am," is appropriated by Jesus who shows us how to embrace our own divinity. The Cosmic Christ is the "I am" in every creature. The divine mystery and miracle of existence is laid bare in the unique existence of each atom, each galaxy, each tree, bird, fish, dog, flower, star, rock, and human. Meister Eckhart says that "in this breakthrough I discover that God and I are one. There I am what I was, and I grow neither smaller nor bigger, for there I am an immovable cause that moves all things" (BR, 218). This "I am" language is mysterious, but it also touches us at a deep place. Our lives are stories of how our "I-am-ness" came to be and how it flowers into its own unique and beautiful expression of the Divine One, that unique image of God that comes to birth once in a universe in us.

In the Gospel of John the "I am" sayings attributed to Jesus play a prominent role:

I am the bread of life [or living bread] (6:35, 51).

I am the light of the world (8:12; 9:5).

I am the [sheep]gate (10:7, 9).

I am the model shepherd (10:11, 14).

I am the resurrection and the life (11:25).

I am the way, the truth, and the life (14:6).

I am the real vine (15:1, 5).

These revelations of "I-am-ness" challenge us to name (or claim) our lives and beings in a similar fashion. How are we the bread of life or living bread to each other? How are we the light of the world, the real vine, the resurrection and the life? How, in other words, are we also expressions of the Cosmic Christ as Jesus was so fully? Johannine scholar Raymond Brown points out that the author of John's Gospel invoked the "I am" sayings in a style patterned after that of Deutero-Isaiah. In Isaiah Yahweh says that . . . Israel has been chosen "that you may know and believe me and understand *that I am*" (43:10; cf. John 8:28). "John draws attention to the implications of divinity in the use of *ego eimi* ["I am"] by Jesus. . . . The use of 'I AM' as a divine name in late Judaism may explain the many Johannine references to the divine name that Jesus bears."[1]

But it is not only John's Gospel that invokes "I am" language. Brown sees the "I am" motif in the many synoptic parables of the kingdom/queendom when Jesus begins his stories with the phrase, "the kingdom/queendom of God is like. . . . " In John Jesus says "I am the vine"; in the other Gospels he is more likely to say "The kingdom/queendom of God is like a vineyard."[2]

Yet there are other "I am" sayings in the Gospels that Brown misses. Those are the "I am" sayings of the *anawim*, the wounded ones without a voice. Consider Matthew 25 where Jesus teaches:

> Then the virtuous will say to him in reply, "Lord, when did we see you hungry and feed you; or thirsty and give you drink? When did we see you a stranger and make you welcome; naked and clothe you; sick or in prison and go to see you?" And the King will answer, "I tell you solemnly, in so far as you did this to one of the least of these brothers or sisters of mine, you did it to me" (Matt. 25:37–41).

Another "I am" saying from Jesus is the eucharistic words, "this is my body, this is the cup of my blood." The Statements that "I am bread" and "I am wine" ground our reverence for food and drink, wheat and wine, soil and vineyard, the processes of photosynthesis and all that makes things grow in an ultimate *reverence*. We revere the everyday because it is so full of the divine, so full of the "I am." In this revelation of the divinity of the bread and wine lies that part of compassion that is celebration. Merriment is as much a part of the divine expression as struggle is. We are to be merry with divine merriment. Joy is ours for the tasting. Divinity is ours for the drinking.

To celebrate our "I am" is to put our *being* before our *doing* or *having* or *proving*. As Meister Eckhart put it, "people ought to think less about what they should do and more about what they are" (ME, 97). "I am" precedes "I do" or "I prove" or "I earn." An "I am" consciousness also affects our attitude toward time. The past and the future are not what exist; it is the now moment that exists most richly. It is the divine "now" that is ours for the drinking.

To experience compassion and to identify with the suffering of others—as well as with their joy—is to experience the Divine One who suffers and rejoices in each person. (See Isa. 58:3–11.) To struggle to birth one's own "I am" is also to experience the divine "I am." In fact, we must all birth the Cosmic Christ in our being and doing for that is why we exist. Is not the purpose of the incarnation in Jesus to reveal the imminence of the Cosmic Christ in the sufferings and dignity of each creature of the earth? As we discover our own "I am" and the ecstasy and pain of the Divine One in us, we gradually grow into an "I-am-with" others (*Emmanuel*, "God-with-us"). We grow into compassion and in doing so the divine "I am" takes on flesh once again. Since God alone is the Compassionate One, as we grow into compassion we also grow into our divinity.[3]

Part V

A Vision of the Second Coming
The Healing of Mother Earth and the Birth of a Global Renaissance

What has been passing for Christianity during these nineteen centuries is merely a beginning, full of weaknesses and mistakes, not a full-grown Christianity springing from the spirit of Jesus.

(Albert Schweitzer)

All flowers and blossoms, apparently without exception, are reproductive organs.

(Guy Murchie)

If life and the soul are sacred the human body is sacred.

(Walt Whitman)

Both religion and sexuality heal the split between ourselves and the universe. We discover that we are indeed "part of everything" and one with the mystery of life. To talk about God in relation to our sexuality means to be aware of love moving in us, for "in God we live and move and have our being."

(Dorothee Soelle)

Except in the modern world, sexuality has everywhere and always been a hierophany, and the sexual act an integral action and also a means of knowledge.

(Mircea Eliade)

The United States in the 1980s may be the first society in history in which children are distinctly worse off than adults.

(Senator Daniel Patrick Moynihan)

The one who makes herself or himself as little as this little child is the greatest in the kingdom/queendom of heaven.

(Jesus)

I can imagine that someday we will regard our children not as creatures to manipulate or to change but rather as messengers from a world we once deeply knew, but which we have long since forgotten, who can reveal to us more about the true secrets of life, than our parents were ever able to.

(Alice Miller)

The negative senex is the senex split from its own puer aspect. He has lost his "child."

(James Hillman)

I, God, am your playmate! I will lead the child in you in wonderful ways for I have chosen you.

(Mechtild of Magdeburg)

Erotic energy is the eternal source of creativity.

(Nicolas Berdyaev)

Art is an antidote for violence. It gives the ecstacy, the self-transcendence that could otherwise take the form of drug addiction, or terrorism, or suicide or warfare.

(Rollo May)

The creation of the world is not only a process which moves from God to humanity. God demands newness from humanity; God awaits the works of human freedom.

(Nicolas Berdyaev)

All things are the works of the Great Spirit. We should know well that He is within all things: the trees, the grasses, the rivers, the mountains, and all the four-legged animals, and the winged peoples; and even more important, we should understand that He is also above all these things and peoples.

(Black Elk)

The passion of justice is a primal embrace between man and all his known universe.

(D. H. Lawrence)

Humanity will find that it is not a diversity of creeds, but the very same creed which is everywhere proposed. . . . There cannot but be one wisdom. . . . Humans must therefore all agree that there is but one most simple wisdom whose power is infinite; and everyone, in explaining the intensity of this beauty, must discover that it is a supreme and terrible beauty.

(Nicholas of Cusa)

From Judaism, Christianity, and Islam to Hinduism, Buddhism, Taoism, and Native American and Goddess religions, each offers images of the sacred web into which we are woven.

(Joanna Macy)

The Shalom of the Holy; the disclosure of the gracious *Shekinah;* Divine Wisdom; the empowering Matrix; She, in whom we live and move and have our being—She comes; She is here.

(Rosemary Ruether)

A Renaissance is a new birth from a spiritual initiative.

(M. D. Chenu)

Henry Adams, the grandson of President John Adams and Abigail Adams, was one of the most impressive feminists in American history. Writing at the dawn of the twentieth century, himself a member of the Bostonian privileged class, Henry Adams spoke with a certain pessi-

mism—a pessimism that we have seen played out since in repeated world
wars, traffic in armaments, decimation of Mother Earth and the mother
principle. About eighty years ago he wrote, "We have no imaginative
race left to reconstruct a faith or an art."[1] Was Henry Adams correct? Is
our civilization as dead as it is deadly, or is something new possible—a
new vision, a new paradigm, a new wisdom, a new civilization? Instead of
a surrender to death, faithlessness, and artlessness, to an earth stripped
of beauty and of hope, is a renaissance possible? M. D. Chenu, the great
historian of European history, defines a renaissance as "a new birth from
a spiritual initiative."[2] Chenu believes that the twelfth century was the
only period in Western history when a renaissance succeeded. Is the human race still capable—in spite of the pessimism voiced by Henry Adams and many writers after him—of a new birth from a spiritual
initiative? If we are not, are we, the creatures of Mother Earth, all
doomed?

If the initiative does not come from the spirit, from the depths of us, it
surely will not come from above, i.e., from our institutions of government and media, education and politics, economics and religion. The
key to Adam's prophetic challenge is the word "imagination." He felt
that it was the death of imagination that was condemning us to sterility,
faithlessness, and life without beauty. Geologist/theologian Thomas
Berry speaks of the need to "reinvent the human."[3] Is that possible or is
that apocalyptic rhetoric? Might a renaissance in fact bring about the
reinvention of the human and might the reinvention of the human bring
about a renaissance?

Robert Bellah underscores the intimate connection between a cultural
and spiritual renaissance when he states that "no one has changed a
great nation without appealing to its soul."[4] The "spiritual initiative"
that Chenu names as the origin of a renaissance must appeal powerfully
to our personal and collective souls. It must truly awaken souls, enliven
their powers, excite their mysticism, ignite their possibilities for beauty
and compassion. This change of heart, this awakening, the *metanoia*, this
revolution which a renaissance can bring about cannot be done without
a renaissance in religion itself, without a recommitment to its own best,
often most hidden and forgotten, history. As Bellah states, "Culture is
the key to revolution; religion is the key to culture. . . . We need tradition as stimulus to rebirth."[5] Roots and tradition, history and the energy
of our ancestors in the communion of saints, are gifts that religion brings
to the spiritual awakening and the essential renaissance of our time. Yet,
in order to contribute to a renaissance, religion must confess some of its
errors and its sins. It must recognize its own need for conversion. As Albert Schweitzer said early in this century, "What has been passing for
Christianity during these nineteen centuries is merely a beginning, full
of weaknesses and mistakes, not a full-grown Christianity springing from
the spirit of Jesus. . . . I call on Christianity to set itself right in the spirit

of sincerity with its past and with thought in order that it may thereby become conscious of its true nature."[6] Schweitzer undertook his effort to recover the full spirit of Jesus by an intellectual commitment to the quest for the historical Jesus and by a personal, compassionate commitment to a lifestyle of work on behalf of the poor in Africa and on behalf of the suffering of animals. He lived out the compassion that Jesus preached.

Ironically a commitment to the full spirit of Jesus today requires that we let go of the quest for the historical Jesus and embark on a quest for the Cosmic Christ. With both elements of the dialectic restored—the historical Jesus and the Cosmic Christ—Christianity might "become conscious of its true nature" and evolve into a "full-grown Christianity," to use Schweitzer's words. The historical Jesus fulfills the meaning of the mystic/prophet outlined in part II. Jesus' life, teaching, and death—his own story as well as the stories of his ministry—reveal a mystic/prophet who possesses the characteristics of mysticism we elaborated earlier (see pp. 66–71). When this historical Jesus is balanced by the Cosmic Christ, then we—and not only Jesus—will be resurrected. We will follow Jesus in becoming true to our vocations as mystic/prophets, as "other Christs." With a resurrection in our spirits, our hopes, and our imaginations will come a renaissance in culture and religion that in turn, will contribute to the resurrection of Mother Earth. This process of resurrection by way of the Cosmic Christ and the living mysticism it engenders in our consciousness will happen as Schweitzer predicted, setting it right with its past. As I demonstrated in part III of this book, the tradition of the Cosmic Christ has a long history within our Scriptures and among Western mystics and prophets. More than that, this tradition is deep in science and art as well. The Cosmic Christ is essential to a living cosmology—to the coming together of science, mysticism, and art in our time. As Einstein put it, "the whole purpose of science and art is to awaken the cosmic religious feeling."[7]

The Cosmic Christ is the archetypal recipient of cosmic religious feeling. But it is the Cosmic Christ with wounds, the Cosmic Christ balanced by the suffering Jesus who was an historical person, a prophet crucified at a particular time in history for trying to usher in the cosmic compassion of the Christ. Suffering is essential to the full, human expression of the Cosmic Christ. In fact, the cosmic suffering of the cross allows all other pain to be acknowledged and entered into. All tears return to the great underground river that Eckhart names as the Divine One. But the tears are saltwater—they salinate and threaten to pollute the creative, divine waters of the underground river. This is yet another reason for acknowledging pain in order that it might be relieved. The recycling of the saltwater of tears into the creative waters of wisdom is still possible; healing is still possible. This is the hope that the Cosmic Christ, wounded but resurrected, holds out to our times.

Otto Rank talks about three levels of healing in a culture. The first is the psychiatrist, who heals, as a rule, on a one-to-one basis. The second is the artist, who heals groups of persons. And the third, he feels, is the religious prophet, who "heals the masses."[8] Does the Cosmic Christ hold the possibility of awakening the religious prophet in all persons and thus of healing the people? Is it possible for religion itself to become prophetic again? Religion would become an instrument of social awakening and deep social change for and by the masses if it let go of the quest for the historical Jesus and moved on to the quest for the Cosmic Christ. It is not enough to find the exact words that Jesus spoke two thousand years ago. We need today *a historical Christ*—a living Christ who can change history once again and ground that change in a living cosmology. The "historical Christ" of which I speak will combine the historical and incarnational rootedness of Jesus the prophet with the spatial and cosmic mysticism of the Cosmic Christ to effect a renaissance, a change of hearts and ways.

Who would dare to speak of a renaissance in our times? Is it a bourgeois dream of an armchair theologian, a romantic cop-out from an academician? Who in their right mind would look at the suffering in today's world and suggest that the human race is, in fact, on the verge of a vast, global renaissance? I suppose it is the mystic in me that dares to suggest such a vision. And why? Because the mystic teaches us to trust all bottoming out, all emptying, all nothingness experiences as the matrix and patrix of new birth. It is precisely the despair of our times that convinces me that a renaissance is right around the corner, that a renaissance is the only answer to the depths of our dilemma. It is either renaissance or planetary extinction. There is no middle ground.

How might this renaissance happen? By the paradigm shift that is possible when a living cosmology bursts on the scene. Recall the reflections by Thomas Kuhn on paradigm shifts in science presented in part III (chapter 15). Consider a new paradigm to be a new wineskin. One does not harvest a new crop of grapes, crush them, and pour them into old, dried-up wineskins. Rather, one seeks a new wineskin that is supple and soft, giving and forgiving, flexible and eager to be made wet, one that welcomes newness and creativity. Such a wineskin is the living cosmology being blended from three rich vineyards: science, from which we derive a universal creation story today; mysticism, from which we awaken the human psyche's powers for unity, wholeness, and imagination; and art, from which the Good News of a living cosmology is born into the hearts, dreams, imaginations, and bodies of persons, and even into the institutions of the culture.

We thus find ourselves at the threshold of naming the paschal mystery anew for the third millenium of Christianity: matricide, mysticism, and the Cosmic Christ name the Paschal story we have understood as the death, resurrection and second coming of Jesus the Christ. The death of Mother Earth (matricide) and the resurrection of the human psyche (mysticism) and the coming of the Cosmic Christ (a living cosmology) name the mystery of the divine cycle of death and rebirth and the sending of the Spirit in our time. Were the human race to believe anew in this mystery, a renaissance would surely occur.

The remainder of this section will outline some elements of this renaissance of culture and of church, of psyche and of institutions. Specifically we will address the following questions: What does the return of the Cosmic Christ do for us today? How does it resurrect the human spirit in regard to sexuality, youth-adult relationships, creative lifestyles, work, education, worship, and deep ecumenism? We will address each of these issues in turn.

25. The Cosmic Christ and a Renaissance of Sexual Mysticism

When religion is anthropocentric and lacks a cosmology, it has very little to tell us that is good news about sexuality, which is so special a gift of the cosmos. When this happens, culture secularizes sexuality and misuses it. Pornography substitutes for mysticism. (In America today we are spending seven billion dollars yearly on pornography.) When I listen to what religion in the West teaches us about sexuality, I hear two things. The first, paradoxically, is *silence:* no puberty rites, no effective rites of passage for our young to celebrate the immense news that they are now fit and able to pass on the mystery of human life. A tap on the cheek at confirmation or a room full of presents at bar mitzvah does not make up for this cosmic silence. A second response to sexuality from our religions is *moralizing.* Telling us all the sins we are capable of performing with our sexual organs does not enlighten us about our sexuality. French philosopher Gabriel Marcel has said that those who reduce a mystery to a problem are guilty of "intellectual perversion." There has been a great deal of intellectual perversion performed by religion in the West during the era that deposed the Cosmic Christ and a living cosmology; in the name of moralizing, the mystery of sexuality has been so often reduced to problems of morality.

If I were asked to name in one word the message I have received from my religion regarding sexuality over the forty-five years of my life I would answer: *regret.* I believe that the Western church, following in the spirit of St. Augustine, basically regrets the fact that we are sexual, sensual creatures. "If only sexuality would go away," the message goes, "we could get on with important issues of faith." But there is another tradition besides St. Augustine's regarding our bodiliness and deep sexual natures—the tradition of *praise.* It is time that the voice of the churches joined the voices of the other creatures to praise the Creator for the surprising and imaginative gift of our sexuality. A living cosmology can and will elicit this praise. It will take sexuality back from pornographers and return it to the sanctuaries where it belongs.

The Song of Songs praises our sexuality as part of the sacred gift of the Cosmic Christ whom lovers encounter in one another. All too many Christians have been led to believe that Christ is not present in lovemaking. That makes no sense. In fact, the Cosmic Christ is radically present to all sexuality in all its dimensions and possibilities. The Cosmic Christ celebrates sexual diversity—"in Christ there is neither male nor female," says Paul (Gal. 3:28). The Cosmic Christ is not obsessed with sexual identity. The Cosmic Christ can be both female and male, heterosexual and homosexual. This is the way nature made the human species, and nothing that is natural to the cosmos is foreign to the Cosmic Christ. The Cosmic Christ rejoices and is intimately at work and play when lovers make love. Angels flap their wings in envy at those times. The Cosmic Christ is ecstatic and excited when babies are born—each one a new expression of the Cosmic Christ. The Cosmic Christ is abused when sexuality is used as a weapon to keep people down or to play out games of control or power-over. The Cosmic Christ is wounded when people are victims of rape, impotence, sterility, or sexual scapegoating (the projection of repressed sexuality onto sexual minorities). The Cosmic Christ is saddened when the mystery and mysticism of sexuality is reduced to moralizing about sexual acts. The Cosmic Christ identifies with the sexual *anawim*. Among the wounds that the Cosmic Christ bears are the sexual wounds that accompany a person or group victimized by sexual oppression of any kind.

The Cosmic Christ in our time is dying over and over again of AIDS. The Cosmic Christ is learning lessons of wisdom and trying to teach them as a result of the tragedy of AIDS. Perhaps first among these lessons is a greater candor and honesty about our sexuality and the rich role it plays in our lives. The Cosmic Christ is becoming less tolerant of those who try to cover up sexuality or pretend that it is not important to psyche and to love and to a living cosmology. Sexual behavior and its expression as the art of lovemaking need to find their expression in committed love relationships between two persons. The Cosmic Christ does not condone sexual expression with multiple partners but would encourage monogamous commitments. The sexual act is a giving of oneself in a very deep way, a deliberate giving of the "I am" that is oneself.

SEXUAL MYSTICISM IN THE SONG OF SONGS

In the poem of sexual mysticism in the Bible called the Song of Songs a woman declares that "My vineyard is mine to give; my fruit is mine to give" (Song of Sg. 8:12). This sense of personhood, of "I am," is essential to a living sexual mysticism. This woman speaks this way because she has a

sense of her own "isness," her own "I-am-ness." Earlier in the poem she
declared, "I am a rose of Sharon, a lily growing in the valley" (2:1). She
has a sense of her beauty, her personhood, her royalty, her original blessing. Because of this, she can praise the beauty in her beloved, "how
beautiful you are, my love, yes, and how pleasant!" (1:16). Of course, her
own beauty is enhanced by the love of her lover who "delights" her and
"strengthens, refreshes, supports, and embraces" her (2:3–6).

Just before the culmination of the poem, before the woman's declaration that "my fruit is mine to give" (8:12) comes another "I am" saying:
"I am a wall and my breasts are like towers/So in the eyes of my lover I
am one who is welcomed" (8:10). Here she is celebrating her "I am" as
including her capacity to say "No" and to commit herself to a single
lover. She is responding to the sages in the chorus that warn young
lovers who are "open doors" that they will be "boarded up with cedar
planks" whereas those who become a "fortified wall will be adorned
with a silver breastplate" (8:9). Infidelity is an offense against the Cosmic
Christ who is seen radiating in one's lover. Is this not part of the new
vision—the living presence of the Cosmic Christ—that lovers experience from one another? Some might call falling in love projection, but
perhaps it is simply the yearning for the Cosmic Christ in another. To do
this well one must enter deeply into the soul and person of one's beloved.
In this sense one must be faithful, patient, and committed to mutual exploration. Consider these words spoken by the woman about her lover.
Clearly she has encountered the Cosmic Christ in him:

My lover is radiant and ruddy, he stands out among ten thousand.
His head is pure gold; his locks are like thick palm leaves,
     and are as black as the raven.
His eyes are like doves beside brooks of water.
His teeth seem bathed in milk,
     and his smile adorns his face like finely set jewels.
His cheeks are like beds of spice, treasures of ripe perfumes.
His lips are red blossoms; they drip liquid myrrh.
His arms are rods of gold,
     his hands crystal olive branches.
His body is a work of ivory with a sapphire veneer.
His legs are pillars of marble supported in sockets of
     precious gold.
His stature, like the trees on Lebanon, is imposing;
     his countenance as noble as cedars.
His mouth is delicious, his whispers are dear,
     and his expressions, "Desire" itself.
Such is my lover, O young ones of the holy city,
     and such is my friend!

(5:10–16)

Her beloved also sings his song, a celebration of the Cosmic Christ he
finds in her.

How beautiful you are, my dearest, O how beautiful!
Your eyes are like doves behind your veil.
Your hair is like a flock of goats streaming down Mount Gilead.
Your teeth are like a flock of ewes ready to be shorn,
    like freshly washed sheep that are big with
    twins, none of them thin or barren.
Your lips are like a scarlet thread,
    and your mouth is lovely when you speak.
The cheeks behind your veil are like a pomegranate
    sliced open in two.
Your neck is like King David's tower.
. . . .
Your breasts are like two fawns, young twins of a mother deer.
. . . .
How beautiful are your breasts, my sister, my bride! . . .
. . . (and) your perfumes are more fragrant than any spices!
Your lips drip honey, my bride,
    Words drop from your mouth like syrup from the honeycomb.
You flourish like an orchard of rare fruits,
    like an orchard of pomegranates.
You are a park full of plants.
. . . .
You are an enclosed garden, my sister, my bride,
    a garden close-locked, with a secret fountain.

                                                    (4:1–5, 10, 11–14)

Observe how the lover *does not take anything for granted* in the beloved but observes so carefully every nuance, every gesture, every limb, every element of the expression of the Cosmic Christ in the beloved. To be in love is to be in love *with the whole* of a person and to experience the divine radiance coming from each and every aspect of the beloved. Notice too how cosmological this poem necessarily is: the lovers exude their radiance back to the universe whence they received it. Love is always about a cosmology. Lovers exist in a universe, not just in a personal relationship. Thus, for example, when the woman responds to her lover's comment on the secret fountain, she includes an incantation to the winds of the universe:

The fountain in my garden is a spring of running water,
    flowing down from Lebanon.
Arise, north wind!
O south wind, come!
Blow upon my garden, let its alluring perfumes pour forth.
Then will my lover come to his garden and enjoy its choice fruits.

                                                    (4:15–16)

The entire poem, so ecstatic about the discovery of the Cosmic Christ in another and indeed in the relationship that two lovers forge, is an example of living cosmology. It ends with a cosmological invitation when the woman sings:

Come! Be swift, my lover!
Be like a gazelle or a wild young stag!
Come! Play on the mountains of myrrh!

(8:14)

She is a mountain of myrrh whose fruit is hers to give—and give it she will. Biblical exegete Phyllis Trible makes the point that the Song of Songs redeems the notion of *garden*, which was a "love story gone awry" in the garden of Eden story in Genesis. The woman in this "symphony of eroticism" is frequently presented as a garden: "the woman is the garden, (*gan*) and to the garden her lover comes." Plants, animals, water, all five senses, all combine to celebrate in this garden. "Testifying to the goodness of creation, then, eroticism becomes worship in the context of grace."[2]

In this poem we are told that the lovers emerged "out of the wild, up from the desert . . . leaning and holding" (8:5) onto one another. To make love is to enter the cosmological wilderness, to go beyond the human artifacts of city and civilization, to return to the depths of darkness where spirit embraces matter and the Cosmic Christ is realized as earthy and untamed. Spirit and instinct need not be at odds. The sexual experience for these lovers is an encounter with the wild, with the wilderness within and among them, with that part of divinity and the Cosmic Christ that is wild, not soft or tamed. The Jewish people first encountered Yahweh "in the wilderness" and the prophets spoke of going into the wilderness where God will speak "heart to heart" (Hos. 2:14). Jesus too wrestled with the cosmic forces of angels and demons and thus came to grips with the Cosmic Christ in him in the wilderness. To speak of playing "on the mountains" is also to suggest a wilderness image. For a mountaintop is not just about beauty but also about its counterpart, terror. Lightning strikes mountaintops; great storms gather there; and clouds often shroud it. Immense silence and aloneness can be tasted at mountaintops. Thus the mountain, too, is a wilderness image. How far this mystical encounter with the divine wilderness is from what Frederick Turner correctly, I believe, has called "the Western spirit against the wilderness."[3] This spirit is characterized by a tame, soft, antibody, and antisexual spiritualism that has dominated Western religion. How far we have strayed from the love and the wisdom of the Song of Songs.

Just as this poem celebrates the Cosmic Christ among lovers and within the love act, it also explores the cosmic pain that absence of the beloved brings. Deep love creates deep vulnerability. An opened heart is opened as much to suffering as to love. The wounds of the Cosmic Christ as well as the radiance of the divine are encountered in love affairs. The *via negativa* is encountered in sexual love.

With my own hands I opened to my lover—but my lover had
turned away and was gone.

> I sought him but did not find him.
> I called him but he did not answer.
> The watchmen met me as they made their rounds of the city.
> They struck me and wounded me
> Then the guards of the wall took away my cloak.
> I charge you, o young ones of the holy city,
>> If you find my lover—
>> What shall you tell him?—
>> Tell him I am faint with love.

> (5:6–8)

Love holds the power to make us faint, to make us suffer deprivation and loss, wounds and misunderstanding. But the young will help with the pursuit of the beloved because they understand what is at stake. The watchmen and security guards, the keepers of law and order and group morality do not understand but instead oppress the lover. They do not grasp the panic in the lover, who feels she has lost touch with the Cosmic Christ of her beloved.

Another dark side raised in sexual love is intimations of our mortality. Love also raises the specter of its cosmological counterpart, death. People in love become sensitized to what the loss of that love might mean—thus to the mystery and power of death. The woman speaks:

> Love is as mighty as death,
> passion as fierce as the grave;
> Its flames are a blazing fire.
> Deep waters cannot quench love, no flood can sweep it away . . . .

> (8:6–7)

Love stands toe to toe with death and stares it down. As awesome as death is, love is at least as great. Love does not flinch before our mortality. No waters can douse the flames of her passionate love and no death will overcome it. In the final analysis, such love is grace, a gift, an unconditional surprise. She declares that "if one were to offer all that he owns to acquire this love, he would be utterly mocked" (8:7). One cannot buy love such as this. It is, one might say, the Cosmic Christ finding its cosmic self in another. It is God loving God through us loving another. Yes, we do make love with the Divine in this lifetime. That is the promise of this poem to the Cosmic Christ of sexuality.

This poem is pre-Christian, as is all the wisdom literature of the Hebrew bible. This fact is one more indication that the Cosmic Christ is not restricted to Jesus.

This poem has generated considerable fear in Christians through the centuries. Consider how, in the lifetime of John of the Cross in sixteenth-century Spain, the Inquisition had actually forbidden the translating of the Song of Songs into Spanish. One poet, Fray Luis de Leon, was put in a dungeon in the Holy Office for five years for having translated this poem into the vernacular.[4] In spite of this ominous situation, St. John of the Cross spent much of his lifetime translating, rewriting, and commenting on this book.

When one considers how many Christian exegetes through the centuries have allegorized this poem to sexual love, one is struck anew by the renaissance that the Cosmic Christ will bring to sexuality. For the richest mystical source the West possesses about sexual love has rarely been heard in its first and most obvious meaning: the Cosmic Christ is encountered in human love and sexuality. Sexuality is revealed in a living cosmology as still one other theophany, one other transfiguration experience. Perhaps this is why the poem ends with an invitation to "Play on the mountains of myrrh"—because the mountain is a common place for theophanies and sacred clouds as we saw in our discussion concerning the transfiguration. The word for "mountain" in Hebrew also means "the Almighty" and it comes from the word for breast. Mountains are the breasts of Mother Earth, thus "Come! Play on my mountain of myrrh."

The psychological depth and insight of this poem is attested to by the manner in which the female and male actors do not merely play out stereotypical sexual roles. It is the woman who is the aggressor. She begins the poem telling us of her desire and where it will lead her:

> I will sing the song of all songs.
> For I desire that my man may kiss me with the kisses of his mouth.
> . . . .
> Take me and we will run together;
> Bring me into your chamber, O my king!

(1:1–2, 4)

She goes looking for her beloved:

> Tell me, you whom my heart loves,
>   where do you pasture your flocks,
>   where do you give them rest at midday?
> Tell me, my true love, lest I find myself picking out lice
>   as I sit among your companions' herds.

(1:7)

She refuses to be bored among her lover's companions. Her lover, though a shepherd, is in her eyes a "king." She seeks after him. She is lonely at night without him:

> Night after night on my bed I have sought my true love;
>   I sought him but did not find him.
>   I called him but he did not answer.
> I said:
>   "I will rise then and go about the city,
>   through the streets and the squares;

> I will seek my true love."
> I sought him but did not find him.
> I called him but he did not answer.

(3:1–2)

In her assertiveness, she is not shy to ask the guardians of the city about the whereabouts of her beloved:

> The watchmen met as they made their rounds of the city,
>   and I asked:
> "Have you seen my true love?"
> Scarcely had I left them when I found my true love.
> I seized him and would not let him go
>   until I had brought him to my mother's house,
>   to the room of her who conceived me.

(3:3–4)

She seizes her beloved and will not let him go. In Jungian terms, this woman displays a well-developed animus. She finds the assertive dimension of her psyche within herself. She is certain that her vineyard is hers to give because she is aware of her "I-am-ness." As Phyllis Trible observes, in the Song of Songs "there is no male dominance, no female subordination, and no stereotypes of either sex. . . . Throughout the Song she is independent, fully the equal of man." Truly there is a "recovery of mutuality in the garden of eroticism."[5]

Conversely, the male lover displays a well-developed anima. He is willing and able to wait, to be patient. Several times he instructs people to let his beloved rest and not to arouse her before her time. He can wait as one waits for flowers to grow and for the moon to emerge. He invokes the earth goddesses in this charge; this man is not out of touch with prepatriarchal spirituality:

> I tell you O young ones of the holy city:
> Do not arouse my lover before her time.
> I charge you by the "spirits and the goddesses of the field,"
>   by the gazelles and the hinds: Do not disturb
>   my love while she is at rest.

(2:7; 3:5; 8:4)

His love is not rapacious and possessive, not demanding and controlling. It is above all *respectful of the natural needs and rhythms of his beloved*—the need for rest, for arousal at the right and full time. He praises her for her relationship to her mother, for being "devoted to the mother who bore her" (6:9). He is not in competition with her womanhood or with her mother—or presumably with his own. He has incorporated a healthy maternal image into himself. He is more given to ecstacy than control and can confess that in her presence "I did not know myself" (6:12). One is reminded of Jesus' teaching that one saves one's soul by losing it. Yet the lover's manhood and royal personhood is enhanced by her who "made me feel more than a prince" (6:12). He does not shirk from his manly nature—he wills to "climb up into the palm tree" *and* "cling to its boughs" (7:9). He "awakens her" under the apple tree (8:5). He is a *whole* person: by fully integrating the feminine dimension of his personality, he has become truly and deeply masculine. This man is not pursuing his anima exclusively outside himself. When he falls in love, he is truly seeking the "other" and not merely the missing parts of his own soul. This man and woman are mature lovers seeking one another's pleasure as well as their own.

The Song of Songs culminates with the man inviting the woman to sing: "Come! Let me hear you sing!" (8:13) he declares. The singing he yearns for appears to be a euphemism for making love. The title of the poem Song of Songs suggests that the true song is lovemaking itself. The woman responds to the man's invitation to sing with her own invitation to "play on the mountains of myrrh!" (8:14). Play lies at the essence of all mysticism, at the essence of all sexuality re-visioned in light of a Cosmic Christ paradigm. This perspective on sexuality links us to that of our earliest ancestors for whom sexuality was essentially play and not reproduction. Carl Jung comments:

> Normal sex life, as a shared experience with apparently similar aims, further strengthens the feeling of unity and identity. The state is described as one of complete harmony, and is extolled as a great happiness ("one heart and one soul")—not without good reason, since the return to that original condition of unconscious oneness is like a return to childhood. Hence the childish gestures of all lovers. . . . It is, in truth, a genuine and incontestable experience of the Divine, whose transcendent force obliterates and consumes everything individual; a real communion with life and the impersonal power of fate.[6]

When was this wisdom about sexuality as play lost and why was it lost, particularly in religious traditions? Otto Rank offers a brilliant response to this question. In contrast to the "naive playful activity"[7] that sex was for thousands of years of human tribal living, about the fourth century A.D. sex became associated with guilt and utter seriousness. At that time, the meaning of the soul or the collective survival of the tribe—its immortality—came to be understood in the context of family blood ties, family trees, inheritance, legitimacy, honor, and obedience. "As an expression of will, sexuality became evil, guilty, and a cause of death," says Rank,[8] because sexuality had to bear the full weight of the tribe's need for survival and immortality. An "ideology of fertilization" characterized this era and sex was understood to rob the male of his strength—interestingly, the ideology of celibacy was being developed simultaneously. The issue "has always been one of immortality and of the salvation of man's soul from dissipation under the sexual era's ideology of fertilization," says Rank.[9] Not only has religion succumbed easily to this negative view of sex, but so have patriarchal cultural figures like Freud,

Nietzsche, and Schopenhauer. Rank believes that this sexual or family era of the human soul when soul became entirely identified with sexuality was laid to rest by the emergence of psychology one hundred years ago. Psychology's great achievement consists in ending the sexual era and freeing people of the excessive seriousness surrounding sexuality. Yet, Rank also believes that the psychological era is only temporary, for "the psychological ideology has never been alive. It came into the world, so to say, with an old mind."[10] Psychology does not believe in anything so it has no vision, no eschatological passion, no future to offer. That is why it is imperative that we move beyond psychology to mysticism and creativity. And that is precisely where the Cosmic Christ can take us—beyond psychology to mysticism and creativity, to a living cosmology whose task is not to moralize about sex but to celebrate the amazing energy and beauty, the intimacy and cosmic connection making that is found wherever the Cosmic Christ, embodied in human lovers, makes love. We must return sexuality to its primal roots in mysticism.

Every time humans truly make love, truly express their love by the art of sexual lovemaking, the Cosmic Christ is making love. The play that the woman in the Song of Songs invites her lover to at the mountain of myrrh with its implications of sensuous oils and fragrances is, as we have seen, of a responsible kind. It is within the context of true love, of genuine commitment, of her being a "wall" and a genuine "I am" whose fruit is hers to give. No wonder she feels as "one who is welcomed." Hospitality reigns in this holy giving and receiving, this sacred play between bodies which are also bodies of the Christ, bodies of the one cosmic and sexual body. The Cosmic Christ is at ease with sexuality and nurturing of its playful side. We have much to learn about sexuality from the living cosmology of the Cosmic Christ.

The Song of Songs may well contain within its profound treatment of sexual love as divine love an entire spirituality of sexuality that could offer a new starting point—indeed a new, though very ancient, wineskin—for a theology for sexuality today. Judaism wisely associates this book with the Sabbath—the day of play and rest—and even includes it as the basic reading for the Passover. Western religion generally has failed to see what it has to teach us about the wisdom of lovers, and the ecstasy, the suffering, and the divine revelation behind human love. However the new era emerging, that of mysticism and creativity, will require the recovery of our spiritual tradition that the Song of Songs so richly represents and the full participation of our religious leaders conscious of these traditions to truly accomplish its promise. We must recover a sense of the theophany, the sacredness of lovemaking. There can be no healthy or full sexuality without mysticism, without a living cosmology, without the origin of sexuality celebrated once again in cosmic praise.

Historian of religions Mircea Eliade maintains our civilization is unique in its secularization and moralization of sex. Eliade writes:

Sexuality . . . everywhere and always . . . is a polyvalent function whose primary and perhaps supreme valency is the cosmological function: so that to translate a psychic situation into sexual terms is by no means to belittle it; for, except in the modern world, sexuality has everywhere and always been a hierophany, and the sexual act an integral action and also a means of knowledge.[11]

The Cosmic Christ urges us to render sexuality a hierophany once again. Theologian Dorothee Soelle does this when she writes that

both religion and sexuality heal the split between ourselves and the universe. We discover that we are indeed "part of everything" and one with the mystery of life. To talk about God in relation to our sexuality means to be aware of love moving in us, for "in God we live and move and have our being."[12]

Physicist Erich Jantsch regrounds sexuality in this cosmological mystery and allows us to celebrate the wonder of it once again. "Sexuality," he says, "was one of two essential factors which resulted in an extraordinary acceleration of evolution and the emergence of a variety of life forms."[13] Sexuality was a creative act of the universe that made our marvelous planet possible. Every flower and blossom *is* a reproductive organ. Sexuality is at the heart of the creative power of the universe. Carl Jung stresses the creative power that is unleashed in our sexuality:

The conflict between ethics and sex today is not just a collision between instinctuality and morality, but a struggle to give an instinct its rightful place in our lives, and to recognize in this instinct a power which seeks expression and evidently may not be trifled with, and therefore cannot be made to fit in with our well-meaning moral laws. Sexuality is not mere instinctuality; it is an indisputably creative power that is not only the basic cause of our individual lives, but a very serious factor in our psychic life as well.[14]

Similarly, Russian Orthodox theologian Nicolas Berdyaev comments on how eros and creativity are connected: "The erotic is connected in the same inseparable way with creativity. Erotic energy is the eternal source of creativity. . . . The erotic shock is the way of revealing beauty in the world."[15] Truly, when sexual love is reset in a cosmological context it becomes sacrament once again, just as Paul commented when he calls it a "mystery with many implications that applies to Christ and the Church" (Eph. 5:32).

The Cosmic Christ recognizes the creativity behind sexuality. The Cosmic Christ also insists on the connection between justice and sexuality. The sad situation in which so many spiritual gurus of the East have come to the West and fallen into bed with numerous disciples is evidence of a lacuna in the Eastern spiritual attitude. Just as the West has lost faith with the spiritual dimension to sexuality, so the East when translated to the West runs the risk of forgetting the justice dimension inherent in all relationships, including sexual ones. Lifestyles must always keep justice as a test of authentic mysticism—just as mysticism is the authentic test for justice. Mysticism is the "yes" dimension, the "I am" dimension, the awareness that "my fruit is mine to give" dimension. Justice is the "no" dimension, the "fortified wall" dimension that the Song of Songs insists is a part of authentic love and real mystical sexuality. No one has carte blanche to bypass the justice dimension to sexuality, for the justice dimension is as much a part of the cosmic law as is ecstacy itself. Without the "no" or the "wall" dimension there is no true giving to a freely chosen partner—there is no commitment of mutuality. One cannot be legitimately welcomed by all—but only by one's freely chosen love.

Of course, the issues of justice and sexuality include justice for sexual minorities and the struggle for a society without sexism. The struggle for justice toward women and toward the mother principle which is being beset by what I refer to as matricide is part and parcel of every authentic cultural sexual awakening today. But matricide also includes within it a kind of patricide as well. The father will become distorted in this process for there is no mother without a father. A distorted fatherhood is what a pathological patriarchy is all about.

The word "mother" is used seven times in the Song of Songs. Mother is a relational term not only to the young, as we saw earlier, but also in relation to a father. Without a father there is no mother. But if the mother is threatened and abused, then father too, is unbalanced—and this is especially the case if the father or father principle is the cause of the abuse of the mother. An era of matricide, then, is also inevitably an era of fatherly distortion. If mother and father are meant to be interdependent principles of relating and interacting and either one is distorted for any reason, then both are affected by this distortion in relationship.

As we saw in the case of astronaut Rusty Schweikert, it took a massive *metanoia* to begin to heal a distorted male psyche. The emergence of male liberation as a movement characterizing our times and the recovery of healthy and virile masculine energy are responses to the fact of the mother dying in our midst. Male liberation will constitute the next important chapter in the awakening of women's consciousness, for men too have been victimized by the system that exploits Mother Earth, women, and children.

Men come to a realization of their own victimization more slowly because, at the level of patriarchal values, it appears that they are *not* victims at all but the successful ones in that system. Wherever male liberation groups are gathering, however, the first lesson learned from honest male sharing is this: men are in deep pain over the very issues I have listed as part of my dream—the threat to Mother Earth and to children, the lack of creativity and compassion, the frustration with mother church, the guilt over genocide toward native peoples. Yet men have been taught to repress and deny their pain. Male liberation groups are learning to help one another get their stories out—preferably not only by verbal means, but by drumming and dancing and using mystical techniques from ancient peoples. When men are enabled to do this they can be healed and they can recognize one another as healers. And this awareness represents a new kind of masculinity, one that is both sensitive and strong. "Soft" masculinity is not called for in the awakening to a healthy mother/father principle. "Strength" must be redefined not as power-over but as power-with.

I recently spoke in Colorado on the wounded child who is in all adults. Afterwards, a man who was present in the audience—a former banker and currently a therapist in his mid-fifties—went home and drew three pictures. The first two were of his childhood. In one he was being attacked by sticklike creatures. The second picture was of a boy's face with a tape over his mouth and tears coming down his cheeks. Under this picture was the caption: "Big boys don't cry—they just keep their cosmic tears inside." The third picture consisted of a flowing river of golden light with a caption saying: "I am divine light flowing into the universe." The last picture would not have been possible without the acknowledgment of the pain expressed in the first two pictures. First this man had to acknowledge and express his pain. When he did this, his mystical self was unleashed to flow with power and grace. This is a lesson for all men wounded by the matricide killing the earth. Matricide and patricide go together. If men and women both have a mother and a father principle within, then we all suffer when either mother or father is distorted.

Women who idolize the father principle outside themselves—a phenomenon common in fascism and fundamentalist religions—are exhibiting a sickness born of patricide, namely the absence of a healthy fatherhood within. A healthy woman needs to find the father within. Otherwise she runs the serious risk of falling victim to projection of fatherhood onto another, be it president, pope, dictator, movie or rock star. A fascist society fans these projections and keeps women "fatherless." Christofascism (Dorothee Soelle's name for religious fundamentalism) makes the same projections when it gives us Jesus without a Creator God. A healthy contribution of the women's movement has been women claiming their own share of masculinity.

Eugene Monick, in a significant book on recovering healthy masculinity entitled *Phallos: Sacred Image of the Masculine*, points out some of the perversions of our worshipping the "great phallic sun god. . . . The nations are constructing nuclear phallos after nuclear phallos, aiming them at one another, playing boys' games of challenge—comparing whose emission might shoot the farthest. Such is the mortal danger of the shadow of self-righteous solar masculinity."[16] It is not difficult to detect this same "self-righteous solar masculinity" in the wars going on within the fundamentalist television movement today or in the Inquisition, Crusades, and witch-burning manias of yesteryear. What is the solution to too much "solar masculinity"? Monick warns that the solution for men can never be a mere return to maternal energy. Such a simplistic solution contains grave dangers and the seed for backlash.

> The unconscious is a man's place of origin. In the evolution of an individual, it is essential to return to "the place" whence one came. . . . If a man's place is the realm of the mother—and thus, in a basic way, antagonistic—the connection will be impeded. If origin is understood only as feminine, male resistance is understandable, given the energy that has been expended in establishing masculinity as independent from the matrix. A man either remains where he is, bereft of the depths, or he gives in to the depth and surrenders what he has sought long to attain.[17]

Where can men turn to recover their origins? To the sacredness of phallos. "Phallos as god–image provides a solution to this quandry. Phallos as masculine source offers a man a way to return to the unconscious without surrendering his phallic identity." Monick argues that the "charm" and "fascination" that phallos holds for people, whether heterosexual or homosexual, is comparable to an "uncontrollable god" that needs to be reverenced. It is part of that holy sphere that philosopher Rudolph Otto called the *numinosum.* "Phallic thrall is a symptom of masculine hierophany," for sexuality "is at bottom a religious issue, opening a door in the psyche which permits the god-image standing behind it an entrance into ego awareness."[18] The oldest of the world religions of today, Hinduism, which dates to 10,000–8,000 B.C., celebrated this hierophany of phallos. The god Shiva is creator and destroyer of things and is lord of the dance. Shiva's symbol is the lingam or phallos. Shiva speaks:

> I am not distinct from the phallos. The phallos is identical with me. It draws my faithful to me and therefore must be worshipped. Wherever there is an upright male organ, I, myself, am present, even if there is no other representation of me. . . . The phallos is . . . the symbol of the god.[19]

This is Cosmic Christ language. The word of God who is present intimately in all things is also present intimately in the reproductive and sexual powers of male and female. Just as Jesus cured the man born blind on the Sabbath and scandalized certain Jews whose concept of the law was literalistic, so there is bound to be scandal today in a genuine effort to bring sexual mysticism back to the realms of the sacred, but the Cosmic Christ insists that we do indeed bring it back. There alone will men recover active respect and reverence for their own amazing powers and thereby cease envying women theirs. From this point of view Monick calls on men not simply to imitate the women's journey into liberation but to dare to make their own. Like women feminists, he critiques the dualism that is behind a pathological patriarchy. "Invisible spirit, as archetypally masculine, manifests itself in flesh; visible flesh, as archetypally feminine, manifests phallos. Phallos, *membrum virile,* is flesh *and* spirit—in a word, psychoid."[20]

But to relearn respect and even reverence for phallos means to enter the power that is chthonic phallos and to resist temptations to spiritualize male sexuality, rendering men soft. According to Monick,

The inbreaking of chthonic phallos, including shadow aspects, is required for transformation and rebirth. Pounding, breaking, forcing, taking are actions of phallos obedient to its nature. The paradox of ravishment as the means of chasteness explains Jung's insistence upon the need for shadow integration. One cannot be pure without knowing impurity as one's own experience; one can find only naive enlightenment without the discovery of evil within oneself.[21]

A particular danger of feminization looms for those men drawn to spirituality—the danger of becoming "prematurely solar in one's life goals, adapting himself to a masculine stance devoid of sexuality," continues Monick. In such a situation one's "spirituality becomes brittle and technical without the hot breath of chthonic phallos, half-there, rational and without inspiration. . . . Fascination and wonder are gone, since both are inextricably related to the rise and fall, death and resurrection, of chthonic phallos."[22] In short, the wilderness needs to be visited by all.

How does one recover the sense of sacred phallos? One way is to return to the chthonic by way of drumming, dancing, and entering into the irrational processes that have been native ways of ritual and wisdom for tens of thousands of years. The key is our learning to embody the sacred and the physical together again. Rituals ought to be developed to help men, especially while they are young, to undergo such awakenings. Puberty rites—which is what sacramental confirmation rites and bar mitzvahs ought to be about—should be accomplishing these tasks of celebrating one's chthonic wholeness in the company of male adults.

Monick is calling men to have more than penises but phalloses as well. Reverence will follow. Ironically, with this reverence will come increased responsibility and moral commitment. The phallos *is* an original blessing. We need to return the sacred dimension, the mystical dimension, to male sexuality once again.

THE COSMIC CHRIST SPEAKS ON SEXUALITY

The Cosmic Christ might speak thus on the topic of sexuality: "Let religion and the churches abandon their efforts to be 'houses of sublimation.' Instead, reenter the cosmic mystery that sexuality is and teach your people, young and old, to do the same, remembering justice, remembering responsibility as intrinsic to the mystical experience. All lovemaking (as distinct from 'having sex') is Christ meeting Christ. Love beds are altars. People are temples encountering temples, the holy of holies receiving the holy of holies. Wings of cherubim and seraphim beat to the groans and passions of human lovers, for the cosmic powers are there eager to enhance the celebration. The sacred moments of sexual

ritual are not inferior to any other cosmic liturgy. Relearn the art of
lovemaking as a genuine art, as meditation experience. Know that in
making love the very process is the way. I am there. I am the way. Go
beyond 'being in love' to being the presence of cosmic love embodied
and reflected in two human lovers. Deanthropocentrize being in love,
yet localize it and ground it in personal commitment to another. Sexual
love will help you to do this, reminding you even of your finiteness in the
midst of infiniteness, of your mortality in the midst of beauty's everlast-
ingness, of the future in the midst of the now."

Meister Eckhart developed a theology of pleasure that may well contribute to a sexual mysticism within the context of a living cosmology
(BR, 81). Applied to sexual experience, it would read thus:

1. Experience of sexual love as "good" or "pleasurable."
2. Experience of sexual love as a gift.
3. Experience of sexual love as "eternally-not-other."

This would seem to be what a divinity who has been incarnated and
become human "in every way save sin" would bring—a revaluing of sexual experience as an encounter with the living God, a theophany, a transfiguration experience, a cosmological gift. To the extent that this truth
of the mysticism of sexuality is lost in our culture and its religious traditions, Carl Jung is correct when he observes that "our civilization enor-
mously underestimates the importance of sexuality."[23]

I believe there is a need to recover the sense of both lust *and* chastity as
powers and therefore virtues within all people. It takes courage to be
lustful, to entertain vulnerability and play and let control go, to enter
what Turner calls the "howling wilderness" and let it enter us. It also
takes courage to let go of attachment to lust and to be chaste as well.
Both spiritual disciplines need to be encouraged in all people, regardless
of their lifestyles, for at times we are called to one, at times to another.
The bridles of Beauty and Love help steer the horse named Lust. Even
at lustful times there will be need for chastity's presence in order that
monogamy and commitment may rule and love may not suffer.

Lust is a great, awesome, and wonderful beast, a stallion that can run
away with people, driving them mad, jealous, or cynical, or deadening
their souls if ignored. Yet, once bridled, it ushers in to lovers and progeny alike all the promise of the universe, all the beauty of cosmic history,
all the music of deep feelings, all the surprise and wonder of bodily,
earthly, sexual adventure wherein humans and animals unite with each
other—and the angels cheer enviously such an expression of a *living* cosmology. Two people riding the great horse of lust can indeed ride more
deeply and swiftly into one another's souls. Good bridling is essential for
this art of riding the horse, as Meister Eckhart said. "If you wish to discipline the flesh, then put on it the bridle of love. Whoever has accepted
this sweet burden of the bridle of love will attain more and come much

further than all the penitential practices and mortifications that all the people in the world acting together could ever carry out" (ME, 58). In this dialectic of chastity and lust we might resurrect a healthy, playful, just—and therefore moral—sexuality once again. But to be all these things sexuality must be grounded in a living cosmology which includes the mystical dimension of how sexual experience is "entering the mysteries" of self, of history, of one's partner, of the universe, of the children yet to be born from such unions; and it must include a recovery of that personal art that lovemaking is about. Such gifts the Cosmic Christ brings to a renaissance of the sexual.

A rebirth of lifestyles and mystical sexuality will require a new attitude, an attitude of valuing process itself. Art as meditation teaches us to value processes—the arts of friendship and conversation; of laughter and conviviality; the great art of creating relationships and creating lifestyle in modes of mutuality; and, of course, the art of lovemaking itself.

Lovemaking needs to find its source again in the spiritual tradition of art as meditation. If art as meditation is about getting in touch with our deepest images and expressing them by way of centering, then clearly lovemaking is art as meditation par excellance. Are not images of the one we love most deeply—the one to whom we freely choose to "give our vineyard"—among the deepest of all the images we live with in our lifetimes? Think of the power our memories possess about such moments in our lives. Think of the sacrifices generous giving people have offered over the years for the one with whom they make love. Think of the results of that loving: the children who are born of art as meditation. To recover lovemaking as an art as meditation would recover mystical sexuality as an important base for cultural renewal and personal spiritual grounding.

Art is just as important to a living cosmology as is mysticism or science. The personal arts ground our cosmological amazement. None of the arts required for a renaissance of lifestyle and love is elitest. All persons are capable of expressing themselves in their fashion in these ways. God is always deeply present in the everyday events of our lives which we enter into fully. The sacred book known as the Song of Songs never uses God's name. It has no need to. God is the way, God is the process—the Cosmic Christ is present deeply and intimately in that process. The Cosmic Christ is present in our most intimate efforts at renewal and love.

The Cosmic Christ paradigm that reawakens us to a sexual mysticism is a necessary part of any authentic renaissance. The greatest sins regarding human sexuality may not be what has gone on behind closed doors by persons who love one another but rather the sins of omission on the part of the churches themselves. Religion has neglected to tell believers of the ways of lovemaking as an art as meditation, has failed to teach spiritual disciplines of the holy art of savoring, has failed to con-

180 / THE COMING OF THE COSMIC CHRIST

nect the theophany of sexuality with other theophanies related in the Scriptures—including that of the Song of Songs—there may lie the greatest danger to the gift of our sexuality. All of life is praised in the Song of Songs—as it is whenever the Cosmic Christ is allowed to emerge. As theologian Dorothee Soelle points out, "In the Song of Solomon, nature, animals, men and women partake of the joy, the abundance, the fullness of life in the garden." The garden becomes a "new creation" which "stands in contrast to the curse tradition of pain, fruitlessness and dominion found in Genesis 2:46–3:24."[24] To recover the Cosmic Christ present in sexuality is to recover the energy and joie de vivre, the love of life and eros that will undergird any and all spiritual awakenings. There can be no renaissance without a mystical sexual awakening.

26. Honoring the Child Within—Youth and the Cosmic Christ

In a newly vitalized culture, one imbued with a living cosmology, the child will be honored and reverenced. The Cosmic Christ can lead the way in the renaissance of relationships between young and old.

How old is the Cosmic Christ? One should not ask "how old" but rather "how young," for the Cosmic Christ is very, very young. Meister Eckhart says God is *novissimus*, "the newest thing" there is. He also says that God is "always in the beginning" (BR, 111–113). Eckhart is referring to the first sentence of Genesis, which begins: "In the beginning." There is an allusion to the first sentence of the New Creation story found in John's Gospel which also begins: "In the beginning." It seems God is always "in the beginning." There is something godlike about all our new beginnings. The Spirit is always there, hovering over the waters. The Cosmic Christ is present at the beginnings and God is somehow in favor of the new. Should we not presume, then, that God is especially present to those still in touch with their beginnings, those nearest their beginnings? One could even say that God is biased in favor of the young. When we experience God, we experience a return to our beginnings, a newness, a rebirth. "Beginning" for Eckhart means compassion, for he also says that "whatever God does the first outburst is always compassion" (BR, 441). In the beginning is compassion; compassion births us; compassion is our origin—it is the origin of our youthfulness. Our journey is indeed a journey from our beginning, to our youth, to our divinity where we rediscover our beginnings and there find the youthful Cosmic Christ who never ceases to play (see Proverbs 7).

Is this bias in favor of the child of God, the child in God, and the child who is God carried through in contemporary church or society? I think not. In this failure to honor our children and the child within lies one of the most critical dangers of our epoch—and, ironically, one of the most powerful sources for a global renaissance. In fifteen years, we are told, over 50 percent of the human race will be under fifteen years of age. Most of these youth will be in so-called Third World countries. In industrial countries—which set the agenda for so much of our cultural and religious institutions—youth are becoming less visible. For example, in 1970 in the United States 40 percent of the population was under twenty-one. By 1980 that percentage had dropped to 34 percent. Statistically, then, our society is becoming more adult. A great danger looms that youth will be even more neglected in the future unless adults are awakened now to their situation. How are we treating our young? Are we preparing them to love life? Are we offering them skills and disciplines for adventure, for sacrifice, for great visions to which they can give themselves?

ADULTISM—A SOCIETY THAT DEVOURS ITS YOUTH

I believe that our civilization, far from honoring our youth and celebrating them, consumes and devours them. Consider the following facts.
• A three-year study conducted by Stanford University found that in the San Francisco Bay Area of California four out of five (80 percent) young people believe there will be a nuclear war in their lifetime. "Nuclear war is very much on students' minds and they are showing a considerable degree of apprehension about it," said Hans Weiler who headed the survey project.[1] Other studies on dreams of young children, for example, indicate that the nuclear bomb has already gone off in our children's dreams.
• One of ten young people in America have attempted suicide according to one study. And on Indian reservations today, one out of ten teenagers succeeeds in committing suicide. Suicide can be entered into directly or indirectly (for example, driving cars while under the influence of alcohol or drugs is a kind of suicide attempt). The suicide rate for fifteen- to nineteen-year-olds has tripled in the last three decades from 2.6 per 100,000 in 1955 to 8.5 per 100,000 in 1980.[2]
• There are ten million alcoholic parents in America and thus twenty-eight million children living in alcoholic homes. In such a situation children have to parent their parents. Children raised in such circumstances are often deprived of their own childhood.
• The young are frequent victims of violence. The primary cause of death in New York City for persons twelve to twenty-six years old is murder. A black youth in the state of California is more likely to die of murder than to graduate from college. In 1982, 30,600 young people destroyed themselves through homicide, suicide, and accidental death due to drinking and driving. One study concludes that "statistics show

quite clearly that the United States has become one of the most dangerous places on earth to pass through the teenage years."[3] A recent study concluded that 77 percent of deaths of Americans fifteen to twenty-four years old come from accidents, homicide, or suicide, a "horribly disturbing" statistic according to the persons who compiled the study. In fact, they concluded that "young people may be headed toward even more acts of depression and desperation. . . . Survey after survey shows these kids are overwhelmingly stressed, suicidal, disenfranchised," said the study's author, Larry Doyle.[4]

• Drug and alcohol abuse is widespread among our young. In areas where there is 90 percent unemployment or more among the young, such as Indian reservations and inner city ghettos, there is hardly a family untouched by drug or alcohol abuse.

• Only within the past eight years has sexual and physical abuse of our children begun to be documented in our society. Prior to this, children who reported such matters were often dismissed as liars or troublemakers. The child pornography industry is expanding 600 percent annually. When I lectured recently to a group on the theme of "the wounded child," a religious sister stood up and told us that in the school where she taught the previous year in a small town in the state of Washington, ten of the twenty-two seven-year-olds in her class had been sexually abused. The religious legitimization of Jansenism—a dualistic heresy exported from seventeenth-century France to Ireland and then America—and the silence on the mysticism and glory of sexuality on the part of the churches is another instance of sexual abuse that feeds the other, more blatant kind of pornography in our culture. The fact that the Catholic bishops of Ireland wrote an entire pastoral to youth in 1985 that never even mentioned the body or sexuality is an example of the sin of omission regarding sexuality in the churches of which I speak.

• Religious and spiritual abuse of our children has become rampant in the past few years of rising fundamentalist aggression in our culture. Rare is the teacher or minister or priest who has not encountered what I have on numerous occasions: children of fundamentalists or young fundamentalists with no ego, no self-respect, no tolerance for diversity, no love of creation, no sense of humor, no sense of sexual identity or joy. The Cosmic Christ within them has been aborted. I know a man in his early thirties who still wakes up at night in cold sweats dreaming about the hell and fire damnation sermons he listened to as a youngster attending Sunday services in a rural church.

• Ineffective education is another concern today. Over 50 percent of America's youth in large cities today never graduate from high school. (This often condemns such youth to no work or very low-paying work and to premature parenthood resulting in still another generation of children with little chance of emotional or cultural success.) Does this statistic indicate that 50 percent of American youth are "dumb"? Or does it call for some alternative education by which to reach those large numbers of the young who are not being reached by our present educational institutions?

• Unemployment among youth is rampant. Increasing numbers the world over are being condemned to no vision, no hope, no opportunity for meaningful work in their lifetimes. Not only in American inner cities and Indian reservations but in Mexico City, Ireland, England, and France as well as in the southern hemisphere, growing numbers of youth are joining the ranks of the unemployed—90 percent are in this category. Unemployed persons frequently experience a sense of inner violence because they have no outlet for offering their gifts to the community. Prisons are becoming increasingly filled with our youth who see no employment in their futures. Today there are more American black youth in prison than in college.

• Sixty–five thousand children die daily of starvation around the world, even though enough food exists for all of them; at the same time adults spend over $1.8 million per minute on weapons.

• The young in the United States will inherit the $200 billion yearly debt that adults are leaving them. A baby born in the United States today arrives owing $65,000 on the national debt.

• One of every four children under the age of six years is living in poverty in America today.

• In the state of California today, one-third of the young men between nineteen and twenty-nine years of age are in jail.

• Consider how often in this century alone young men have been sent into battle by old men to kill or die or be wounded for the sake of old men's ideological battles.

• I have spoken to one youth leader who was raised in an inner city project and underwent all the violence and deprivation associated with that kind of living situation—alcoholism, murder, drugs, unemployment, physical, and sexual abuse. Yet he declares that the greatest deprivation of his youth was not being challenged enough, not being given a vision or an adventure into which he could channel his considerable talents. Children deprived of a living cosmology, of an affirmation of their cosmic calling and cosmic destiny, are experiencing another kind of abuse, that of life without adventure.

These facts remind one of the slaughter of the children portrayed in the infancy story of Matthew's Gospel where the lamentation of the prophet Jeremiah is repeated: "A voice was heard in Ramah, crying and loud lament; Rachel weeping for her children, and she refused to be comforted, because they were no more" (Matt. 2:18). How poignantly and appropriately this lamentation from the prophet Jeremiah (see Jer. 31:15) applies to the sad state of affairs for the children if Mother Earth cannot survive. She too will refuse to be comforted becuase they will no longer be. How near we are to repeating a slaughtering of the innocents—

only this time on a grand scale unimagined even by Herod's cruel standards of behavior.

What do all these problems of today's young people have in common? A loss of reverence for life—*one's own*—is at issue among our young, as youth leader Victor Lewis puts it. Where does one learn this loss of reverence for one's own divinity, one's own beauty, one's own *doxa* or "glory," *and for the Cosmic Christ that one is,* if not from those who run the society—the adults? Children are so vulnerable for so long. They learn to love themselves from adults who love them or mislove them. They love self and others as they have been loved or not been loved. Is not the Cosmic Christ sexually abused? the victim of physical violence? the victim of alcoholic homes when children are so treated? Uneducated? Unemployed? In prison? Certainly Jesus made this clear when he said: "I tell you solemnly, in so far as you did this to one of the least of these brothers or sisters of mine, you did it to me" (Matt. 25:41). And again,

> Anyone who welcomes a little child like this in my name welcomes me. But anyone who is an obstacle to bring down one of these little ones who have faith in me would be better drowned in the depths of the sea with a great millstone round his neck. . . . See that you never despise any of these little ones, for I tell you that their angels in heaven are continually in the presence of my Creator in heaven. . . . It is never the will of your Creator in heaven that one of these little ones should be lost (Matt. 18:5, 6, 10, 14).

As we have seen, Dorothee Soelle warns that it is endemic to an unjust civilization to cover up the pain of its victims. The youth are paying a tremendous and painful price for our current civilization. The major price is the killing of Mother Earth, the very source of life and sustenance for our youth. If the youth cannot grow up in a world of beauty and diversity, of healthy soil, of animals and forests, of air and food, of birds that sing and porpoises that play purposelessly, then should they want to grow up at all? Is a life that is only about survival even worth living? Is not the quality and grace of life intrinsic to belief in the blessing that life is?

To assist in uncovering the pain of the young who are victims in our culture it is helpful to name the cause of the suffering. Twenty-five years ago "racism" was named on a cultural scale; eighteen years ago, "sexism"; seventeen years ago, "homophobia." Today it is necessary to name another cause of suffering: *adultism.* Its opposite is respect for youth, for youth as spiritual directors to adults. Senator Daniel Patrick Moynihan has commented that "the United States in the 1980s may be the first society in history in which children are distinctly worse off than adults." Why? Because adultism reigns. Harold Howe II says in a report to the National Association of School Psychologists, "The overwhelming fact faced by children in our country today is that they are losing ground. The self-interest of adults is moving center stage, and the interests of children are shoved toward the wings."[5] The adultist issue is especially pressing in the United States because our culture is unique in prolonging the dependency of our youth. A 1979 study found that "the average age of maturity for all urbanized, technologically advanced nations of the world other than the United States was 16 to 17 years of age. For the United States it was 24 years of age. It took eight years longer to achieve the same level of functional adulthood or maturity in the United States than in any other comparable nation on earth."[6] Yet, because so much of American culture is being exported these days, the situation of prolonged adolescent dependency that exists here may harbor a kind of advance warning to other Western cultures: Beware! Your youth too may be affected by this dependency phenomenon in the near future. An adultist society not only creates excessive dependency on the part of the young. It also dictates to these young people what their education will be as well as what jobs and housing, worship, political, and economic options will be. Where are the school boards or church boards with the youth actively engaged in defining their roles and contributions? Prolonged dependence is still another example of the devouring of our youth.

CHRISTOS OR CHRONOS?

The ancient Greeks had a god who names the devouring of youth phenomenon that is occurring in our times. Chronos (known among the Romans as Saturn) was the father of six children. He sat by his wife Rhea as she gave birth and ate each of the first five children to emerge from her womb. Chronos was the ultimate consumer. He was determined to consume all his children because he was afraid of losing his throne to one of them. Only his sixth child, Zeus, escaped the fate of his siblings because Rhea hid him from Chronos and substituted a rock wrapped in baby's clothes which Chronos swallowed in place of the child. As it turned out, Chronos eventually vomited up all his children who, after a fierce ten-year battle, overcame him.

A strong argument could be made, based on the statistics about the situation of youth in our society presented earlier, that ours is a society that worships the god Chronos. Chronos—the ultimate consumer and the ultimate waster—is the god of Western civilization, encouraging us in our consumption and waste of youth, of Mother Earth, of minorities, of imagination itself, of mysticism, of our powers of compassion, of our sexual energy, of good work. We consume and waste our prophets and our mystics. We are wasting Christ and Christianity as well. During the Vietnam War the word "waste" became a synonym for "kill." Our killing of Mother Earth is taking the form of ecocide, biocide, geocide, genocide—all of which add up today to suicide. We are involved in the last analysis, then, in wasting ourselves and in consuming ourselves. In this respect we even outdo Chronos who limited his excessive cannibalism to his own children. When we waste or kill Mother Earth we are actively engaged in eating our children. When we ignore or kill the mystic in us we are also engaged in eating the child within and killing it. When we prefer adultist games of military spending to feeding, training, and educating our children, we are choosing to kill them—and this even before we send them on battlefields to kill one another with all the weapons that adults conjure up in the name of our ideologies.

A consumer society deserves a patron saint like Chronos. For a consumer society, by offering objects one buys as the ultimate adventure to the young, is also subtly eating away at the soul of the young and its potential for great things and great visions. Chronos has been the god whom we have worshipped. But an alternative exists.

That alternative is the Cosmic Christ, Christos. Instead of consuming his children Christos loves them, and indeed, as in the Eucharist, Christos allows his children to eat him. Christos is sacrificed for his children. The Cosmic Christ has the power to flush out the Chronos syndrome of jealousy, fear, and resentment of the young and to recycle such cannibalistic consumerism into a renaissance of respect. Alice Miller asks why Jesus turned out so well—why he fulfilled his destiny so totally. Her answer is: because his father Joseph "regarded Him *as the child of God*" (italics mine). Then she poses the question: what if all parents and all adults in society "regarded our children *as children of god*?"[7] This is, after all, what Jesus came to teach persons, is it not? We are all divine sons and daughters with divine dignity and responsibilities. The Divine Father or Parent whom Jesus calls *Abba* and to whom Jesus prays is certainly not a devourer of children or a consumer at all. Jesus' parent is a lover—a lover of the sparrow that falls from the tree, a lover of the lost sheep in a herd of one hundred, a lover of the lilies of the field, a lover of the human race, and a cosmic lover of the cosmic beloved, of creation itself. "God so loved *the world* that God sent the only begotten divine son," says the Scriptures (John 3:16; emphasis mine). Perhaps one of the most radical of Jesus' messages—one that certainly contributed to his downfall and crucifixion at the hands of the adultist powers of his society—was his teaching about young people. He did not see children as objects for abuse or manipulation but as spiritual directors and sources of wisdom, as does Alice Miller when she envisions: "that someday we will regard our children not as creatures to manipulate or to change but rather as messengers from a world we once deeply knew, but which we have long since forgotten, who can reveal to us more about the true secrets of life, than our parents were ever able to."[8]

Consider the following passages in the Gospels where the Cosmic Christ incarnated in Jesus addresses the adults about their adultism.

> At that time Jesus exclaimed, "I bless you, Creator, Lord of heaven and earth, for hiding these things from the learned and the clever and revealing them to mere children [the childlike]. Yes, Parent, for that is what it pleased you to do" (Matt. 11:25–26; Luke 10:21–22).

Children of wisdom will be wiser than the learned ones of one's generation, Jesus is saying. When his disciples entered into a typical adult argument about who would be greatest among them, Jesus' answer was that "the greatest among you must behave as if he were the youngest, the leader as if he were the one who serves" (Luke 22:26). Several times Jesus calls his disciples "little ones" or children. "If anyone gives so much as a cup of cold water to one of these little ones because he is a disciple, then I tell you solemnly, he will most certainly not lose his reward" (Matt. 10:42). In Jesus' understanding there is a child in every adult and it is precisely this child who rejoices and responds to hear the Good News of the kingdom/queendom of God. Yet this child can be buried by the adult responding to the adultist demands of our society. Change of heart or *metanoia* is necessary for the child to be released.

> At this time the disciples came to Jesus and said, "Who is the greatest in the kingdom/queendom of heaven?" So he called a little child to him and set the child in front of them. Then he said, "I tell you solemnly, unless you change and become like little children you will never enter the kingdom/queendom of heaven. And so, the one who becomes as little as this little child is the greatest in the realm of heaven."
>
> (Matt. 18:1–4)

Notice how Jesus combats adultism—the quest for competitive greatness—with the lesson of the child. His disciples often acted more out of their adult selves than out of their childlike selves and for this Jesus rebuked them.

> People brought little children to him, for him to lay his hands on them and say a prayer. The disciples turned them away, but Jesus said, "Let the little children alone, and do not stop them coming to me; for it is to such as these that the kingdom/queendom of heaven belongs." Then he laid his hands on them and went on his way.
>
> (Matt. 19:13–15)

We are not asked to tolerate the young in this context but to understand that it is to them that the royal realm of heaven belongs. They are prophets, bearers of divine wisdom. A large part of the scandal of the Jesus story lies in the mystery of the incarnation of the Cosmic Christ in Jesus: the Cosmic Christ was a child and subject to growing "in wisdom and grace" (Luke: 2:52). Yet, the divine presence and the cosmological glory is celebrated at the birth events of this child. Simeon saw this in the child Jesus and remarks to Mary his mother, "You see this child: he is destined for the fall and for the rising of many in Israel, destined to be a sign that is rejected" (Luke 2:34–35). Jesus himself never lost his childlikeness and the relationship of awe and wonder to creation and Creator (whom he addressed as *Abba*, or "Papa"). The child in him is evident in all his parables and is part of his prophetic personality and work.

The Cosmic Christ who represents the youthfulness of God and of the

Divine Spirit, who "makes all of creation new" (Rev. 20:5), who became incarnated in Jesus and wants to become ever more incarnated in us, is biased in favor of the youth. Far from consuming the young, this God blesses the young; employs the young as examples of wisdom for their elders; insists on his disciples reclaiming the spirit of youth; and teaches persons how to be young like God is. A clear option is set up between the spirit of Chronos and the spirit of Christos.

PUER AND SENEX—THE PUER AS PROPHET TO A TIRED CIVILIZATION

Another name for the god Chronos is "Senex," which is the archetype of the senator, the wise old man. In tension with the Senex is the "Puer" archetype, the child, the youth, the mystic within us all. In a healthy psyche and culture both Senex and Puer operate together. In our culture— and I suspect in many of our psyches—Senex and Puer are at odds and when this happens we display, instead of a happy polarity of youth and age, negative aspects of each. A generation gap becomes a generation chasm that operates within the psyche and extends outwards into our social institutions, rendering them ageist and dualistic. Psychologist James Hillman writes that "the negative senex is the senex split from its own puer aspect. He has lost his 'child.' "[9] In other words, the negative senex is the person or culture that has lost the mystic within. Having repressed the child within, such a senex is a Chronos who wants to consume youth and creativity out of envy and repressed youthfulness. Hillman believes that cynicism and tyranny result from the loss of the child within the senex.

> Without the enthusiasm and eros of the son, authority loses its idealism. It aspires to nothing but its own perpetuation, leading but to tyranny and cynicism; for *meaning cannot be sustained by structure and order alone.* . . . The old is always preferred to the new. Sexuality without young eros becomes goaty; weakness becomes complaints; creative isolation only paranoid loneliness. . . . Cut off from its own child and fool the complex no longer has anything to tell us. Folly and immaturity are projected onto others. Without folly it has no wisdom, only knowledge—serious, depressing, hoarded in an academic vault or used as power.[10]

Aspects of the senex are present in all of us even as children. But negatively, the senex engages in a dryness and coldness that comes about from the "absent feminine."[11] I find Hillman describing with painful accuracy many of the cultural and religious institutions of our time.

What are some positive aspects of senex? The ability to "go back," Hillman believes, is intrinsic to a time of renaissance or rebirth. When a culture is lost, it needs to return—as happened in the sixteenth-century Renaissance. "This is a move made by artists, by thinkers, by cultures, the move of going back so that one stands somewhere." In the twelfth-century Renaissance also the driving force was a return to the biblical sources—what kind of poverty did Jesus live was the hottest question of the time. What a healthy senex offers a tired culture or a negatively puer culture is "the old eye, the call of the old, and it may be the essential eye. . . . Distance, depth, and essence are given by the old. . . . The old doesn't belong to the senex in some sterile dusty way." The issue is one of getting to the essential images of living and the living archetypes of our consciousness in order to revivify both. Negative senex renders history a "big burden . . . a statue in the park for pigeons." In contrast, healthy senex offers wisdom and a tradition that has the power to inform what we do and feel. This senex is pictured as the old wise man, the old whale, the old ape. But healthy senex requires a healthy puer partner, since without puer the senex becomes "soulless concretism"—power with no anima overtones.[12]

The rise of "puer power" will prove to be an essential prophetic gift to a senex civilization provided, of course, that that puer power is balanced itself by a healthy senex. What constitutes the essential gift of senex to puer? A healthy senex is in touch with living traditions and stories of the past that have significance to the emerging story of the present. For example, a healthy senex contribution would be a living knowledge, heart as well as head, of the mystical tradition of the West and a capacity to pass on the stories of cosmology and the search for cosmology that have been a rich tradition of Western religion. Just as the senex knows the allies to today's puer needs for a living cosmology, the senex also knows the enemies from the past and the battles that have been waged and often lost on behalf of the Cosmic Christ. It is important to recognize, for example, that Kant and Descartes, Newton and Augustine, had no place for a Cosmic Christology in their philosophy. Puers have trouble making distinctions and therefore in making commitments. The puer needs to feel the struggle and to develop the strength to undertake it. A healthy puer needs a developing senex within in order to make commitments based on realities of history to balance a well-developed sense of mystery. The puer needs to know the limits of the quest for the historical Jesus and how this Enlightenment agenda has so dominated the most recent religious epoch and has systematically ignored the Creator and creation, a Cosmic Christ, the spirit, creativity and mysticism.

It is important that these and many other stories be told to the puer from the tradition that the senex ought to hold dear, for with them the puer is armed for the adult struggle of responsibility and commitment (of facing the enemy within and without) that constitutes the authentic adventure to which the puer so longs to surrender. The puer's sense of mystery and living in the "now" seeks a balance from the senex' gift of history and storytelling based on those adventures from persons of the past who also gave themselves to the "now" of their times. The history of the communion of saints, of theological inquiry which attempts to reclaim the Cosmic Christ, of spirituality understood as the experience of both mysticism and prophecy—all these are gifts from senex to puer. As puer assimilates them, puer moves from child to adult-with-child. The puer grows up but need not lose the power of being puer. Quite the opposite, such a puer, steeped in knowledge of the past, is grounded and prepared for the adventures of the future.

And adventures there will be, for part of the shared sickness of a one-sided puer and a one-sided senex is that both ignore the future: the senex, because he feels all that is important has already happened in the past and because his tired state disempowers him to imagine contributing to a living future; and the puer because he lives only in the "now." But a healthy senex also gifts the puer with an awareness of eschatology—of how history is not only the glory of the past but also the urgency of the future. All the power we amass as mystics and as citizens in a living cosmology is meant to bless future generations, future puers who will in turn grow up to be healthy adults with both puer and senex alive in them. A healthy senex is passionate about the future that needs to be born from responsibility and commitment and aroused vision. That is why the prophet Joel promised that on the healthy day, "the young shall see visions and the old shall dream dreams" (Joel 2:28). Together puer and senex bring about a New Creation. Yet this birthing cannot occur without roots in the living tradition of the past (senex) as well as the daring, challenging, joyful, visionary dreams of the present (puer). Puer and senex are destined to awaken hope to the extent that they excite one another eschatologically, i.e., with the possibility that there *is* a future; that the future lies as near as the open heart and the hands willing to commit themselves to bringing about a new future. Poet and symbolist Juan Eduardo Cirlot speaks of the puer archetype as

a symbol of the future, as opposed to the old man who signifies the past; but the child is also symbolic of that stage of life when the old man, transformed, acquires a new simplicity. . . . Hence the conception of the child as symbolic of the "mystic Centre" and as the "youthful, re-awakening force." . . . Psychologically speaking, the child is of the soul—the product of the *coniunctio* between the unconscious and consciousness: one dreams of a child when some great spiritual change is about to take place under favorable circumstances.[15]

Is it little wonder that St. Benedict, in his monastic rule advised monks always to listen to the youngest of the community first, since the Holy Spirit was nearest to them?[14] If the senex would take seriously the deep contribution of the puer and the deep yearning of the puer within the senex to be reborn, then the youth and mystic in the adult would indeed be born. The result would be that the repression of youth that expresses itself in such violent projections onto the young would cease. The slaughter of the innocents—in war and preparations for war, in unemployment and lack of education, in suicide and despair, in being alienated from and in trivializing tradition—might cease. Finally, the birthing required by a marriage of senex and puer might finally begin to happen. The puer and senex do not gift one another from outside-in. Rather, each educes from the other the latent element that has been sleeping there: in the puer there lurks a senex waiting to be born; in the senex there lurks a puer eager to be released. This mutual education, this common eduction from inside-out, this art as meditation, is the essential gift that each bestows on the other.

Given Hillman's reflections on the nature of healthy and negative senex, it seems appropriate to suggest that a certain amount of our cultural life today—religion included—is swamped in negative senex power. This should come as no surprise, since the mystical or puer element is so rare, as we discussed in part II. But the key to health, Hillman believes, is the coming together of the two: "The two, senex and puer, have to appear together. You can't have one without the other somewhere near."[15] This coming together of parent and child, senex and puer, is explicitly accomplished in the Cosmic Christ as represented by Jesus who so often speaks of how "the Creator and I are one." And "I do the works of the Father" (John 5:36). Perhaps Christians who have used such texts to demonstrate apologetically how Jesus is like God have missed the point—the point is how child and parent, puer and senex *together form the divine dynamism.* Indeed, this would seem to be the deep meaning behind the trinitarian doctrine in Christianity: only a relationship of mutuality between the Parent and the Child, i.e., the senex and the puer, truly births the Spirit. The Spirit cannot and never will be birthed by senex (the Parent) alone. Nor will it be birthed by puer (the Child) alone. Only senex and puer, Parent and Child, can truly enspirit the world.

Of the two, Parent and Child, senex and puer, it is important that the Cosmic Christ became incarnate *as Child.* Why? Might it be because the puer factor, the youth factor, was most lost in religion and the human psyche during the deep patriarchal period of Hellenism, the Roman Empire, and Judaism of the first century A.D.? The Cosmic Christ draws needed attention to the puer dimension in psyche and history if the Spirit is to be born. "A little child shall lead them," the prophet Isaiah foretold, a "prince of peace, a comforter, a healer, a child of God" (Isa. 11:7)—a mystic child who is a royal person of the house of David. "Wisdom," the Scriptures teach us, "gave speech to the tongues of babes" (Wis. 10:21). Christianity, then, in its most basic tradition, celebrates the puer in a unique way. It is meant to be a religion of youth, a religion to bring back youth, a religion to birth youth, to birth the divine child who is the Cosmic Christ—a religion of resurrection. To resurrect is one of the special gifts of puer. "Puer resurrects because resurrection in the psyche *is* puer. Always there is something incipient, some new theme or movement, and that beginning is itself psyche's puer."[16] If God is always "in the beginning," as Eckhart has said, then God is uniquely indebted to and expressive of puer.

What are some other dimensions to the puer in both its negative and positive aspects? Jungian analyst Marie-Louise von Franz writes that the puer is meant to be "a symbol of renewal and of the total inner man for whom the neurotic pueri aeterni of our days are unknowingly searching." Such a puer possesses the power to renew a senex civilization, one that is characterized by a "worn-out image of God and world order." The reclamation of the Cosmic Christ can restore a truly living cosmology which will give us newer, more powerful and more life-giving images for God and our world. After all, to be a child is to be in awe and in wonder. The child is "fully alive" because "the child has a naive view of life, and if you recall your own childhood, you remember you were intensely alive. The child . . . is constantly interested in something." Vitality is key to the child's world. Von Franz asks: "How can one pull out of this fantasy life of youth and youthfulness without losing its value? How can one grow up without losing the feeling of totality and the feeling of creativeness and of being really alive, which one had in youth? . . . How can one grow up and not lose it?"[17]

Von Franz believes that an unhealthy or one-sided puer lives in an utter world of complete fantasy and that disillusionment and cynicism await such a person. Hillman comments that the "high-flying, fire-eating puer" ought to be allowed to feel "inferior and moody and confused" and "a little lonely and outcast and misunderstood like the senex," if it is to make healthy contact with the senex.[18] Von Franz accepts that there is a need to revolt and to assert individuality on the part of the puer and the expression of this revolt can be either constructive or destructive. There is also the call to play and to unite disparate parts, to make connections. In this regard the puer is like the creative personality[19] (the artist has been defined by Baudelaire as "one who can recover childhood at will").[20]

When the puer loses its balanced connection to senex it becomes fanatical. The puer has a kind of "wanderlust," an attitude of "don't fence me in." The puer struggles with responsibility, with living beyond just the "now," with remaining grounded on the earth. The archetype of a one-sided puer is Icarus who flew too near to the sun and paid the consequences by falling violently to earth. A negative puer may express itself in hyperactive ways or in ways of passive withdrawal. Though the puer does not age, neither does it develop or mature—it learns nothing because it concentrates only on the present. It is easily tempted by narcissism because it boasts a certain self-containment and self-perfection. Hillman maintains "the puer never learns with time and repetition: he resists development and is always unique. No precedents, no past— that's how it feels to him." A negative puer will despise the past as old and forlorn. Hillman believes that American culture displays deep aspects of this unhealthy onesidedness, that ours is a culture that is preoccupied only with "what is immediately topical. America is a complete immersion in what is happening; it's a Now-culture, utterly Now." One way out of excessive "nowness" is myth or history—qualities that senex brings. History provides a gestalt background to the present events. "Historical references, figures from the past release the foreground event from being stuck in only what it says it is."[21]

One might say, then, that our culture and its institutions simultaneously suffer very often from the worst elements of puer and senex. Lacking a healthy puer we cannot support a healthy senex. The result is cynicism, pessimism, dualism between generations, and a paralysis of imagination and creativity. Just as the Spirit is born of a healthy puer/ senex alignment, so too all creativity is born of this marriage of new and old, foreground and background. Is it little wonder, then, that a healthy puer shoulders a profoundly prophetic calling in our civilization? Without the healthy puer resurrected and rediscovered the Cosmic Christ, who binds healthy senex and puer together, is stillborn. With a healthy puer the senex can be rendered healthy and alive, "green and juicy" as Hildegard of Bingen says. Renaissance and rebirth can happen psychically and culturally. Hillman himself speaks of the prophetic call of the puer in our time when he says, "the 'puer problem' of today is not only a collective neurosis; it is a psychic expression of an historical claim, and as such is a call."[22]

One of the prophetic contributions made by a realigned puer/senex relationship has to do with the father/son struggle in our culture. It is rare to find sound and invigorating father/son relationships among middle-aged persons in our culture. Many male liberation groups discover this when men begin sharing their stories. Much healing takes place when somehow the puer/senex tension can be laid to rest between generations. Hillman believes that this tension of senex and puer, father and son (in my words, Chronos and Christos), lies "at the heart of our culture."[23] Freud agrees. The truth is that father needs son, senex need puer, puer needs senex. What is needed is son and puer within, not just the puer outside, but a puer outside who arouses and awakens the slumbering and often forgotten puer on the inside. The mystic comes alive. The Cosmic Christ is reborn just as Eckhart predicted when he said "we are all meant to be mothers of God" (BR, 329).

Another prophetic demand the puer makes on a tired culture or religion is the demand for adventure. Without the puer alive in us, Hillman points out, "there would be no spiritual drive, no new sparks, no going beyond the given, no grandeur and sense of personal destiny." In fact, Hillman continues, those psychoanalysts who reduce the puer to a psychological complex in the puer spirit "would thus deny the puer's legitimate ambition and art of flying" because the one "who cannot fly cannot imagine."[24] Another prophetic contribution of the puer is the connection of past and present. As Hillman puts it, "our other half is not only of the same sex. The union of opposites—male with female—is not the only union for which we long and is not the only union which redeems. There is also the union of the sames, the re-union of the vertical axis which would heal the split spirit."[25] The father/son split is at heart a split between sames which demands healing.

Who has not tasted this bitter struggle between past and present, old and new, authority and youth, in our times? Who has not been victimized directly or indirectly by the inability of our race to deal with fanaticism on the one hand (the negative puer) or tired complacency on the other (the negative senex)? Who could say that religion itself has not succumbed repeatedly to killing the puer, that is, to crucifying the Christ all over again? How many times must the Christ be crucified before people and religions themselves will resurrect puer power? The crucifixion event redeems because it forgives the killer child who would kill even God's child. "Father forgive them, they know not what they do" (Luke 23:24). The wounded child (puer) in each of us is healed insofar as the Creator (senex) is linked with the divine child once again. This is one more instance of the prophetic work of Jesus in carrying out the destiny of the pattern that connects. Truly the Cosmic Christ, who is the "pattern that connects" will usher in an age of puer/senex connection. Then the dynamics of mutuality between old and young in this age will be more balanced, and the wisdom of the young will be welcomed and valued.

While writing this book I received a letter from a five-year-old child. He tells me that "there are four kinds of beans—green beans, pork and beans, jelly beans, and human beings. Human beings are special." "Why are human beings special?" he was asked. He replied, "People eat green beans, jelly beans, and pork and beans and God eats human beings. God likes us and eats us. We become part of God and live in God's belly all our life. . . . God's belly is the whole earth." "Where did you get these ideas?" he was asked. "From inside myself," he replied. It is good to know that panentheism is alive and well in the minds and imaginations of our children, even if it has only begun to penetrate the minds of many of our theologians and clergy. In a kindergarten class in Colorado, children were asked to draw a picture of Jesus. They all obliged but only one six-year-old girl drew a picture different from the bearded figure all the other students drew. She drew a picture of herself. Her teacher explained to me that she responded almost indignantly, but held back and gave the incident some thought. When she heard me lecture on the Cosmic Christ she understood what the six-year-old was saying. The puer are working overtime in our society today. We need to listen because the divine child may be lurking within them—or any of us. This is the tradition of the creation-centered mystics who always recognized the Cosmic Christ in the child.

THE MYSTICAL CONTRIBUTION TO AWAKENING THE PUER. Adultism is caused by adults. It is caused by that aspect of the adult that kills the child inside who is the mystic. Alice Miller observes that this suppression of the child in the adult

> permeate[s] so many areas of our life that we hardly notice it anymore. Almost everywhere we find the effort, marked by varying degrees of intensity and by the use of various coercive measures, to rid ourselves as quickly as possible of the child within us . . . in order to become an independent, competent adult deserving of respect.[26]

The creation mystics can shed some light on the puer/senex discussion, for mystics are adults who welcome the child inside them. Mechtild of Magdeburg writes:

> God leads the child God has called in wonderful ways. God takes the soul to a secret place, for God alone will play with it in a game of which the body knows nothing. God says: "I am your playmate! Your childhood was a companion of my Holy Spirit."

> (MM, 54)

And again:

> I, God, am your playmate! I will lead the child in you in wonderful ways for I have chosen you. Beloved child, come swiftly to Me, for I am truly in you. Remember this: The smallest soul of all is still the daughter of the Creator, the sister of the Son, the friend of the Holy Spirit and the true bride of the Holy Trinity.

> (MM, 47)

Julian of Norwich also understands the divine child in all of us: "I understand no higher state in this life than childhood" (JN, 119). Julian admonishes people who "foolishly dwell on their sinfulness" and reminds them that "God joyfully calls saying: 'Let all your love be, my child, turn to me. I am everything you need' " (JN, 62). The reader will recall that in the Song of Songs, which we considered in the previous chapter, the lovers appeal to the young who understand the pain and the ecstasy of love. The woman trusts the young to understand her love and she entrusts her deepest images of her beloved with them, making herself deeply vulnerable in the process. Among the young she knows her love will not be mocked or laughed at. The man also speaks to the young as being able to grasp the beauty of his beloved. Clearly the puer is celebrated in these mystical texts as the companion of love and of beauty, of play and of renewal, of creativity and of the divine presence.

Meister Eckhart's legend about encountering God while encountering puer depicted divinity as a beautiful, naked boy.

MEISTER ECKHART AND THE NAKED BOY

Meister Eckhart met a beautiful, naked boy.
He asked him where he came from.
He said: "I come from God."
Where did you leave him?
"In pure hearts."
Where are you going?
"To God."
Where do you find God?
"Where I let go of all creatures."
Who are you?
"A King."
Where is your kingdom?
"In my heart."
Be careful that no one take it from you.
"I shall."
Then he led him to his cell and said to him: Take whatever jacket you
would like.
"Then I would be no king!"
And he disappeared.
For it was God who had been amusing the divine self at Eckhart's
expense.[27]

Notice that the divine puer in this story is naked and beautiful; is a king
who goes from God and to God; whose kingdom is the heart itself; who is
capable of letting go of all creatures and is possessing nothing (no clothes)
yet in possession of all things (otherwise he would be no king). And notice
too how the naked divine child plays games with Eckhart. There is a hint
in this legend of the "emperor with no clothes" story as well.

Elsewhere, Eckhart develops the puer side to God and us at still greater length and depth. He declares: "I am younger today than I was yester-
day and if I am not younger tomorrow than I am today I would be
ashamed of myself" and further, "when we say God is eternal we mean
God is eternally young" (ME, 32). He is fond of citing the psalmist who
promised that "your youth will be renewed like the eagle's." Eckhart is
acknowledging puer power when he defines mysticism as "unselfcon-
ciousness" and as a "return to our origins." Our origins are the wellsprings where we are revigorated with puer power. Eckhart's insistence
that we learn to "live without a why, love without a why and work without a why" is also an affirmation of play which is always "without a why"
and therefore another instance of the necessity and indeed prophetic
contribution of puer power (BR, 472–475). This puer power is also part
of how we experience the eternal now even in this lifetime. Eckhart
writes, "What is eternity? Pay attention. Eternity is the peculiarity that
being and being young are one" (BR, 111). He continues by saying God
always creates in the present. The act of creation does not fade into the

past but is always in the beginning and in process and new" (BR, 111). Here Eckhart is promising puer power as a fruit of our being near God. He teaches that newness is the first gift of the Spirit. Our contact with God makes us new. "By ascending to God, by drawing near to God, by running back to God, by returning to God—all things are made new, all things become good, are purged, cleansed, made holy. On the other hand, by receding from God they grow old, they perish, they sin as Paul says: 'The wages of sin are death' " (Rom. 6:23) (BR, 112).

Eckhart is saying that negative senex comes from distancing ourselves from the beginning, from God. This is sin and death. Eckhart talks of how we return to a state of being "unborn" and reexperience our preexistence (BR, 213–225). This is truly Cosmic-Christ-as-puer imagery.

Eckhart equates the puer with the "inward person" dwelling in this eternally fresh and new "now." Eckhart maintains "the outward person is the old person, the earthly person, the person of this world, who grows old 'from day to day.' His end is death. . . . The inward person on the other hand, is the new person, the heavenly person, in whom God shines" (BR, 71). He goes on to say that "the inward person is not at all in time or place but is purely and simply in eternity. It is there that God arises, . . . [and] is heard, there God is; there God, and God alone, speaks" (BR, 71). What does God speak? God speaks the word of the Cosmic Christ, who is the "pattern that connects" all and is "all in all." Furthermore, in Eckhart's theology we are the puer of God, we are truly God's sons and daughters, images of the childhood of divinity: "The Father bears his Son in the soul in the same way that he bears him in eternity, not in any other way" (BR, 310).

Eckhart derives much of his celebration of ourselves as the puer of God from the Scriptures: "Think of the love that the Creator has lavished on us, by letting us be called God's children; and that is what we are" (1 John 3:1). The divine puer depends on us for its continual birth into history—that is Eckhart's refreshing teaching on the role of the youthful Cosmic Christ. What a renaissance would occur if the West, beginning with its religious traditions, were to return to this ancient teaching of puer power as spiritual power that we find in creation mystics in the Scriptures and throughout history.

Much life and energy, money and opportunity is squandered among adults who grow addicted to drugs, alcohol, eating, shopping, or almost anything because they have lost their puer and do not know how to play. The Church has not instilled healthy puer either in its children or its adults. The Cosmic Christ will need to instruct humans in play again. Both psyche and culture, young and old, need awakening to the power of healthy puer and senex. It will take a divinely endowed "pattern that connects" to connect the divine child, the godly puer, to our psyches and our institutions once again. When this happens an authentic renaissance will truly be on its way.

THE COSMIC CHRIST SPEAKS ON YOUTH

The Cosmic Christ speaks "I am eternal youth. I am always young, always new, always fresh, always eager, always in the beginning. Why aren't you? The beginning is not in opposition to the past, it fulfills it, complements it, invigorates it. I am also the past made fresh and new, powerful and exciting. Bring these parts together—the new and the past—in your present "now." Look about you at those who are actively doing this. Consider the young. Be like them—awestruck and wonder-filled, enthusiastic (meaning full of divine energy). Do not confuse *childlike* and *childish*. Be childlike—as I am, but not childish, which is indeed something to outgrow. The childish person has no roots, no sense of the past, no respect for the future and one's responsibility to birth it. Living in the "now" does not mean you remain ignorant of the past or oblivious of the future—it means you bring past and future, old and young, together in you. Now. This is always renaissance, new birth, deep vision, new energy. Expect divinity to appear and reappear as a child. Expect it in yourselves. Adults should not envy the youth or neglect them or project resentment onto them and burden them with debts, scorched earth, scarce waters, devastated forests, dwindling species, despoiled beauty, fossilized institutions. Attend to the youth in yourself and you will heal your relationships with the young and with the generations still unborn. To the young I say: bear your wisdom within you. Nurture it in one another. Start your own culture. Do not depend overmuch on adults but seek out allies among them who can pass on wisdom from living traditions of the past. Learn to be adult. Learn both history and mystery, commitment and hard work. And always play, play, play. Stay young. Like me."

Perhaps it is time that our institutions, so indebted to a senex spirit, pay more attention to the puer spirit potential within them. Perhaps it is time, for example, to ordain young people *while they are young*—young in spirit and in age. The young might communicate with the young and lead them. Spiritual leaders should emerge from the community they are serving. What would happen if churches were to ordain the young with a minimum of academic seminary training but with a grounding in the spirituality and mysticism of the Cosmic Christ? Perhaps the young persons these priests and ministers served would in turn get excited about the adventure the Cosmic Christ extends to the young. The result might be an upcoming generation that, instead of being ignorant, indifferent, and cynical about religion, might prove to be leaders in the renaissance that Mother Earth needs. "For Wisdom opened the mouths of the dumb/and gave speech to the tongues of babes" (Wis. 10:21).

27. The Cosmic Christ and Creativity— The Return of the Personal Arts

The Cosmic Christ will usher in an era of renewed folk art, of the awakening of the divine powers of creativity in all persons. There is no renaissance without a vast outburst of creativity—new images, new risk taking, new relationships, new dreams and visions. As Einstein put it, "the whole purpose of science *and art* is to awaken the cosmic religious feeling."[1] Another name for the cosmic religious feeling is *reverence*. The word "reverence" comes from a root word meaning to show fear or to exhibit respect based on awe. Reverence is one's response to an *awesome* experience. Reverence is integral to a cosmological spirituality in which awe names the mystical experience known as the *via positiva*, the first of the four paths of Creation Spirituality. A morality of reverence will also be a morality of responsibility—not a responsibility based on duty and fear of disobedience but a responsibility based on *care for what we cherish and revere*.

AWAKENING THE ARTIST

The artist's task is awakening awe and providing vehicles of expression so that we can express our awe and wonder at existence. There is an artist in each one of us, and so the artist's task belongs to us all. Sharing our experiences of awe will lead to an experience of reverence. We will reform our moralities grounded in reverence rather than in precept. Reverence will become the test of our moralities: is what I am doing, are the choices we are making, reverential to others—to Mother Earth, to generations of humans to come, to the particular individuals with whom I am currently interacting, to our non-two-legged brothers and sisters with whom we share Mother Earth? Reverence can only grow out of a living cosmology. It can only find a home in our instincts and images, our psyches and bodies, and thereby in our institutions with the help of the artist who sings it there, who dances it there, who writes poetry or tells stories about it there, and who colors it and molds it there. The task of the artist is to excite humans to reverence all that is precious and meaningful in life. The Cosmic Christ, by awakening the artist, ushers in an age that excites young and old alike to reverence.

FOLK AND PERSONAL ARTS AND THE REINVENTION OF THE HUMAN

We have spoken of the new wineskins and the new paradigm that the Cosmic Christ announces. Thomas Berry talks of the need to "reinvent the human species" with a worldview and a moral commitment to Mother Earth and her nonhuman children that is no less a leap than the invention of consciousness by our planet millions of years ago. Surely the task of "reinventing the human" requires a vast awakening of creativity. But what does it mean to "reinvent the human?" I believe this reinvention will happen primarily in our imaginations with the gifts of our imaginations and our powers of imaging. It will happen when art becomes truly *folk* art once again, when all people wake up to their powers and responsibilities for creativity. This awakening to the power of folk art will be eminently local; it will find expression in neighborhoods and communities, in work places and schools, in churches and synagogues, in families and in homes where singles dwell. It will happen within individuals themselves as they take more responsibility for birthing their own personalities, lifestyles, relationships, and citizenship.

Otto Rank prophesies that an era of deep political, economic, and religious change will demand "new personality types." Rank is speaking of the responsibility we all share to birth our personalities and the basic relationships of our lives in fresh ways. He warns professional artists that they are in no way exempt from this responsibility to put their energy into the everyday arts, or what I refer to as the "personal arts." He writes:

> The new type of humanity . . . must grow out of those artists themselves who have achieved a renunciant attitude towards artistic production. A man with creative power who can give up artistic expression in favour of the formation of personality . . . will remould the self-creative type and will be able to put his creative impulse *directly* in the service of his own personality. . . . The creative type who can renounce this protection by art and can devote his whole creative force to life and the formation of life will be the first representative of the new human type.[2]

What are the personal arts that we all need to start birthing anew? They include the art of friendship, the art of making beauty where we dwell, the art of conversation, of massage, of laughter, of preparing food, of hospitality, of the sharing of ideas, of growing food and flowers, of singing songs, of making love, of telling stories, of uniting generations, of putting on skits, of satirizing human folly. The personal arts include the arts of listening and of healing, of enjoying oneself with others in simple ways; the art of creating our lifestyles and our communities; the art of conviviality; the art of parenting and of forgiving. These personal arts are, I propose, what constitute the "formation of personality" which Rank insists will usher in "the new human type." More and more prophets, puer and senex alike, are committing themselves to these personal arts. As they make this commitment more fully they will indeed begin to birth that "new personality type" Rank feels must necessarily accompany a renaissance or new spiritual era.

In recovering the personal arts we will be recovering folk art and redeeming art from the elitism it has acquired during the patriarchal era. As Erich Fromm observed, the artist has become a specialized profession in Western civilization. "We have no word," he points out, for the art of ritual, or folk dance, or community singing, "because art in a wide and general sense, as a part of everybody's life, has lost its place in our world."[3] Zen poet Kenji Miyazawa, who laments the professionalizing of the title "artist," defines the artist as "one who is free to let his or her inner mind speak to him or her."[4] Releasing the "inner mind" is what this new art will do.

This awakening of the inner mind will not be satisfied with personal expression alone. Its power will find its true fulfillment in returning the social arts of politics and economics to the folk. When this happens politics will no longer be defined in the tired, pessimistic, and negatively senex manner as "the art of compromise" but as the *art of expression of the people's will and needs*. Politics will itself become the art of the people, the art of preserving and celebrating Mother Earth, the art of doing justice and keeping balance and harmony. Economics will become the *art of planetary management*, the art of living harmoniously within the necessary limits that the goods of the earth set for us, the art of common survival wherein all of creation and its immense wealth—which is its health—is celebrated in balance and harmony. In this context, then, the arts of politics and economics can be expressions of shared reverence for our shared existence.

PLAY, CREATIVITY, AND THE COMIC CHRIST

Clearly the Cosmic Christ will have to be reincarnated many times in persons' minds and imaginations for this creativity to take charge in human history. Co-creation will be important for understanding our role of creativity in light of that of the Creator. A mutuality is presumed in the term *co*-creation. Divinity and we are co-creators, equally responsible one might say, for the survival of Mother Earth and for the kinds of personalities, relationships, lifestyles, politics, and economics that we birth. A co-creator is one who births the mystic self or allows it to be born. In allowing the "true self" or mystic to be born one is already involved in a deep process of birthing the Cosmic Christ. In allowing one's authentic awe and wonder to be born again and in welcoming the puer, the child and playfulness, to come to self-expression one is already involved in co-creation. For there is no creation without play. The Cosmic Christ is a *comic* Christ with a universal sense of humor. Carl Jung celebrates the necessary connection between play and creativity when he writes:

> Every creative individual whatsoever owes all that is greatest in his life to fantasy. The dynamic principle of fantasy is play, a characteristic also of the child. . . . Without this playing with fantasy no creative work has ever yet come to birth.

The creation of something new is not accomplished by the intellect but by the play instinct acting from inner necessity. The creative mind plays with the objects it loves. . . . The creative activity of the imagination frees man from his bondage to the "nothing but" and raises him to the status of one who plays. As Schiller says, man is completely human only when he is at play.[5]

An explosion of creativity will constitute a revelation of the Cosmic Christ at play, "at play everywhere in the world, delighting to be with the sons and daughters of the human race" (Prov. 8:30–31). True reverence is more about play than it is about pious noddings of the head. For play is our response to *feeling* that we are part of a living and dynamic whole. We are players in the universe, actors and actresses on a cosmic stage in a twenty-billion-year-old awesome unfolding display of creation and generativity. Our play is not only prayer and art as meditation, it is also the expression of our role in the universe—it is a revelation of *dis*play of the unique image of God, that unique "I am" that is our unique way of being in the world. Each of us displays a different aspect of the divine face, divine humor, and divine hands by the ways we choose to live out our spirituality and our lives. Our co-creation is a display and revelation of the divine essence.

THE VIRTUE OF CREATIVITY

The living cosmology ushered in by the Cosmic Christ will do more than redeem creativity itself; it will propose creativity as a moral virtue—indeed as *the most important moral virtue of the upcoming civilization.* During the Newtonian era obedience became the most important moral category: if we live in a machine universe, then our primary task is to obey the machine. The doctrine of obedience fit well the patriarchal impulses to control and be controlled that have characterized so much in society and religion during the Newtonian era. The Spirit of the Cosmic Christ will call upon an era of creativity to displace the era of mechanistic obedience.

The word "virtue" comes from the Latin word for "manly excellence" and the old French word for strength, virility or power. Creativity is the most neglected and most needed power today. Creativity constitutes a redefinition of the word "power" that has been so abused in the patriarchal era. Creativity is the source of empowerment in an era of the Cosmic Christ. Not only every individual but each of our institutions—religious, educational, political, economic—will need to acknowledge and embrace creativity as the fundamental law of the universe because we know that from the first instant of the original fireball the whole universe has been constantly generating. Creativity is the fundamental law of the human psyche which constitutes a microcosm of the universe. In beginning to imitate the law of the universe, human communities and social institutions will need to reinstate creativity at their core. Wisely does scientist Erich Jantsch, reflecting on the dynamic creativity so intrinsic to the laws of the universe, urge humankind to move from an excessive preoccupation with individual "rights" to the moral demands of responsibility—especially the responsibility to create.

> There is so much talk of rights, of basic human rights as well as of rights of particular groups, minorities, privileged and underprivileged people— and almost never of responsibility. . . . Rights constitute a static and defensive, structure-oriented concept, whereas *the acceptance of responsibility implies creative participation in the design of the human world.* The ethics which dominates in the Western world is therefore an individualistic ethics in the guise of a socially committing behavioural code. It is not a multilevel ethics in the true sense.[6]

I believe that Jantsch is calling for a renewed *devotion* to creativity and the responsibility inherent in creativity, the basis of a renewed morality. Our dualistic culture has reduced the word "devotion" to the level of pious sentiment. Yet the term "devotion" comes from the Latin meaning to "make a vow," to "devote oneself fully to." If communities of citizens today were to devote themselves fully to encouraging one another's creativity at all levels of living, educating, and healing, we would indeed embark on a renaissance of vast proportions. Religion itself would be the first recipient of the new spiritual energy since the virtue known as devotion constitutes the basis of healthy religion.

CREATIVITY—A VOW FOR THE NEW SPIRITUAL ERA

In the Renaissance of the Middle Ages, poverty became the ruling virtue of the new civilization. Francis of Assisi took up this mythological love of "Dame Poverty" and incarnated her as the foundation of his new order. The vow of poverty understood as a commitment to a new social and economic order—one that was neither the feudalism of the outgoing paradigm nor the rapacious capitalism of the new order—became the rallying cry of the movements committed to a new world order. Battles were waged in the streets as well as in the Vatican over whether Jesus had been "poor" in the sense of the meaning behind the new vow of poverty.

I propose that just as Dame Poverty represented the fundamental virtue of the new society and a commitment to a new vision in the Renaissance of Francis's day, so today the prime virtue is creativity. We need a new vow (one not limited to members of Roman Catholic religious orders), a new "mystic bride" or groom to which people can devote themselves, to which they can surrender their immense gifts. I am speaking of a promise to creativity itself: a promise to remain creative, to endure creativity, to commit ourselves to it as individuals and communities, and to support one another in solidarity to it. This encouragement, this mutual

204 / THE COMING OF THE COSMIC CHRIST

building up of courage for creativity must occur at the level of personality, personal relationships, and the personal arts as well as at the level of politics and economics on a global scale. Mahatma Gandhi put such emphasis on the taking of vows that he felt that there could be no purification of politics or transformation of society without it. "He believed that a life without vows is like a ship without an anchor or like an edifice built on sand instead of rock. A vow is a deliberate commitment to a moral principle."[7] Today that moral principle needs to be creativity itself.

Behind all creativity there lies not just a tolerance for diversity but a reverence for it, a passionate need for it. Those who willingly take a vow of creativity will be the leaders in revitalized lifestyles, education, religion, politics and economics as they midwife the Cosmic Christ yearning to be born anew. Artist and mystic Peter Rogers, in his beautiful book, *A Painter's Quest*, comes to the conclusion that Jesus' teaching to "love God with your whole heart and soul and your neighbor as yourself" (Matt. 22:36–39) represents the ultimate artistic truth: that there is no artist who does not deal both at the cosmic level—which is God—*and* at the level of detail—which is one's "neighbor." Rogers says, "the broader our perspective, the closer we come to loving God; the greater our attention to detail the closer we come to loving our neighbor." This is a truth all artists have experienced—among them Jesus himself. Rogers writes:

> Artists know from continual experience that this dual focus works and, furthermore, that it is the only sort of focus that does work. They rely on this focus every time they put brush to canvas, and know that without it they are lost. Similarly, Christ's two commandments are not a question of ethics, they are pure pragmatism.[8]

True creativity, Rogers is saying, combines the local and the cosmic. By his incarnation in the artist/parable-teller Jesus Christ, the Cosmic Christ celebrated the spiritual way of the artist and underscored the theme of love of God/love of neighbor. A vow of creativity would bring together the local need for grounding and incarnation with the cosmic need for breadth and space. It would connect time and space along with old and new, senex and puer, male and female, North and South, rich and poor. It would be fulfilling those two commandments of Jesus—to love God and neighbor—which are the fulfillment of the law. Cosmic Christ, the "pattern that connects," would be at home and at work in such a creative situation.

Those who take a vow of creativity would be ushering in a new spiritual era because they would be ushering out pessimism—a characteristic of the tired senex and patriarchal civilization. Otto Rank observes that pessimism comes from repressed creativity.[9] If Rank is correct, then a commitment to creativity is a commitment to banish pessimism.

Creativity can, as Rollo May points out, help us to eliminate the excessive violence in our lives. In fact, May sees this role of being an "antidote to violence" as constituting the "function of beauty and art in human experience." He writes, "Art is an antidote for violence. It gives the ecstasy, the self-transcendence that could otherwise take the form of drug addiction, or terrorism, or suicide or warfare." Why is this possible? Because we are violent when we lose the sense of our own significance. Art restores that sense by reimmersing us in a living cosmology where we learn that we are "part of a universe of beauty." May continues:

> One purpose of art, and the beauty which is its inspiration, is to counteract this experience of insignificance. People have to have a sense of transcendence of their boring, day-to-day existence, and to live with some adventure, joy, zest, and a sense of meaning and purpose in their existence.[10]

Or, as Dante put it, "beauty awakens the soul to act."[11]

CREATING WORK

If the world is conceptualized as a machine then all work is mechanistic in nature. Defining work mechanistically has prevailed during the Newtonian era of the past four centuries. If the new cosmology teaches that the world is not primarily a machine but a mystery, then those who lead others more deeply into mysteries are the primary workers of the emerging culture. This would mean that artists, fools, and mystics are in fact workers! Perhaps a clue lurks here for banishing unemployment. What gifts would return to our planet were humans to commit themselves reverentially to the awesome power called creativity, not in the context of creating weapons or walls between us, but in the context of the work of healing, celebrating, and justice making? What would be the results, for example, of a vast effort by the human imagination to *create work*, good work for our vast armies of unemployed adults and youth the world over? Would not much of this newly created work consist of the "work" of recovering play, of recovering the personal arts, of recovering creativity itself? The industrial revolution and the Newtonian era effectively eliminated art as work. The Cosmic Christ would bring art back as *the* basic work of the universe, as the basic work-form of human societies. With the burgeoning of reemployed artists, life will become something to reverence again, something to fill us with awe. When the artist in everyone finds an authentic outlet in work and when that work is grounded in one's mysticism, then, as Eckhart puts it, the work "receives and draws all its being from nowhere else except from and in the heart of God" (ME, 99). This is truly a Cosmic Christ image applied to our work. The toil we put into it is nothing less than the toil we sow in the very heart of the Cosmic Christ. Eckhart says:

> The outward work will never be puny if the inward work is great. And the outward work can never be great or even good if the inward one is puny or of little worth. The inward work invariably includes in itself all expansive-

ness, all breadth, all length, all depth. Such a work receives and draws all its being from nowhere else except from and in the heart of God.

(ME, 99)

No wonder Hildegard can say that good work by humans makes the cosmic wheel go around and that every human is a "flowering orchard" needing to give back the fruits of one's labor to the community as a gift (HB, 54).

When one looks around the universe one finds work everywhere—good work of birthing, midwifing, celebrating, and being. Only among the two-legged species do we find that strange invention called unemployment. There is so much good work that needs to be done. How can we tolerate unemployment any longer? The Cosmic Christ leads the way to full employment, to the task of creating work. "The world is our soul," Meister Eckhart declared (BR, 117). By this he means that we live in the world we create for ourselves. If we deserve better than what we have, we must birth it from our souls.

CREATING LIFESTYLES

One area in which creativity could prevail and a powerful sense of community could emerge is in the area of creating our own lifestyles. Part of the problem with sexual theology in the West is its Newtonian piecemealness. We have almost entirely isolated different lifestyles from one another: heterosexuals are threatened by the idea that there might be other legitimate forms of sexual expression and are thus isolated in a privileged ghetto; homosexuals (who were all raised in heterosexual homes and environments but were rarely allowed to be honest about their sexuality there) are forced into their own ghetto, often a lonely and desperate place; celibates more or less hide out in convents, monasteries, or rectories with others of their own sex and lifestyle; single people feel isolated with their own unique struggles. The result is that *none of our lifestyles are allowed to touch the others with its unique wisdom*. No group truly profits from the others' experience. No group truly enters into the suffering of the other groups nor into their unique ecstasies. The parts-mentality of Newton reigns in our sexual lifestyles and the result is boredom. Otto Rank teaches that diversity is the primary principle for creativity. Yet a Newtonian culture allows no real diversity because it isolates lifestyle types instead of encouraging them to intermingle and interconnect. The result is predictable: creativity and mysticism seep out of sexual relationships. The wineskin is dry, parched, brittle, and leaking.

John Boswell of Yale University has published a significant work on homosexuals who were allowed a place in the twelfth-century church. This was the century of Chartres Cathedral and five hundred other churches of comparable size all dedicated to Mary, the Christian name for the mother goddess; of Hildegard of Bingen; of the first universities in the West; of the birth of Francis of Assisi; of the end of feudalism and the rise of capitalism; and of lay communes that resisted both capitalism and feudalism. In short, it was an immensely creative time for society and church. Boswell puts his finger on one of the causes for the creativity: what he calls "tolerance" in the title of his work, *Christianity, Social Tolerance and Homosexuality.*[12] The tolerance Boswell researches might also be understood as a respect for diversity. In his study on the *berdache* or androgynous persons of the primal peoples of America, Walter Williams demonstrates the unique sacred powers that sexual minorities were understood to possess for the healing of the people.[13] European colonists wiped out this tradition savagely and one can only wonder what was lost in the European soul for doing so. The Cosmic Christ, I believe, calls us to embrace diversity as a civilization if our creativity is to emerge and if each person is to truly live out her or his lifestyle and vocation with passion and responsibility. Why should a heterosexual be threatened by a homosexual or vice versa? Vive la différence! Let diversity and creativity flow within the parameters of moral responsibility and committed love that we have seen celebrated in the Song of Songs and that truly reflect the moral laws the universe teaches us. Let new communities with new visions of living together be born—with a conscious and deliberate vow to create together, to sustain one another's creative powers, to stand in solidarity with other creators and co-creators in society and the cosmos. Who can predict how this commitment to creativity would invigorate a community and what it might accomplish therein? The Cosmic Christ would be allowed freedom to dance, to play, to create anew.

Many persons ask about what role—if any—celibacy plays in a nondualistic or mystical spirituality. Once celibacy is extricated from its role in an ideology of virginity, its expressions may change. This does not, however, mean that celibacy has no role to play in a living cosmology. Celibacy is truly a prophetic option when it calls attention *not* to virginity but to the needs of the sexual *anawim* of a culture. The sick, the prisoner, the mentally retarded, the single, the divorced, the widowed, the homosexual, the poor—all of these persons lead less than satisfying sexual lives in our civilization. A celibate can stand in solidarity with such persons for he or she has chosen to be a sexual minority. Like voluntary poverty, voluntary celibacy allows solidarity to emerge among the voiceless ones in society—especially a society as preoccupied with sex as Western culture is today. For example, a true celibate will offer solidarity with the sexual *anawim* who are victims of scapegoating such as homosexuals. The homosexual has been a particular victim of scapegoating in Western culture and in Western religion of late. A homosexual is a sexual minority. Studies now confirm that approximately 10–13 percent of any given culture will be homosexual, about one of every ten of our children. Yet homosexuals in our society are driven into a ghetto-like existence.

208 / THE COMING OF THE COSMIC CHRIST

Anthony Stevens sees the act of scapegoating as "obscene," deriving from displacement which is, "next to projection, the defense mechanism with the most sinister social implications." He considers scapegoating to be "an obscene practice by which the aggression that we dare not direct against someone stronger than ourselves is turned against someone [we see as] weak and helpless." A group that is a minority will be seen as "weak and helpless." Unhealthy people try to conceal their own shadows by "rationalization" to justify what they do and say, or by "intellectualization"—the use of dry, abstract terminology—to defuse emotionally explosive issues. The cause of scapegoating, according to Stevens, is that feelings experienced by the ego are regarded as too dangerous to deal with. The result is a displacement of human aggression "against the 'enemy within.' "[14]

In addition to being in solidarity with the sexual *anawim*, the celibate also offers a prophetic voice to the sexual struggle insofar as he or she can laugh at his or her own sexuality. "All dressed up with no place to go" is one working definition of a celibate. A society that takes sexuality too seriously—as ours does either on the right by excessive moralizing or on the left by excessive license and preoccupation—needs sexual fools or jesters. That is one role the celibate plays in such a cultural situation. The celibate is also one who has dared to dance with the demons of loneliness. Loneliness is a dark and dreadful spirit that haunts our civilization today and the voluntary celibate has risked much to wrestle with these cosmic demons in the night. The emptying that results from such dancing allows the celibate an avenue of understanding and compassion by which to enter the lives of others who have been touched by loneliness. The celibate has often been driven "into the wilderness" to seek a cure for the cosmic loneliness of our times. A living cosmology comes as an antidote to this deep loneliness and celibates can often help lead this quest for the Cosmic Christ.

As women increasingly develop their awareness and consciousness and to the extent that men resist doing the same, a sociological situation will prevail where many women will in fact not be able to find men of their calibre and consciousness with whom to share their lives. A similar sociological situation prevailed in the Middle Ages when, because of the Crusades, there was a shortage of men. The result was the emergence of the Beguine movement, where unmarried women lived together without taking religious vows. Interest in celibacy is rising today especially among women who are learning to live together or in solitude, independent of male partnership. The fact that among men who are coming to greater self-awareness a rather high percentage are gay men also suggests that women will need to find alternatives to living with men. It may happen that new forms of celibacy and alternative forms of sexual mysticism will emerge from this struggle. Biblical scholar Elisabeth Schüssler Fiorenza points out that Pual's admonitions to remain free from marriage constituted a "frontal assault" on the mores of his culture and a "severe infringement of the right of the *paterfamilias*." The celibate lifestyle he advocated "offered a possibility for 'ordinary' women to become independent" in a patriarchal culture.[15]

People ought to acknowledge a well-kept secret in our society—much celibacy is being practiced by single persons and others every day. Celibacy is not restricted to the formally vowed individual. Many gay persons today, for example, are finding celibacy preferable to the threat of AIDS. Many young persons are not rushing into sexual relationships but are waiting for the right partner and the right time in their life for a committed relationship. Many women, as I alluded to above, are finding celibacy a better alternative than being victimized in an abusive relationship. Many widows and widowers are living lives of celibacy. Celibacy is not nearly as rare a lifestyle as our Playboy and Penthouse philosophers would have us believe. Perhaps groups of "out of the closet" celibates should become more public so that they can be playfully supportive of one another!

One example of artists of lifestyles in Western culture have been the founders of religious orders. Benedict, Francis, and Dominic—to name three such artists—responded creatively to a yearning for lifestyles of substance in a time of spiritual vacuity. A lifestyle is an art form. It brings life and wonder, joy and hope to persons otherwise condemned to superficial living. Our times call for the creation of lifestyles of spiritual substance.

EDUCATION—EDUCING THE COSMIC CHRIST

This entire book is about *educing* what is already present in our midst: the image of God, the Cosmic Christ present in every individual. True empowerment happens when we *educe* the divine beauty and power from one another. In this sense this book is part of the art of education, a folk art very much in need of renewal. Education can become creative again by centering its energies on educing the Cosmic Christ by educing wisdom and creativity. "There is wisdom in all creative works," Hildegard of Bingen declares (IHB, 49). Thus, to foster creativity is to unleash wisdom and the kinds of radical questions that wisdom poses. In ten years of directing an educational program consciously devoted to educing wisdom and eliciting the new cosmology from adult students, I can say unequivocally that excitement and learning happen anew when art as meditation—centering by way of giving birth in arts of painting or massage, clay or dance, ritual or music listening—is engaged in. I look forward to the day when our model of education at the Institute in Culture and Creation Spirituality is finally appreciated and utilized in other educational settings ranging from high schools to colleges, universities and seminaries. The key to de-Newtonianizing education, to letting go of its parts-mentality, will always be art. As Adrienne Rich has written, "They're luckiest who know they're not unique:/ But only art or common interchange/ Can teach that kindest truth."[16] I have written extensively on the art as meditation tradition in spirituality elsewhere.[17] The key to its success is its playfulness and truthfulness. As Meister Eckhart put it, "the truth cannot come from outside to the inside but must emerge from the inside and pass through an inner form" (BR, 399). Students and adult learners of all ages need to be empowered as artists by way of art as process. Awakening students to the new cosmology which includes the scientific creation story, mysticism, and art will revitalize education. In classrooms ecstacy will replace boredom. Persons in institutions such as prisons will also profit immensely from this kind of education. A greater peace will prevail therein, for as M. C. Richards has written, "There lives a creative being inside all of us and we must get out of its way for it will give us no peace unless we do."[18] The awakening of professionals, who are burning out rapidly because their Newtonian education has robbed their bodies and imaginations of their true power, will be a major achievement of a reeducation in creativity. Clergy, therapists, doctors, lawyers, business people—all could come alive under the influence of such a retooling in learning.

This retooling in learning, because it would awaken adult awe and wonder and with it reverence and the true meaning of devotion as commitment to creativity, would constitute the basis for a renewed morality in all our professions. Given the news reports on Wall Street immoralities, on governmental ones à la Contragate, on television evangelists and on teachers, it is clear that a reburst of morality is greatly needed in all of our educational efforts. Learning grounded in a living cosmology—when science, art, and mysticism are allowed both right brain and left brain interaction—constitutes the key to this moral awakening. A moral depth can only be achieved on the basis of reverence, which in turn is a consequence of awe. But awe comes from an awakened cosmology, or as Einstein put it: "All religions, arts, and sciences are branches of the same tree."[19]

BERDYAEV ON CREATIVITY AND THE NEW SPIRITUAL ERA

Russian Orthodox theologian Nicholas Berdyaev offers food for thought on the subject of creativity and the new spiritual era. He maintains that "the new spirituality will be first and foremost an experience of creative energy and inspiration. . . . The Christian renaissance can only be a creative renaissance. . . . The problem of creativeness is the fundamental problem of the new spirituality."[20] Art is creative transfiguration, not yet real transfiguration, but an anticipation of that transfiguration. The beauty of a dance, a poem, a symphony or a picture enters into eternal life. Art is not passive, but active, and in a sense theurgic.[21] God waits eagerly on our creativity, for "God expects from me a free creative act."[22] Creativity constitutes a responsibility from humans to God. According to Berdyaev, "it is imperative to bear in mind that human creativity is not a claim or a right on the part of humanity, but God's claim on and call to humanity. God awaits humanity's creative act, which is the response to the creative act of God."[23]

Indeed, God expects from us who are Cosmic Christs free, and therefore creative, acts. Such a Christ ushers in a new era, one that connects the divine power of creativity with the human power of co-creation. As Meister Eckhart put it: "we are heirs of the fearful creative power of God" (BR, 405). The Cosmic Christ challenges us to take this fear and dare to dance it, to make an adventure of it, to mold a world from it. For the cosmos we live in is the one we choose to make. The worlds we live in *are* the worlds we choose to give birth to. Our soul *is*, as Meister Eckhart says, the world.

THE COSMIC CHRIST SPEAKS ON CREATIVITY

The Cosmic Christ challenges us to embrace our powers of creativity: "Do not hide your light, your divine creative powers, under a bushel and thus allow human creativity to be manipulated and misused by forces of war making, destruction, pessimism, and bureaucracy. Find the creative person, the 'I am,' the divine child at play and at generativity in yourself. Give birth to yourself—your lifestyles, your relationships, your learning, your sexuality, your joys, your healing, your work—and build up in one another this same courage to create. Enter the great power of the universe, a power of constant generativity and do not be afraid. For I am with you always when you are creating. I, too, am a Creator, sometimes called *the* Creator. But in fact I ask you to be my companions, to share the birthing of images with me, to be my co-creators. Do not bore me by refusing. Do not scandalize me by saying 'I can't.' Do not oppress Mother Earth and her future by refusing to create and re-create. Come, play with me. Let us create together."

28. The Cosmic Christ—Redeemer of Worship

The coming of the Cosmic Christ will mean a thorough renewal of worship in the West. I believe that if our civilization could truly redeem worship it could itself be redeemed. Liturgy, which means the "work of the people," has the power to make a people, to create a people, to re-create a people by healing them and allowing them to feel again the deep wellsprings of reverence for being that we all have in us. Who can predict what teaching the people to again celebrate a living cosmology might accomplish? What unleashing of imagination and creativity, of the child and the mystic, of the prophet and healer might happen were worship itself immersed in a new wineskin that was supple and wet, flexible and cosmic. Worship makes wet the heart, ignites the magic of imagination, connects disparate and separate parts, and thus plays out the lesson of the universe itself in our local, microcosmic settings of church and synagogue, neighborhood and community. Worship *is* the playing out of the cosmic drama in our psyches and social groupings. As such it is the ultimate folk art—the ultimate work of creativity in the emerging era of creativity. Living worship, based on a living cosmology, creates a people and heals a people; it celebrates a people and their amazing place in the universe. It enkindles kinship with all God's blessed works or words, with all the creatures of the universe. Ritual, or the folk art of worship, is the proper place and the living space in which to pass on the new cosmic story—the story of the universe revealed by science. Ritual passes on the story through experiences of mysticism. Thus we have in true worship a living cosmology of science, mysticism, and art that ushers in a new civilization and a real renaissance. But are we up to this? Can our worship take on the new wineskin of the new cosmology? Clearly, worship deserves our attention. It deserves our criticism and our best efforts at thorough renewal.

SIX STEPS TO REDEEMING WORSHIP IN THE WEST

What are some practical steps that would allow the Cosmic Christ to refashion and thus redeem our worship?

1. RESET ALL OF WORSHIP IN A COSMOLOGICAL CONTEXT. This means, negatively speaking, letting go of that "personality cult" emphasis that has crept into Roman Catholic worship with the Second Vatican Council's turning of the altar to face the people. If the smile or comments by a priest take precedence over the presence of the angels and the stars, the atoms and the galaxies, then we have already thoroughly trivialized worship. While some good was accomplished by the Vatican Council's decrees on liturgical reform, much has occurred since that has been anthropocentric and therefore essentially boring and lacking in mystery. The Council's decree on liturgy was the first document it issued. Liturgical questions were not examined within the full theological context eventually developed by the Council. In addition, the Council—which did not invite the contributions of a single artist—lacked a cosmological awareness.

The wisest remarks on liturgy from that Council are not found in the decree on liturgy but in its more mature document on non-Christian religions, *Nostra Aetate,* which was issued much later. There the Council had the intuition to recognize that non-Christian peoples possess something powerful and authentic in their worship experiences that the Western churches need. That "something" is, of course, a cosmological sense. Native peoples do not worship anthropocentrically. They worship as citizens in a universe—a living, teeming, diverse, moving, sacred universe. In doing so, they realize the power and importance of ritual to celebrate this connection between humanity and the rest of creation. In this context the Cosmic Christ as the "pattern that connects" takes on striking power and proportions.

The essential role of worship is to link together microcosm and macrocosm once again in the context of thanksgiving or praise for our amazing (and therefore reverential) existence in the universe. Worship is the microcosm (human) giving thanks for the macrocosm (universe and all its creative wonders). Carl Jung comments on the potential power of recovering a micro/macro psychology: "The ancient and long obsolete idea of man as a microcosm contains a supreme psychological truth that has yet to be discovered."[1] Worship's task is to allow us to discover—or rediscover—this supreme psychological truth of our being microcosms of the universe. This discovery must take place not in our heads but in our whole beings by way of shared play and ritual. Native peoples have never lost faith with this essential, core meaning of worship. Otto Rank offers some significant observations on this gift from earlier eons, from prepatriarchal eras of worship which we now call native peoples' worship. He writes that all experience of art implies "a spiritual unity between the artist and the recipient. . . . It is more than a matter of the passing identification of two individuals, . . . it is the potential restoration of a union with the cosmos, which once existed and was then lost." To restore this lost cosmic sense and unity is the work of the Cosmic Christ in worship, and indeed of all living ritual and worship. What results culturally when such unity—which psychologically is the unity we experienced once in the womb—is restored? Culture itself is renewed and values are renewed! Rank comments that "the individual urge to restore this lost unity is . . . an essential factor in the production of human cultural values" for "cultural development has advanced by way of the cosmic . . . the artistic working-out of a culture remains inexplicable unless we posit a macrocosmization of the earthly."[2]

Worship in the East and among more primitive peoples, Rank observes, has always held true to a cosmic relationship, an identification with the universe. "The Eastern culture-peoples systematized in their micro-macro-cosmic structure a general human feeling which we find in a more primitive form in all nature-peoples. . . . the world-outlook of the uncivilized is founded on the same identity with the universe." Rank sees a Cosmic Christ in the worship of Babylonia in the fifth to sixth century before Jesus Christ. "The whole universe is the great world, the macrocosm; its parts are small universes in themselves, microcosms. Such a microcosm is man, who is in himself an image of the universe and a perfect being. But the great universe is likewise a man, and as it is 'god,' God has human form."[3]

What ritual essentially does is to awaken the human to his or her cosmic identity. The ancients knew this. According to Rank, "Certain celestial processes had to be imitated in cult-form on earth in order that man's cosmic identity, and with it his immortality, might be assured." In fact, Rank believes that the very idea of God comes from this cosmic awakening which is always an awakening in creativity. God was born from a "creative urge that is no longer satisfied with self-reproduction, but must proceed to create an entire cosmos as the setting of that self." In such an act the human becomes transformed "from creature to creator."[4] We discover our callings as co-creators. No wonder Carl Jung believed that a "supreme psychological truth" lurks in the micro/macro psychology. It is precisely the task of worship to recover this sense of micro/macro and not at a theoretical or head level but at the level of practice, participation, body, and play.

One can begin to sense that the recovery of some of the ancient wisdom surrounding native ritual holds the power to detrivialize worship. Consider, for example, what detrivializing would occur regarding eucharistic belief if Christians were taught that the body of Christ that they eat and drink was in fact the *real* (what Bateson calls the Roman Catholic belief of sacrament as distinct from the Protestant belief of metaphor or "sort of") eating and drinking of the cosmic body and blood of the Divine One present in every atom and ever galaxy of our universe. What is more grounding, more intimate, more local, and more erotic than eating and drinking? And if Jesus Christ is Mother Earth crucified, then the eating and drinking at the Eucharist is the eating and drinking of the wounded earth. The ingesting of the sacrifical victim brings about an awakening of consciousness to the sufferings of Mother Earth and all her children. But it also brings eschatological hope, that is, hope in a future where the blessed earth will be reverenced appropriately for all the awesome gifts it bestows on us. The law of the cosmos of universal sacrifice, of the giving of our lives so that others might thrive, is reenacted and played out—indeed it is *displayed* in the eating and drinking of the bread and cup of the Cosmic Christ. We are all food for one another. "Take and eat for this is my body." The body we eat together is no longer limited to a matter of bread, whether leavened or unleavened, but the bread is seen for what it is: a cosmological gift, twenty-billion-years old, a gift of earth, air, fire, water, of photosynthesis and the sun, of supernova explosions and of original fireballs—indeed the ingenuity to make the bread from wheat and soil and to harvest the grapes is itself a cosmic gift of light waves and brain energies that allowed such imagination into the human consciousness.

The Eucharist stands as a complete affirmation of the Cosmic Christ's yearning for intimacy with the human ones—that is, the Cosmic Christ's need to be eaten. All of creation is present at such a moment, such a feast and festal gathering—no one is excluded for this is truly a cosmological event. This is why the angels are invoked in the preface to the Eucharistic Prayer when the cosmic hymn of "Holy, Holy, Holy" is introduced by the invitation to join with seraphim and cherubim and the whole host of heavenly angels in singing. As Origen put it centuries ago: "I have no doubt that there are angels in the midst of our assembly too, not only the Church in general, but each church individually. . . . Thus we have here a twofold Church, one of men, the other of angels." St. John Chrysostom, preaching at an Easter Mass declared: "It is not only earth, but heaven as well which has part in today's feast. . . . The Angels exult, the Archangels rejoice, the Cherubim and the Seraphim join us in the celebration of today's feast. . . . What room is there for sadness?"[5] The "Gloria in Excelsis Deo" is a cosmological hymn uttered by the angels to the shepherds at Bethlehem. The Nicene Creed has significant cosmological imagery in it, yet this is invariably missed when worship remains in an anthropocentric wineskin. Consider the following cosmological references in that creed, including references to the Cosmic Christ.

> We believe in one God, the Father, the Almighty,
> *Maker of heaven and earth,*
> *of all that is seen and unseen.*
> We believe in one *Lord* Jesus Christ,
>
> . . . .
> *through him all things were made.*
>
> . . . .
> He *ascended into heaven*
> and is seated at the right hand of the Father.
> He will come again *in glory* to judge the living and the dead.

The italicized lines point to the cosmological language that is present in this traditional creed. Yet how often this is missed by worshipers and liturgical leaders whose minds are not yet awakened to a living cosmology.

The traditional prayers are not the only liturgical source of rich cosmological imagery usually overlooked in our Western worship. Last year I was at Chartres Cathedral for the Ascension Thursday Mass celebrated by a bishop and numerous priests. The Scripture readings for the day were immensely cosmological yet the preacher did not make one reference to this fact. The young man who accompanied me at the Mass said, as the parade of celebrants came in, "this is a very old church," meaning that the bishop appeared to be the youngest priest in the service. The dominant presence of older persons was magnified by the fact that young were not visible in any aspect of the liturgy, even though the service was to commemorate a group of pilgrims, many of whom were young, who had marched from Paris to Chartres for the occasion. The old, senex wineskin in which our liturgical leaders have been trained has actually blinded them to their own cosmological tradition present in the Scriptures. Consider, for example, the following readings from Ascension Thursday liturgy:

"You will receive power when the Holy Spirit comes down on you; then you are to be my witnesses in Jerusalem, throughout Judea and Samaria, yes, even to the ends of the earth." No sooner had he said this than he was lifted up before their eyes in a cloud which took him from their sight. They were still gazing up into the heavens when two men dressed in white stood beside them. "People of Galilee," they said, "why do you stand here looking up at the skies? This Jesus who has been taken from you will return, just as you saw him go up into the heavens."

(Acts 1:8–11)

We have in this passage indications of cosmology: the cloud, angels (men dresssed in white), the exit and return from the heavens to the earth, the power of the Holy Spirit that will send disciples to "the ends of the earth." The Epistle read for Ascension Thursday is among the most cosmological texts of the New Testament, Ephesians 1:17–23.

The God of glory . . . has seated Christ at the right hand of divinity in heaven, high above every principality, power, virtue and domination, and every name that can be given in this age or the age to come. God has put all things under Christ's feet and has made him thus exalted, head of the church, which is his body: the fullness of the one who fills the universe in all its parts.

(Eph. 1:17–23)

It is difficult to imagine a more cosmic text—one that brings together the themes of "glory" and angels and exaltation over the angels and the filling of the universe in all its parts.

I had an experience similar to that Ascension Thursday Mass in the United States when I attended a Mass for the feast of Pentecost. Again, the texts are deeply cosmological. The readings of the vigil for the feast of Pentecost utilize the cosmic imagery of the prophet Joel (3:1–5) promising the Spirit will come upon all humankind, and that young and old shall see visions and dream dreams: "I will work wonders in the heavens and on the earth, blood, fire, and columns of smoke; the sun will be turned to darkness, and the moon to blood." The Epistle is Romans 8:22–27, a statement on all creation groaning and hoping. Pentecost itself offers readings from Acts 2:1–11 about the universality of the breakthrough by the Spirit. The Epistle, 1 Cor. 12:3–7, 12–13, speaks of the one body having many members, yet being one body: "And so it is with Christ. It was in one Spirit that all of us, whether Jew or Greek, slave or free, were baptized into one body." Yet the cosmology inherent in these rich texts was again ignored by an anthropocentrically-trained preacher. It is especially painful to behold the anthropocentric deterioration of worship in the West in light of the fact that the great cosmic hymns that we considered in part III were invariably liturgical songs sung by the earliest followers of Jesus.

Liturgy in its present context is not redeemable. It needs to yield to a fuller and fresher wineskin. It needs to conform to a living cosmology and not the other way around. It needs an immediate recycling of our leaders and preachers, and reimmersion into the tradition of the Cosmic Christ. All worship leaders need to be instructed in both left and right brains and in body awareness and awakening. How can they be expected to lead the micro/macro experience that worship is meant to be without an appreciation of a living cosmology? Our places of worship deserve a setting that is not anthropocentric by its linear, Newtonian benches (an insult to the curved universe of Einstein and all native peoples whose architecture for worship is invariably the circle because the universe is believed to be rounded). We need to worship in circles again, preferably on the soil of Mother Earth wherever possible. Circles invite all creatures to be part of the grateful event and they allow the humans present to look each other in the eye while rounding and connecting themselves in step with the universe.

We need to realize that the liturgical calendar as presently designed is not adequate to a reclamation of Mother Earth as the Cosmic Christ. Mother Earth does not observe the resurrection of an Easter event once a year but every day. Easter is a daily event. Does this fact not provide awesome possibilities with which our artists, scientists, and mystics might resurrect worship? Does the Cosmic Christ not challenge us to excitement over a renewed cosmological worship? Is not worship the primary avenue by which we can be reeducated and reenthused in a living cosmology?

2. BRING THE BODY BACK. The body has been effectively banished from most white worship in the West. That is one role stationary benches play in the churches—they assure that no dance, no celebration of body-spirit, might break loose. Books play a similar role in worship—if people have to hold books, then their hands are also occupied and they aren't free to move the body. But there can be no living worship without the body. We *are* our bodies—though more than our bodies. Our bodies are the temple that con-temples us with other temples, other bodies of the universe, bodies of stars, of suns, of earth, of winged, finned, four-legged and two-legged brothers and sisters, children all of a living God. Until the body is back the body of the Cosmic Christ is only an idea in the head. The Cosmic Christ wants to dance, to express itself bodily, to respond to Good News and to cosmic grace. The angels cannot worship with body—this is an instance in which they envy us with good reason. Why would we want to worship more like angels than like the animals we are? If "ritual dance" is too threatening a concept, then let us think in terms of "processions." Our worshiping ancestors were deeply into processions—around the church, out of the church, under the church, through the church, through the streets of towns and villages, into the countryside to cemeteries and back again. All these processions were

forms of body worship. They move the breath-spirit, the muscles, and the blood. They move us together into a shared sense of community care and celebration. Hildegard of Bingen teaches that prayer is essentially the inhaling and exhaling of the one breath of the universe—*ruah* or spirit. But to get us inhaling and exhaling again in worship is to get our bodies in motion again. Worship needs more of an athletic dimension to it.

Again, lessons abound from the native peoples of the power of dancing together with the beating of the drum providing a common heartbeat. This heartbeat reminds us of the time in our mother's womb when we were so much at peace; it reminds us of the heartbeat of Mother Earth—beating still on our behalf; it reminds us of the heartbeat of the Cosmic Christ which fills the universe with overflowing, wet love binding all things together on earth and in heaven. Yet the heartbeat we hear today is that of an ever more wounded heart—a victim of matricide. The earth's healthy heartbeat is being threatened severely—one more reason for dancing deeply from shared feelings of the heart in hopes of restoring its health.

3. BRING PLAY BACK. Worship is not lugubrious; it is not about rules and regulations and conformities and obediences. It is about replaying in the universe, about eros returned to our collective lives and individual psyches. Hildegard says that the purpose of worship is to "cheer the inner strength of people" (IHB, 91). If worship is not joyful it is not transformational and is as good as dead. If a proper test of living mysticism is, in Eckhart's phrase, "unselfconsciousness," then worship requires mountains of unselfconsciousness—especially in our day when selfconsciousness is the rule and unselfconsciousness is so rare. The puer in each of us needs to be challenged to come out at worship. If not at worship, where else in our culture is there space ample enough and relaxed enough to invite the divine child out to play? Starhawk, in bringing back simple and basic chants and spiral dances from ancient women's religions, is doing much to awaken us all to the power of play in worship. If eros is not being celebrated in the heart of a community—in the powerful setting of cosmic worship—it will sneak around behind closed doors and pornographic playhouses to corrupt youth and adult alike. Thomas Aquinas wrote that "joy is the human's noblest act."[6] Is worship, then, not to partake of so noble an act? Is there room for joy in our worship—and for instruction in joy?

Eros belongs at the heart of worship, at the heart of our cosmology. Our lives are as erotically humorous as they are divinely tragic. The clown of God dwells in each of us and it needs nourishment to grow into its destiny. As Eckhart says, "in the heart of the Trinity the Creator laughs and gives birth to the child. The child laughs back at the Creator and together they give birth to the Spirit. The whole Trinity laughs and gives birth to creation" (ME, 131). If we were born of laughter, if laughter is among our divine origins and our source, then a living mysticism in worship will not settle for less than playful ritual. Not books, but body and heart prayer will reawaken us to living ritual. For if ritual and worship cannot bring the puer and the senex healthily together again, then what can? If the Cosmic Christ cannot make patterns that connect in worship, then where will they be made? If our times and spaces of worship are not the places and occasions for nourishing eros, then when are such times and where are such places?

4. MAKE ROOM FOR THE *VIA NEGATIVA*—DARKNESS, SILENCE, SUFFERING. An acutely embarrassing dimension to a good deal of white worship in the West today and in Roman Catholicism since the Second Vatican Council has been the almost complete absence of the *via negativa*. By the *via negativa* I mean the path of mystery and darkness as well as the path of silence and suffering. Rare are the liturgical occasions when the *via negativa* is allowed its appropriate time and space. The familiar result of this lacuna is often an experience of so-called celebration that is not about the *via positiva* at all for it lacks the awe and wonder that comes only in a nonanthropocentric context. Instead, worshipers are subjected to a pitiful *positivism* that attempts, by human-made balloons and home-made smiles, to render ritual alive again. Such efforts are doomed to failure for *what* we celebrate is nothing less than the cosmos and *that* we celebrate is directly proportionate to admission of shared suffering. Just as our joy is cosmic and ripe for celebration, so too is our pain cosmic and ripe for celebration. Living worship, placed in a living cosmology, represses no side of this dialectic between fullness and emptiness, joy and sorrow, light and dark. The Cosmic Christ is not one-sided. The Cosmic Christ comes to worship with wounds in hands, feet, and sides. All of us do. This deserves and indeed demands to be acknowledged at all ritual. How is this done?

First, we need silent spaces and silent times—the spaces between the drumbeats and heartbeats—for being with the silence which is so rich a part of a living mysticism. Rare is the liturgical minister who can let silence be, who can let persons pray not out of books but out of the depths of their silent hearts. Quaker worshipers have not lost faith with this sense of letting the Spirit speak through a community gathered around silence.[7] Were we worshiping outdoors more often the silence would come naturally as it does whenever native people gather to worship. The poet Rilke writes about silence: "Being-silent. Who keeps innerly/silent, touches the roots of speech."[8]

Behind all authentic speech there lies silence. Thus, behind all authentic worship, there lies silence as well. But silence should not simply be taken literally to mean absence of speech or noise. Silence is also letting other images go. It is "being-with-being." This kind of silence, this group emptying, has a deep role to play wherever people and angels and creation gather to worship. Silence becomes an occasion for emptying ourselves of our projections and letting others be. And letting ourselves be. And letting the Divine One be. There is much silence in the universe—astronauts have often been awakened to their mysticism by the awesome silence of space—and the gift of silence is part of the gift that a living cosmology brings to worship. Teresa of Avila teaches that until we let go of verbal prayer and enter the realms of silence we are nowhere near maturity in our prayer.[9] Yet rare is the liturgical event that allows for such letting go of excessive prayer talk. "Quit flapping your gums about God," Meister Eckhart advises (ME, 44).

In addition to welcoming silence, a cosmological worship will welcome darkness as well, and in the process instruct people to embrace the dark and not fight it. Of course, we cannot read in the dark and since so many worshipers in the West have learned to equate prayer with reading, the idea of turning out the lights may threaten many people. Yet prayer is mostly about responding with the heart, not with the written word. Worship that takes the heart as the starting point for prayer would be sure to attract many who have given up on worship precisely because it has banished mystery and darkness. In the Roman Catholic church up to the Second Vatican Council there was much darkness—the Latin service was essentially "in the dark" because people did not "get the meaning." They got rhythms and tones and general moods from the vernacular sermons, vestment colors or the title of the feast. In many respects that was enough, for other, more mystical and mysterious gifts were passed on by the smell of candles and incense, by the Gregorian chant, and even by the banishment of the left brain's unceasing quest for the verbal. It is telling that a whole generation of spiritually serious American youth went East to pray in Sanskrit while American Catholics dropped Latin altogether and started praying in English. Putting liturgy into English was an invitation to turn on the lights in church. How often I see people reading in church who might instead be praying.

I am not proposing that we will take up Latin again and return to that particular expression of darkness. I believe we had to let go of Latin to let go of the worldview inherent in that particular culture. But listening to and reading English prayers does not a living worship make. Now that the new cosmology introduces us again to the basic *mystery of the universe* we can reenter that mystery and begin our prayer anew. The mysterious universe of which I speak includes, of course, the universe that is our bodies and our imaginations. Neither the old Latin Mass nor the current vernacular one offered a living cosmology. The old Mass, however, was at home enough in the dark to invite the magic of imagination to entertain possibilities of a cosmology; the vernacular is so hopelessly anthropocentric and in-the-light that all cosmic mystery is effectively banished (except, of course, for Holy Saturday night when the lights are—thankfully—turned off). The Roman Catholic church has lurched from one era without cosmology to another. The Protestant churches have done even worse things to the possibility of a cosmology. Pietism, as Lutheran theologian Joseph Sittler has pointed out, effectively banished the Cosmic Christ. Early in the century, theologian Allan Calloway concurred with this assessment of the Protestant pietistic dilemma, built as it is on a dualism between inner and outer worlds. He believed that Kant's dualistic distinction between the "starry heavens without" and "the moral law within" (Kant's words) set Western religion up—and Protestantism in particular—for a sentimental and acosmic piety. This very separation of the within from the without, the psyche from the cosmos, "is the source of its religious appeal and of the wide-spread acceptance of this kind of world-view in some forms of pietistic Christianity," according to Galloway.[10]

It is time to place worship within the cosmological setting that the human species throughout the world is embracing. We should explore the rituals of the native peoples, whose ceremonies appreciated the power of darkness and night. Sweat lodges, for example, allow us to be immersed in the holy darkness of our origins in the womb. The great ceremonial dances are another example: they often take place during the night when the drum is best heard in heart as well as in head and body, and when fire takes on special meaning. Moon rituals may threaten a light-oriented patriarchal slant on worship, but for that very reason they ought to be explored for their power to evoke mystery and to call forth the spirit as embodied in women's experience through the centuries.

Another dimension to be considered in restoring a viable *via negativa* to our worship is suffering. So often people come to church covering up their suffering—all clean and dressed up with fancy ties, hats, and shoes. Where is the possibility that tears might soil one's pristine facial creams or cut through the masculine defenses of accomplishment and ego attainment? People who cannot share their cosmic pain cannot worship together. Worship is the emptying of all we have, and pain and suffering are deep within us all. In worship among black people or native peoples, pain is not covered up. It it spoken out, it is chanted out, it is sung out, it is danced out. In short, it is connected to the rest of our lives and to the universe itself. Simone Weil advises us to return all suffering to the universe.[11] This is what worship ought to accomplish. Otherwise we spend our lives concealing our pain and wasting immense energy in doing so. The *via negativa* and the *via positiva* come together in living worship. The Cosmic Christ appears in both instances and indeed is the "pattern that connects" the cross with the creation, the sorrow with the jubilation. In an era without a living cosmology, our deepest pain has to go underground because it is so very real and so very large, in fact, cosmic in size. One reason for placing worship within a cosmological context is to *let the pain out.* This will prove to be one of the most prophetic contributions that the Cosmic Christ can make to our worship and culture. Only when the pain is out, can the creativity flow to do something with the pain. If the pain remains inside, rancid terror results and with it sentimentalism, violence, and the stifling of creativity. In these circumstances, ever-increasing pessimism, guilt, and abortion of the Cosmic Christ ensues. Joanna Macy's remarks about suffering parallel the teachings of the mystics through the ages who urge us not to be afraid of the dark night of the soul. As Macy teaches, "it is in darkness that birth takes place" and "we are in grief together."[12] Worship is an occasion for naming our pain and grieving together. Lamentations are in order given today's crises of earth, of youth, of sexuality, of injustice. Without naming our pain and lamenting our situation, no prophets are shaped or born. No true healing or creativity can occur. Alice Miller points out that in her experience of working with the deeply wounded of our society, "the prerequisite [for creativity] is the work of mourning. . . . If the personal roots of an aggressive or even destructive way of acting are understood, . . . then psychic energy will of itself be transformed into creativity. Mourning over what has happened, over the irreversibility of the past, is the prerequisite for this process."[13]

White worshipers could learn much from the native religions about the art of wailing and lamentation. Our Institute once sponsored a wailing ceremony in which white people could grieve the pain of Mother Earth. It got a bit out of hand when an individual or two more or less "flipped out." A black advisor told me afterwards that this must be expected if true grieving is entered into, and that in the black church elders are assigned to usher out those who are in such deep personal pain that they cannot withstand the public wailing. One lesson I learned from this is how alienated from deep grief our white worship is—our liturgies are not structured to allow the kind of emotional catharsis that would accompany deep mourning—or deep joy. Even though we possess a Book of Lamentations in our Bible, we have lost the ways of doing lamentations in our worship. Dorothee Soelle has a similar observation to make. "Organized religion, especially among white northerners," she writes, "has often extinguished all sparks of ecstasy from its forms of worship."[14]

5. AWAKEN AND NURTURE THE PROPHET. Worship has a deeply prophetic task to perform. It is meant to nurture prophets, to challenge them, to refresh them, to bring them together for community conviviality and the sustenance and enrichment of a prophetic imagination. Each of the four elements of living worship I have just outlined contributes in its way to a prophetic awakening.

Awakening the prophet through worship will require that we choose meaningful themes for worship. Liturgy must embrace a cosmological agenda in order to detrivialize our heritage and awaken the power inherent in our tradition. Lamentations for Mother Earth, lamentations for the lost or wounded child, celebrations of the mystery of the human body and sexuality, rites of passage, celebrations of the power of play, celebrations of animals, confessions of the Church's sins through history—such cosmological themes need to be addressed in our worship. What if a year of the liturgical calendar were to be dedicated to the celebration of the mystery known as the human body—what Jesus and Paul refer to as a "temple"? This would enable religion to atone for its dualistic past and to assist culture in moving from Cartesian and Augustinian negations of the body to a celebration of its amazing history and mystery. Each Sunday could be dedicated to celebrating a different organ of the body. One Sunday would be Liver Sunday; another Spleen Sunday; another Brain Sunday; another Pancreas Sunday, and so on. Scientists, poets, dancers, and others would awaken us to the awe, wonder, amazement, reverence of that particular organ as part of our healthy bodies. (As a rule we recall we have a liver only when it is acting up—a typical fall-redemption spiritual attitude that admits of something's existence only when there is a problem.) A scientist or doctor could tell us how our livers serve us; a dancer could perform a liver dance and elicit everyone's participation; a poet could proclaim an "Ode to a Liver." What would a people who worshiped in this fashion be like after one year of such celebrations? I am quite sure that they would be more in touch with their bodies and the amazing gifts we otherwise take for granted. We would not be so bored. We would learn unity around the gift of the human body we all have in common. Child and adult alike would be amazed and thankful for being alive and well, for being part of a living cosmos and a living, mystical body of Christ.

6. BRING PARTICIPATION BACK. Participation is key to a living ritual just as participation is key to the cosmos itself. We cannot sit passively and watch the universe happen *around* us or *outside* us, for we, along with all other creatures, *are that universe*. Boredom comes from lack of participation. The boredom that dominates so much Western worship reflects the boredom of an anthropocentric culture that is attempting to live out a paradigm and worldview that are just plain tired.

Where there is authentic ritual there is always full participation—according to each person's capabilities.[15] One serious deficiency in the anthropocentric worship that has dominated in the West is most worshipers are rendered passive or semipassive spectators to the specialist, be that the "ordained priest" in Roman Catholicism, the "theological preacher" in Protestantism, or the "church choir" in either tradition. While there is certainly a place for leading, preaching, and singing in worship, the emphasis should be how *all participants can give and receive fully* in the ritual. In an Indian sweat, all persons participate and sweat to their utmost, yet there are leaders of the chants and the songs. In a living cosmology all creatures are "busy expressing God and gladly doing their best to express God," as Meister Eckhart puts it (BR, 59). Worship needs to afford humans that holy opportunity. Liturgy needs to become the work of the people once again—of the people, by the people, and for the people, and for "all our relations" as the native peoples say in their worship contexts.

Each of the elements I have listed above as essential for worship contributes to increasing participation: cosmology, body, play, darkness, the prophetic—none of these dimensions can be vicariously experienced. All demand the calling forth of the priest in each person.

Recently, I led a class in "Renewing Christian Ritual" at our Institute, using the criteria laid out in this chapter as the basis for thirty-three students and myself creating three "Cosmic Masses." In October, we held a Cosmic Mass of Lamentation for Mother Earth (held on the feast of Francis of Assisi); in November, we held a Cosmic Mass in Thanksgiving for our Bodies; in December, we held a Cosmic Mass in Honor of the Child, Wounded and Divine. We learned much from these gatherings of 200–250 people in our gymnasium with the use of spiral dances and Indian smudging, of small circle dances and slide shows of the organs of our bodies (commented on by a biophysicist and accompanied by a litany set to ancient chant honoring the organs of our bodies). Reverence and awe were elicited. Healing occurred. Awakening happened. One woman said to me, "It was an honor to have been here worshiping in the manner in which all people will worship forty years from now." What we did with the ideas in this chapter is only a modest effort at worship renewal. Students of this book will, I am sure, be able to carry these efforts further. The redemption of worship in the West is a necessary prelude to any authentic renaissance. As Native American scholar Jamake Highwater puts it in his book, *Ritual of the Wind*, "we are myth makers. We are legenders. Of all the animals we alone are capable of dreaming ourselves into existence."[16] Worship that lives is so powerful because it gathers the dreams of past and future into the hearts of those desiring to live fully in the present. There lies its ultimate power—the power to translate dreams into tribal myths, a power of educing and indeed of educating for a new cosmology. In the Newtonian era ritual virtually died from anthropocentrism. Today the human heart yearns for ancient and new cosmic visions. If they cannot be born, expressed, and celebrated in worship, where can this happen? Worship is the ultimate folk art.

The test of authentic worship will be awakened awe and reverence among peoples of a culture. The excitement of a new cosmology grafted onto traditional wisdom will lead artists of all kinds to come alive and excite others with their passion for existence. Worship will be the gathering place where the many stories are told and retold by dance, poetry, music, color, song, laughter, drama and art forms still to be created. Renewed worship will allure the youth to dream bigger dreams, to test their incipient adulthood with visions of greatness. Authentic worship will excite scientists to contribute their gifts to the cosmological awakening. It will arouse the *anawim*, the oppressed and voiceless ones, to find their voices and express them. It will enable all of us to find ears that listen to the impassioned voices that suffering creates.

I believe that Protestants, Catholics, and Jews alike are today yearning for the vitality and rebirth that a living worship can bring about. I believe the youth—and the youth or *puer* in every adult—yearn for a living worship. I was once invited to preach at two Episcopal Eucharists on a Sunday morning in Connecticut. At neither of these liturgies did I see anyone under thirty-eight years of age. What might happen to worship in the West if its leaders were retrained in a cosmological context? What if, for example, at wedding ceremonies, instead of the usual sentimental, senex, and secularized ceremony, the bride and groom were to read the Song of Songs to each other with the congregation—their supportive community—playing the role of the chorus? The same could be done in a renewal of marriage vows. The renaissance I call for in worship does not consist in abandoning our traditions but of delving more deeply into them. As Howard Thurman cautions us, the only way we can be sure of being at home everywhere is to be sure that we are at home somewhere.[17] The persons who do not know or experience a living cosmology in their liturgical and biblical traditions are at home neither everywhere nor somewhere. They are adrift. The greatest gift that the senex can give to the younger generation is a rich and living tradition. Such a tradition has at its heart a living cosmology.

Potentially, worship is more powerful than the media in its ability to awaken people and therefore a culture. The six steps I have outlined in this chapter could launch the renewal of worship that the Cosmic Christ desires for us.

LESSONS LEARNED FROM NATIVE WORSHIP

Praying with native peoples has always been a source of deep spiritual renewal for me. Sweat lodges and powwow dances, pipe ceremonies and vision quests are just some of the ways of worship that have been employed by native peoples for tens of thousands of years on this land.[18] Last year, at the time of the Harmonic Convergence, I had the privilege of praying with Lakota peoples at a Sun Dance in South Dakota. It was a deeply spiritual experience. A few lessons came home to me:

1. I was reminded of Gandhi's belief that worship without sacrifice is a sin. Sacrifice is very much a part of the Sun Dance where pray-ers fast from food and water for four days while dancing in the hot sun. In addition, those who choose to pierce (that is, to attach ropes by way of pegs embedded in their backs or chests) sacrifice a piece of their flesh so that the people might live. This raises questions about the level of *comfort* that

white churches require in order to make worship. How can the West recover a sense of sacrifice in its worship? Those who dare to do civil disobedience, for example, are worshiping in the ancient tradition of sacrifice.

2. Gratitude is what motivates us in worship. Worship is about thanksgiving. The West knows this conceptually—the word "eucharist" is Greek for "thank you"—but is Western worship *in fact* built around gratitude? And if so, gratitude for what? One Indian at the Sun Dance performed the sacrifice of dragging four buffalo heads attached to the skin on his back around the dancing circle four times. Before he did this he spoke to the gathering and said he was doing this in thanksgiving for the good health he had enjoyed in his life. He told us how his son was to be sentenced the next day to twenty-five years in jail. It is moving that the oppressed can feel so deeply the experience of gratitude and can express it at the level of sacrifice. Has something been lost in Western worship to the extent that we project too much of the sacrifice of worship onto the accomplishment of Jesus Christ in his death and do not take enough responsibility for the sacrifice of other Christs that goes on in our own day?

3. Closely related to the above points is the matter of bravery and heroism. The Sun Dance is a brave and heroic way to worship. I do not mean "brave or heroic" in the macho sense—in fact any sun dancer tempted to pierce or dance out of macho motivation is quickly shorn of such temptations, for ego and willpower do not see one through such a trying spiritual discipline. In the Sun Dance, the opportunity for bravery and heroism is offered to anyone who cares to dance. How vital an invitation this is, especially for persons who have been victimized as often as native peoples have been. Their internalized oppression is manifested in tragedy in their daily lives, marked as they are by unemployment, crime, drugs, alcohol, imprisonment, and suicide. Worship needs to offer the *anawim* an expression of their greatness—an expression of the power of the Cosmic Christ in us all. Are bravery and heroism part of Western worship?

4. Community is a necessary part of the Sun Dance. The dancers need the presence of the community to sustain them in their sacrifice and their brave prayer. The community offers spiritual support and often dances with the Sun Dancers. After all, the community is the purpose of the gift the sun dancers give—they dance so that the people might live. Solidarity is experienced and formed when the community worships richly and deeply together. It includes mutual laughter and feasting as well as fasting and sweating. "Being-with" is integral to community support and sustenance. To be with one another in deep, sacrificial prayers of thanksgiving is a highpoint in the community's year. The Indian Sun Dance is folk mysticism. It is for the people and by them. It does not conceal their pain—rather, it dives into the pain. The Sun Dance is an

ultimate group expression of what Rank calls the "irrational" dimension of life that is so essential to a living mysticism. The left brain will never grasp or possess the work of the Spirit occurring therein. The Sun Dance awakens the collective right brain, the mystical energy of the community.

5. The Cosmic Christ is present in so many ways in the Sun Dance and its surrounding prayer forms—the sweat, the pipe giving, the vision quest. All twenty-one "running definitions" of mysticism presented in part II can be found in Native American worship such as the Sun Dance. Consider, for example, the Cosmic Christ present in the rich expression of panentheism that Black Elk speaks of:

> We should understand well that all things are the works of the Great Spirit. We should know that He is within all things: the trees, the grasses, the rivers, the mountains, and all the four-legged animals, and the winged peoples; and even more important, we should understand that He is also above all these things and peoples.[19]

In the sacred pipe we experience a living cosmology, a Cosmic Christ, a universal person who awakens the universal person in all of us. Black Elk speaks through his recorder, Joseph Epes Brown:

> In filling a pipe, all space (represented by the offerings to the powers of the six directions) and all things (represented by the grains of tobacco) are contracted within a single point (the bowl or heart of the pipe), so that the pipe contains, or *really is*, the universe. But since the pipe is the universe, it is also man, and the one who fills a pipe should identify himself with it, thus not only establishing the center of the universe, but also his own center; he so "expands" that the six directions of space are actually brought within himself. It is by this "expansion" that a man ceases to be a part, a fragment, and becomes whole or holy; he shatters the illusion of separateness.[20]

The fire at the center of tepee, pipe, or of sweat lodge represents *Wakan-Tanka*, the Great Spirit within the world. How close this comes to Meister Eckhart's teaching that an *ancilla animae*, a "spark of the soul," burns within every creature and every human that will never be extinguished and that this spark of the soul is the divine presence within us all. All of creation shares in this holiness. Black Elk prays: "Everything is *wakan* that is on our Mother, the earthly source of all life. The steps of our people are upon Her. May they be firm and strong! . . . All together as one we send our voice to *Wakan-Tanka*. Help us to walk in a *wakan* manner pleasing to You!"[21]

THE COSMIC CHRIST SPEAKS ON WORSHIP

The Cosmic Christ calls us to renewed worship: "Come to me all you who are burdened by lack of praise, lack of beauty, lack of vision in your lives. Look about you at the starry heavens and the deep, deep sea; at the amazing history that has birthed a home for you on this planet; at the surprise and joy of your existence. Gather together—you and your communities—in the context of this great, cosmic community to rejoice and give thanks. To heal and let go. To enter the dark and deep mysteries, to share the news, to break the bread of the universe and drink blood of the cosmos itself in all its divinity. Be brave. Let your worship make you strong and great again. Never be bored again. Create yourselves, re-create your worlds, by the news you share and the visions you celebrate. Bring your sense of being microcosm in a vast macrocosm; bring your bodies; bring your play; bring your darkness and your pain. Gather and do not scatter. Learn not to take for granted and learn this together. Become a people. Worship together."

29. The Cosmic Christ and Deep Ecumenism

The Cosmic Christ and the living cosmology that the Cosmic Christ ushers into society and psyche have the power to launch an era of what I call deep ecumenism. Deep ecumenism is the movement that will unleash the wisdom of *all* world religions—Hinduism and Buddhism, Islam and Judaism, Taoism and Shintoism, Christianity in all its forms, and native religions and goddess religions throughout the world. This unleashing of wisdom holds the last hope for the survival of the planet we call home. For there is no such thing as a Lutheran sun and a Taoist moon and Jewish ocean and a Roman Catholic forest. When humanity learns this we will have learned a way out of our anthropocentric dilemma that is boring our young, killing our souls, trivializing our worship, and exterminating the planet. Universalism is a common characteristic to all the traditions of the Cosmic Christ in the Scriptures and in Western history that we have considered above.

Why am I so confident that the Cosmic Christ can usher in an age of deep ecumenism? Remember that cosmology is three things: the scientific story, mystical experience, and art. The scientific story is today being heard and believed globally. East Indians and Africans, Russians and Latin Americans, Europeans and North Americans, Chinese and Australians are beginning to hear the same story—that this planet was not an accident, that we have been "loved from before the beginning" in the original fireball itself, that the universe wanted us and awaited us eagerly. We have a responsibility to give back the cherished blessing of our lives with grace and gratitude. We must return blessing for blessing. Generativity and creativity have been built into the universe from the start; intrinsic to our destiny as cosmic citizens as well as they are images of God the Creator.

Like science, art too is transcultural. As I write this it is July 4, 1987, and on this day an unprecedented event is occurring in Moscow as some of America's finest rock singers team up with Russian rock groups for a six-hour concert. Music, dance, drama, ritual—all the arts—have long held the power to connect, the power to make whole what was separate, the power to move the human heart to wholeness instead of piecemealness. With today's instant communications and satellite hookups much can happen that holds promise for a global artistic awakening, one that hopefully incarnates the new, global, and therefore radically ecumenical cosmology into our psyches, dreams, and bodies, and even our bodies politic. A global renaissance *is* possible and the proof of this statement is that it is so necessary. The emergence of folk arts and personal arts that will put people to good work, which will bind together communities at the neighborhood level, and which will revitalize our lifestyles is equally a part of the hope that a new cosmology brings to a suffering planet.

MYSTICISM—A UNIVERSAL EXPERIENCE

A living cosmology cannot happen from science and art alone. Mysticism too must be integral to this awakening, basic to this global renaissance. Indeed, the new science is demanding a mystical awakening as we saw in part II. Yet mysticism—which represents the depth of religious traditions the world over—has *never been tried on an ecumenical level.* I cannot emphasize this fact enough. We have no inkling what power would ensue for creativity, for employing one another, for exciting the young to deep adventures once again (other than that dated adventure called war) were mysticism to be unleashed on a global scale. Because it has never been tried, we cannot predict the consequences. Why have we never tried it? Because the West has been so thoroughly out of touch with its own mystical heritage. How could the West dialogue on mysticism with the East when it did not know its own mystical roots? What can Christianity say to native peoples whose mystical traditions are so rich when Christians don't know their own mystical experience? After all, the great encounters between Christianity and native peoples and between Christianity and the Eastern religions *have occurred only in the past few centuries, i.e., during that exact period in the West when Newton and the Enlightenment extinguished the Cosmic Christ.* The point cannot be emphasized too much: We have never attempted a rapprochement between the Cosmic Christ in Christianity and the Cosmic Christ in the universe and the Cosmic Christ in other religions. Yet the Divine One is present in them all, as Joanna Macy points out:

> From Judaism, Christianity, and Islam to Hinduism, Buddhism, Taoism, and Native American and Goddess religions, each offers images of the sacred web into which we are woven. We are called children of one God and "members of one body;" we are seen as drops in the ocean of Brahman; we

are pictured as jewels in the Net of Indra. We interexist—like synapses in the mind of an all–encompassing being.[1]

A year ago a young man from mainland China joined our Institute of Culture and Creation spirituality in Oakland. He was not a Christian and had in fact never opened the bible in his life. He was a practicing Taoist in deep connection with his own mystical tradition. His grandmother had hid him in the basement during the cultural revolution in China and had taught him the ancient ways of chi chung and t'ai chi meditation. He had plumbed the well of his own tradition to reach what Eckhart calls the "great underground river" of divinity. What was the result? This young man wrote papers for me—comparing Meister Eckhart to Lao-tzu and Hildegard of Bingen to Confucius—that were as fine as any papers I have received in teaching these mystics to Westerners over the past twelve years.

How was this possible for someone not familiar with the Christian tradition? It was possible because mysticism is, like art, a common language, uttering a common experience. There is only *one* great underground river, though there are numerous wells into it—Buddhist wells and Taoist wells, Native American wells and Christian wells, Islamic wells and Judaic wells. A Sufi master of our day says:

> Sufism is not different from the mysticism of all religions. Mysticism comes from Adam (God's Peace upon him). It has assumed different shapes and forms over many centuries, for example, the mysticism of Jesus (God's Peace upon him), of monks, of hermits, and of Muhammed (God's Peace and Blessings upon him). A river passes through many countries and each claims it for its own. But there is only one river.[2]

The awakening of the mystic in our time means that many more wells are being sunk into the wet, creative, greening powers of that one underground river. The Cosmic Christ—the "pattern that connects"—can connect all persons in the context of the shared sacredness, the shared reverence and awe of our existence. I have seen this happen on a small scale with students and workshop participants I have taught over the years. For example, when I gave a series of lectures at a Mennonite seminary in the Midwest, a woman in an Indian sari, who was very attentive throughout my stay, approached me at the end of my visit. "You are the first Christian theologian I have ever met," she commented, "who spoke Hindi." "Goodness!" I replied, "I was trying to speak English." "No," she said. "I mean that you speak in images that are thoroughly Hindu and speak to my heart from my own deepest Indian roots. And those slides you showed from Hildegard (I had shown Hildegard of Bingen's twelfth-century illumination mandalas)—they too are deeply Hindu." I was not altogether surprised by this exchange. I knew of the influence of Hinduism on Celtic spirituality, and I knew that Hildegard was part of that Celtic movement along the Rhine. But I was moved by this Eastern woman's power of making connections at the level of mysticism. After all, it was the Japanese Zen Buddhist D. T. Suzuki who first convinced Thomas Merton to take Meister Eckhart seriously, just as it was the Hindu scholar Coomaraswamy who first alerted me to Meister Eckhart.

Other personal stories abound regarding my experience of the deep ecumenical nature of mysticism. I gave a lecture on creation spirituality and showed slides of Hildegard's illuminations several years ago in New Mexico. Afterwards an old Native American man with only one tooth came up, hugged me, and kissed me. "You are a red man," he said. "While you were talking all my ancestors came and sat on my shoulder and said, 'Listen to this man, he is one of us.' And the painter of those paintings you showed—she is one of us also." Living out a creation-centered mysticism prepares one for such beautiful encounters as this. Recently, I was lecturing at Pacific Lutheran Theological Seminary in Berkeley, California. When I finished a gentleman came up to me, his eyes as large as grapefruits. He was a visiting scholar from Switzerland whose field is Jewish mysticism. He had received his doctorate under the internationally renowned scholar, Gershom Scholem. He was quite ecstatic and said to me: "You are the first Christian theologian I have heard who has consciously rejected the three paths of Plotinus and Proclus. The four paths you present are deeply Jewish. Now, finally, we can pursue ecumenism between Judaism and Christianity at the level of spirituality. Your emphasis on Jesus as wisdom is the perfect bridge between our two faiths and it has never been tried!" At that time I was not lecturing on the Cosmic Christ. In this book, however, I have developed the incipient idea of Jesus as wisdom. Wisdom is the key to the Cosmic Christ in Judaism and is evidence of a Cosmic Christ tradition long before Christianity.

Buddhism boasts its own tradition of cosmic wisdom. Like its Western counterpart Sophia, this tradition speaks of wisdom as female—she is the "Mother of all Buddhas" who is teacher and nourisher of compassion. She is immeasurable and incalculable and deep like space itself, yet she is also the "ground of being."[3] She is also the void, the hole in the nave of the wheel through which the axle can turn. She is, in Western categories, prophetic; that is, a defender of the oppressed. She announces the bodhisattva path for the first time in Buddhist history, which is the path of the prophet, the path of the via transformativa, the path of acting boldly, simple, courageously for the sake of justice and peace for all creatures.

> In this dwelling of Perfect Wisdom . . . you shall become a saviour of the
> helpless, a defender of the defenseless . . . a light to the blind, and you shall
> guide to the path those who have lost it, and you shall become a support to
> those who are without support.[4]

Buddhism has a well-developed tradition of the Cosmic Christ or the "buddha nature" in all things. Consider these reflections by the Vietnamese Zen master, Thich Nhat Hanh.

> This capacity of waking up, of being aware of what is going on in your feelings, in your body, in your perceptions, in the world, is called Buddha nature, the capacity of understanding and loving. Since the baby of that Buddha is in us, we should give him or her a chance.[5]

Hanh has written an "I am" or Cosmic Christ poem.

> I am the frog swimming happily in the clear water of a pond,
> and I am also the grass-snake who,
>   approaching in silence,
>   feeds itself on the frog.
> I am the child in Uganda, all skin and bones,
>   my legs as thin as bamboo sticks,
> and I am the arms merchant, selling deadly
>   weapons to Uganda.[6]

To be in touch with our "true self" is to be at the "source of wisdom and compassion." This is something that children understand, namely "that the Buddha is in themselves."[7]

> A Buddha should be smiling, happy, beautiful, for the sake of our children.... A flower is a Buddha. A flower has Buddha nature.... It is really beautiful to begin the day by being a Buddha. Each time we feel ourselves about to leave our Buddha, we can sit and breathe until we return to our true self.[8]

When historian Arnold Toynbee commented that the coming together of Christianity and Buddhism will prove to be the most important event of the twentieth century,[9] perhaps he had an intuition about the power of the Cosmic Christ to unleash deep ecumenism.

Deep ecumenical possibilities emerge when we shift from the quest for the historical Jesus to the quest for the Cosmic Christ. This shift requires making mysticism central to our faith once again. What the human race needs today is *mystical solidarity*. We need to pray together in deep and ancient mystical ways. Especially do the oppressed peoples need to be leaders of such prayer, for their suffering is redemptive of all other peoples' suffering. The *anawim* are our natural spiritual leaders. Such a mystical solidarity will prove to be at least as valuable as political solidarity. In fact, it can promote and sustain political solidarity. Native Americans need to lead white people in prayer as do blacks; women need to lead men; "Third Worlders" need to lead "First Worlders;" gay people need to lead straight people.

For this mystical solidarity to happen, some confession of sin is in order. Jesus wisely advised that if one is offering a gift at the altar and realizes one's brother or sister has something against one then one should leave the gift at the altar and be reconciled first (Matt. 5:24). Reconciliation is in order today at the level of religions themselves. It is time that Western, white, European Christianity apologized publicly to the native peoples of America, Africa, Asia, and Europe and asked for forgiveness. With this reconciliation, we might gather at our altars with power once again. (One Christian church, the United Church of Canada, has had the courage and imagination to do this. I reproduce their apology in the Appendix of this book.) It is also time for Christianity to embrace more fully the wisdom of these peoples and to recognize the saints, heroes, and heroines of these traditions: Gandhi, Chief Seattle, Sojourner Truth, and groups of Indians and black slaves who were martyrs to their faiths—often at the hands of so-called followers of Christ—come to mind immediately. It is also time that the Western soul be cleansed by confessing its sins of omission—by banishing a living cosmology it invited religious sectarianism and war. Confession is good for the soul, including the soul of a people. Today we need public confessions from entire traditions, not just from individuals. With the forgiveness and letting go that is sure to come from such confession, deep ecumenism will be free to happen.

No one has seen this global ecumenism happen on a large scale for it has yet to be tried. The urgency of Mother Earth's plight at the hands of matricidal forces which imperil all peoples, nations, and religions would seem to indicate that the coming of the Cosmic Christ—and of the era of global ecumenism—cannot be put off any longer. This ecumenism can be described as deep because it will be truly cosmological—affecting our scientific myths along with our mystical ones—and it will be expressive of a deep art born of authentic dreams and the naming of our shared pain.

DEEP ECUMENISM—A PRELUDE TO WORLD PEACE AND JUSTICE

This era of deep ecumenism promises hope in the nuclear arms madness. The movement beyond war and militarism will take a great change of heart, a *metanoia*. Yet the mystical traditions of the world offer both theory *and practice* to bring about such change of heart. War is by definition anthropocentric dualism carried to its logical conclusion: I kill you; you kill me; we kill them; they kill us. It is the essence of all healthy mysticism to move persons beyond dualism. To do this would be to end war whose very essence is dualism. Martin Heldman of Stanford University is an expert on statistics, probability, and cryptography. He has come to the conclusion that nuclear war is mathematically inevitable, just as Russian roulette inevitably concludes in death if you play the game often enough. He points out that

no one in his right mind would play Russian roulette even once. Yet we are continually playing nuclear roulette in which the entire world is at stake.

... I'm convinced that the only way to survive nuclear roulette is to stop playing the game, to put down the gun globally, to move beyond war. If we want to avoid the world's imminent suicide, we must shift totally the way we think about war. We no longer can accept it as a means of settling disputes, as an extension of politics or as an innate ingredient in the nature of man.[10]

It is the mystical traditions that offer promise that we can indeed "shift our way of thinking about war" or indeed anything else. This is the very meaning of *metanoia* or change of heart. As Mechtild of Magdeburg put it in the thirteenth century, "I have the power to change my ways" (MM, 112). So do we! The Cosmic Christ ushering in an era of living cosmology, represents just such a power.

Deep ecumenism leads to an era of world peace and justice in still another way. Justice is a cosmological issue. In the Bible the universe is said to stand on two pillars—one is political justice and the other is psychic justice or what I would call mysticism. To heal injustice is to right relationships in the universe itself. To suffer injustice is to suffer cosmic rupture, which leads to chaos within creation. Justice is an integral part of a cosmological spirituality because justice is not a human invention. It has been integral to creation from the very first second of the fireball when order (not chaos) emerged and when harmony and balance emerged from the struggle and the destruction of the evolving creation. This quest for justice has been integral to creation's unfolding ever since. It is evident even in our bodies and in our psyche's search for balance by way of dreams, for example, when it suffers damage. As D. H. Lawrence said, "the passion of justice is a primal embrace/between man and all his known universe." Lawrence calls passionately for embracing a "new justice, new justice/between men and men, men and women, and earth and stars and suns."[11] *Homeostasis*, the scientific word for justice or equilibrium, is now recognized as a basic principle of the universe.

The unleashing of world religion's wisdom about creating justice and about increasing sensitivity to injustice will happen with the awakening to a living cosmology. The Cosmic Christ would settle for nothing less. In our century the Cosmic Christ has taken form in Gandhi, in Martin Luther King, Jr., in Dorothy Day, and in other prophets of peace and justice. But in the era of deep ecumenism the Cosmic Christ who is a warrior for justice and peace founded on justice will need to be embodied on a wider scale—among ordinary people and ordinary institutions. Renewed religious traditions living out a cosmology will make this possible.

Kabir defines a holy person as "one who is aware of others' suffering."[12] The cosmic Christ is the suffering one found in every person and creature who suffers unjustly. The suffering of injustice unites us all, and from a common grasp of that shared pain holiness emerges. With the power of holiness unleashed, anything can happen. Is there any world religion that does not call its people to compassion? Is compassion not what all world religions are about? Is compassion not a cosmic law? Meister Eckhart thought it was for he says that "the first outburst of everything God does is always compassion" (BR, 441). How then could an era of compassion—an era of celebration and justice making—not erupt globally when deep ecumenism is allowed to happen? If religious traditions cannot birth global peace and justice, can we honestly believe that state departments will? Religious traditions hold collective power—especially because they are more in touch with the *anawim* or voiceless ones—to motivate governments to interact on behalf of peace and justice.

SOME EXAMPLES OF DEEP ECUMENISM

Today we can respond to the challenge deep ecumenism poses. Does the fact that the Christ became incarnate in Jesus exclude the Christ's becoming incarnate in others—Lao-tzu or Buddha or Moses or Sarah or Sojourner Truth or Gandhi or me or you? Just the opposite is the case. In fact Paul's letter to the Galatians talks of the Christ becoming incarnate in him: "I live now not with my own life but with the life of Christ who lives in me" (Gal. 2:20). Paul challenges the recipients of his letter to "form Christ in you" (4:20) and be "sons and daughters of God" (3:27). "The proof that you are sons and daughters is that God has sent the Spirit of God's Child into our hearts: the Spirit that cries, 'Abba,' and it is this that makes you a child, you are not a slave any more; and if God has made you child, then God has made you heir" (4:6–7). The Cosmic Christ still needs to be born in all of us—no individual, race, religion, culture, or time is excluded. "Christ" is a generic name. In that sense we are all "other Christs." Deep ecumenism is the very matrix in which the Cosmic Christ is nourished and comes to birth.

One of the more surprising areas of deep ecumenism may well prove to be that between goddess religions and Christian mysticism. We are instructed, for example, that Gaia, the ancient mother goddess, is from the netherworld.[13] This is not unlike Eckhart's talking of divinity as a "great underground river that no one can dam up and no one can stop" (ME, 16). Or his statement that God is "superessential darkness" (ME, 43), for what comes from the netherworld emerges from the dark. The chant to Gaia in ancient Greece went as follows: "Earth sends up fruits so we praise Earth the Mother."[14] How alike this is to Hildegard's song to the earth: "She is the mother of all, for contained in her are the seeds of all" (HB, 58).

Furthermore, Gaia is celebrated for being "free of birth or destruction, of time or space, of form or conditions. . . . From the eternal Void, Gaia danced forth. . . ."[15] When I read the scholars of the goddess religions, I am continually struck by how similar the mystical concept of the

Godhead is to that of the goddess. For example, consider the following comments on the goddess: "The great goddess was regarded as immortal, changeless, omnipotent. The concept of father-god had not been introduced into religious thought."[16] And, "The goddess is the giver of all, life, moisture, food, happiness and taker of all. She is the mother or source . . . the mother of crafts, of spinning, of weaving. . . . The goddess is rebirth, renewal, transcendence."[17] When you compare these understandings of the ancient goddess religions with the mystical tradition of Meister Eckhart on the Godhead, for example, you find remarkable common ground that has never been explored. Meister Eckhart writes about the Godhead that God acts but the Godhead never acts. He continues:

> When I dwelt in the ground, in the bottom, in the stream, and in the source of the Godhead, no one asked me where I was going or what I was doing. Back in the womb from which I came, I had no God and merely was myself. . . . And when I return to God and to the core, the soil, the ground, the stream and the source of the Godhead, no one asks me where I am coming from or where I have been. For no one misses me in the place where God ceases to become.

(ME, 10–11)

The side of divinity that is mysterious, changeless, and the source of all birth and rebirth is expressed in Eckhart's treatment of the Godhead. There may be an important connection between "goddess" and "Godhead" that has not been seen previously because the West has not delved deeply enough into its own mystical roots. When it does so, deep ecumenism will flourish.

Mechtild of Magdeburg could write freely about the goddess as a Christian mystic and social activist in the thirteenth century: "God says to the soul: I am the God of all gods; but you are the goddess of all creatures" (MM, 33). Hildegard of Bingen calls Mary a goddess in the twelfth century. Otto Rank declares that Christianity is essentially a mother goddess religion that sought to distinguish itself from the other goddess religions of the Mediterranean by emphasizing Mary's perpetual virginity; it did this to distance itself from those religions wherein the divine son had intercourse with his mother.[18] Deep ecumenism will delve deep asking questions and exploring terrain seldom explored before. Like all authentic ecumenism the result will not be to abandon one's tradition but to demand more of it.

Part of the demand we must make on our own tradition consists in challenging the Protestant traditions to let go of their fear of mysticism and to reclaim from the spirit of their founders a living mysticism. Time and again I have found more mysticism in Protestant origins than in contemporary interpretations of those origins. Deep ecumenism requires going more deeply into one's roots and stirring up the repressed or forgotten elements. How can Lutherans, for example, be true to Luther's spirit and continue to ignore the Rhineland mystics when Luther himself acknowledges in his preface to the *Theologia Germanica*—a Rhineland mystic book—that they influenced a full third of the work? How can Lutherans be Lutherans without knowing Eckhart, Hildegard, and the Rhineland mystic/prophets who inspired Luther in so many ways? Luther's first follower in Nuremberg, Osiander, considered Hildegard to be the first Protestant (IHB, 17). It is time that Lutherans and other Protestants let go of pietism, Kantian dualism, and the Enlightenment's fear of the Cosmic Christ in order to recover the healthy mysticism of the Middle Ages. The Middle Ages were filled with protestors, among whom the creation mystics were the greatest: Hildegard (who wrote Pope Anastasius IV that "Rome stinks" and accused him of being surrounded by injustice and evil), Francis of Assisi, Thomas Aquinas, Mechtild of Magdeburg, Meister Eckhart, and Julian of Norwich. The Middle Ages do *not* belong exclusively to the Roman Catholic Church. Christianity in the West was very diverse at that time and Protestants have a right and a *need* to reclaim it.

More radical Protestant wings of prophetic mysticism such as the Quakers, the Mennonites, and the Moravian Brethren will also find allies in the prophetic mysticism of the Middle Ages. The radical Protestants of the sixteenth century—Hans Hut, Sebastian Franck and Hans Denk—deserve much more careful scrutiny than they have received from mainline Protestantism. Their prophetic mysticism—their support of the peasants—flows directly from Meister Eckhart's theology of the Cosmic Christ, from a nonelitist theology of the Word of God and of how "every creature is a word of God."[19] The first time I lectured on Meister Eckhart was in a Friends Meeting House in Highland Park, Illinois. The moment I finished, the woman who ran the Meeting House exclaimed, "My God, that sounds exactly like George Fox!" Her enthusiastic response represented the "aha" experience that can happen through deep ecumenism. Methodists need to return to the mystical roots of the Wesley brothers, as many are doing, and relate that to the larger church history that preceded it. Presbyterians may be surprised to learn that Calvin had more mystical leanings than most of his interpreters have had. Unitarians owe it to themselves to rediscover the creation mysticism of their sources such as Thoreau and Emerson. Too few Protestants know any pre–Enlightenment history—including their own—and that is one reason why letting go of the Newtonian worldview comes with so much difficulty.[20] But deep ecumenism demands such a letting go in order to renew. Part of deep ecumenism consists in reclaiming roots that go back far beyond the sixteenth and seventeenth centuries. Allies are to be found from many eras and places—the communion of saints is no small gathering—and those who are serious today about a living cosmology need all the allies they can muster. Newton has left us an inheritance that is deeply antiecumenical. Piecemeal thinking contributes to sectarianism. The splintering of the Christian Church into competitive pieces increased geometrically with Newton's worldview. The breaking up of that worldview allows ecumenism to flow.

This past year, while I was lecturing in Omaha, Nebraska, a woman came up to me and told me the following story. "I live on a farm in Minnesota three hundred miles from here," she said. "I drove all the way the attend this conference to hear you speak because all my neighbors have been telling me for a couple of years that you are the Martin Luther of our time. After hearing you speak, I agree. And I am a Lutheran. Boy, does the church need a Martin Luther today." I have spent some time meditating on this revelation, and what I believe is most true in it is the heart-felt yearning for a religious renewal and awakening in our time. While much about me is decidedly *not* Martin-Luther-like—for one thing, I have been trained as a Dominican and not as an Augustinian; for another, I have no desire whatsoever to reform the church or to see new churches started—nevertheless I cannot shirk the truth of the challenge this woman puts to all of us. For me the truth lies in the fact that creation spirituality and the recovery of a living cosmology and Cosmic Christ mysticism does indeed constitute a basis for church *renewal* (as distinct from reformation) for our time—and with it a potential for spiritual renewal that touches every element of society from small farming and education to challenging the youth and putting artists to good work.

Also implied in this woman's challenge is something about the religious moment through which we are passing. Just as the sixteenth century was a watershed for religious awakening and reform, so the late twentieth century needs to be a watershed moment for religious renewal of a deep and mystical/prophetic kind. The sixteenth century split religion up in the West so that by the time Newton's paradigm of piecemealness came along in the seventeenth century, all the parts were in place—Lutheran parts and Anglican parts, Roman Catholic parts and Presbyterian parts. But the twentieth century, beginning with the ecumenical movement in the early part of this century, has been striving to make religion whole again. We live today in a time of *post-denominational* religion. I have much more in common with an Anglican, a Methodist, or a Quaker who is committed to social justice than I do with a crippled and vengeful right-wing cardinal of the Roman Catholic Church. I derive more healing power from worshiping with the former than with the latter. Today in Boston—so Irish and Italian and Roman Catholic—I encounter the best of the Second Vatican Council Catholics who have left their church and attend Unitarian or Quaker services because they feel so deeply unrepresented by the current Catholic hierarchy of that city. The deep ecumenism about which I have written in this chapter vis-à-vis Western religions and religions of the East, North, and South (native religions) will probably imply new alignments and realignments of religious traditions of the West. Just as the Lefebvre Catholics have now left the Roman Catholic Church (the present papal regime's extraordinary efforts to keep them aboard notwithstanding), so too I believe that this is just the beginning of new alignments and realignments. At a recent summer workshop on creation spirituality in North Carolina there were not only Roman Catholics and Quakers, Anglicans and Methodists, but Southern Baptists and Seventh-Day Adventists. Mother Earth cannot wait for all the churches to get their houses perfectly in order. The Spirit is greater than any one church, yet present in some fashion in all traditions, subject always, of course, to authentic "tests of the spirit," such as justice.

EDUCATION FOR DEEP ECUMENISM

Courses in the mystics, and above all courses that *bring out the mystic* in each minister, rabbi, or priest-to-be, must be taught in our seminaries. Such courses will necessarily include art as meditation courses; every seminary needs more of these to awaken the mystic within and to empower future spiritual leaders with skills with which they can train others in church and synogogue settings. A healthy seminary on American soil would eagerly employ Native Americans to build sweat lodges and to instruct spiritual leaders in how the ancient Americans prayed. One result of this training would be a healthy situation where every church or synogogue would have a sweat house on its property. Think, among other things, how this development would put Native American people to good work and would help to heal the devastating breach between European Christians and Native American peoples. Also, there would be clay and dance and massage as meditation in the church basements for evening meditation classes.

Along with artists teaching art as meditation to awaken wisdom and the right brain, seminaries needs scientists to stimulate imaginations and minds about the reverential cosmos in which we live. Without a renewal of seminary training built around a living cosmology of artists, mystics and scientists, future so-called spiritual leaders may prove to be obstacles to the deep ecumenism that needs to happen if Mother Earth is to survive. Graduates of our seminaries may actually obstruct the coming of the Cosmic Christ. This renewal of seminary education might precipitate a renewal in public education itself so that the time would come when it would be unthinkable for persons to graduate from high school or college without the right-brain skills of art as meditation. Sweat lodges ought to become a regular feature on the campuses of every high school, college, and university, as well as every seminary, church, and synagogue.

Persons of color will invariably find that their ancestors were deeply imbued with a living cosmology before the white colonists arrived bearing a religion that, at that time in history, had lost practically all contact with the Cosmic Christ. The power of native religions to regenerate Christianity and to reconnect the old religion with the prophetic Good News of the Gospels has yet to be tapped. The essential nonanthropocentrism of these ancient religions will bring a powerful corrective and a mirror of judgment to Westerners trying, somewhat clumsily at first, to rediscover their heritage. The connections that are made in this interaction are what one would expect from the Cosmic Christ, the "pattern that connects."

THE AGE OF WISDOM—THE RENAISSANCE USHERED IN BY THE COSMIC CHRIST

If an era of a living cosmology is to occur in our time, its basic sign will be that wisdom will count more than knowledge. Wisdom will mark all aspects of a culture's existence, from its schools and training centers for spiritual leaders to its homes, places of work, of play, and of worship. Wisdom will impact political and economic life. If the Cosmic Christ has the power to come again in the hearts, minds, and bodies of the humans on this planet, then surely that Christ will come as wisdom awakened, sought after, and celebrated. The Cosmic Christ *is* the "pattern that connects" and connecting is what all wisdom is about, as the philosopher Gabriel Marcel points out: "The true function of the sage is surely the function of linking together, of bringing into harmony. . . . the sage is truly linked with the universe."[21] This is done by humans fitting anew into the cosmological order of things whence creation comes. When humans fail to do this, chaos or disaster (whose root meaning is "to be cut off from the stars") occurs. Marcel elaborates:

The important thing—and I think it is hardly possible to insist on it too much—is that in this outlook the true aim of knowledge and of life is to be integrated in the universal order, and not at all to transform the world by bringing it into subjection to the human will, to man's needs or his desires.[22]

The renaissance we hope for will be notable for its democratization of wisdom. Humanity will seek to live in harmony with the cosmos rather than to subjugate it.

Wisdom is also the lesson learned from our suffering and from the breaking of our hearts. These broken and opened hearts make compassion possible.

> I call forth tears,
> the aroma of holy work.
> I am the yearning for good.

(HB, 31)

Through wisdom, all pain can be recycled and invested in relieving the suffering of others. The wounds of the Cosmic Christ, so visible in all of our lives and Mother Earth herself today, are not in vain. Wisdom becomes the source and the end of our creative activity, for "wisdom resides in all creative works" (IHB, 49). The ongoing creation of the world will be a wise one in such hands as these. For "he who hates me [wisdom] loves death" (Prov. 8:36), but those who love wisdom experience life eternal and pass it on to others. Wisdom is the legacy of a living cosmology, the gift of the Cosmic Christ resurrected. Science, mysticism, and art come to life in order to awaken us all to wisdom.

> I came forth from the mouth of the Most High,
>   and I covered the earth like mist.
> I had my tent in the heights,
>   and my throne in a pillar of cloud.
> Alone I encircled the vault of the sky,
>   And I walked on the bottom of the deeps.
> Over the waves of the sea and over the whole earth,
>   and over every people and nation I have held sway.
> Among all these I searched for rest,
>   and looked to see in whose territory I might
>   pitch camp.
>
> (Sir. 24:3–12)

Notice the expansive cosmology and the deep ecumenism of this promise that people of "every nation" are held sway by wisdom. Dare wisdom pitch her camp among humans in our time? Might this actually happen? What are the consequences if it does not happen? We and our children need to be and indeed deserve to be showered by wisdom, ravished by wisdom, watered by wisdom. As Nicholas of Cusa put it, "Even though you are designated in terms of different religions, yet you presuppose in all this diversity *one religion which you call wisdom.*"[23] The Cosmic Christ ushers in an era of such wisdom.

IS THE "COSMIC CHRIST" A TERM THAT IS ANTI-ECUMENICAL?

The question logically arises as to how ecumenical the term "Cosmic Christ" is. Can persons not of the Christian heritage be at home with it, or is it an ever more subtle term for Christian proselytizing? Throughout the writing of this book it has become increasingly evident to me how the concept of the Cosmic Christ is pre-Christian. The image of God in every atom and galaxy is not exactly a property of Christians. The divine "I am" in every person and every creature is no particular tradition's private legacy. Indeed, many non-Christians and post-Christians have written at length and quite happily about the "Cosmic Christ" including Paramahansa Yogananda, Rudolf Steiner, and Carl Jung. Bede Griffiths has written a book on the Cosmic Christ in Hinduism. I have demonstrated in this book that the Cosmic Christ concept is deep in

242 / THE COMING OF THE COSMIC CHRIST

the Jewish tradition of wisdom and is also found in the Jewish prophets and apocalyptic literature long before Jesus Christ. Scientists, like Ken Wilber, who talks of the "isness of each thing-event" as being "the most fundamental and elemental starting point for all mystical traditions,"[24] are talking of the Cosmic Christ, of the divine "isness" present in every creature. Physicist David Bohm says that "the whole is present in each part, in each level of existence. The living reality, which is total and unbroken and undivided, is in everything."[25] A name for this "living reality" is the Cosmic Christ. Non-Christian people I meet do not tell me of their displeasure at Jesus Christ, who they invariably believe was indeed an incarnation of the Cosmic Christ. Their problems lie with Christians.

The word *christos* or "christ" means in the original Greek, "the anointed one." Kings and priests were anointed in ancient Israel. The Messiah too was understood to be "Christ" or an anointed one. Is the Cosmic Christ not an archetype about how we are all in some way anointed kings, queens, priests, and messiahs? Are we not all called to do what D. H. Lawrence writes about, "to distill the essential oil out of every experience"?[26] Didn't Jesus do this, namely to distill the essential oil out of his Judaic heritage? Are religious believers not called to do this today?

The word *christos* suggests a royal person since royalty are anointed. Is there any religion that does not celebrate the royalty of all creatures patterned after the royal dignity of the Creator? Being anointed involves oil. Oil makes smooth, it limits friction, it lubricates. Lubrication is especially important in our day of connection making, global awakening, and deep ecumenism. We need help in times like this to minimize friction between diverse and disparate traditions, peoples and creatures so that we can get on with our common work: building community. Just as the word "harmony" comes from the Greek for "shoulder" because the joints of the shoulder work together with so little friction, so too the work of harmony today requires oil, christos, as we struggle together to make cosmic and local connections.[27] Hildegard of Bingen talked of how Christ brings the "oil of compassion" (BDW, 321), a happy phrase that indicates the lubricant that compassion is about, the healing powers of justice and of celebration that compassion brings. In this context *christos* can also mean anointed as prophets, for the prophet is one who brings compassion or justice. Jesus came explicitly as one oiled or "anointed" as prophet. "The Spirit of the Lord has been given to me, for God has anointed me . . . to bring the good news to the poor" (Luke 4:18). Elisabeth Schüssler Fiorenza points out that all four Gospels tell the story of the woman who anoints Jesus (Mark 14:3–9; Matt. 26:6–13; Luke 7:36–50; John 12:1–8). This anointing is a "prophetic recognition of Jesus, the Anointed, the Messiah, the Christ. According to the tradition it was a woman who named Jesus by and through her prophetic sign-action. It was a politically dangerous story."[28] Would it be any less politically dangerous for persons today to be anointing one another as other

Cosmic Christs? The fact that it was an unnamed *woman* who did the anointing tells us more about the way the Christ comes: the Christ comes most readily through those without a voice. Can he also come as other Christs, that is as ones oiled and anointed to be prophets? Abraham Heschel taught that "there is the grain of the prophet in the recesses of every human existence."[29] Can we anoint one another, celebrate and empower one another, to be prophet? As we do so, are we not anointing one another as other Christs, as Cosmic Christs?

Given these explanations of the term *christos*, it may still be that, because of the sins of Christians toward persons of other faiths over the centuries, the term "Cosmic Christ" carries too much baggage with it that might hinder deep ecumenism. If that is the case, there is another phrase which carries a similar message: "Cosmic Wisdom." Hildegard of Bingen teaches that every person is born with "original wisdom" (IHB, 57). Thus the term "Cosmic Wisdom" bears most of the meaning of the term "Cosmic Christ." I prefer the term "Cosmic Christ" because I am a Westerner and the term "Cosmic Christ" is our term for "Cosmic Wisdom." Furthermore, I choose to be a creation-centered Christian and part of this commitment is to accept responsibility for my role in awakening Christians to that shadow side of their tradition known as creation spirituality or the Cosmic Christ tradition. It is important that ecumenism not be applied only to those traditions outside one's own. A deep ecumenism will critique and attempt to renew one's own roots, as Carl Jung advised when he said: "Of what use to us is the wisdom of the Upanishads or the insight of Chinese yoga, if we desert the foundations of our own culture as though they were errors outlived and, like homeless pirates, settle with thievish intent on foreign shores?"[30]

Christianity needs to contribute its riches to an awakening of Cosmic Wisdom and it will do so by way of a tradition known as that of the "Cosmic Christ." One of the principle gifts of Judaism and Christianity to world religions is the tradition of the prophets. Gandhi taught Indians that they needed to learn to say no from the West.[31] The prophets are experts, one might say, at *time*. They choose to interfere with history in order to render it more sacred, more just. Just as a tremendous mystical awakening occurs when native spiritualities offer their gifts of mysticism and space consciousness to Westerners, so too the West has a gift of an awareness of the sacredness of time and of the need for prophetic interference with injustice in human history: this is the gift the West has to offer to these more nature-based religions. The fact that the Cosmic Christ is wounded is another important Western contribution to a Cosmic Wisdom spirituality. Persons of other faiths will have to decide for themselves on the appropriate terminology for them. The purpose of this book has been to explore the meaning behind the term and the tradition of the Cosmic Christ in the West and to offer that meaning as a common ground for understanding and responding to the challenges of our time.

THE COSMIC CHRIST SPEAKS ON DEEP ECUMENISM

Listen to the Cosmic Christ, to Cosmic Wisdom calling all the children of God together: "Come, children, drink of my waters which are all common waters. They are free and available to all my children. Drink of my wisdom from your own unique well. Let the Taoists drink and the Muslims drink; let the Jews drink and the Buddhists drink; let the Christians drink and let the native peoples drink. And then tell me: What have you drunk? How deeply have you imbibed my refreshment? What wet and running wisdom drips from inside you to the outside? What have you to share with others of my wisdom and harmonious living, of the dripping of the oils of compassion and the lubricants of your common anointings as my images, my other "Christs," my co-creators of wisdom on earth? I am tired of your religious wars, your sectarian divisions, your crusading spirits that arise from disharmony. I long for harmony. If there must be competition let it take place at the level of shared gifts and bountiful outpouring of wisdom. Pray together. Create harmony and healing together. Celebrate, praise, and thank together. Cease using religion to divide. Use it for its purpose, to reconnect to Mother Earth, to blessings, to the underground river that I am and that you all share. And cease scandalizing the young by your indifference to these awesome blessings, by your competition, and your boredom. Praise one another. Praise the earth. In doing so, you praise me."

Epilogue: Vatican III—A Dream

Since this book began with a dream it seems reasonable to end it with another dream—one that came to me after I thought I had finished writing the book.

The year is 1992. Mother Africa and the so-called Third World has now penetrated Western religion, and the newly elected pope, John XXIV, is the first African pope. Mother Africa, where the human race began, is now represented at the symbolic center of Western faith. Pope John XXIV has called for a new ecumenical council, Vatican III. The purpose of this Council is to define the doctrine of the Cosmic Christ as being intrinsic to faith. The Council will also consider as immediate corollaries to this doctrine the issues of sexuality as mysticism, cosmic worship, deep ecumenism, folk art as a basic means to employ the one billion unemployed adults around the world, and youth and adult relationships. Expected at the Council are not only bishops from around the world but leaders of all the world's religions including representatives of the native religions of Africa, Australia, America, Asia and Europe. The goddess religions are represented as well. Expected also is a large delegation of artists whose interest in the Cosmic Christ and in the renewal of worship in particular is electric. How is it possible that so much creativity and so much hope are coming together in one place in the name of a spiritual awakening of the human race?

Perhaps it has to do with the first action taken by Pope John XXIV, which was to offer a public apology in the name of Western Christianity to native peoples, women, homosexual people, scientists (this action was begun under Pope John Paul II when he removed Galileo from the condemned list) and artists, for the sins of the Church against them. These groups, after considerable debate among their constituencies, have accepted the papal apology and will play a prominent part in the forthcoming, truly ecumenical, Council. All seem interested in celebrating the divine image in all creatures, even human ones. All appear excited about calling forth the Cosmic Christ traditions from their spiritual heritage and offering them as a gift to redeem Mother Earth, as a gift to our children and theirs for generations to come.

Another action taken by Pope John XXIV has been to dismantle entirely the Office of the Inquisition (lately known as the Congregation of the Doctrine of the Faith) and to replace it with a board of grandmothers who will counsel the overall church on implications of doctrine and movements for the young. Still another action taken by this pope has been to gather all the Opus Dei bishops of the world on one island where, it is said, they are undergoing a two-year spiritual retreat that includes a critique of the history of fascism and Christianity on the one hand and an inculcation of creation spirituality on the other. It is said these bishops do body prayer three times daily and art as meditation four hours per day. The native people of the island are the instructors for their art as meditation classes. Women have assumed the office of bishop in their respective diocesan sees.

At the United Nations plans are underway for the great global happening of the year 2000. That happening is, in religious terms, the celebration of the Jubilee Year. The Jubilee Year of 2000 will mark a global switch-over from the current economic and banking system to a new one. It includes the letting go of all debts from so-called Third World countries and the reconstituting of a system of monetary security that includes all nations. The starting point for this economic system is not humanly conceived monetary systems but the shared wealth of the world beginning with the earth's treasures of the waters, forests, soil, animals, birds, fishes, and plants. Preparations for this vast act of global "letting go" and global creativity are occupying the creative minds of all nations. The planet is alive with excitement. To stimulate the countdown for this act of giving and beginning anew there has been, beginning in 1992, a 10 percent *annual* reduction in armaments spending by every nation on the earth. Persons and nations alike are astounded by the amount of available capital and available jobs as a result of this tithing by the military to the defense of Mother Earth. Preparations are underway to convert *all* defense departments of all nations from defending nations against armies to defending Mother Earth against the human species. It is agreed that the changeover in human attitudes required of such a conversion will require a spiritual basis. With this end in sight, spiritual disciplines and traditions are being taught in all educational programs, East and West, from kindergarten through graduate schools. No lawyers, engineers, doctors, or business persons are graduating without knowing the cosmic story of the origins of the universe and of the powers and possibilities of the human species. All are learning both ancient and new ways to praise. The human race is relearning the meaning of reverence: the shared awe about its own existence and responsibilities. Artists are at the forefront—along with native spiritual leaders and regenerated spiritual leaders from West and East—in awakening persons to their own Cosmic Wisdom. In this context a global renaissance seems well underway. And Pope John XXIV, it is widely felt, is lending powerful impetus to this movement. The Third Vatican Council is expected to do the same.

Appendix A
Apology to Native Congregations—
United Church of Canada

Submitted by the United Church of Canada General Council to Native Elders and accepted by the Same on August 15, 1986:

Long before my people journeyed to this land
your people were here, and you received from
your elders an understanding of creation, and of the
Mystery that surrounds us all that was deep, and rich and
    to be treasured.
We did not hear you when you shared your vision.
In our zeal to tell you of the good news of Jesus Christ
we were closed to the value of your spirituality.
We confused western ways and culture with the depth and breadth
    and length and height of the gospel of Christ.
We imposed our civilization as a condition of accepting the Gospel.
We tried to make you be like us and in so doing
we helped to destroy the vision that made you what you were.
As a result you, and we, are poorer and the image of the Creator
    in us is twisted, blurred and we are not what we are meant
    by God to be.
We ask you to forgive us and we ask you to walk with us
    in the spirit of Christ so that our peoples may be blessed
    and God's creation healed.

Prayers were offered in four languages—Mohawk, Cree, Kwaquilth, and English—and a native dance of victory was held. Pledges of commitment and solidarity with native people and their needs were exchanged.

Appendix B
Apology to Native Congregations—
Pacific Northwest Church Leaders

On November 21, 1987, in Seattle Washington, the following Public Declaration was presented by the Christian church leaders whose names are at the bottom of the page to the "Tribal Councils and Traditional Spiritual Leaders of the Indian and Eskimo Peoples of the Pacific Northwest in care of Jewell Praying Wolf James, Lummi."

Dear Brothers and Sisters,
    This is a formal apology on behalf of our churches for their

long-standing participation in the destruction of traditional Native American spiritual practices. We call upon our people for recognition of and respect for your traditional ways of life and for protection of your sacred places and ceremonial objects. We have frequently been unconscious and insensitive and have not come to your aid when you have been victimized by unjust Federal policies and practices. In many other circumstances we reflected the rampant racism and prejudice of the dominant culture with which we too willingly identified. During the 200th Anniversary year of the United States Constitution we, as leaders of our churches in the Pacific Northwest, extend our apology. We ask for your forgiveness and blessing.

As the Creator continues to renew the earth, the plants, the animals and all living things, we call upon the people of our denominations and fellowships to a commitment of mutual support in your efforts to reclaim and protect the legacy of your own traditional spiritual teachings. To that end we pledge our support and assistance in upholding the American Religious Freedom Act (P.L. 95-134, 1978) and within that legal precedent affirm the following:

1) The rights of the Native Peoples to practice and participate in traditional ceremonies and rituals with the same protection offered all religions under the Constitution.

2) Access to and protection of sacred sites and public lands for ceremonial purposes.

3) The use of religious symbols (feathers, tobacco, sweet grass, bones, etc.) for use in traditional ceremonies and rituals.

The spiritual power of the land and the ancient wisdom of your indigenous religions can be, we believe, great gifts to the Christian churches. We offer our commitment to support you in the righting of previous wrongs: To protect your peoples' efforts to enhance Native spiritual teachings; to encourage the members of our churches to stand in solidarity with you on these important religious issues; to provide advocacy and mediation, when appropriate, for ongoing negotiations with State agencies and Federal officials regarding these matters.

May the promises of this day go on public record with all the congregations of our communions and be communicated to the Native American Peoples of the Pacific Northwest. May the God of Abraham and Sarah, and the Spirit who lives in both the cedar and Salmon People be honored and celebrated.

Sincerely,

The Rev. Thomas L. Blevins,
  Bishop
Pacific Northwest Synod
Lutheran Church in America

The Most Rev. Raymond G.
  Hunthausen
Archbishop of Seattle
Roman Catholic Archdiocese of
  Seattle

The Rev. Dr. Robert Bradford,
Executive Minister
American Baptist Churches of the
   Northwest

The Rev. Elizabeth Knott,
Synod Executive
Presbyterian Church
Synod Alaska-Northwest

The Rev. Robert Brock
N.W. Regional Christian
   Church

The Rev. Lowell Knutson,
Bishop
North Pacific District
American Lutheran Church

The Right Rev. Robert H.
   Cochrane,
Bishop, Episcopal Diocese of
   Olympia

The Most Rev. Thomas
   Murphy
Coadjutor Archbishop
Roman Catholic Archdiocese of
   Seattle

The Rev. W. James Halfaker
Conference Minister
Washington North Idaho
   Conference
United Church of Christ

The Rev. Melvin G. Talbert,
Bishop
United Methodist Church—
Pacific Northwest Conference

Appendix C
Apology to Native Congregations—
United Church of Christ
A Statement to the United Church of Christ and the
Indian Community of the United Church of Christ
Expressing Penitence and the Hope of
Reconcilation

WHEREAS: 1987 is a Year of Reconciliation in Minnesota between
the dominant culture and the Indian people. Part of the remembrances
is dealing with the 1862 Indian and White conflict.

AND WHEREAS: Last year the United Church of Canada apologized
to native people for their historical and present lack of sensitivity to
them and to their religious heritage.

AND WHEREAS: Our Indian Concern Committee believes that the
Minnesota Conference should lead the United Church of Christ in ad-
dressing our Church's wrongs against the Indians.

THEREFORE, BE IT RESOLVED: The Sixteenth General Synod
adopts the following statement:

The United Church of Christ through its long involvement with Indian people bears a heavy burden of responsibility—as part of the dominant culture—for the ongoing injustice and religious imperialism that have been so disruptive of the inherent values of Indian life and culture.

The United Church of Christ through its antecedent bodies was the first Protestant church to have a mission relationship with the Indians of North America. Beginning with the initial overtures between the Pilgrims and the New England tribes; through the first translation of the Bible into a native tongue by John Eliot; the missionary efforts of Jonathan Edwards, David Brainerd, and many others; down through the major mission outposts among various Indian tribes, established by the American Board of Commissioners for Foreign Missions in the mid-Nineteenth Century—mission has been understood to mean the conversion of the Indians to Christianity and to western civilizations.

The cumulative effect, unfortunately, of the missionary legacy and the larger Christian influence has been the disparagement and undermining of the Indian culture and the way of life and a spiritual impoverishment affecting both Indian and all people. Often the missionaries were blinded by the pervasive cultural and religious ethnocentrism of western society. We must acknowledge that the church—our church—has with few exceptions, treated the Indian as a child in need of direction, as a savage in need of civilizing, and as a heathen in need of salvation.

The result has been to create an overall sense of loss, which has distorted the Indian people's self image, along with cultural and spiritual traditions. The depth of this tragedy, and how it has hurt not only Indian, but all people, has only begun to be realized.

The United Church of Christ takes responsibility for its part in this ongoing atrocity, and expresses to you, our Indian brothers and sisters, a deeply felt sorrow and a penitent spirit. At the same time, we seek an ongoing reconciliation that can be expressed in dialogue, mutual concern, and, furthermore, a reconciliation that seeks to share your wisdom, truth, and sensitivity. We affirm as essential your struggle to reclaim cultural traditions and pledge our support.

Appendix D
A Litany of Deliverance

From Patriarchy's dualism,
From Patriarchy's proneness to self-pity,
From Patriarchy's sentimentalism,
From Patriarchy's violence,
From Patriarchy's lack of imagination,
From Patriarchy's intellectual laziness,

From Patriarchy's lack of authentic curiosity,
From Patriarchy's separation of head from body,
From Patriarchy's separation of body from feelings,
From Patriarchy's preoccupation with sex,
From Patriarchy's fear of intimacy,
From Patriarchy's reptilian brain,
From Patriarchy's anthropocentrism,
From Patriarchy's cosmic loneliness,
From Patriarchy's crucifixion of Mother Earth,
From Patriarchy's envy and manipulation of children,
From Patriarchy's abuse of women,
From Patriarchy's homophobia,
From Patriarchy's righteousness,
From Patriarchy's idolatry of nationhood and national security,
From Patriarchy's forgetfulness of beauty and art,
From Patriarchy's impotence to heal,
From Patriarchy's sado-masochism,
From Patriarchy's parental cannibalism and devouring of its children,
From Patriarchy's lack of balance,
From Patriarchy's savaging of the earth,
From Patriarchy's quest for immortality,
From Patriarchy's ego,
From Patriarchy's waste of talent and resources, human and earth,
From Patriarchy's human chauvinism,
From Patriarchy's compulsion to go into debt to finance its bloated
   lifestyles,
From Patriarchy's matricide, spare us O Divine One.

Notes

Prologue

1. Matthew Fox, *Breakthrough: Meister Eckhart's Creation Spirituality in New Translation* (Garden City, NY: Doubleday & Co., 1980), 309. Scientist Erich Jantsch says: "Our search is ultimately devoted not to a precise knowledge of the universe, but to a grasp of the role which we play in it—to the meaning of our life. The self-organization paradigm which lays open the dimensions of connectedness between all forms of unfolding of a natural dynamics, is about to deepen the recognition of such a meaning. . . . It is no longer the *re-ligio* to the origin which mediates this highest intensity in mystical rapture. It reappears also with the progressing of evolution. The highest meaning is in the non-unfolded as well as in the fully unfolded; both reach up to the divinity." In Erich Jantsch, *The Self-Organizing Universe* (New York: Pergamon Press, 1980), 310–11.
2. Wendell Berry asks: What is our defense against this sort of language—this language-as-weapon? There is only one. We must know a better language. . . . The only defense against the worst is a knowledge of the best. By their ignorance people enfranchise their exploiters." In Wendell Berry, *A Continuous Harmony* (New York: Harcourt Brace Jovanovich, 1972), 172.
3. Cited in Philip Shabecoff, "Action is Urged to Save Species," *New York Times*, 28 September 1986, 28.
4. Harold Gilliam, "State of the World," *San Francisco Chronicle*, 25 October 1987, This World section, 18.
5. Alice Miller, *The Drama of the Gifted Child* (New York: Basic Books, 1981), 57.
6. "Introduction to the Prophets," in *The Jerusalem Bible*, ed. Alexander Jones (Garden City, NY: Doubleday & Co., 1966), 1140–41.
7. Ibid., 1141.
8. Gregory Bateson, *Mind and Nature* (New York: Bantam Books, 1980), 19.
9. Berry, *Harmony*, 6.
10. The term is bluntly used by Dorothee Soelle in *Beyond Mere Obedience* (New York: Pilgrim Press, 1982), xvi.
11. Gerard Manley Hopkins, "That Nature is a Heraclitean Fire and of the comfort of the Resurrection," in *Poems of Gerard Manley Hopkins*, ed. Robert Bridges and W. H. Gardner (New York: Oxford Univ. Press, 1948), 112.
12 Bateson, *Mind*, 109.
13. Jolande Jacobi and R. F. C. Hull, eds., *C. G. Jung: Psychological Reflections* (Princeton: Princeton Univ. Press, 1978), 206.

PART 1

Epigraph 1: This quote from an aboriginal woman appeared on a greeting card I received.
Epigraph 2: Gabriel Uhlein, *Meditations with Hildegard of Bingen* (Santa Fe, NM: Bear & Co., 1982), 58.
Epigraph 3: Monica Sjöö and Barbara Mor, *The Great Cosmic Mother* (San Francisco: Harper & Row, 1987), 51.
Epigraph 4: Rosemary Ruether, *Mary—The Feminine Face of the Church* (Philadelphia: Westminster Press, 1977), 45.
Epigraph 5: Lao-tsu, *The Way of Life*, trans. Witter Bynner (New York: Capricorn Books, 1962), 40.
Epigraph 6: Adrienne Rich, *Of Woman Born* (New York: W. W. Norton & Co., 1977), 280.
Epigraph 7: Glenys Livingstone, *Motherhood Mythology* (self-published, 1984), 64.

Epigraph 8: Guy Murchie, *The Seven Mysteries of Life* (Boston: Houghton Mifflin Co., 1978), 1–2

Epigraph 9: Cited in Joseph Epes Brown, *The Spiritual Legacy of the American Indian* (New York: Crossroad, 1986), 92.

Epigraph 10: Buck Ghosthorse, *Red Nations Sacred Way* (Oakland, CA: self-published, 1987), 10.

1. Mother Earth Is Dying

1. "Position Paper of the Native American Project of the Theology in the Americas Conference" (Detroit, MI, July/August, 1980), 2.
2. Cited in William Tuohy, "Europe Faces an Ecological Nightmare," *Oakland Tribune*, 16 November 1986, C–7.
3. I am indebted for many of these facts to the work and study of Dr. Brian Swimme of the Institute in Culture and Creation Spirituality, Oakland, CA. See Samuel S. Epstein et al., *Hazardous Waste in America: Our Number One Environmental Crisis* (San Francisco: Sierra Club, 1983) and Paul R. Ehrlich and Anne H. Ehrlich, *Extinction: Causes and Consequences of Disappearances of Species* (New York: Random House, 1981).
4. See Frances Moore Lappe, *Diet for a Small Planet* (New York: Ballantine Books, 1975) and Frances Moore Lappe and Joseph Collins, *World Hunger: Twelve Myths* (New York: Grove Press, 1986).
5. Cited in Philip Shabecoff, "Action is Urged to Save Species," *New York Times*, 28 September 1986, 28.
6. James M. Markham, "Chernobyl Fuels Nuclear Anxieties in Europe," *New York Times*, 18 May 1986, sec. 4, p. 1.
7. Rainer Maria Rilke, *The Sonnets to Orpheus: Rainer Maria Rilke*, trans. Stephen Mitchell (New York: Simon & Schuster, 1986), 41.

2. The Mystical Brain Is Dying

1. Laurens van der Post, "Wilderness: A Way of Truth," *One Earth* (Summer/October, 1984), 6.
2. Ken Wilber, ed., *The Holographic Paradigm and Other Paradoxes* (Boulder, CO: Shambhala, 1982), 2.
3. Ibid., 3. Italics Wilber's.
4. Fritjof Capra, "Holonomy and Bootstrap," in Wilber, *Holographic*, 114.

3. Creativity Is Dying

1. Jacobi, *Jung*, 196.
2. Rollo May, *The Courage to Create* (New York: W. W. Norton & Co., 1975), 120–22.
3. Joanna Rogers Macy, *Despair and Personal Power in the Nuclear Age* (Philadelphia: New Society Publishers, 1983), 2–16.
4. May, *Courage*, 124.
5. Ibid., 134.

4. Wisdom Is Dying

1. May, *Courage*, 132.

5. The Youth Are Dying

1. Alice Miller, *For Your Own Good* (New York: Farrar Straus Giroux, 1984), xi.
2. Alice Miller, *Thou Shalt Not Be Aware* (New York: New American Library, 1986), 97.
3. Alfred North Whitehead, *Science and the Modern World* (New York: Macmillan, 1927), 276.

6. Native Peoples, Their Religions, and Cultures Are Dying

1. Frederick Turner, *Beyond Geography: The Western Spirit Against the Wilderness* (New York: The Viking Press, 1980), 248.

2. Cited in Charlene Spretnak, *Lost Goddesses of Early Greece* (Boston: Beacon Press, 1978), 14.
3. Ibid.
4. Tzvetan Todorov, *The Conquest of America: The Question of the Other*, trans. Richard Howard (New York: Harper & Row, 1984), 133; Pierre Vilar, *A History of Gold and Money 1450–1920*, trans. Judith White (London: Verso Editions, 1976), 67. I am indebted to Marvin Anderson for his scholarship on these topics. See Marvin Anderson's "On 'the Beaten Christ of the Indies,' Bartolomé de las Casas' Polemic on the Annihilation of the Indians in New Spain" (Class paper, University of Toronto, 1985).
5. Juan Friede, "Las Casas and Indigenism in the Sixteenth Century," in *Bartolomé de Las Casas in History: Toward an Understanding of the Man and His Work*, ed. Juan Friede and Benjamin Keen (Dekalb, IL: Northern Illinois Univ. Press, 1971), 209, 212.
6. Bartolomé de Las Casas, *History of the Indies* (New York: Harper & Row, 1971), 190.
7. Friede, "Indigenism," 324–25.
8. Cited in Matthew Fox, *Whee! We, wee All the Way Home* (Santa Fe, NM: Bear & Co., 1981), 22.
9. Cited in Enrique Dussel, *A History of the Church in Latin America: Colonialism to Liberation (1492–1979)*, trans. Alan Neely (Grand Rapids, MI: William B. Eerdmans Publishing Co., 1981), 313.
10. This story is recounted in Joseph G. Donders, *Non-Bourgeois Theology* (Maryknoll, NY: Orbis Books, 1985), 2.
11. Laurens van der Post, "Wilderness," 4.
12. Robert Boissiere, *Meditations with the Hopi* (Santa Fe, NM: Bear & Co., 1986), 100.

7. Mother Church Is Dying

1. Anthony Stevens, *Archetypes: A Natural History of the Self* (New York: William Morrow & Co., 1982), 132.
2. Ibid., 133–34.
3. Ibid., 132–33.
4. Ibid., 133.
5. Ibid., 134. Italics Stevens's.
6. Ibid., 91.
7. Ibid., 96–97.
8. Ibid., 129–30.

8. Mother Love (Compassion) Is Dying

1. Otto Rank, *Beyond Psychology* (New York: Dover Publications, 1958), 140–43. Rank believes that Christianity, "by giving the ancient Oriental mother-cult a new human meaning, for the first time translated the psychology of the son into a mother-concept, whereas formerly it was derived from the father-relation, that is, was a social concept." For him, Christianity "lifted the father-son problem from its biological base as manifested in Jewish tradition and from its socialized crystallization in Roman Law into a timeless and stateless spiritual philosophy" of love (142).
2. Says Augustine: "As regards the woman alone, she is not the image of God, but, as regards the man alone, he is the image of God as fully and completely as when the woman too is joined with him in one." (*de Trinitate* 7.7, 10).
3. Rusty Schweikert, lecture given at Institute in Culture and Creation Spirituality, Holy Names College, Oakland, CA, Spring 1985. Astronaut Edgar Mitchell speaks of similar mystical experiences in Murchie, *Mysteries*, 618.

9. Our Mother Is Dying, but Not Dead

1. At least one author provides substantive evidence that this pope's sudden death was not accidental. See David A. Yallop, *In God's Name: An Investigation into the Murder of Pope John Paul I* (New York: Bantam Books, 1984).

PART II

Epigraph 1: Rainer Maria Rilke, *The Selected Poetry of Rainer Maria Rilke*, trans. Stephen Mitchell (New York: Vintage Books, 1984), 135.

Epigraph 2: Jelaluddin Rumi, *The Ruins of the Heart: Selected Lyric Poetry of Jelaluddin Rumi*, trans. Edmund Helminski (Putney, VT: Threshold Books, 1981), 26, 32.

Epigraph 3: Abraham Joshua Heschel, *The Earth is the Lord's* (New York: Farrar Straus Giroux, 1978), 70–71.

Epigraph 4: *Teresa of Avila: The Interior Castle*, trans. Kieran Kavanaugh (New York: Paulist Press, 1979), 196.

Epigraph 5: Thomas Berry, "Future Forms of Religious Experience," in *Riverdale Papers*, vol. 5, ed. Thomas Berry (Riverdale, NY: Riverdale Center, n.d.), 2.

Epigraph 6: Patrick Kavanagh, *Collected Poems* (London: Martin Brian & O'Keefe, 1972), 149.

Epigraph 7: Gregory Bateson, *Steps to an Ecology of Mind* (New York: Ballantine Books, 1972), 146.

Epigraph 8: Guy Murchie, *The Seven Mysteries of Life* (Boston: Houghton Mifflin Co., 1978), 258–59.

Epigraph 9: Otto Rank, *Beyond Psychology* (New York: Dover Publications, 1958), 250.

Epigraph 10: Matthew Fox, *Breakthrough: Meister Eckhart's Creation Spirituality in New Translation* (Garden City, NY: Doubleday & Co., 1980), 427.

Epigraph 11: Fritjof Capra, "The Tao of Physics Revisited," in *The Holographic Paradigm and Other Paradoxes*, ed. Ken Wilber (Boulder, CO: Shambhala, 1982), 243.

Epigraph 12: Dorothee Soelle, *To Work and To Love: A Theology of Creation* (Philadelphia: Fortress Press, 1984), 137.

Epigraph 13: Rilke, *Selected Poetry*, 221.

Epigraph 14: Gabriel Uhlein, *Meditations with Hildegard of Bingen* (Santa Fe, NM: Bear & Co., 1982), 85.

Epigraph 15: Sehdev Kumar, *The Vision of Kabir* (Concord, Ontario, Canada: Alpha & Omega, 1984), 123.

Epigraph 16: *The Poems of St. John of the Cross*, trans. John Frederick Nims (Chicago: Univ. of Chicago Press, 1979), 19.

Epigraph 17: Henry David Thoreau, *Walden*, cited in Frederick Turner, *Beyond Geography: The Western Spirit Against the Wilderness* (New York: The Viking Press, 1980), ix.

Epigraph 18: Wendell Berry, *A Continuous Harmony* (New York: Harcourt Brace Jovanovich, 1972), 14.

10. The Etymology of Mysticism

1. John Baptist Scaramelli, S.J., *The Directorium Asceticum, or Guide to the Spiritual Life*, vol. 2 (New York: Benziger Brothers, 1908), 15–16, 96, 99.
2. See Arthur J. Deikman, "Deautomatization and the Mystic Experience," in *Altered States of Consciousness*, ed. Charles T. Tart (Garden City, NY: Doubleday & Co., 1972), 25–46; Matthew Fox, *Whee! We, wee All the Way Home: A Guide to Sensual, Prophetic Spirituality* (Santa Fe, NM: Bear & Co., 1981), 55–72.
3. Brian Swimme, *The Universe is a Green Dragon: A Cosmic Creation Story* (Santa Fe, NM: Bear & Co., 1985), 151.
4. Murchie, *Mysteries*, 113, 121.

11. The Denial of the Mystic

1. See Alice Miller, *For Your Own Good* (New York: Farrar Straus Giroux, 1984), 108.
2. José A. Arguelles, *The Transformative Vision* (Berkeley, CA: Shambhala, 1975), 36.
3. Frithjof Schuon, *The Transcendental Unity of Religions* (Wheaton, IL: Theosophical Publishing House, 1984), xv–xvi.
4. A student of Neibuhr's told me he said this in class. In Neibuhr's defense it should be said that his criticism of mysticism was aimed at a mysticism that fled the world, was

dualistic, Hellenistic, ascetic, without a sense of prophetic criticism or a love of creation. Unfortunately, Neibuhr never had the creation-centered mystical tradition named for him. See Reinhold Niebuhr, *An Interpretation of Christian Ethics* (New York: Meridian, 1956), 27–39, 69–71, 189–92.

5. Anders Nygren, *Agape and Eros* (New York: Harper & Row/Harper Torchbooks, 1969), 650.

6. A woman seminarian has written me a similar letter: "You said in your book that more seminary students should 'come out of the closet' and admit that they are mystics. I did that several years ago and met with anger and ridicule. . . . They couldn't understand my relationship with God at all and therefore concluded that I had none; worse, that I had no God." The woman left the seminary.

7. Cf. Rosemary Ruether, *Mary—The Feminine Face of the Church* (Philadelphia: Westminster Press, 1977), 25–26; Eloise McKinney-Johnson, "Egypt's Isis: The Original Black Madonna," *Journal of African Civilizations* 6 (April 1984): 64–71; Ean Begg, *The Cult of the Black Virgin* (Boston: Arkana, 1985).

12. The Rise of Pseudo-Mysticism

1. Jacobi and Hull, *Jung*, 161.
2. Jacobi and Hull, *Jung*, Ibid.
3. James Hillman, "Senex and Puer: An Aspect of the Historical and Psychological Present," in *Puer Papers*, ed. James Hillman (Dallas, TX: Spring Publications, 1987), 67.
4. Albert Einstein, *Ideas and Opinions* (New York: Crown, 1982), 11.
5. Cited in Willis W. Harman, *The Post-Modern Heresy: Portents of a Fundamental Shift in Worldview* (Paper delivered at the Conference on a Post-Modern World, Santa Barbara, CA, 16–20 January 1986).
6. Capra, "Tao," 243.

13. Twenty-one Running, Working, Experiential Definitions of Mysticism

1. Kumar, *Kabir*, 128, 134.
2. *Rilke on Love and Other Difficulties*, trans. John J. L. Mood (New York: W. W. Norton & Co., 1975), 93–94.
3. Cited in David J. Garrow, *Bearing the Cross: Martin Luther King, Jr. and the Southern Christian Leadership Conference* (New York: William Morrow & Co., 1986), 58.
4. Jacobi and Hull, *Jung*, 193–94.
5. Kumar, *Kabir*, 183, 184. Cf. Rumi: "I have put duality away and seen the two worlds as one. One I seek, One I know, One I see, One I call. He is first, He is the last. He is the outward, he is the inward" (Rumi, *Ruins*, 22).
6. For further elaboration on compassion, see Matthew Fox, *A Spirituality Named Compassion* (San Francisco: Harper & Row, 1979). For a fuller treatment of panentheism, see Matthew Fox, *Original Blessing* (Santa Fe, NM: Bear & Co., 1983), 88–92.
7. Potter and poet M. C. Richards elaborates beautifully on this point in her *Centering in Pottery, Poetry and the Person* (Middletown, CT: Wesleyan Univ. Press, 1962).
8. Cited in John C. Merkle, *The Genesis of Faith: The Depth Theology of Abraham Joshua Heschel* (New York: Macmillan & Co., 1985), 170, 172.
9. Einstein, *Ideas and Opinions*, 11. "Being rapt in awe" is another translation of Einstein's phrase cited on page 92.
10. For a fuller elaboration of the four paths of creation spirituality and how they differ from the three paths of fall-redemption spirituality, see Matthew Fox, *Original Blessing*.
11. Josef Pieper, *Leisure: The Basis of Culture* (New York: New American Library, 1963), 62.
12. Raghavan Iyer, *The Moral and Political Thought of Mahatma Gandhi* (New York: Oxford Univ. Press, 1973), 91.
13. Andrew Weil, *The Natural Mind* (Boston: Houghton Mifflin Co., 1972), 179.
14. Anthony Stevens, *Archetypes: A Natural History of the Self* (New York: William Morrow & Co., 1982), 255–56.
15. Jacobi and Hull, *Jung*, 206, 340.

16. Kavanagh, *Poems*, 149.
17. *John of the Cross*, 19.
18. Rank, *Beyond Psychology*, 289.
19. Ibid., 250, 289.
20. Ibid., 289. Italics Rank's.
21. Ibid., 290–91.
22. Kavanagh, *Poems*, 155.
23. Kumar, *Kabir*, 123.
24. John of the Cross, "Although by Night," trans. Lynda Nicholson, in *St. John of the Cross*, ed. Gerald Brenan (New York: Cambridge Univ. Press, 1973), 165.
25. Mary Giles, *The Feminist Mystic* (New York: The Crossroad Publishing Co., 1985), 6.
26. Dorothee Soelle, *Beyond Mere Obedience* (New York: Pilgrim Press, 1982), xviii–xvix.
27. See Matthew Fox, "Meister Eckhart and Karl Marx: The Mystic as Political Theologian," in *Understanding Mysticism*, ed. Richard Woods (Garden City, NY: Doubleday/Image, 1980), 556–57.
28. Evelyn Underhill cited in Brendan Doyle, *Meditations with Julian of Norwich* (Santa Fe, NM: Bear & Co., 1983), 11.
29. Kumar, *Kabir*, 82.
30. Mood, *Rilke on Love*, 71.
31. Kumar, *Kabir*, 170.
32. M. C. Richards, Lecture at Institute in Culture and Creation Spirituality, Oakland, CA, Spring 1987.
33. Gregory Bateson and Mary Catherine Bateson. *Angels Fear: Towards an Epistemology of the Sacred* (New York: Macmillan Publishing Co., 1987), 80–81. Italics theirs.
34. Jacobi and Hull, *Jung*, 298.
35. Joanna Rogers Macy, *Despair and Personal Power in the Nuclear Age* (Philadelphia: New Society, 1983), 4–5.
36. Cited in Garrow, *Bearing*, 149.
37. Jacobi and Hull, *Jung*, 199.
38. Ibid., 198–200.
39. Ibid., 199–200.
40. See Matthew Fox, *On Becoming a Musical, Mystical Bear: Spirituality American Style* (New York: Paulist Press, 1972) and William Ernest Hocking, *The Meaning of God in Human Experience* (New Haven, CT: Yale Univ. Press, 1963).
41. Film Interview in "Deitrich Bonhoeffer: Memories and Perspectives" (Minneapolis, MN: Trinity Films).
42. Alice Miller, *Thou Shalt Not Be Aware* (New York: New American Library, 1986), 191.
43. Kumar, *Kabir*, 14.
44. See *The Documents of Vatican II*, ed. Walter M. Abbott, S. J. (Chicago: Follett, 1966), 661, 662.
45. Ibid., 660, 668.

14. The Historical Jesus as Mystic and Teacher of Mysticism

1. Edward Schillebeeckx, *Jesus: An Experiment in Christology* (New York: Seabury Press, 1979), 652–53.
2. Norman Perrin and Dennis C. Duling, *The New Testament—An Introduction* (New York: Harcourt Brace Jovanovich, 1982), 415.
3. Cited in ibid., 417.
4. C. H. Dodd, *The Parables of the Kingdom* (London: Collins, 1967), 64–65, n. 4.
5. Ibid., 133.
6. See ibid., 138.
7. Ibid., 140.
8. Ibid., 144.
9. Pheme Perkins, *Hearing the Parables of Jesus* (New York: Paulist, 1981), 89.
10. See Albert Schweitzer, *The Mysticism of Paul the Apostle* (New York: Seabury Press, 1968), 105–9.

PART III

Epigraph 1: Col. 1:16.

Epigraph 2: Cited in Jaroslav Pelikan, *Jesus Through the Centuries* (New Haven, CT: Yale Univ. Press, 1985), 63.

Epigraph 3: Cited in Ibid., 68.

Epigraph 4: Matthew Fox, *Illuminations of Hildegard of Bingen* (Santa Fe, NM: Bear & Co., 1985), 40.

Epigraph 5: Thomas Aquinas *In Jn.* n. 116. Translation from James A. Weisheipl and Fabian Larcher, *Commentary on the Gospel of St. John* (Albany, NY: Magi Books, 1980), I, 15, 2.

Epigraph 6: Thomas Aquinas *In Eph.* 3, lectio 5. Translation from Matthew Lamb, *Thomas Aquinas Commentary on St. Paul's Epistle to the Ephesians* (Albany, NY: Magi Books, 1966). Cf. 2 Pet. 1:4.

Epigraph 7: Sue Woodruff, *Meditations with Mechtild of Magdeburg* (Santa Fe, NM: Bear & Co., 1982), 32.

Epigraph 8: Matthew Fox, *Breakthrough: Meister Eckhart's Creation Spirituality in New Translation* (Garden City, NY: Doubleday & Co., 1980), 66.

Epigraph 9: Brendan Doyle, *Meditations with Julian of Norwich* (Santa Fe, NM: Bear & Co., 1983), 39.

Epigraph 10: James Francis Yockey, *Meditations with Nicolas of Cusa* (Santa Fe, NM: Bear & Co., 1987), 28–29.

Epigraph 11: Pelikan, *Jesus*, 182.

Epigraph 12: Krister Stendahl, *Paul Among Jews and Gentiles* (Philadelphia: Fortress Press, 1976), 39. Stendahl continues: "That is one of the aspects of Christianity which might be opened up with the help of Paul—if we restore Paul to his fullness and do not translate him into a biblical proof-text for Reformation doctrines. . . . His searching eyes focused on the unity and the God-willed diversity of humankind, yes, of the whole creation" (39–40).

Epigraph 13: Thomas Kuhn, *The Structure of Scientific Revolutions* (Chicago: The Univ. of Chicago Press, 1970), 103.

Epigraph 14: Matt. 9:17.

Epigraph 15: Pierre Teilhard de Chardin, *The Heart of Matter* (New York: Harcourt Brace Jovanovich, 1978), 93.

1. Pelikan, *Jesus*, 182.
2. Joseph A. Sittler, "Called to Unity," *The Ecumenical Review* 14 (October–December 1961): 181. This is an excellent article based on Col. 1:15–21, calling for a cosmic Christology with one caveat: Sittler, like Pelikan, ignores the medieval mystics' accomplishment regarding the Cosmic Christ. See also Gustaf Wingren, "The Doctrine of Creation: Not an Appendix but the First Article," *Word & World* 4 (Fall 1984): 353–371: "The doctrine of creation has not only been neglected; it has been the object of pointed opposition ever since the 1920s, especially on the part of Karl Barth and his disciples" (353).
3. Leo Scheffczyk, *Creation and Providence* (New York: Herder and Herder, 1970), 100.
4. Krister Stendahl's phrase in Stendahl, *Paul*, 78–96: "With Augustine, Western Christianity with its stress on introspective achievements started. . . . The introspective conscience is a Western development and a Western plague" (16–17).
5. Stendahl, *Paul*, 24–25.
6. Pelikan, *Jesus*, 182.

15. The Quest for the Cosmic Christ—A Paradigm Shift

1. Kuhn, *Structure*, 53, 77, 116, 120, 150–51, 109, 111.
2. Otto Rank, *Beyond Psychology* (New York: Dover Publications, 1958), 163.
3. Kuhn, *Structure*, 57, 56.

4. Ibid., 98, 76, 121, 90.
5. Ibid., 85, 103, 111.
6. Ibid., 77.
7. Otto Rank, *Art and Artist*, (New York: Agathon Press, 1975), 428–29.
8. Ibid., 429.
9. Robert N. Bellah, *The Broken Covenant* (New York: Seabury Press, 1975), 162.
10. Philosopher Charles Fair believes that the notion of soul dies at the end of a civilization and a new notion of soul accompanies a new civilization. See Charles M. Fair, *The Dying Self* (Garden City, NY: Doubleday, 1970), 106, 121.

16. Biblical Sources for Belief in the Cosmic Christ

1. Sittler, "Unity," 183.
2. Chardin, *Heart*, 93.
3. Edward Schillebeeckx, *Christ: The Experience of Jesus as Lord* (New York: Seabury Press, 1980), 528.
4. Abraham J. Heschel, *The Prophets* (New York: Harper & Row, 1962), 172.
5. Ibid., 186.
6. Ibid., 169.
7. Rob van der Hart, *The Theology of Angels and Devils* (Norte Dame, IN: Fides, 1972), 16, 80–81.
8. Leonard Doohan, *Mark: Visionary of Early Christianity* (Santa Fe, NM: Bear & Co., 1986), 92.
9. C. H. Dodd, *The Interpretation of the Fourth Gospel* (Cambridge, England: Cambridge Univ. Press, 1970), 241–49.
10. Jon Sobrino critiques this "cross mystique" very well in his *Christology at the Crossroads* (Maryknoll, NY: Orbis Books, 1978), 227–28.
11. Schillebeeckx, *Christ*, 176, 178, 168.
12. Sittler, "Unity," 179.
13. Schillebeeckx, *Christ*, 189.
14. Ibid., 196.
15. Ibid., 208.
16. Ibid., 210.
17. Ibid., 254.
18. Robert A. Spivey, *Anatomy of the New Testament* (New York: Macmillan Publishing Co., 1974), 433.
19. Raymond E. Brown, *The Gospel According to John* (Garden City, NY: Doubleday, 1970), 2:753–54.
20. Elisabeth Schüssler Fiorenza, *Invitation to the Book of Revelation* (Garden City, NY: Image Books, 1981), 72.
21. Ibid., 64.
22. Louis Hartman and P. van Imschoot, in "Lord," in *Encyclopedic Dictionary of the Bible*, 1373–74.
23. Schüssler Fiorenza, *Revelation*, 72.
24. Ibid., 77.
25. Ibid., 94.
26. Ibid., 125, 131, 177.
27. Ibid., 205.
28. As Schillebeeckx puts it, "Belief in creation is simply taken for granted and is the background for the whole of the Jesus event" (*Christ*, 523). He goes on to say, "Both the New Testament and early Judaism understand belief in creation as the all-supporting basis for the Jewish-Christian kerygma" (Ibid., 529). As Oscar Cullmann has indicated, the quest for the historical Jesus is not what occupied the writers of the Gospels or the epistles. See *Christ and Time: The Primitive Christian Conception of Time and History* (Philadelphia: Westminster, 1949).
29. Schillebeeckx, *Christ*, 519.
30. Raymond E. Brown, *The Birth of the Messiah* (Garden City, NY: Doubleday, 1977), 31.

Brown points out that the infancy narratives of Matthew and Luke as well as the Prologue to John all echo Genesis. "The tendency to resort to Genesis to explain Jesus' origins reflects the Christian concept of a new creation or a new beginning" (231, n. 1).

31. Ibid., 168. Brown says that the magi from the East are "the wise and learned among the Gentiles. Precisely since they are Gentiles, they receive their proclamation through created nature (see Rom. 1:19–20; 2:14–15)" (Ibid., 182).
32. Ibid., 183.
33. Ibid., 290, 314–15.
34. Ibid., 426–27.
35. Brown talks of his "discovery" that the infancy narratives are "just as profoundly Christian and as dramatically persuasive as the last two chapters, the story of the passion and resurrection" (Ibid., 38).
36. D. E. Nineham, *Saint Mark* (London: Penguin, 1979), 56.
37. Ibid., 59.
38. Ibid., 64, 63.
39. Jean Danielou, *The Angels and Their Mission* (Westminster, MD: Christian Classics, 1956), 3.
40. Nineham, *Saint Mark*, 64.
41. Doohan, *Mark*, 90.
42. See Exod. 24:11 and 1 Kings 19:11–12.
43. Nicolas Berdyaev, "Salvation and Creativity: Two Understandings of Christianity," in *Western Spirituality: Historical Roots, Ecumenical Routes*, ed. Matthew Fox (Sante Fe, NM: Bear & Co., 1981), 123–24, 129.
44. Schillebeeckx, *Christ*, 419.
45. Ibid., 205.
46. Raymond E. Brown, *The Virginal Conception & Bodily Resurrection of Jesus* (New York: Paulist Press, 1973), 89, 92.
47. Ibid., 105, n. 174.
48. Ibid., 123, n. 208.
49. Cited in ibid., 105, n. 174.
50. Ibid., 113. Italics Brown's.
51. Brown, *John*, 1:504. "Since John conceives of passion, death, and resurrection as the one 'hour,' John sees the theme of glory throughout the whole hour. In fact, the hour is the time for the Son of Man to be glorified."
52. Schillebeeckx, *Christ*, 200.
53. Brown, *John*, 2:1037.
54. Van der Hart, *Theology of Angels*, 40–41.
55. Nineham, *Saint Mark*, 235.

17. The Cosmic Christ and Creation Mystics—The Greek Fathers

1. Pelikan, *Jesus*, 58, 59, 62, 63, 64, 65, 66.
2. Ibid., 67.
3. Ibid., 68.
4. *Five Books of S. Iranaeus Against Heresies*, trans. The Rev. John Keble (London: James Parker and Co., 1872), 281–82. Iranaeus repeats this theme; see 225, 449–50.
5. Ibid., 69.
6. For a discussion of the considerable lacunae among the Greek Fathers, see Rosemary Ruether, "Misogynism and Virginal Feminism in the Fathers of the Church," in *Religion and Sexism*, ed. Rosemary Ruether (New York: Simon & Schuster, 1974), 150–183.

18. The Cosmic Christ and Creation Mystics—The Medieval West

1. Reproductions of these and twenty-three other paintings along with her own commentaries on them are available in Matthew Fox, *Illuminations of Hildegard of Bingen* (Santa Fe, NM: Bear & Co., 1985). Her music is available in several records and also in an English edition in *Hildegard of Bingen's Book of Divine Works with Letters and Songs*, ed. Matthew Fox (Santa Fe, NM: Bear & Co., 1987).
2. See, for example, Dr. Wighard Strehlow and Gottfried Hertzka, M.D., *Hildegard of*

Bingen's Medicine (Santa Fe, NM: Bear & Co., 1988).

3. See Edward A. Armstrong, *Saint Francis, Nature Mystic* (Berkeley, CA: Univ. of California Press, 1976), 33–41.
4. Translation from Eloi Leclerc, *The Canticle of Creatures: Symbols of Union* (Chicago: Franciscan Herald Press, 1970), xvii–xviii.
5. Thomas Aquinas *De veritate* iv. 1. Translation from Thomas Gilby, *St. Thomas Aquinas: Theological Texts* (Durham, England: The Labyrinth Press, 1982), 63.
6. Ibid., 63. *De veritate*, 1 ad 6.
7. Ibid., 64. *sum. theol.* 1a xxxix.3.
8. Thomas Aquinas *In Eph.* 4, lectio 7. Translation from Matthew Lamb, *Thomas Aquinas Commentary on St. Paul's Epistle to the Ephesians* (Albany, NY: Magi Books, 1966), 183.
9. Thomas Aquinas *Contra gentes*, II.3. Translation from Thomas Gilby, *St. Thomas Aquinas: Philosophical Texts* (Durham, England: The Labyrinth Press, 1982), 129.
10. Ibid., 127. *Contra gentes*, II.2.
11. Ibid.
12. Thomas Aquinas *In Jn.* n. 116. Translation from James A. Weisheipl and Fabian Lascher, *Commentary on the Gospel of St. John* (Albany, NY: Magi Books, 1980), 65.
13. Ibid., n. 136, 74–75.
14. Ibid., n. 86, 55; n. 93, 57.
15. Aquinas *Sum. theol.* I.15.2. Translation from Josef Pieper, *The Silence of Saint Thomas* (Chicago: Henry Regnery, 1966), 66.
16. Aquinas *Sum. Theol.*, I.14.7. Translation mine. Cf. Gilby, *Philosophical Texts*, 181.
17. Aquinas *In Jn.* n. 136. Translation mine.
18. In Pieper, 56. (Aquinas *Liber de Causis* I.6.)
19. Thomas Aquinas *Compendium Theologiae*, 214. In Gilby, *Theological Texts*, 305.
20. Aquinas *In Eph.* 3, lectio 5. In Lamb, *Aquinas Commentary*, 147.
21. Thomas Aquinas *de Trinitate* ii.1 ad 7. In Gilby, *Theological Texts*, 267.
22. Ibid., 365. Italics Gilby's. *Breviary Lessons, Corpus Christi*.
23. Aquinas *Sum. theol.* 2a–2ae.xiv.6. In Gilby, *Theological Texts*, 261.
24. James Collins, "Introduction," in James Collins, *Meditations with Dante Alighieri* (Santa Fe, NM: Bear & Co., 1984), 8. One of the principle influences on Dante as a student was Thomas Aquinas's pupil in Paris, Fra Remigio Girolami.
25. See Matthew Fox, "Meister Eckhart and Karl Marx: The Mystic as Political Theologian," in *Understanding Mysticism*, ed. Richard Woods (Garden City, NY: Image Books, 1980), 541–63.
26. John Dolan, in the Introduction to his book, *Unity and Reform: Selected Writings of Nicholas of Cusa* (Notre Dame, IN: Univ. of Notre Dame Press, 1962), summarizes Cusa's contributions in the following manner: "If every man is a microcosmos, then Christ is the same in a maximal way . . . Christ is the Principle of all creative activity both human and divine. . . . The prologue of the Johannine Gospel runs through his theology" (41–45). Dolan indicates that in contrast to Cusa's Cosmic Christ theology, "Augustinianism was a failure in fitting Christ into the material universe" and Aristotle "completely obscured Christ's vital role in all creation as well as in all creative activity" (42–43).

PART IV

Epigraph 1: Wis. 1:7.
Epigraph 2: Exod. 3:13–14.
Epigraph 3: John 8:58.
Epigraph 4: Rainer Maria Rilke, *The Selected Poetry of Rainer Maria Rilke*, trans. Stephen Mitchell (New York: Vintage Books, 1984), 255.
Epigraph 5: Pierre Teilhard de Chardin, *Human Energy* (New York: Harcourt Brace Jovanovich, 1969), 23, 130–31. See also *Nature Thoughts*, ed. Louise Bachelder (Mount Vernon, NY: Peter Pauper Press, 1965), 8.
Epigraph 6: Abraham Joshua Heschel, *The Earth Is the Lord's* (New York: Farrar Straus

Giroux, 1978), 71–72. Italics mine.

Epigraph 7: *Walt Whitman's Leaves of Grass*, ed. Malcolm Cowley (New York: Penguin Books, 1959), 49, 83.

Epigraph 8: Gregory Bateson, *Mind and Nature* (New York: Bantam Books, 1980), 8.

Epigraph 9: Col. 1:15–17.

Epigraph 10: 2 Cor. 3:18.

Epigraph 11: Eph. 1:9–10.

Epigraph 12: Heb. 1:3.

Epigraph 13: John 1:1–3.

Epigraph 14: Sehdev Kumar, *The Vision of Kabir* (Concord, Ontario, Canada: Alpha & Omega, 1984), 144.

Epigraph 15: Joanna Rogers Macy, *Despair and Personal Power in the Nuclear Age* (Philadelphia: New Society Publishers, 1983), 156, 30.

1. Bateson, *Mind*, 109.
2. See Matthew Fox, "On Desentimentalizing Spirituality," *Spirituality Today* 30 (March 1978): 64–76.
3. Thomas Aquinas *Contra gentiles* II.3. Translation from Thomas Gilby, *St. Thomas Aquinas: Theological Texts* (Durham, England: The Labyrinth Press, 1982), 76.

20. Naming the Cosmic Christ

1. Bateson, in his introduction to *Mind and Nature*, says that he "offers the phrase *the pattern that connects* as a synonym, another possible title for this book" (italics Bateson's). He defines the aesthetic as being "responsive to the pattern that connects" (8–9).
2. John Donne, "An Anatomie of the World: The First Anniversary." Sociologist Robert Bellah cites this passage from Donne in his exposition on contemporary culture as "the culture of separation." See Bellah's *Habits of the Heart: Individualism and Commitment in American Life* (New York: Harper & Row, 1985), 277–81.
3. J. B. Lightfoot, *Saint Paul's Epistles to the Colossians and to Philemon* (Grand Rapids, MI: Zondervan Publishing Co., 1957), 154.
4. Edward Schillebeeckx, *Christ: The Experience of Jesus as Lord* (New York: Seabury Press, 1980), 207.
5. Teilhard de Chardin, "La Vie Cosmique," in *Ecrits du temps de la guerre* (Paris: Editions du Seuil, 1965), 67–69. This paraphrase is offered by J. A. Lyons, *The Cosmic Christ in Origen and Teilhard de Chardin* (Oxford: Oxford Univ. Press, 1982), 38. Though we have seen the *concept* to be rich in Christian history, the precise *term* "Cosmic Christ" was first used in the United States by Yale Divinity School Professor G. Stevens in *The Christian Doctrine of Salvation* (1905); the following year it was used by J. W. Buckham of the Pacific Theological Seminary in Berkeley in his *Christ and the Eternal Order*. In England its first use was by W. R. Inge in 1907. Teilhard de Chardin picked up on the term and used it over thirty times in his early writings (1916–24). During the last ten years of his life, including his last essay, "le Christique," Chardin also employed a synonym, "universal Christ" (Lyons, *Cosmic Christ*, 29, 38–39).
6. Evelyn Underhill, *Mysticism* (New York: E. P. Dutton & Co, 1961), 118.
7. Rob van der Hart, *The Theology of Angels and Devils* (Notre Dame, IN: Fides Publishers, 1972), 37. Italics mine.
8. Jacobi and Hull, *Jung*, 363.
9. For more on this rich theme of the "royal person," see Helen A. Kenik, "Toward a Biblical Basis for Creation Theology," in *Western Spirituality: Historical Roots, Ecumenical Routes*, ed. Matthew Fox (Santa Fe, NM: Bear & Co., 1981), 25–72. See also Matthew Fox, *Original Blessing* (Santa Fe, NM: Bear & Co., 1983), 93–102.
10. Jacobi and Hull, *Jung*, 353.

21. Jesus Christ as Mother Earth Crucified and Resurrected

1. Thomas Berry, "The Human Venture," in *Riverdale Papers on the Earth Community* (Riverdale, NY: Riverdale Center, n.d.), 2.
2. Notker Fuglister, "Passover," in *Encyclopedia of Theology*, ed. Karl Rahner (New York:

Seabury Press, 1975), 1168.

3. Otto Rank, *Beyond Psychology* (New York: Dover Publications, 1958), 236.

4. Ibid., 15.

22. A Paschal Mystery for the Third Millennium of Christianity

1. Fulgister, "Passover," 1166.

2. Ibid., 1168.

3. Ibid., 1169.

23. Redeeming Redemption—The Cosmic Christ as Redeemer of Cosmic Pain

1. Kumar, *Kabir*, 144.

2. Van der Hart, *Theology of Angels*, 69, 68.

3. Schillebeeckx, *Christ*, 255.

4. Macy, *Despair*, 156, 30.

5. Ibid., 37.

24. The Cosmic Christ—Revealer of The Divine "I Am" in Every Creature

1. Raymond E. Brown, *The Gospel According to John* (Garden City, NY: Doubleday, 1970), 1:537.

2. Ibid., 535, 538.

3. See Matthew Fox, *A Spirituality Named Compassion* (Minneapolis: Winston Press, 1979).

PART V

Epigraph 1: Cited in Thomas Kiernan, *A Treasury of Albert Schweitzer* (New York: Philosophical Library, 1965), 123.

Epigraph 2: Guy Murchie, *The Seven Mysteries of Life* (Boston: Houghton Mifflin Co., 1978), 363.

Epigraph 3: *Walt Whitman's Leaves of Grass*, ed. Malcolm Cowley (New York: Penguin Books, 1959), 122.

Epigraph 4: Dorothee Soelle, *To Work and To Love: A Theology of Creation* (Philadelphia: Fortress Press, 1984), 138–39.

Epigraph 5: Mircea Eliade, *Images and Symbols* (New York: Sheed & Ward, 1969), 14.

Epigraph 6: Cited in Fred M. Hechinger, "America Lacks Agenda on Needs of Its Children," *Oakland Tribune*, 11 May 1986, sec. C–7.

Epigraph 7: Matt. 18:4.

Epigraph 8: Alice Miller, *For Your Own Good* (New York: Farrar Straus Giroux, 1984), xi.

Epigraph 9: James Hillman, "Senex and Puer," in *Puer Papers*, ed. James Hillman (Dallas, TX: Spring Publications, 1987), 20.

Epigraph 10: Sue Woodruff, *Meditations with Mechtild of Magdeburg* (Santa Fe, NM: Bear & Co., 1982), 47.

Epigraph 11: Nicolas Berdyaev, *The Meaning of the Creative Act* (New York: Harper & Row, 1955), 224.

Epigraph 12: Rollo May, *My Quest for Beauty* (New York: Saybrook, 1985), 215.

Epigraph 13: Nicolas Berdyaev, *The Divine and the Human* (London: Geoffrey Bles, 1949), 53.

Epigraph 14: Cited in *The Sacred Pipe*, ed. Joseph Epes Brown (New York: Penguin Books, 1987), xx.

Epigraph 15: D. H. Lawrence, "The Primal Passions," in *D. H. Lawrence: A Living Poet*, ed. Charles Davey (London: Brentham Press, 1985), 39.

Epigraph 16: James Francis Yockey, *Meditations with Nicolas of Cusa* (Sante Fe, NM: Bear & Co., 1987), 110–11.

Epigraph 17: Joanna Rogers Macy, *Despair and Personal Power in the Nuclear Age* (Philadelphia: New Society Publishers, 1983), 29.

Epigraph 18: Rosemary Ruether, *Sexism and God-Talk: Toward A Feminist Theology* (Boston:

Beacon Press, 1983), 266.

Epigraph 19: M. D. Chenu, *Nature, Man, and Society in the Twelfth Century* (Chicago: Univ. of Chicago Press, 1968), 3.

1. Cited in R. P. Blackmur, *Henry Adams* (New York: Harcourt Brace Jovanovich, 1980), 282.

2. According to Chenu, a renaissance "literally involves new birth, new existence in all the changed conditions of times, places, and persons; it represents an initiative all the more irreducible to the ancient materials it uses because it is a spiritual initiative. Imitation is subordinate to inventiveness even when providing it with material" (Chenu, *Nature*, 3).

3. Thomas Berry, "Economics: Its Effect on the Life Systems of the World," *Thomas Berry and the New Cosmology*, ed. Anne Lonergan and Caroline Richards (Mystic, CT: Twenty-Third Publications, 1987), 19.

4. Robert H. Bellah, *The Broken Covenant* (New York: Seabury Press, 1975), 162.

5. Ibid., 144.

6. Cited in Kiernan, *Albert Schweitzer*, 123.

7. Albert Einstein, *Ideas and Opinions* (New York: Crown, 1982), 38.

8. See E. James Lieberman, *Acts of Will: The Life and Work of Otto Rank* (New York: The Free Press, 1985), 81.

25. *The Cosmic Christ and a Renaissance of Sexual Mysticism*

1. For this chapter I employ the excellent adaptation of David Granville. I am indebted to him. His adaptation, presented as a choral reading, is available for group use. See David Granville, *Song of Songs* (Oakland, CA: Friends of Creation Spirituality, 1988).

2. Phyllis Trible, *God and the Rhetoric of Sexuality* (Philadelphia: Fortress Press, 1987), 144, 152–53, 161.

3. Frederick Turner, *Beyond Geography: The Western Spirit Against the Wilderness* (New York: Viking, 1980), xi.

4. Gerald Brenan, *St. John of the Cross: His Life and Poetry* (Cambridge, England: Cambridge Univ. Press, 1976), 7.

5. Trible, *Sexuality*, 161, 160.

6. Jacobi and Hull, *Jung*, 105.

7. Cited in Ira Progoff, *The Death and Rebirth of Psychology* (New York: Julian, 1956), 219.

8. Otto Rank, *Psychology and the Soul* (Philadelphia: Univ. of Pennsylvania Press, 1950), 164.

9. Ibid., 42.

10. Otto Rank, *Modern Education*, trans. M. E. Moxon (New York: Knopf, 1932), 112.

11. Eliade, *Images*, 14. Frithjof Schuon points out that Islam, Judaism, Hinduism, and Chinese religions teach "the essential or qualitative aspect of sexuality, or what we might call its cosmic aspect." Only Christianity "unavoidably and as it were incidentally rejoins the Judaeo-Islamic perspective" in its teaching on the sacrament of marriage. See Frithjof Schuon, *The Transcendent Unity of Religions* (Wheaton, IL: Theosophical Publishing House, 1984), 118–19. I am proposing that Christianity return to its Jewish roots on this issue of sexual mysticism.

12. Soelle, *To Work*, 139.

13. Erich Jantsch, *The Self-Organizing Universe* (New York: Pergamon Press, 1980), 126.

14. Jacobi and Hull, *Jung*, 104.

15. Nicolas Berdyaev, *The Meaning of the Creative Act* (New York: Harper & Brothers, 1955), 224.

16. Eugene Monick, *Phallos: Sacred Image of the Masculine* (Toronto: Inner City Books, 1987), 106–7. Dr. Helen Caldicott senses the same connection between perverse sexuality and the arms race. See her *Missile Envy* (New York: Bantam, 1986).

17. Monick, *Phallos*, 62.

18. Ibid., 62, 27, 36. I have dealt with this same subject at some length in *Whee! We, wee All the Way Home: A Guide to Sensual, Prophetic Spirituality* (Santa Fe, NM: Bear & Co., 1981).

19. Cited in Monick, *Phallos*, 29–30.

20. Ibid., 68.
21. Ibid., 100.
22. Ibid., 97.
23. Jacobi and Hull, *Jung*, 103.
24. Soelle, *To Work*, 150.

26. Honoring the Child Within—Youth and the Cosmic Christ

1. Richard Colvin, "Study: Fear of Nuclear War Haunts Bay Area Teens," *Oakland Tribune*, 28 Feb. 1986, sec. B–1.
2. Larry Doyle, "Violence is top Teen Killer, Studies Say," *Philadelphia Inquirer*, 26 June 1987, sec. A–3.
3. Stephen Glenn, "Strategies and Self-Esteem," a talk delivered at Cedar Falls, IA on 2 March 1984. Cited in Andy LePage, *Transforming Education* (Oakland, CA: Oakmore House Press, 1987), 88. For much of this section on adultism I am indebted to conversations and insights received from Mr. Victor Lewis, a young man in touch with his pain and his promise.
4. Doyle, "Violence," A–3.
5. Fred M. Hechinger, "America Lacks Agenda on Needs of Its Children," *Oakland Tribune*, 11 May 1986, sec. C–7.
6. Cited in LePage, *Transforming Education*, 88.
7. Alice Miller, *Thou Shalt Not Be Aware* (New York: New American Library, 1986), 97 Italics mine.
8. Miller, *Own Good*, xi.
9. Hillman, *Puer*, 20.
10. Ibid., 21. Italics his.
11. Ibid., 19.
12. James Hillman, *Inter Views* (New York: Harper Colophon Books, 1983), 114, 115, 116, 122.
13. J. E. Cirlot, *A Dictionary of Symbols* (New York: Philosophical Library, 1962), 43–44.
14. "The Lord often reveals to the younger what is best," says the Rule. *St. Benedict's Rule for Monasteries*, trans. Leonard J. Doyle (Collegeville, MN: The Liturgical Press, 1948). See chapter 3, "On Calling the Brethren for Counsel," p. 3.
15. Hillman, *Inter Views*, 123.
16. Tom Moore, "Artemis and the Puer," in Hillman, *Puer*, 200.
17. Marie-Louise von Franz, *Puer Aeternus* (Boston: Sigo Press, 1981), 292, 291, 98, 13.
18. Hillman, *Inter Views*, 212.
19. Von Franz, *Puer Aeternus*, 99–100, 26.
20. Cited in Matthew Fox, *Original Blessing* (Santa Fe, NM: Bear & Co., 1983), 227.
21. Hillman, *Inter Views*, 118, 114, 117.
22. Hillman, *Puer*, 10.
23. James Hillman, "Puer Wounds and Ulysses' Seas," in Hillman, *Puer*, 123.
24. James Hillman, "Peaks and Vales," in Hillman, *Puer*, 65.
25. Hillman, "Senex and Puer," in Hillman, *Puer*, 34.
26. Miller, *Own Good*, 58.
27. *Meister Eckhart: Deutsche Predigten und Traktate*, ed. Josef Quint (Munich, Germany: Carl Hanser Verlag, 1963), 444–45. Translation mine.

27. The Cosmic Christ and Creativity—The Return of the Personal Arts

1. Albert Einstein, *Ideas and Opinions* (New York: Crown, 1982), 28. Italics mine.
2. Otto Rank, *Art and Artist* (New York: Agathon Press, 1975), 430–31. Italics Rank's.
3. Erich Fromm, *Sane Society* (New York: Fawcett, 1955), 301.
4. Kenji Miyazawa, "Life as Art," (unpublished translations from his thoughts of 1926 done in 1962), 1.
5. Jacobi and Hull, *Jung*, 199–201.
6. Jantsch, *Universe*, 265. Italics mine. Swimme makes the same point—that creativity lies

at the heart of the fiery universe of which we now know we are a part. See Swimme, *The Universe Is a Green Dragon: A Cosmic Creation Story* (Santa Fe, NM: Bear & Co., 1985), 157–171.

7. Raghavan Iyer, *The Moral and Political Thought of Mahatma Gandhi* (New York: Oxford Univ. Press, 1973), 73.

8. Peter Rogers, *A Painter's Quest* (Santa Fe, NM: Bear & Co., 1987), 152.

9. Cited in E. James Lieberman, *Acts of Will: The Life and Work of Otto Rank* (New York: The Free Press, 1985), 324.

10. May, *My Quest*, 215.

11. Dante, *Purgatorio*, Canto 18.

12. John Boswell, *Christianity, Social Tolerance, and Homosexuality* (Chicago: Univ. of Chicago Press, 1980).

13. Walter L. Williams, *The Spirit and the Flesh: Sexual Diversity in American Indian Culture* (Boston: Beacon Press, 1986).

14. Anthony Stevens, *Archetypes: A Natural History of the Self* (New York: William Morrow & Co., 1982), 236–37.

15. Schüssler Fiorenza, *In Memory of Her* (New York: Crossroads, 1984), 225–26.

16. "Stepping Backward," in Adrienne Rich, *The Fact of a Doorframe: Poems Selected and New 1950–1984* (New York: W.W. Norton & Co., 1984), 6–7.

17. See Matthew Fox, *Original Blessing*, Path III.

18. M. C. Richards, *Centering* (Middletown, CT: Wesleyan Univ. Press, 1962), 27. See also M. C. Richards, *Toward Wholeness: Rudolf Steiner Education in America* (Middletown, CT: Wesleyan Univ. Press, 1980).

19. Albert Einstein, *Out of My Later Years* (Secaucus, NJ: The Citadel Press, 1974), 9. A graduate of the Institute in Culture and Creation Spirituality, Dr. Andy LePage, has written a fine book, *Transforming Education*, that develops methods from our Institute and applies them to the public school system's needs today. He bases his renewal of education on the "New 3R's" of reverence, responsibility, and renewal. The study forms a useful basis for applying the contribution of the Cosmic Christ to education.

20. Nicolas Berdyaev, *The Spirit and Reality* (London: Geoffrey Bles, 1939), 192–93. Berdyaev, *Meaning*, 9. Berdyaev, *Slavery and Freedom* (New York: Scribners, 1939), 171–72.

21. Berdyaev *Slavery*, 241.

22. Nicolas Berdyaev, *Freedom and the Spirit* (New York: Scribners, 1935), xviii.

23. Nicolas Berdyaev, *Dream and Reality* (New York: Collier Books, 1962), 204. For this section on Berdyaev I am deeply indebted to the excellent work by Russell Becker, *Meditations with Nicolas Berdyaev*, to be published shortly.

28. The Cosmic Christ—Redeemer of Worship

1. Jacobi and Hull, *Jung*, 353.

2. Rank *Art and Artist*, 113, 125.

3. Ibid., 114, 115.

4. Ibid., 125, 134–135.

5. Cited in Jean Danielou, *The Angels and Their Mission* (Westminster, MD: Christian Classics, 1956), 61–62, 67.

6. Thomas Aquinas, *Contra gentiles* III.35. Translation mine.

7. See John Punshon, *Encounter with Silence* (Richmond, IN: Friends United Press, 1987).

8. *Rilke on Love and Other Difficulties*, trans. John J. L. Mood (New York: W. W. Norton & Co., 1975), 71.

9. See "The Fourth Dwelling Places," in Teresa of Avila, *The Interior Castle*, trans. Kieran Kavanaugh (New York: Paulist Press, 1979), 67–84.

10. Allan D. Galloway, *The Cosmic Christ* (London: Nisbet, 1951), 212.

11. Cited in Susan Griffin, *Woman and Nature* (New York: Harper & Row, 1978), 219.

12. Macy, *Despair*, 29, 22.

13. Alice Miller, *The Drama of the Gifted Child* (New York: Basic Books, 1981), 101; Miller,

Own Good, 270.

14. Soelle, *To Work,* 138. Soelle continues: "As a white person coming from a rationalistic tradition, attending worship in the black community has taught me more about my own religious needs than white forms of religious ritual ever could."

15. See my chapter on "Dancing Sarah Circle," in Matthew Fox, *A Spirituality Named Compassion* (Minneapolis: Winston Press, 1979), 36–67.

16. Jamake Highwater, *Ritual of the Wind* (New York: Alfred Van Der Marck Editions, 1984), 9.

17. Howard Thurman's entire theology was deeply centered in creation and in the Cosmic Christ tradition. See, for example, Howard Thurman, *The Search for Common Ground* (New York: Harper & Row, 1971). Thurman was significantly influenced by his teacher, Rufus Jones, and the mystics, especially Meister Eckhart, and he remained attuned all his life to the black spiritual experience of his people.

18. I can make mine the words of Otto Rank: "Here, too, the primitives disclose to us the deeper sources" (*Beyond Psychology,* 245). Is it mere coincidence that contemporary art was birthed when Picasso encountered Native American and native African culture? Might there be a lesson here for rebirthing contemporary worship?

19. Black Elk, cited in *Sacred Pipe,* xx.

20. Ibid., 21.

21. Ibid., 23 (n. 10), 25. A white man of good intentions produced a book of "Christian-Sioux Dialogue" that fails in its efforts because the author has no Cosmic Christ and no creation theology by which to represent Christianity. See William Stolzman, S.J., *The Pipe and Christ* (Pine Ridge, SD: Red Cloud Indian School, 1986).

29. The Cosmic Christ and Deep Ecumenism

1. Macy, *Despair,* 29.

2. Cited in Sheikh Ragip Frager, *Love is the Wine: Talks of a Sufi Master in America* (Putney, VT: Threshold Books, 1987), 1.

3. Joanna Macy, "Perfection of Wisdom: Mother of All Buddhas," *Anima* 3 (Fall 1973): 75, 77.

4. Cited in ibid., 78.

5. Thich Nhat Hanh, *Being Peace* (Berkeley: Parallax Press, 1987), 9.

6. Ibid., 64.

7. Ibid., 86.

8. Ibid., 114–15.

9. Cited by Joanna Macy in "The Cosmic Christ and the Way of the Boddhisattva," a conference given with Matthew Fox at La Casa de Maria Center in Santa Barbara, California, 30 April 1988. Deep ecumenism between African religions and creation spirituality is found in Marlene De Nardo, "Listening to the Deepest Wisdom of Mother Africa," (M.A. thesis, Holy Names College, 1987) and with Jewish mysticism in the work of Daniel Matt, "Loss and Discovery of Self in Hasidism," (Berkeley: unpublished paper, 1988).

10. Lloyd Shearer, "Nuclear War is Inevitable—Unless . . . ," *Parade Magazine,* 24 Aug. 1986, 18.

11. Lawrence, "Primal Passions," 39.

12. Sehdev Kumar, *The Vision of Kabir* (Concord, Ontario, Canada: Alpha & Omega, 1984), 144.

13. Charlene Spretnak, *Lost Goddesses of Early Greece* (Boston: Beacon Press, 1978), 42.

14. Cited in ibid., 43.

15. Ibid., 45.

16. Robert Graves, cited in Merlin Stone, "The Great Goddess: Who Was She?" in *The Politics of Women's Spirituality,* ed. Charlene Spretnak (Garden City, NY: Doubleday, 1982), 17.

17. Marija Gimbutas, "Women and Culture in Goddess-Oriented Old Europe," in Spretnak, *Politics,* 27–28.

18. Otto Rank, *Beyond Psychology* (New York: Dover Publications, 1958), 143, 237.

19. More of the works of these remarkable mystic-prophets is becoming available. See, for example, *Sebastian Franck: 280 Paradoxes or Wondrous Sayings*, trans. E. J. Furcha (Lewiston, NY: The Edwin Mellen Press, 1986); *Selected Writings of Hans Denck*, ed. Walter Fellman (Pittsburgh, PA: The Pickwick Press, 1975).

20. A recent and largely successful contribution to the hitherto unheralded cosmic theology of John Calvin is found in William J. Bouwsma, *John Calvin: A Sixteenth Century Portrait* (New York: Oxford Univ. Press, 1988), especially pages 69–80. Though this work shows some common ground between Calvin and creation theology, it also has severe limitations: for example Calvin "attacks imagination and creativity" in the human person (p. 80).

21. Gabriel Marcel, *The Decline of Wisdom* (New York: Philosophical Library, 1955), 42.

22. Ibid.

23. *Unity and Reform: Selected Writings of Nicholas of Cusa*, ed. John Dolan (Notre Dame, IN: Univ. of Notre Dame Press, 1962), 202.

24. Ken Wilber, ed., *The Holographic Paradigm and Other Paradoxes* (Boulder, CO: Shambhala, 1982), 140.

25. Ibid., 192. Cf. Meister Eckhart who says "isness is God" in Matthew Fox, *Breakthrough: Meister Eckhart's Creation Spirituality in New Translation* (Garden City, NY: Doubleday & Co., 1980), 89–90.

26. D. H. Lawrence, "Courage," in Davey, *D. H. Lawrence*, 6.

27. I am indebted to conversations with M. C. Richards for these ideas on oil in a time of friction.

28. Elisabeth Schüssler Fiorenza, *In Memory of Her* (New York: Crossroad, 1984), xiii. See also 153–54.

29. Abraham Joshua Heschel, *God in Search of Man* (New York: Harper & Row, 1955), 255.

30. C. G. Jung, *The Secret of the Golden Flower* (New York: Harcourt Brace Jovanovich, 1962), 144.

31. Raghavan Iyer, *The Moral and Political Thought of Mahatma Gandhi* (New York: Oxford Univ. Press, 1973), 132.

General Index

Index to Biblical References

ABOUT THE COVER ILLUSTRATION

COVER ARTIST ROBERT LENTZ WRITES:

There is a traditional icon of Christ as Holy Wisdom from Russia. This is a modern variant of that theme. The child-Christ is based on Matthew Fox's discussion of God as a child and Meister Eckhart's vision of the beautiful naked boy. He is Asian, indicating the wisdom of native peoples, and androgynous, like Sophia. He holds the earth like a ball, with the moon revolving around it. His hand has a wound from the crucifixion. The halo with cross and Greek letters signifies in an icon that the figure is Christ. At the bottom are wild waves among rocks, and clouds, representing the chaotic forces of nature at the beginning of creation.

A Leader's Guide is available for
The Coming of the Cosmic Christ

Harper's Adult Study Leader's Guides have been prepared for a wide range of books suitable for adult discussion groups.

The Leader's Guide for *The Coming of the Cosmic Christ* provides an adult discussion group with step-by-step instructions, discussion questions, journaling exercises, and group activities for a six-session program.

The Leader's Guide makes it easy to conduct lively, stimulating discussion programs that participants will respond to with enthusiasm.

The Coming of the Cosmic Christ, Leader's Guide
80 pages, paperback
Matthew Fox
ISBN 0-06-062959-2
$00.00

The *Coming of the Cosmic Christ* Leader's Guide is available from your local bookstore or from:

> Customer Service Department
> Harper San Francisco
> 1160 Battery Street
> San Francisco, CA 94111-1213
> 800-328-5125